Neal-Schuman

Guide to Recommended Children's Books and Media for Use with Every Elementary Subject

Kathryn I. Matthew and Joy L. Lowe

Neal-Schuman Publishers, Inc.
New York   London

Published by Neal-Schuman Publishers, Inc.
100 Varick Street
New York, NY 10013

Printed and bound in the United States of America

Library of Congress Cataloging-in-Publication Data

Matthew, Kathryn I.
    Neal-Schuman guide to recommended children's books and media for use with every elementary subject / Kathryn I. Matthew, Joy L. Lowe.
        p. cm.
    Includes bibliographical references.
    ISBN 1-55570-431-X (alk. paper)
    1. Children's literature—Bibliography. 2. Children—Books and readings.—United States—Bibliography. 3. Best books—United States. 4. Children's literature—Study and teaching (Elementary)—United States. 5. Content area reading—United States.
6. Video recordings for children—United States—Catalogs. 7. Children's software—United States—Catalogs. I. Lowe, Joy L. II. Title.

Z1037 .M2865 2002
011.62—dc21

                                                                    2001044490

In Loving Memory of
Colleen Werner Lowe.

Contents

Chapter 6   Sports, Recreation, and Dance

Preface

The *Neal-Schuman Guide to Recommended Children's Books and Media for Use with Every Elementary Subject* will help teachers and librarians integrate the best of a broad range of children's literature into the excitement of everyday learning. This comprehensive, easy-to-use guide will lead teachers and librarians to the best resources available. In an effort to foster a love of reading in children in a range of curriculum areas, the guide explores more than 1,200 books, videos, software, CDs, cassettes, and Internet sites. The list is extensive — including classics as well as new publications through the end of 2001. Strategies for incorporating these selected resources into curricular areas are also provided.

As Dorsey-Gaines (1994) and many other researchers have demonstrated, children should encounter books frequently throughout their school day. Quality literature should be an important part of the learning experience in every elementary school classroom. Sharing books with children throughout the day illustrates the joy and importance of reading. As reading becomes an enjoyable habit, students will find their own feelings and experiences reflected in books. When children perceive the wonders of their world captured between the pages of a book they are on their way to becoming lifelong readers and learners. Teachers and librarians know this and are eager to incorporate literature into classrooms in all content areas. The challenge for busy educators is to find quality media that fit naturally into core curricular topics.

The current reading cycle involves moving away from using literature to teach reading toward a skills-based approach to reading instruction, Charlotte Huck noted in an interview (Carpenter and Peterson, 1997). This same trend was decried by Kathy Short (1998), which she described as "the worst of times." With this trend in literacy instruction, teachers and librarians are striving to strike the right balance. How can educators make the best of children's literature an integral part of the content area curriculum? Librarians' knowledge of current, appropriate materials combined with the teachers' knowledge of the content area curricula can offer children the greatest variety of appropriate books. Insights about curriculum content should be shared and discussed by teachers and librarians. The key is collaboration. It is essential that teachers and librarians work together with the common goal of choosing and using books and media that will expand the mind of each child.

The *Neal-Schuman Guide to Recommended Children's Books and Media for Use with Every Elementary Subject* contains annotations for contemporary children's books, videos, and related media, as well as presenting inventive ideas for exploring them. It carefully and completely explores each of the eight major subject areas: mathematics, science, language arts, social studies, physical education, health, art, and music. Each chapter begins with a brief overview of the concepts included in the curricular area. Ever mindful of the necessity of preparing students for the inevitable rigors of testing, the guide assembles — in one resource — each of the current subject area content standards. Each of the eight chapters is subdivided into useful, smaller topics (for example, math is arranged into a dozen topics — counting, fractions, time, money, and so on). Each of these subtopics are followed by book and media annotations and suggested ideas for exploring the texts. Chapters end with teacher references.

The annotations in each section are arranged by grade level with books for the youngest readers listed first. P represents preschool, K represents kindergarten, and grade levels 1 through 8 are indicated with their respective numerals. "And up" signifies books that can be used beyond eighth grade. The annotations include bibliographic information and suggested grade levels with the realization that teachers and librarians must rely on their own judgments as to the appropriateness of the books and media for their children. The annotations in each section are arranged by grade level with books for the youngest readers listed first. Following the annotations there are suggested explorations for books and media related to the particular curriculum area under discussion and general ideas for using other materials on the same topic. Each chapter concludes with teacher resources — including books, professional organizations, and Internet sites.

The *Neal-Schuman Guide to Recommended Children's Books and Media for Use with Every Elementary Subject* is equally effective as a collection development tool for elementary school libraries and district/regional curriculum libraries, as a planning tool for developing or updating units, or as a quick source for materials that will enhance a specific lesson. Please take the time to read the Introduction on page xvii. It provides critical information on meeting the needs of individual students, making personal connections, extending learning, and responding to literature through writing, discussing, questioning, and exploring. Also included is information on selecting materials and general suggestions for using children's literature routinely as learning resources.

Chapter 1 introduces books and other media that present math concepts in meaningful contexts as a part of children's everyday lives. In addition to the topics mentioned earlier, the guide explores numeration and number sense, shapes, addition, subtraction, multiplication, division, measurement, and problem solving. These materials provide opportunities for exploring and discussing math concepts in a natural, relaxed atmosphere.

Chapter 2 offers suggestions for interesting ways to explore pure and applied science concepts by a variety of noted authors. The section examining life science begins with the human body and senses. It continues with an exploration of animals including birds, mammals, reptiles, dinosaurs, insects, fish, animal adaptations and habitats, and exploring animals. Life science concludes with plants, environmental issues, and ecology. Earth sciences explore volcanoes and earthquakes, landforms, soil, and water. Space science reveals the adventures of stars, planets, and space travel. Light, energy, machines, weather, and seasons are all a part of physical science. This chapter also contains a section on scientists and inventors. Material selections exhibit the colorful graphics, enticing photographs, and engaging text that enhance students' learning with intriguing scientific explorations.

Chapter 3 focuses on the elements that enable children to identify, understand, and utilize components of English language arts. This subject is divided into the alphabet, parts of speech, word play, writing, speaking, and poetry. These materials easily lend themselves to children's exposition and expansion of concepts through discussion, listening, and writing.

Social studies, as seen through the eyes of characters that help students experience life in other times and places, are examined in Chapter 4. American history is presented chronologically. Exploration begins with individual sections on the age of discovery of the New World and proceeds through to the American Revolution and struggle for freedom, a new nation, a nation divided by the Civil War and the era of the changing nation that followed it, the troubled times of the first half of the last century to the challenges of life from the end of World War II to the present. This chapter also investigates people and places, geography, government, and biography. These books and media amplify information of historical and contemporary significance in lively, entertaining ways that capture the imagination and interest of children.

Chapter 5 discusses ways to use books and other media to examine the many aspects of good health. Topics include hygiene, safety, and nutrition. The inclusive and contemporary segment on families includes family constellations, divorce, adoption and foster care, and homelessness. Growth and development examines birth and growth, feelings, friendship, self-esteem, manners, aging, and death. These topics are presented in an informative manner that engages the attention of children and presents essential information.

Recommendations for teaching students about sports, recreation, and dance comprise Chapter 6. Topics include sports, athletics, recreation, dance, and dancers. These materials are of great interest to children and help develop lifelong skills for maintaining a healthy lifestyle.

Chapter 7 contains books and media that open up the world of art to children. This chapter illustrates artists, art appreciation, art in children's literature, and creating art. These materials enable children to explore the world of art and encourage them to create their own works of art.

Chapter 8 covers materials related to music, musical instruments, musicians and composers, types of music, and songs. Children learn about the different instruments, examine the sounds and effects of music, and learn to appreciate music and songs.

The appendix contains a comprehensive listing of teacher and librarian resources including journals, professional organizations, and Internet sites. Media sources include videotapes, audio books, and software. A subject index is complemented by a full title/author index.

We, the authors, constructed the *Neal-Schuman Guide to Recommended Children's Books and Media for Use with Every Elementary Subject* to be the best resource of its kind. It focuses on a great variety of subject areas, spells out the subject area content standards, displays complete and current book and media annotations, and includes innovative activities for responding to literature. We trust you will find it to be an effective, practical, and useful tool. We wish you the best of luck greeting this important challenge. Librarians and teachers know that the search for creative and interesting approaches to the successful integration of great literature into core curricula is rewarding. The fact that teaching and learning can become as much fun for adults as it is for children is simply a wonderful bonus.

REFERENCES

Carpenter, Marilyn, and Barbara Peterson. 1997. "Charlotte Huck — Children's Literature in the Classroom." *Language Arts* 74, no.7 (November): 546–556.

Dorsey-Gaines, Catherine. 1994. "Growing into Literacy Via Children's Literature, Children's Music, and Movement." In *Resources for Early Childhood: A Handbook*, ed. Hannah Nuba, Michael Searson, and Deborah Lovitky Sheiman. New York: Garland Publishers.

Short, Kathy. 1998. "The Best and Worst of Times." In *Literature-Based Instruction: Reshaping the Curriculum*, ed. Taffy E. Raphael and Kathryn H. Norwood, Mass.: Christopher-Gordon Publishers.

Introduction

BUNNY CAKES ARE NOT JUST ANOTHER PIECE OF CAKE

Red-Hot Marshmallow Squirters, earthworms, and caterpillar icing are Max's idea of ingredients for Grandma's perfect birthday cake. Ruby, his sister, decides on traditional ingredients of sugar, eggs, and flour for Grandma's cake. In the end Grandma is delighted with both cakes and has difficulty deciding which one to eat first. In *Bunny Cakes* (Wells, 1997) Max and Ruby each create a birthday cake in their own very different ways using their own very different ingredients. Other Max and Ruby books include *Bunny Money* (Wells, 1997), *Max's Chocolate Chicken* (Wells, 1999), *Max's Dragon Shirt* (Wells, 2000), and *Goodnight Max* (Wells, 2000).

Through encounters with characters like Ruby and Max, young children find pleasure in books. They relate to the characters because they see themselves as Ruby or Max or both. As they listen to stories, they learn about a great variety of worlds and situations, learn to love reading, and discover the joys and benefits of learning to read. Parents, other primary care givers, teachers, and librarians are often the first to share books with children, long before they are ready for school.

Many parents start their children's reading experience by taking them to the public library when they are quite young. In fact they may view their public library as a "pre-school learning center." They may solicit help from the children's services librarian or they may attempt to find what they want on their own. Many children as young as one or two years benefit from special infant and toddler story times and other programs. Many parents take part in these programs with them and learn how to take the book experiences home. But the important thing is that they take their children to the library. Children's early social, emotional, and cognitive development is greatly enhanced by learning how to read and learning also to love to read. One of the great myths in education is that literacy springs from knowing the mechanics, the skills of reading. Long before learning to decode words, children who acquire an emerging literacy foundation of familiarity with books have a head start on reading instruction. With guidance from parents, teachers, and librarians, children learn to enjoy reading as they read.

Just as Ruby and Max select different ingredients, parents, teachers, and librarians select different books for different children. Ruby and Max follow their own set of instructions for creating their cakes. Parents, teachers, and librarians recognize the uniqueness of each child by finding books appropriate to each child. This book provides teachers and librarians with clues to finding or creating interesting response ideas and resources to adapt to use to suit the needs of individual children.

When possible, literature should directly serve to implement the curriculum and not just be used as an introduction to a topic or as an extension of the textbook. The integration of literature and content area curriculum allows students to dive into the experience rather than just using literature as a springboard for the content (Schiro, 1997). Children's literature has been shown to foster language development, facilitate writing evolvement, encourage life-long reading habits, and nurture personal development (Funk and Funk, 1992).

Fortunately, many teachers question the efficacy of using a single textbook for content area instruction and understand the importance of providing students with a collection of resources written at different reading levels (Blintz, 1997). Additionally, teachers have come to understand the importance of allowing students to explore and discover their world rather than using didactic instruction to cover the required content. Teachers know that providing students with choices and giving students a high degree of self-determination motivates them to learn.

Children's literature presents information in a variety of formats and on a variety of reading levels with colorful illustrations and photographs. These books capture students' attention, and excite them about reading as they learn. Children's literature has the power to motivate students to read independently, to go beyond the walls of the classroom and the required content.

Content standards have been written by the professional organizations representing that subject area. Since the standards were written by different organizations they were written in different formats. The standards seek to provide all students with similar opportunities and experiences to assure that they learn the information they need to be productive citizens. These standards are guidelines to assist teachers as they make curriculum decisions. The books and media annotated in this book support the content area standards.

MEETING THE NEEDS OF INDIVIDUAL STUDENTS

Quality literature facilitates students' understanding because it can accommodate the different backgrounds and life experiences of the students, their prior general background knowledge, their purpose for study, and their reading levels. When children read an information or nonfiction book, they establish a framework or schema to assist them in reading more complex material about the topic in the future. Information books engage children in learning about their world and its inhabitants. A selection of carefully chosen books can address individual differences, focus on a topic in great detail, and present the material in a comprehensible manner. Literature has the power to "integrate all the dimensions of learning in a manner that reflects meaning and child appeal" (Hornburger, 1994:338). Using a variety of quality literature in the classroom helps assure that teachers reach all of the students in their classrooms.

MAKING PERSONAL CONNECTIONS

Children's literature enables students to live through others' life experiences and view the world through their eyes. "Before children can learn anything, they must love it, experience awe of the subject, and engage themselves with the content" (Cullinan, 1994:327). Ross presents a strong argument for incorporating literature in the content classroom:

> Because of their obligation to present the facts, textbooks often fail to communicate the feeling related to the tragedy of war, the horror of the Holocaust, the wonder of birth, or the beauty of nature. (1994:8)

Literature has the power to gather children into the story as they make connections between their lives and the lives of the characters. Making personally meaningful connections between the text and their own lives enables children to more fully comprehend and remember the concepts presented.

EXTENDING LEARNING

In literature, moral and social concerns are portrayed in such a way that help students to understand life in other times and places (Ross, 1994). Ross contends that the authors' sensitive, insightful writing leads students to greater understanding than can be accomplished by the presentation of facts alone. Carefully chosen literature enhances students' understanding, enjoyment, and interest in learning. Further, literature provides opportunities for students to examine subjects from multiple perspectives with great detail and imagination (Goforth, 1998; Ross, 1994). Students discover and develop an understanding of the different perspectives on a topic as they gain a broader understanding of material presented in literature (Goforth, 1998).

Children's authors take the time to fully define terms in meaningful contexts that allow students to make connections between the material they are learning and their own prior knowledge. Connections between subjects have the potential to enhance student understanding and retention of the material (Shutes and Peterson, 1994). Morrow, Pressley, Smith, and Smith found that integrating literature into literacy and science instruction resulted in significant gains in science facts and vocabulary (1997). Literature can be used to make connections between subjects. For example, David Macaulay's book, *Pyramid* (1975), connects social studies, science, and art, subjects students often study separately (Carter and Abrahamson, 1993). Hence, books found in a specific content area chapter may indeed be useful in other content areas.

RESPONDING TO LITERATURE

In his mathematics classroom, Schiro (1997) has students reread and reexamine *The Doorbell Rang* (Hutchins, 1986). "After experiencing, responding to, and reflecting on their literary encounter, children focus their attention on the book's mathematics, analyzing the meaning of that mathematics and the adequacy of its presentation" (Schiro, 1997:16). Using creative innovations, such as writing out the math problems on sticky notes applied to the pages, students change the book's presentation of mathematics to extend and enhance the text. Their innovations reflect careful, thorough attention to the text and illustrations.

Cohn and Wendt (1993) used *The Doorbell Rang* (Hutchins, 1986) and other children's literature selections in their math classes. They found that using examples from students' favorite books to model mathematical concepts enhanced their math class as well as captured students' attention. Using *Where Do You Think You Are Going, Christopher Columbus?* by Fritz (1981) enabled them to combine social studies and math as they examined maps and created charts. Throughout students' interactions with text, the teacher's role is to support and guide students as they construct their own meanings from the text. One way teachers do this is by modeling higher order questions that require the students to think deeply and question the text. Additionally, teachers encourage students to use metacognitive strategies to examine and extend ideas presented in the text (Campoy, 1997).

WRITING

When reading expository texts, students need opportunities to explore the text structure as well as opportunities to respond to the text in writing (Moss, Leone, and Dipillo, 1997). They contend that written responses facilitate the development of critical thinking and problem solving skills. Schroder discovered that her sixth grade students' understanding of chemistry elements was enhanced as they wrote picture books on the elements for younger students (1996). As they wrote, the sixth graders discovered gaps in their understanding that required them to return to their resources. They used critical thinking and problem solving to not only understand the elements themselves, but to be able to explain the elements in terms simple enough for younger students to understand. Bosma and Brower provide additional support for the use of literature in the science classroom (1995). They integrated children's literature into Brower's first grade science lessons on animals and found that students critically examined and compared the different books on animals. Students wrote about their science explorations and shared their responses during group discussions thus enhancing their literacy development.

DISCUSSING

Small and large group discussions provide students opportunities to explore books with their classmates and teachers in order to fully comprehend the concepts presented. These discussions are one way for students to continue their interactions with the books, to deepen their understanding of the content, extend what they have learned, to question the material presented, and to realize that there is no one interpretation for a text. Allowing students opportunities to talk provides these benefits: 1) enhances learning, 2) clarifies thoughts, 3) increases comprehension, 4) improves writing, 5) develops confidence, and 6) enables teachers a glimpse into their students' thinking processes (Cullinan, 1993).

QUESTIONING

McKeown believes that an effective way to assure that students fully probe the text is by having them question what the author is trying to say and to determine what the author means as they carefully examine passages of the text (1998). Students reading fiction should be encouraged to question the characters' reasons and actions. Why did he do what he did? What else could she have done? Having some students take on the roles of the characters provides the rest of the class with an opportunity for lively face-to-face interviews (Matthew, 1994). Students should be encouraged to return to the text while questioning the author and the characters. Teachers know that "when children seek out information for themselves, identify what is relevant, and use it for meaningful goals, they become more efficient at storing and retrieving facts" (Cullinan and Galda, 1994:314). Rosenshine, Meister, and Chapman's review of research on questioning shows that teaching students to generate questions results in comprehension gains (1996). Students must look critically at the text and extend their thinking beyond the text. When reading fiction, students should look for intertextual links between the books, and when reading nonfiction, they should look for the author's persuasive writing techniques (McKeown, 1998). These types of critical thinking activities involve children in using higher levels of thinking as they interact with literature in the content area (Davis and Palmer, 1992).

EXPLORING

Opportunities for exploration of text includes literature logs, dialog journals, writing workshop, reading workshop, partner reading, dramatization, readers' theater, projects, illustrations, cooking, and demonstrations. These activities require students to delve deeply into the book and create their own personal responses to share with others. *Using Literature with Young Children* (Coody, 1997) contains practical, detailed explanations of ways to extend children's responses to literature with examples of activities using a variety of texts. Yopp and Yopp's *Literature-Based Reading Activities* (1996) provides prereading, during reading, and after reading activities as well as a chapter on book making. Directions for activities, such as anticipation guides, feeling guides, and polar opposites, are followed by examples showing how the activities can be used with specific books. Anticipation guides ask students questions that require them to think about what they think happens in the story. Feeling guides require students to reflect on the characters' feeling throughout the story and to consider their own feelings about what they are reading. Polar opposites require students to think about character's actions on a continuum. For example in Jack and the Beanstalk, was Jack stealing from the giant or was he retrieving his belongings?

With technology, students are able to extend their responses to literature in a variety of ways. One way is by creating multimedia presentations to share with their classmates and other students in the school. Placing the presentations on a centrally located computer in the library or on a computer network provides students with an authentic audience for their presentations. These multimedia presentations with sounds, narration, and graphics facilitate the understanding of students from diverse backgrounds. Students can create electronic databases of book reviews to share their reactions to the stories with their classmates. Carefully selected activities extend and enhance students' interactions with the text as well as require them to use critical thinking skills.

SELECTING BOOKS

Galda urges teachers to carefully select the best books, because books that students can connect with can transform them (1998). Further, Galda advises teachers to select books that expand ideas and concepts of importance to the students, that reflect the students' world, and that relate to the classroom content. Teachers may be uncertain as to which books are appropriate for their students, and they may feel uncertain as to whether or not they can adequately cover the content when they use a variety of literature genres in their classrooms. Additionally, they may not have adequate resources to locate the books they need. Many have not participated in an extensive examination of children's literature since a children's literature class in college. Librarians at their schools and the local public libraries are excellent resources to help teachers locate the books they need. Other teachers may be willing to share books and other resources they use in their classrooms. Annotated bibliographies are found in the October issues of *The Reading Teacher* that has "Children's Choices" and *Language Arts* that has "Notable Children's Books in the Language Arts (K-8)." *Book Links* is another source of essays and reviews that link students and books. Additionally, *Using Literature with Young Children* (Coody, 1997) provides teachers with ideas for using books in the classrooms as well as for helping parents find books for their children. Carefully searching for and locating a variety of appropriate books requires time and up-to-date resources.

GENERAL SUGGESTIONS FOR USING CHILDREN'S LITERATURE

Just as Max and Ruby had different ideas about Grandma's birthday cake, teachers and librarians have different ideas about extending literature for content area learning. This book is intended to be a starting point to help teachers and librarians decide on their own "ingredients" and methods for creating the perfect "cake" for their children.

1. Share the books for pleasure and encourage the students to offer their personal responses to the books. Some books are for reading aloud to the children and others should be introduced to the students prior to their independent reading and exploration of the books.
2. Children enjoy opportunities to read and reread books. Younger students want the teacher to read certain books again and again. Older students want to read the books themselves once the teacher has read them aloud. Once read these books can be placed in the classroom collection, many of which can be on long-term loan from the school library for the students to explore independently.
3. Students enjoy responding to books in a variety of creative, open-ended ways. They like having choices as to how they respond to the books, and to be given opportunities to suggest ways to respond to the books.
4. Students need assistance in making connections between the books, the content area material, and their lives. Activating children's prior knowledge or filling in some gaps

in general background knowledge before reading and encouraging them to discuss the book after reading helps assure that the book becomes personally meaningful to them.

5. Literature presented in this book is suitable to a variety of ages, interests, abilities, and reading levels. When selecting books for children it is important to remember that children who are very interested in a topic are often able to read books above their normal reading level.

6. Many of the books discussed in these chapters can be integrated into more than one subject area. Connecting books across subject areas enhances children's comprehension and fosters retention of the concepts presented.

REFERENCES

Blintz, William P. 1997. "Exploring Reading Nightmares of Middle and Secondary School Teachers." *Journal of Adolescent and Adult Literacy* 41, no. 1 (January): 12-24.

Bosma, Bette, and Marilyn Brower. 1995. "A First-Grade Literature-Based Science Program." In *Children's Literature in an Integrated Curriculum: The Authentic Voice*, eds. Bette Bosma and Nancy D. Guth. New York: Teachers College Press.

Campoy, Renee W. 1997. "Creating Moral Curriculum: How to Teach Values Using Children's Literature and Metacognitive Strategies." *Reading Improvement* 34, no. 2 (Summer): 54-65.

Carter, Betty, and Richard F. Abrahamson 1993. "Factual History: Nonfiction in the Social Studies Program." In *Fact and Fiction: Literature across the Curriculum,* ed. Bernice E. Cullinan. Newark, Del.: International Reading Association.

Cohn, D., and S. J. Wendt. 1993. "Literature Adds Up for Math Class." In *Fact and Fiction: Literature across the Curriculum*, ed. Bernice E. Cullinan. Newark, Del.: International Reading Association.

Coody, Betty. 1997. *Using Literature with Young Children*. 5th ed. Madison, Wis.: Brown and Benchmark.

Cullinan, Bernice. E. 1993. "Introduction." In *Children's Voices: Talk in the Classroom*, ed. Bernice E. Cullinan. Newark, Del.: International Reading Association.

——————. 1994. "The Rhythms of Language, Literature, and Life." In *Resources for Early Childhood: A Handbook*, eds. Hannah Nuba, Michael Searson, and Deborah Lovitky Sheiman. New York: Garland.

Cullinan, Bernice E., and Lee Galda. 1994. *Literature and the Child*, 3d. ed. Orlando, Fla.: Harcourt Brace.

Davis, John C., III, and Jesse Palmer. 1992. "A Strategy for Using Children's Literature to Extend the Social Studies Curriculum." *The Social Studies* 83, no. 3 (May-June): 125-128.

Fritz, Jean. 1981. *Where Do You Think You're Going, Christopher Columbus?* New York: Putnam.

Funk, Hal, and Gary D. Funk. 1992. "Children's Literature: An Integral Facet of the Elementary School Curriculum." *Reading Improvement* 29, no. 2 (Spring): 40-44.

Galda, Lee. 1998. "Mirrors and Windows: Reading as Transformation." In *Literature-Based Instruction: Reshaping the Curriculum,* eds. Taffy E. Raphael and Kathryn H. Au. Norwood, Mass.: Christopher-Gordon.

Goforth, Frances S. 1998. *Literature and the Learner.* Belmont, Calif.: Wadsworth.

Hornburger, Jane. 1994. "Bringing Children and Books Together: Learning through Literature." In *Resources for Early Childhood: A Handbook*, eds. Hannah Nuba, Michael Searson, and Deborah Lovitky Sheiman. New York: Garland.

Hutchins, Patricia. 1986. *The Doorbell Rang.* New York: Mulberry.

Macaulay, David. 1975. *Pyramid.* Boston, Mass.: Houghton Mifflin.

Matthew, Kathryn I. 1994. "Questioning Storybook Characters." *The Oklahoma Reader* 293 (Spring): 8-12.

McKeown, Margaret G. 1998. "Discussion of Text for Understanding." In *Literature-Based Instruction: Reshaping the Curriculum,* eds. Taffy E. Raphael and Kathryn H. Au. Norwood, Mass.: Christopher-Gordon.

Morrow, Lesley M., Michael Pressley, Jeffrey K. Smith, and Michael Smith. 1997. "The Effect of a Literature-Based Program Integrated into Literacy and Science Instruction with Children from Diverse Backgrounds." *Reading Research Quarterly* 32, no. 1 (Jan/Feb/Mar): 54-76.

Moss, Barbara, Susan Leone, and Mary Lou Dipillo. 1997. "Exploring the Literature of Fact: Linking Reading and Writing through Information Trade Books." *Language Arts* 74 (October): 418-429.

Rosenshine, Barak, Carla Meister, and Saul Chapman. 1996. "Teaching Students to Generate Questions: A Review of the Intervention Studies." *Review of Educational Research* 66, no. 2 (February): 181-221.

Ross, Elinor P. 1994. *Using Children's Literature across the Curriculum.* Phi Delta Kappa Educational Foundation Fastback No. 374. Bloomington, Ind.: Phi Delta Kappa Educational Foundation.

Schiro, Michael. 1997. *Integrating Children's Literature and Mathematics in the Classroom: Children as Meaning Makers, Problem Solvers, and Literary Critics.* New York: Teachers College Press.

Schroder, Ginnie. 1996. "The Elements of Story Writing: Using Picturebooks to Learn about the Elements of Chemistry." *Language Arts* 73, no. 6 (October): 412-418.

Shutes, Robert, and Sandra Peterson. 1994. "Seven Reasons Why Textbooks Cannot Make a Curriculum." *NASSP Bulletin* 78, no. 565: 11-20.

Wells, Rosemary. 1997. *Bunny Cakes.* New York: Dial Books for Young Readers.

————————. 1997. *Bunny Money.* New York: Dial Books for Young Readers.

————————. 1999. *Max's Chocolate Chicken.* New York: Viking.

————————. 2000. *Max's Dragon Shirt.* New York: Viking.

————————. 2000. *Goodnight Max.* New York: Viking.

Yopp, Hallie Kay, and Ruth Helen Yopp. 1996. *Literature-Based Reading Activities.* 2nd ed. Needham Heights, Mass.: Allyn and Bacon.

Chapter 1

Mathematics

Children's literature presents math concepts in a natural way that makes sense to children. Literature enables them to see the connections between math and their everyday lives as they discover math concepts all around them. Through literature children can be exposed to math in natural everyday occurrences in meaningful contexts. These meaningful contexts are established when mathematical concepts are incorporated in stories (Whitin and Wilde, 1992). Students need time to explore and discuss math concepts. Sharing a variety of children's literature with them provides opportunities for exploration and discussion of these concepts in a natural relaxed atmosphere. Responding to literature through discussion and writing enables students to develop and use the language of math as they learn math problem solving, reasoning, and thinking (Schiro, 1997).

The National Council of Teachers of Mathematics' *Principles and Standards for School Mathematics* (NCTM, 1999) are guidelines for determining the content and processes of mathematics programs. NCTM recognizes the societal need for mathematical knowledge: mathematical literacy, cultural literacy, workplace mathematics, and active mathematics users. The standards provide guideposts to help determine students' progress as they develop the mathematical knowledge they need to be productive members of society. NCTM realizes that students need multiple opportunities to discover mathematical concepts in a variety of contexts, to analyze, solve, and reflect on mathematical problems, in addition to opportunities to create their own mathematical problems. The first five standards are content standards that focus on the content students should learn including:

1. Number and operations
2. Algebra
3. Geometry
4. Measurement
5. Data analysis and probability

Standards six through ten are process standards including:

6. Problem solving
7. Reasoning and proof
8. Communication
9. Connections
10. Representations

These standards focus on how students acquire and use the content knowledge and include activities such as visualizing, writing, reasoning, making connections, communicating, illustrating, and dramatizing. The process standards are met through the explorations found in each section.

Students experiencing failure in math may become frustrated. Through literature the teacher can minimize this frustration and provide excitement and encouragement as students delve into the mysterious, ordered world of mathematics. Frustration, discovery, and excitement are part of learning math; poems such as the ones in *Marvelous Math* (Hopkins, 1997) are a wonderful introduction to math concepts as they provide children with the feeling that someone else understands how they feel about mathematics. For example, children relate to Sammy who has a long division problem stuck in his head. These poems show children that their struggles with math are common occurrences and that mistakes can be used as a mechanism to aid in their learning. Students can be encouraged to write their own poems depicting their math frustrations and understandings.

Hopkins, Lee Bennett, editor. *Marvelous Math: A Book of Poems*. Illustrated by Karen Barbour. 1997. New York: Simon and Schuster. 32p. Grades: K–8.

This engaging collection of poems with large, colorful illustrations depicts how pervasive math is in the world. Sometimes math is confusing and overwhelming, until the order and wonder of math is discovered. The magical and mysterious side of math is presented in this poetry. These poems can be used as brief introductions to a variety of math concepts and to assure students that they are not the only ones who at times find math challenging or very exciting.

This is just one example of the way children's literature can enhance content area teaching. More and more children's books with a math theme are being published each year as evidenced by the books presented in this chapter. These books and other media described in this chapter demonstrate math as a natural part of life and provide the background knowledge children need to recognize math all around them. Literature is another resource for math teachers as they seek a variety of ways to present math concepts to students to assure that each student understands. Sections in this chapter include numeration and numbers sense, counting, shapes, addition, subtraction, multiplication, division, fractions, measurement, time, money, problem solving, and teacher resources.

NUMERATION AND NUMBER SENSE

Young children's introduction to mathematics begins with counting, comparing, and sorting objects they can hold in their hands and explore. Content standard one focuses on students' development of a sense of numbers and number operations. From the concrete, they move to the abstract as they learn numerals. Children need natural experiences with numeration at home and then at school. They need to count objects in their surroundings, such as the number of oranges in a basket, and then draw pictures of oranges to count. Comparing, sorting, and counting familiar objects helps to develop their number sense. Simple everyday objects like silverware being moved from the dishwasher to its proper place in the drawer provide explorations of comparing, sorting, and counting. Books and media contain natural explorations to help reinforce what children have learned and provide them with ideas for further investigations.

Standard two calls for an understanding of algebra, which includes working with patterns, relations, and functions. A basis for understanding algebra develops gradually from prekindergarten to high school beginning oftentimes with the discovery of patterns. From experiences with patterns, students begin to develop knowledge of functions (NCTM, 1999). Some of the books and media in this section introduce students to patterns.

BOOK AND MEDIA CHOICES

Florian, Douglas. *A Pig Is Big*. 2000. New York: Greenwillow Books. Unp. Grades: P–1.

Comparative size is introduced in this book for young readers with rhyming text and vibrant illustrations. The illustrations include familiar objects such as a pig, a cow, a car, and a truck doing fanciful things like the cow driving the pig to town in the car.

Swinburne, Steve. *Lots and Lots of Zebra Stripes: Patterns in Nature*. 1998. Honesdale, Penn.: Boyds Mills Press. Unp. Grades: P–2.

This photo-essay introduces children to patterns found in nature. The patterns in spider webs and snake skins and flowers are all waiting to be discovered. But the patterns are not just for looks; they also provide information. For example, tree rings tell the age of the tree. Simple questions encourage young readers to set off and find patterns in nature.

ifsrtfr*Millie's Math House*. 1991. Mac/Win. Redmond, Wash.: Edmark. Grades: P–2.

The engaging activities and cute animated characters entice young children to explore math concepts. Students learn about numbers, shapes, patterns, counting and have opportunities to practice simple addition and subtraction.

Swinburne, Steve. *What's a Pair? What's a Dozen?* 2000. Honesdale, Penn.: Boyds Mills Press. Unp. Grades: K–2.

The colorful, charming photographs in this book depict mathematical concepts such as first, second, pair, dozen, odd, and even. Children encounter familiar objects and scenarios as they learn the concepts. At the end of the book are review questions whose answers are displayed in both pictures in words.

Atherlay, Sara. *Math in the Bath (and Other Fun Places, Too!).* Illustrated by Megan Halsey. 1995. New York: Macmillan. 32p. Grades: K–3.

This book was written by a teacher as she helped her students discover that math was all around them wherever they are. Math is there in the morning when they awake, during the day, and at night as they fall into bed. Math becomes less abstract as students find it in every part of their lives. Included in this book are ideas for encouraging students to estimate, problem solve, and recognize math in their own environment.

Hubbard, Patricia. *Trick or Treat Countdown.* Illustrated by Michael Letzig. 1999. New York: Holiday House. Unp. Grades: K–3.

Using a Halloween theme the reader counts up to twelve and back down to one with haunted houses, ghosts, goblins, trick-or-treaters, and witches. Colorful pages, with animated characters, numbers, numerals, and easy-to-count objects enhance the enjoyment of basic counting. The author mentions in the text that all is make-believe.

McMillan, Bruce. *One, Two, One Pair!* 1991. New York: Scholastic. Unp. Grades: K–3.

Charming photographs of a pair of twins getting ready to ice skate serve as an introduction to the math concept of number sets. Patterns, matching, and predicting reinforce the concept. The left side of each two-page spread has two pictures with, for example, one boot in each picture and then the right side has a picture of a pair of boots.

Schwartz, David M. *How Much Is a Million?* Illustrated by Steven Kellogg. 1985. New York: Lothrop, Lee and Shepard Books. 40p. Grades: 1–5.

How Much Is a Million? introduces students to large numbers such as a million, a billion, and a trillion. Marvelosissimo the magician leads the way as he travels through the world in search of large numbers. This book engages children in a variety of problem-solving activities and includes information as to how he figured out the calculations. Older students want to figure out the calculations on their own. Steven Kellogg's whimsical illustrations extend and expand the math concepts being explored.

How Much Is a Million? **2000. Video. Norwalk, Conn.: Weston Woods Studios. 10 min. Grades: 1–5.**

This beloved book has been made into a video. Marvelosissmo leads them on this adventure through the world of large numbers.

Math Rock. **1996. Mac/Win. Minneapolis, Minn.: The Learning Company. Grades: 1–5.**

Games, videos, and songs are all used to reinforce a broad range of math skills in this interactive software program. Equations, sequence, geometric shapes, and patterns are some of the concepts presented in this software. Students find the program challenging as the games have five levels of difficulty.

Wells, Robert E. ***Can You Count to a Googol?*** **2000. Morton Grove, Ill.: Albert Whitman. Unp. Grades: 2–3.**

In order to try to get to a googol students have to multiply some very big numbers and as the author explains it's really no use trying to get to a googol, it is just too big. A googol is a number with 100 zeroes. To try and explain a googol, large numbers are explored and described in familiar terms. The book ends with a note about the mathematician who had his nephew name the googol.

Stienecker, Daniel L. ***Discovering Math Numbers.*** **Illustrated by Richard Maccabe. 1995. Tarrytown, N.Y.: Marshall Cavendish. 32p. Grades: 4–6.**

This book appears to be very elementary and simple in design but actually contains problems of varied levels of complexity. It introduces numbers and numerical concepts with a large variety of hands-on activities. This discovery approach to numbers helps develop children's problem-solving ability and enables students to develop their own problems to solve. This book is one of the Discovering Math series.

How the West Was One + Three x Four. **1997. Mac/Win. Pleasantville, N.Y.: Sunburst Communications. Grades: 4–8.**

While racing through the Old West students learn about order of operations and negative numbers while they develop their problem-solving skills in this challenging program. Students have the opportunity to play against the computer, against each other, or to work cooperatively as they race down a number line trail. This is a game they play over and over again.

Smoothey, Marion. *Let's Investigate Number Patterns*. Illustrated by Ted Evans. 1993. North Baltimore, N.Y.: Marshall Cavendish. 64p. Grades: 5–7.

Through a variety of problems and games older elementary students investigate the intriguing patterns found in numbers. Dots, patterns, magic squares, square numbers, and triangular numbers help students discover the order and logic of math. The Fibonacci Sequence is explored in addition to a variety of other number patterns. The wide variety of activities in this book assures that the needs of all students are met as they explore these intriguing patterns.

EXPLORATIONS

1. After reading *Lots and Lots of Zebra Stripes: Patterns in Nature* (Swinburne, 1998) take the students on a walk through the school grounds looking for patterns. This is also a great book to read to students prior to a visit to the zoo where they are sure to find an abundance of patterns in nature.

2. Before reading *Math in the Bath* (Atherlay, 1995) students' prior knowledge can be activated by asking them to recount what they did the previous evening. The teacher or librarian can use this discussion to lead students to talk about things in their houses they can count.

3. After reading *Math in the Bath* (Atherlay, 1995) students can illustrate examples of mathematics in their homes.

4. *One, Two, One Pair!* (McMillan, 1991) introduces students to pairs. This book can be introduced by asking students to tell about items they have two of at home or in the classroom. These items can then be listed on chart paper at the front of the room. After reading this book, students can then determine which items on the list are pairs.

5. Having them create their own book of pairs can assess students' understanding of the concept of pairs.

6. Students enjoy working with large numbers even before they fully comprehend them. *How Much Is a Million?* (Schwartz, 1985) challenges students to visualize large numbers and provides them opportunities to work with large numbers. Calculators enable students to manipulate these fascinating, large numbers.

7. To help students develop skills in estimation, fill a large jar with small candies. Help the students estimate the number of candies by modeling estimation strategies, such as counting the number of candies on the bottom layer of the jar and counting the approximate number of layers.

8. Working through the problems in *Discovering Math Numbers* (Stienecker, 1995) enables students to construct new mathematical knowledge from which they can then create their own problems. Students enjoy working with partners to create problems to stump their classmates. Modeling problems that require higher order thinking skills provides students with patterns and ideas for writing their problems.

9. As students read about magic squares, they begin to solve them. Once they understand magic squares, they want to create their own. *Let's Investigate Number Patterns* (Smoothey, 1993) encourages children to examine, analyze, and create their own number patterns.

10. Students can create math logs as chronicles of the problems they solve and the ones they create. These math logs enable the students to see their growth in mathematical knowledge.

COUNTING

The largest category of books available for use in the math classroom is the counting books. Animals, candy, feet, and clothing are just some of the objects found in counting books. These books are often children's first introduction to the number system. The best counting books have the numeral, the number, distinct objects to count, and only the objects to be counted on the page. In order to understand counting, students need extensive opportunities to manipulate a wide variety of common objects. They need to have their own sets of objects to count again and again. Providing students with counters to use while a book is being shared enable them to more fully understand the concept of counting. Counting helps students develop a sense of number and operations, which is reflected in content standard one.

BOOK AND MEDIA CHOICES

Cousins, Lucy. *Count with Maisy*. 1997. Cambridge, Mass.: Candlewick Press. Unp. Grades: P–K.

Children everywhere are crazy for Maisy! They can count along with Maisy as she explores one ladybug, two flowers, three buckles, and more. This board book with large colorful pictures captures the attention of very young children just learning to count. It is one they want to return to again and again on their own.

Miranda, Anne. *Vroom, Chugga, Vroom-Vroom*. Illustrated by David Murphy. 1998. New York: Turtle. Unp. Grades: P–1.

Brightly colored, numbered racecars with animated faces speed to the finish line. Just as real racecars encounter problems during the course of the race, so do these cars. Young children enjoy picking out the cars in the illustrations by number as the rhyming text is read. Excitement builds as the cars race around the track. The book begins and ends with two page spreads of the cars lined up with their numbers spelled out just below them. Young readers want to point to and count the cars on these pages before and after reading the book.

Marzollo, Jean. *Ten Cats Have Hats: A Counting Book*. 1994. New York: Scholastic. 24p. Grades: P–1.

This predictable, rhyming text means students will be chiming along as the teacher reads the repeated refrain on each page. An assortment of animals each with an assortment of possessions is depicted along with a girl with a hat. Her hat matches the animals' possessions. For example, on the nighttime visit to nine snails with trails she wears a lighted-miner's cap. On the last page ten cats have hats and so does the girl.

Lewis, Steve. *Cock-a-Doodle-Do: A Farmyard Counting Book*. 1996. New York: Lodestar Books. Unp. Grades: P–1.

Not only do students count with this book, they also get to make a variety of farmyard noises as they count. For example, after counting the four woolly sheep, students can then "Baaaaaa" four times. The numerals and animal sounds are written on the pages. Adding to the fun is a small mouse lurking on every page. Watercolor pictures depicting easily counted farm animals with their sounds make this a fun book to enjoy again and again.

MacDonald, Suse. *Look Whooo's Counting*. 2000. New York: Scholastic. Unp. Grades: P–1.

Stunning cut paper illustrations are a delight to examine as young readers search to find first the woodland creatures to count and then the numerals cleverly displayed in the owl's open wings. Children are enchanted by the unique art form found in these illustrations. They learn to count along with Owl as she travels through the night sky.

Lifesize Animal Counting Book. 1994. New York: DK. 32p. Grades: P–1.

This oversized book can easily be seen by a large group of children seated on the floor surrounding their teacher. Children can easily see the numeral, the number, and the phrase describing the cuddly, adorable animals that fill the pages. In the top right corner of each page, and just above the numeral, is the corresponding number of ladybugs. This book goes beyond ten to twenty and one hundred. This is a book that can be used again and again by children as they increase their number sense. The end-pages of the book are covered with rows of ladybugs that can be counted by advanced counters.

Krudwig, Vickie Leigh. *Cucumber Soup*. Illustrated by Craig McFarland Brown. 1998. Golden, Colo.: Fulcrum. Unp. Grades: P–3.

When a cucumber falls from the vine and lands on an ant mound, ten determined ants attempt to move the cucumber. They are joined by other groups of animals in the garden counting down from ten, such as nine noisy mosquitoes and two praying mantises. By working together the animals succeed in moving the cucumber and sit down to enjoy cucumber soup. A recipe for cucumber soup is included. This book won a Benjamin Franklin award.

Schlein, Miriam. *More Than One*. 1996. New York: Greenwillow Books. 24p. Grades: P–3.

Advance counting concepts are presented in *More Than One* as children discover how the number one can actually be more than one. For example, one pair of shoes is actually two shoes, one family can have an unlimited number of members, and one dozen eggs are actually twelve eggs.

Bohdal, Susi. *1, 2, 3 What Do You See? An Animal Counting Book.* 1997. New York: North-South Books. 32p. Grades: K–1.

In *1, 2, 3 What Do You See?* animals from around the world cavort across the pages of this book. A freckle-faced little girl who brings them whimsical gifts visits the animals. Below the border on the bottom of the page the animals are shown using their gifts. Each two-page layout depicts the numeral, the number, and the correct number of animals.

Hamm, Diane Johnston. *How Many Feet in the Bed?* Illustrated by Kate Salley Palmer. 1991. New York: Simon and Schuster Children's Books. Unp. Grades: K–2.

Dad's quiet morning alone in bed is interrupted when his daughter asks how many feet are in the bed. In response to his reply of two, she climbs in bed with him and increases the number to four. The number of feet in the bed continues to increase by twos as her little brother, her mom, and finally, the baby join them. They keep a count until each person leaves the bed and eventually goes to breakfast. Colorful, charming illustrations enhance this Saturday morning counting adventure.

Sierra, Judy. *Counting Crocodiles.* Illustrated by Will Hillenbrand. 1997. New York: Scholastic. Unp. Grades: K–2.

A clever monkey living in a lemon tree and longing to cross the sea to get to a banana tree devises a clever plan to convince the hungry crocodiles to aid him. He tricks the crocs into allowing him to count them to see how many of them there actually are. He lines them up from one to fifty-five spread across the sea. As he counts he hops across them to get to the island with the banana tree. He then counts them back from fifty-five to one as he crosses the sea back to his own island, his arms laden with bananas. This rhythmic story with its appealing illustrations is a fun way to practice counting.

Wells, Rosemary. *Emily's First 100 Days of School.* 1999. New York: Hyperion Books for Children. Unp. Grades: K–2.

As Emily and her classmates begin the long count to the first one hundred days of school, they discover that numbers are all around them. Emily's family becomes involved in the class project as they help her find numbers, such as Grandpa's sixty-eight bulbs, and the eighty-nine calories in her aunt's soup. This bright, colorful book is a joyous celebration of numbers, counting, family, and school projects that involve everyone.

Cuyler, Margery. *100th Day Worries*. Illustrated by Arthur Howard. 1999. New York: Simon and Schuster. Unp. Grades: K–2.

Every child and parent who has ever been faced with finding one hundred objects to bring to school to celebrate the one hundredth day of school appreciates this story of a child's search for just the right objects to bring. In the end her collection of one hundred objects includes ten sets of objects with ten items in each set. But the most important thing about her collection was that all of the members of her family contributed to the collection. This book is available as an audiocassette produced by Spoken Arts, New Rochelle, NY.

Michelson, Richard. *Ten Times Better*. Illustrated by Leonard Baskin. 2000. Tarrytown, N.Y.: Marshall Cavendish. 40p. Grades: K–3.

Vibrant watercolors, clever wordplay, whimsical verse, and charming animals make learning to count by ten fun. This is a book for reading aloud at story time. The book concludes with one hundred bumblebees waiting to be counted and multiplied.

EXPLORATIONS

1. Large animal pictures from magazines such as *National Geographic* or *Audubon* can be mounted on tag board and the numeral, number, and the animal's name can be written on the back and then laminated. Once shared with the students, they can be placed in the math center for independent explorations.

2. Popsicle stick puppets of cats and paper hats created by the children can be used to dramatize the story, *Ten Cats Have Hats* (Marzollo, 1994). The cats and hats can also be used for a variety of counting and classifying activities.

3. Students can bring hats from home and create their own class counting book based on the variety of hats brought to school. These hats can also be sorted and classified.

4. Students can bring their favorite stuffed animals from home and count with the young girl in *1, 2, 3 What Do You See?* (Bohdal, 1997) as she counts the animals. Students can then brainstorm ideas for gifts for their stuffed animals and tell how the stuffed animals would use the gifts.

5. Challenging students to determine the number of feet in their family, their classroom, the cafeteria, and the school bus can extend the counting by twos explored in *How Many Feet in the Bed?* (Hamm, 1991).

6. With a selection of counters, students can count along with the monkey as it counts the crocodiles lined up in the sea in *Counting Crocodiles* (Sierra, 1997).

7. After reading *Look Whooo's Counting* (MacDonald, 2000), provide children with a variety of wallpaper samples to create their own woodland counting scenes.

8. Students can look around the classroom, school, and library to find examples of when one is more than one. A note can be sent home to parents asking them to help students find additional examples at home, on the television, and in the community. Students can share examples they find with their classmates.

9. Walking around the neighborhood provides children with opportunities for counting items they see. Students can record items they see one of, then items they see two of, then three of until they get to an appointed number such as ten or twenty. Once back in the classroom, they can create a wall frieze putting their items in numerical order.

10. After reading the story *Emily's First 100 Days of School* (Wells, 1999), have students involve their families in finding numbered items in their households.

11. After reading the story *100th Day Worries* (Cuyler, 1999) list the ten sets on the board and have students try to remember who contributed each set of objects to the collection. Demonstrate to the students how to look back in the text to check their answers.

SHAPES

Active explorations with two- and three-dimensional shapes enhance students' understanding of geometric objects. Content standard three addresses the importance of students developing their spatial sense and understanding of geometry. Students need to analyze, describe, draw, classify, and create shapes. Those students who struggle with numerical skills may find it easier to understand geometric concepts. Literature provides students a variety of informal examples of geometric principles in the environment. Students need a strong foundation in order to succeed in the more formal geometric applications they will encounter in later years.

BOOK AND MEDIA CHOICES

Rikys, Bodel. *Red Bear's Fun with Shapes*. 1993. New York: Dial. Unp. Grades: P–K.

Designed for very young children, this book uses large, colorful illustrations to show the concepts of different shapes in everyday life. Red Bear explores the shapes in his world, both inside (egg, horn, blocks, toast, etc.) and outside (fence, ball, kite, moon, etc.). Bright colors and simple drawings entice youngsters.

Hoban, Tana. *Cubes, Cones, Cylinders, and Spheres*. 2000. New York: Greenwillow Books. Unp. Grades: P–1.

This wordless picture book is filled with bright, clear, color photographs of cubes, cones, cylinders, and spheres found both inside and outside. The photographs show children how these shapes are part of their everyday lives, such as traffic cones and ice cream cones. Once they become familiar with the shapes, children begin finding them in their own environment.

Rogers, Paul. *The Shapes Game*. Illustrated by Sian Tucker. 1990. New York: Henry Holt. Unp. Grades: K–2.

This book is designed with young children in mind, but adds verse to the pictures and plays a game with readers and listeners. All basic and traditional shapes are included with some that are not so basic. Riddles are used to attract the attention of children to the shapes around them. The pictures are kaleidoscopes of brilliant colors that appeal to toddlers, as well.

Murphy, Stuart J. *Let's Fly a Kite*. Illustrated by Brian Floca. 2000. New York: HarperCollins. 33p. Grades: 1–3.

Children with siblings relate to this book as Bob and Hannah insist that everything be divided equally and that they each get half. As their kite, the back seat, a picnic blanket, and a sandwich are divided young readers discover the symmetry in the objects. The book ends with activities for exploring symmetry and a short list of other books that explore the same concept. This book is part of the MathStart series.

Adler, David. *Shape Up!* Illustrated by Nancy Tobin. 1998. New York: Holiday House. Unp. Grades: 2–5.

In this book everyday items such as cheese slices, pretzels, and bread are used to create and explore triangles and other polygons. Large colorful illustrations guide students to create their own shapes. Puzzling, enticing terms such as vertex and isosceles are drawn and explained.

King, Andrew. *Exploring Shapes*. 1998. Brookfield, Conn.: Copper Beech Books. 32p. Grades: 3–5.

Hands-on activities, games, and projects enable students to create and explore two- and three-dimensional shapes. Step-by-step instructions, simple materials, helpful hints, and color-coding to specify difficulty level assure that the activities in this book can be used in every classroom.

***TesselMania! Deluxe*. 1997. Mac/Win. Minneapolis, Minn.: The Learning Company. Grades: 3–12.**

Not only do students learn about tessellations, symmetry, and patterns with this software, they also get to create projects such as calendars, t-shirt designs, puzzles, stationery, cards, and holiday decorations with their designs. A teacher's guide is provided with the software.

Wyler, Rose, and Mary Elting. *Math Fun with Tricky Lines and Shapes*. 1992. New York: Simon and Schuster. 64p. Grades: 4–7.

Games, tricks, and puzzles are used to explore geometric concepts and discover that math is all around even in some rather surprising places. Tangrams, tessellations, and pi are explored in fun activities that encourage students to stop and think about the concepts.

EXPLORATIONS

1. Geometric shapes are hidden everywhere. A field trip through the school halls can become a hide-and-seek adventure as children look for triangles, circles, squares, and rectangles. Parents can be encouraged to extend this activity at home by having students discover shapes in their homes.

2. Students and parents can work together to create a journal of common shapes they encounter in their neighborhood, such as stop signs and yield signs. Giving students opportunities to illustrate the shapes fosters retention.

3. Prior to reading *Cubes, Cones, Cylinders, and Spheres* (Hoban, 2000) introduce these shapes to the children. Then, after reading the book take them on an exploration to find the shapes in the classroom and on the playground. A note can be sent to parents inviting them to help their children find these same shapes in their home.

4. *Math Fun with Tricky Lines and Shapes* (Wyler and Elting, 1992) can be introduced to students by placing one of the problems on the overhead for the students to solve with a partner. Then, the book can be placed in the math center for students to explore and solve the problems in small groups. Students' understanding is deepened as they work with others to explore and extend their knowledge.

5. After students have determined which shapes tessellate and which ones do not, they will enjoy using *Tesselmania! Deluxe* software to rapidly create colorful tessellations.

6. Creating their own three-dimensional shapes helps students understand the often-abstract concepts of area and volume. Activities in *Exploring Shapes* (King, 1998) can be placed in a classroom center for students to complete with partners.

7. Students' personal dictionaries of mathematical terms can be started as they encounter new words, such as those found in Adler's (1998) *Shape Up!*

ADDITION

Children need extensive experiences manipulating physical objects as they practice addition computations (Sheffield and Cruikshank, 1996). Content standard one focuses on students' development of a sense of numbers and number operations. They need opportunities to model and act out the operations described in these books using a variety of math manipulatives. These manipulatives should be kept within easy access for students to practice adding. Learning addition requires that students be given practice sorting and classifying a variety of objects prior to counting. Additionally, students' understanding of mathematical concepts is enhanced when they engage in conversations with their peers about their learning. As students communicate and discuss their learning with others they are developing the skills described in process standard eight, communication. Books and media included in this chapter enhance children's understanding of addition.

BOOK AND MEDIA CHOICES

Chorao, Kay. *Number One, Number Fun*. 1995. New York: Holiday House. 32p. Grades: P–3.

Pigs, chickens, and other farm animals prance and balance in piles, for students to add and subtract. This book could be used as a counting book as well as an introduction to number sentences. The number sentence is on the left side of the page and the answer is displayed on the right side of the page with the problem depicted in the center of the two-page spread.

Leedy, Loreen. *Mission Addition*. 1997. New York: Holiday House. 32p. Grades: P–3.

Miss Prime's class is busy using addition to solve everyday problems in everyday situations. Ample opportunities are provided for students to practice adding along with Miss Prime's students. The answers to the problems are in the back of the book and provide immediate reinforcement for children as they work. Addition terms, addend, and sum are explained in an easy-to-understand manner. Miss Prime's students can also be found hard at work subtracting in *Subtraction Action* (Leedy, 2000).

Merriam, Eve. *12 Ways to Get to 11*. 1996. New York: Simon and Schuster. Unp. Grades: P–3.

Ordinary, everyday experiences are used to present twelve different fact families that all add up to the number eleven. This imaginative counting exploration uses words rather than numbers. As they read the book students can work together to write out the fact families.

Walton, Rick. *One More Bunny: Adding from One to Ten*. 2001. Illustrated by Paige Miglio. New York: Lothrop, Lee and Shepard. Unp. Grades: K-2.

Enchanting illustrations of bunnies frolicking on a wooded playground set the stage for learning simple addition as bunnies arrive one by one to join in the merriment. The brief, rhyming text with the repeated refrain "Here comes one more bunny" has children chiming in as the text is read. The fact families for each number are included on the page. Additionally, each page has objects to count other than the bunnies, and the number sentences for them are found at the end of the book.

Duke, Kate. *One Guinea Pig Is Not Enough*. 1998. New York: Dutton Children's Books. Unp. Grades: K–2.

One lonely, little guinea pig is soon joined by one more guinea pig and then another until they number ten. This colorful, humorous book shows loveable, huggable guinea pigs joining in a variety of activities. They are all introduced by name on the title page of the book. Simple addition number sentences are prominently displayed on the pages of the books as each guinea pig is added to the scene. At the end of the day all ten guinea pigs are joined by one parent making for twenty smiling, happy guinea pigs.

Appelt, Kathi. *The Bat Jamboree*. Illustrated by Melissa Sweet. 1996. New York: Scholastic. 32p. Grades: K–2.

These rollicking bats entertain the crowd at a drive-in movie. First one bat sings, then two bats flap, next three bats cha-cha-cha, and the numbers increase until the ten Acro-Bats perform. For the grand finale all the bats form a pyramid with the ten Acro-Bats on the bottom and the one bat lady singing at the top. This fun, zany book is an engaging way to practice counting and addition.

Goldstone, Bruce. *Ten Friends*. Illustrated by Heather Cahoon. 2001. New York: Henry Holt. Unp. Grades: K–3.

What better way to learn the fact families that equal ten than by inviting ten friends to tea, but be careful because ten groups of ten equal one hundred which leads to a very large tea party. Rhyming text and colorful, cheerful illustrations are used to introduce these simple addition equations. A chart at the end of the book shows all of the number combinations.

EXPLORATIONS

1. *Number One, Number Fun* (Chorao, 1995) serves as an excellent pattern for students to use to create longer number sentences for their classmates to solve. Creating number sentences gives students practice at representing numbers and depicting the relationships among numbers.
2. *Mission Addition* (Leedy, 1997) is an example of a book that students can use as a model for their own addition missions. Using their own classroom experiences allows students to build on their own knowledge as they demonstrate their understanding of addition.
3. *Storybook Weaver* software provides children with room at the top of the screen to illustrate their addition problems. At the bottom of the screen, they can write number sentences to accompany their illustrations.
4. After reading *12 Ways to Get to 11* (Merriam, 1996) students can search the classroom or school to find groupings that add up to eleven. Parents and siblings could help children explore their home for additional groupings.
5. While reading *12 Ways to Get to 11* (Merriam, 1996), students can use calculators or counters to work the complete fact families as the book is read aloud.
6. *One Guinea Pig Is Not Enough* (Duke, 1998) shares a pattern for students to model as they create their own addition books incorporating addition by twos or threes. These books can be shared with students in younger grades.
7. As the teacher reads *The Bat Jamboree* (Appelt, 1996), students can add the bats on

paper to see if they all get to fifty-five. Some students may want to work with counters to add the bats rather than using paper and pencil. This zany look at bats can be used to entice children to do their own research to discover information about bats.

8. *The Bat Jamboree* (Appelt, 1996) could be extended by having students work with different numbers of bats on the bottom row to look for a pattern to enable them to predict the total number of bats in pyramids with different numbers in the base.

SUBTRACTION

To understand the concept of subtraction, students need to be able to classify and sort objects, and to see subsets within groups of objects. Students need opportunities to manipulate concrete objects as they learn to classify and group. Additionally, manipulatives help students to discover, compare, and reflect on the four models of subtraction including take away, missing addend, comparison, and set within a set. Using manipulatives to recreate problems shared in books read in the classroom fosters students' understanding and retention of subtraction facts. As students develop their understanding of subtraction they are addressing content standard one, which focuses on students' development of a sense of numbers and number operations.

BOOK AND MEDIA CHOICES

Thaler, Mike. *Seven Little Hippos*. 1994. New York: Simon and Schuster. 40p. Grades: P–1.

In this variation of a familiar counting rhyme, seven little hippos persist in jumping on the bed, only to fall off one by one and bump their heads. Children want to sing along with the teacher as this book is read. The delightful, chubby hippos bouncing up, down, and off the bed can be counted again and again. Children enjoy seeing the hippos pursuing a familiar activity with predictable consequences.

Hutchins, Pat. *Ten Red Apples*. 2000. New York: Greenwillow Books. Unp. Grades: P–2.

Starting with ten red apples dangling on a tree, students enjoy subtracting by ones as the farmer's animals eat the apples one by one. The rhyming text, the repeated refrain, and the animal sounds have youngsters chanting along as the story is read. The end papers of the book show the farmer and his wife counting ten apples and provide the students with additional opportunities for counting to ten and back again to zero.

Hoban, Tana. *More, Fewer, Less*. 1998. New York: Greenwillow Books. Unp. Grades: K–2.

A wordless picture book with colorful photographs of various collections encourages children to count the collections and then compare them. Everyday objects are beautifully photographed, including shoes on racks, sheep in a field, and stacked red and green baskets. The simple, colorful pictures can easily be used to invoke higher-order thinking skills as students make the comparisons suggested at the end of the book. Asking students which pictures contain fewer objects, how many fewer objects, and which contain less helps introduce students to the concept of subtraction.

Sheppard, Jeff. *The Right Number of Elephants*. Illustrated by Felicia Bond. 1990. New York: HarperCollins Publishers. Unp. Grades: K–2.

The right number of elephants is a phrase repeated throughout this predictable subtraction book as the number of elephants needed to solve a variety of problems decreases by one as each problem is solved. A whimsical herd of elephants assist a young girl as she pursues activities such as painting a ceiling, playing cards, and escaping a rainstorm. This imaginative story introduces subtraction by one using a predictable phrase and pattern.

Duke, Kate. *Twenty Is Too Many*. 2000. New York: Dutton Children's Books. Unp. Grades: K–3.

Twenty amusing guinea pigs set sail only to discover that twenty guinea pigs are too many to have on board, so ten jump ship. Then, one by one the other guinea pigs depart in a variety of ways until only one is left. The subtraction equations are included on the pages. The book ends with all twenty guinea pigs cavorting on an island.

Murphy, Stuart. *Shark Swimathon*. Illustrated by Lynne Cravath. 2001. New York: HarperCollins. 33p. Grades: 2–3.

The focus of this math book is on subtraction of two-digit numbers. The Ocean City Sharks have to swim seventy-five laps in one week to earn the money to get to swim camp. With their coach's encouragement and their own determination they furiously swim as many laps as they can each day to reach their goal. The coach tallies the laps and records them on a chart demonstrating two-digit subtraction as the sharks race to their goal. At the end of the book are activities for further exploring subtraction of two-digit numbers. This book is part of the MathStart series.

Wells, Alison. *Discovering Math Subtraction*. Illustrated by Richard Maccabe. 1995. Tarrytown, N.Y.: Marshall Cavendish. 32p. Grades: 3–5.

Fifteen exercises are explained with problems solved by subtraction in this intriguing math book. Answers are in the back of the book along with a glossary of pertinent terms. These problems deal with popcorn, checkers, noodles, money, and guppies among other familiar things. Practicing math skills is fun when they are turned into games such as the ones in this book. This book is one of the Discovering Math series.

Toft, Kim, and Allan Sheather. *One Less Fish*. Illustrated by Kim Toft. 1998. Watertown, Mass.: Charlesbridge Publishing. 32p. Grades: 3–6.

The exotic, colorful creatures of Australia's Great Barrier Reef and their precarious existence are explored in this underwater subtraction book. Ten clownfish become nine when drilling for oil disrupts their habitat and so the subtraction begins. With each turn of the page one creature disappears as the countdown from ten begins. Along the bottom of the two-page spread is information on taking care of the creatures and their habitat. The book includes a picture glossary of the fish and other creatures as well as a glossary of terms used in the book.

EXPLORATIONS

1. *Read The Right Number of Elephants* (Sheppard, 1990) aloud to the students. Read the story again, stopping to write out subtraction word problems found in the books on the chalkboard, overhead, or chart paper. Then, work together with the students to solve the problems.

2. Using small counters, students can subtract by one as the teacher reads the *Seven Little Hippos* (Thaler, 1994). Students can be encouraged to see if they and their neighbors have the same number remaining.

3. *Seven Little Hippos* (Thaler, 1994) can be sung by the students to help them as they learn to count backwards. The sounds and rhythm aids students' retention.

4. Collections of objects in a math center can be used to encourage students to create their own *More, Fewer, Less* (Hoban, 1998) comparisons. After scanning collections of objects into the computer, students can create *HyperStudio* stacks posing questions such as those at the end of the book.

5. Prior to reading *Shark Swimathon* (Murphy, 2001) review two-digit subtraction with the students.

6. *Discovering Math Subtraction* (Wells, 1995) provides a variety of subtraction activities that students can work in groups to solve using a collection of simple materials.

7. Older students can be encouraged to create their own environmental count-down book using environmental problems in their community based on *One Less Fish* (Toft and Sheather, 1998). Internet explorations provide them with information specific to their area as well as provide them with information about similar environmental problems in other communities.

8. Students can devise their own subtraction activities and desktop publish their collections to share with other classes using word processing software such as AppleWorks or desktop publishing software such as The Print Shop.

MULTIPLICATION

Memorizing multiplication tables in order to complete a work sheet of multiplication problems is not much of an incentive to learn them. However, needing to memorize them in order to play games and complete activities might be just the incentive students need. Manipulatives provide students hands-on opportunities to portray multiplication problems using grouping for example by creating row-by-row displays to enable them to see multiplication as repeated addition. As students learn the multiplication tables they develop an understanding of numbers and number operations that address content standard one.

BOOK AND MEDIA CHOICES

Pinczes, Elinor J. *One Hundred Hungry Ants*. Illustrated by Bonnie MacKain. 1993. New York: Scholastic. 32p. Grades: K–3.

The youngest ant is disturbed by the fact that marching in a single line will take the one hundred hungry ants way too long to arrive at the picnic. He decides that the fastest way to get to the picnic is to march in rows rather than in a single line. Throughout the book the ants regroup into more and more rows to hasten their travels as they march past a variety of critters coming from the picnic carrying food. This clever story depicts multiplication in a painless, entertaining manner.

Appelt, Kathi. *Bats on Parade*. Illustrated by Melissa Sweet. 1999. New York: Scholastic. 32p. Grades: 2–5.

Join the animals in the grandstand as the bat parade rolls past. In lively verse the parade unfolds and as the Bat Marching Band appears, the multiplication fun begins. Starting with one drum majorette all the way to one hundred sousaphones, each group multiplying by itself (2 piccolos × 2 = 4), then all are added together for the finale.

Leedy, Loreen. *2 × 2 = BOO! A Set of Spooky Multiplication Stories*. 1995. New York: Holiday House. 32p. Grades: 2–5.

Six funny Halloween stories of pumpkins, black cats, bats, and funny witches introduce the multiplication facts from zero to five. For example, multiplying a vampire, bats, and snakes by zero makes them disappear. What better way to dispose of Halloween beasties and remember that multiplying by zero equals zero. At the end of the book the multiplication facts are written out and a multiplication table is provided.

Stienecker, David L. *Discovering Math Multiplication*. Illustrated by Richard Maccabe. 1995. Tarrytown, N.Y.: Marshall Cavendish. 32 p. Grades: 3–6.

Multiplication is presented through a variety of activities and games. Students are able to practice their multiplication skills as they play games. These problems solved by multiplication skills seem game-like to beginners in multiplication as well as more advanced students. This book is one of the Discovering Math series.

EXPLORATIONS

1. While reading *One Hundred Hungry Ants* (Pinczes, 1993) or *Bats on Parade* (Appelt, 1999) have students work with partners using manipulatives to rearrange the ants in rows and write out the multiplication problems. These activities provide students opportunities to use concrete objects to aid their understanding.

2. After reading *One Hundred Hungry Ants* (Pinczes, 1993) have students use what they learned to line themselves up in rows of different lengths while lining up outside after recess.

3. Students can write out the number sentences using the figures in *One Hundred Hungry Ants* (Pinczes, 1993) or *Bats on Parade* (Appelt, 1999). After writing the sentences on sticky notes, they can be placed in the book for others to solve.

4. Using manipulatives, students can work together with a partner to create multiplication problems for their partners to write as number sentences.

5. Once students are familiar with *2 × 2 = Boo* (Leedy, 1995), they can then create their own books of multiplication problems based on other holidays. Providing students with activities that let them visualize and demonstrate their knowledge gives teachers valuable insights into students' understanding of multiplication.

6. *Discovering Math Multiplication* (Stienecker, 1995) provides students with a variety of multiplication activities to explore with a friend. Students working together to construct their knowledge and share their learning assures a deeper understanding of the content.

DIVISION

Division may present problems for children who have not fully grasped their addition, subtraction, and multiplication facts. Students need opportunities to explore division in literature as they use manipulatives to work out the division problems found in books. Explorations with manipulatives and with writing out their own algorithms enhance their understanding of division. Grouping and regrouping manipulatives enhance students' understanding of division as repeated subtraction, fair sharing, and distribution. As students come to an understanding of division they are addressing content standard one, focusing on number and operations.

BOOK AND MEDIA CHOICES

Hutchins, Pat. *The Doorbell Rang.* 1986. New York: Mulberry Books. 24p. Grades: K–2.

Students can relate to this delightful story about sharing cookies with friends. As more and more friends ring the doorbell, the cookies have to be divided and divided again to see how many cookies each child will receive. Then, Grandma rings the doorbell and brings a surprise. Students can be encouraged to work together to write the number sentences to accompany the story. This book is also available on cassette in both English and Spanish from Live Oak Media, Pine Plains, New York.

Pinczes, Elinor J. *A Remainder of One*. Illustrated by Bonnie MacKain. 1995. New York: Scholastic. 32p. Grades: K–3.

The formations of the twenty-five marching bugs in the twenty-fifth squadron always have a remainder of one, Joe. Unfortunately, the queen does not like rows that are uneven, so Joe gets left behind. They try out a number of different marching formations until they find the one that will allow Joe to march in formation with them.

Stienecker, David L. *Discovering Math Division*. Illustrated by Richard Maccabe. 1995. Tarrytown, N.Y.: Marshall Cavendish. 32p. Grades: 4–7.

Using stars, decks of cards, pyramids, honey pots, and other items, this book shows how to solve problems in an entertaining way using the mathematical skill of division. Puzzles, games, and riddles introduce division concepts and capture the attention of youngsters. Answers and a glossary are located in the back of the book. This book is one of the Discovering Math Series.

EXPLORATIONS

1. With a bag of chocolate chip cookies, students can reenact *The Doorbell Rang* (Hutchins, 1986), as well as write out the various number sentences to accompany the story.
2. Purchasing bags of different brands of chocolate chip cookies sets the stage for students to explore a variety of math problems. Students can chart the number of their classmates who prefer a particular brand of cookies. Cookies can be taken apart and the average number of chips in each cookie can be graphed.
3. Once familiar with *The Doorbell Rang* (Hutchins, 1986), students can be challenged to divide a number of objects among differing numbers of students. Handfuls of small pretzels given to small groups of students will allow them to practice division as well as provide a nutritious snack.
4. After reading *A Remainder of One* (Pinczes, 1995), provide students with manipulatives and challenge them to discover which formations will allow the bugs to march in straight rows without leaving a remainder of one. Then, they can write out the division problems to accompany their calculations.
5. Using paper and pencil, a deck of cards, calculators, and mental arithmetic, students can solve the division problems in *Discovering Math Division* (Stienecker, 1995). Students' solutions can be orally presented and demonstrated to the class.
6. Students can write their own version of *Discovering Math Division* (Stienecker, 1995) using integrated programs such as AppleWorks or Microsoft Works.
7. Students can be challenged to tackle complex long division problems with their calculators in a division bee. Whoever comes up with the correct answer first wins.

FRACTIONS

Fractions are befuddling. Children learn that 1 + 1 = 2. Then, they discover that with fractions one whole equals two parts, or four parts, or even thirty-two parts. In literature children discover that fractions are all around them and are a natural part of their lives. They have all had experiences sharing food with siblings or friends. They know the importance of having things divided equally, of getting their fair share. These experiences can form the basis of their understanding of fractions. Literature can build on those experiences and help them to comprehend the logic of fractions. Using everyday occurrences students can become aware of the importance of fractions in their lives. As students make connections between fractions and their daily lives they are addressing content standard nine. Literature provides teachers with another way of presenting fraction concepts to students by providing realistic opportunities to explore fractions. The materials below provide a way to extend the fraction concepts presented in textbooks and make them meaningful to students. Many activities used to teach fractions involve measurement as for example, in cooking. This helps to address content standard four, measurement.

BOOK AND MEDIA CHOICES

Stienecker, David L. *Discovering Math Fractions*. Illustrated by Richard Maccabe. 1995. Tarrytown, N.Y.: Marshall Cavendish. 32p. Grades: 1–5.

Using decks of cards, flags, charts, and puzzles, Stienecker explains fractions with easy-to-understand examples. The drawings are colorful and appeal to first graders as well as older children. The book includes answers to the problems as well as a glossary and index. This book is one of the Discovering Math series.

Leedy, Loreen. *Fraction Action*. 1994. New York: Holiday House. 32p. Grades: 2–3.

Students enjoy learning the basic principles of fractions as they divide with Miss Prime's students. Cookies, sandwiches, shapes, apples, and marbles are all divided in the book and can easily be divided in a classroom setting.

McMillan, Bruce. *Eating Fractions*. 1991. New York: Scholastic. 32p. Grades: 2–3.

A variety of foods are used to show how fractional parts make wholes. These colorful photographs of a boy, a girl, and a dog hold students' attention. The left side of the two-page spread depicts the food as a whole and on the right side the food has been divided into equal parts. The sequence of dividing into halves, thirds, and fourths is repeated twice, which helps to reinforce the concepts. A banana is sliced in half, cloverleaf rabbit rolls are divided into thirds, and pizza is divided into fourths.

Adler, David. *Fraction Fun*. Illustrated by Nancy Tobin. 1996. New York: Holiday House. 32p. Grades: 2–4.

Fractions are fun when explored through a variety of hands-on activities, such as the ones in this book. Students quickly understand that they use fractions on a daily basis when they divide food and describe their ages as for example, eight years and five months. Once introduced to the concepts, students can explore them on their own using the activities in the book. The cartoon-like quality of the illustrations is especially appealing to children.

Schwartz, David M. *If You Hopped Like a Frog*. Illustrated by James Warhola. 1999. Berkeley, Calif.: Tricycle Press. Unp. Grades: 3–5.

From fractions students learn about ratio and proportion. Students delight in determining what their bodies could do if they had capabilities similar to those of various animals. Clever illustrations show animals and humans engaged in similar actions. For example, with tongues like chameleons children could slurp the food off their plates without using their hands. Just behind the slurping child is a rather dismayed mother. Short descriptions at the end of the book describe the proportions used to determine human capabilities based on animal capabilities.

ceb*Fraction Attraction*. 1997. Mac/Win. Pleasantville, N.Y.: Sunburst Communications. Grades: 3–8.

Fractions, percents, and rational numbers are the focus of this software program. Students make their way through four activity areas with three to four difficulty levels. The Analyze mode provides a visual explanation when students get stuck on a problem.

ceb*Math Mysteries: Fractions*. 2000. Mac/Win. Watertown, Mass.: Tom Snyder Productions. Grades: 4–7.

In this software program students find themselves in the town of Balancing Rock just as gold fever strikes. As they proceed through the word problems to unravel the mystery of who will strike it rich, students learn the skills they need for solving word problems. This is one of the Math Mysteries series, which includes whole numbers, advanced whole numbers, measurement, and advanced fractions. There is an Internet link that provides additional activities for students, www.teachtsp2.com/mathmysteries/.

ceb*Fizz and Martina's Math Adventures: Lights, Camera, Fractions*. 1998. Mac/Win. Watertown, Mass.: Tom Snyder Productions. Grades: 5–6.

With this software program students develop their problem-solving skills and they learn to communicate using mathematical vocabulary. Only one computer is needed to get the entire class involved in helping Fizz and Martina with their new cable TV detective show. This program is part of the Fizz and Martina's Math Adventures series. It received a Technology & Learning Award of Excellence.

EXPLORATIONS

1. Activities in *Discovering Math Fractions* (Stienecker, 1995) lend themselves easily to independent student explorations of fractions. They require simple materials, such as buttons, checkers, or colored squares of cardboard, that can be gathered and placed in the math center for students to explore as they extend their comprehension of fractions.

2. Groups of students can be divided into portions to provide a living-fraction display. Students can be asked to quietly divide the class in half, then into thirds, and so on.

3. Following along with Miss Prime's students, children can draw the fractions with her students. They can also divide marbles or counters along with Miss Prime's students.

4. After reading *Eating Fractions* (McMillan, 1991), provide students with snacks to enable them to eat their own fractions. Exploring fractions using food places students in a familiar context of having to evenly divide food with siblings and friends. Easily divided food such as popcorn, pretzels, and cheese cubes can be used to replicate the activities in this book.

5. Folding squares or circles of paper provides students with opportunities to practice the fraction problems presented in books independently or with partners.

6. Origami paper folding provides students with fraction practice as they make a variety of fanciful animals.

MEASUREMENT

Measurement requires active involvement of the students using both standard and nonstandard units of measure. Literature enhances students' understanding as they examine different forms of measurement in a variety of real-life contexts (Whitin and Wilde, 1992). Students enjoy measuring with nonstandard units of measure, as there seems to be something special about getting to measure objects with other objects. Content standard four addresses students' understanding of measurement and its uses in their everyday lives. Materials in this section help students to understand measurement.

BOOK AND MEDIA CHOICES

So Big! Illustrated by Dan Yaccarino. 2001. New York: HarperCollins. Unp. Grades: P–K.

This interactive flap book entertains the youngest readers as they repeat the refrain "So big!" and flip the pages to reveal how big the animals are. At the end of the book is a ruler to measure how big the readers are.

Pinczes, Elinor J. *Inchworm and a Half.* **Illustrated by Randall Enos. 2000. Boston: Houghton Mifflin. Unp. Grades: K–3.**

A curious inchworm decides to measure the vegetables in the garden where he lives. As he measures he calls on a quarter inchworm, a one-third inchworm, and a one-fourth inchworm. Together this group of inchworms introduces children to the concepts of measurement and fractions. Young readers listen for the refrain and chime in as the book is read.

Wilkes, Angela. *Children's Quick and Easy Cookbook.* **1997. Portsmouth, N. H.: Heinemann. 96p. Grades: 1–7.**

Fast, easy-to-follow recipes provide students with realistic experiences using measuring. Not all of the recipes require cooking, so they can be done in the classroom. Kitchen rules and a picture glossary provide students with support materials as they explore the world of cooking and measuring.

Leedy, Loreen. *Measuring Penny.* **1998. New York: Henry Holt. 32p. Grades: 2–4.**

Challenged to measure something in different ways using standard and nonstandard measures, Lisa decides to measure her dog, Penny. Using Penny and other dogs in the park, Lisa measures their ears with swabs and their tails with dog biscuits. She compares their weights by putting them on opposite ends of the seesaw. Students eagerly turn the pages to find out what will be measured next and how it will be measured. Then, they can venture out on their own to measure their own pets with standard and nonstandard units.

Math Mysteries: Measurement. **2000. Mac/Win. Watertown, Mass.: Tom Snyder Productions. Grades: 4–6.**

In this program students answer a series of word problems to solve the mystery of the crew members missing from a deep-sea outpost, and to determine the source of earthquakes. Students use their measurement skills to solve the problems. The software package includes a CD for use with the whole class, a CD of mysteries for students to solve, and a teacher's guide.

EXPLORATIONS

1. Using some of the noncooking recipes in *Children's Quick and Easy Cookbook* (Wilkes, 1997), students can measure and prepare classroom treats. This gives students an authentic way to work with fractions.

2. In order to make enough treats for the classroom, the recipes in *Children's Quick and Easy Cookbook* (Wilkes, 1997) will have to be doubled and tripled. Students can work with a partner and a calculator to write out the recipe adjustments.

3. Just as Penny (Leedy, 1998) is measured in a variety of ways, students can measure things in the classroom with a variety of standard and nonstandard measures. For example, students can measure their desks with the chalkboard erasers or their pencils.

4. Prior to actually measuring objects, students are encouraged to estimate the length of the object being measured. Once measured, they compare their estimates with the actual length.

5. When the students are gone for the day, the teacher can measure different objects in the classroom. These measurements are then placed on a chart. The next day the students first estimate which objects correspond to which measurements, then they take their rulers to determine the actual measurements of the objects.

TIME

We use the measurement of time more than any other measure in our daily lives. Young children are first exposed to time when they are told that lunch will be ready in one-half hour. Then, the child asks how long a half hour is, and the parent responds by explaining time in relation to the length of the child's favorite television show. Children mark time in holidays, birthdays, and summer vacations. Time is an abstract concept that is not readily explained with manipulatives. Students need a variety of opportunities to explore the concept of time in order to develop their understanding. The materials in this section provide students opportunities for exploration.

BOOK AND MEDIA CHOICES

Axelrod, Amy. *Pigs on the Move: Fun with Math and Travel*. Illustrated by Sharon McGinley-Nally. 1999. New York: Simon and Schuster. Unp. Grades: P–3.

Based on the author's real-life experience, the pig family misses their flight and ends up zigzagging across the country as they try to reach their cousin's house in Bean Town in time for Christmas. A map of the United States is included for students to be able to see the pigs' flight path. The cities on the map are labeled by their nicknames—for example, Boston is labeled Bean Town. Also included are activities involving time zones and mileage between the cities. This is one of the Pigs Will Be Pigs math series that focus on the NCTM standards.

Harper, Dan. *Telling Time with Big Mama Cat*. Illustrated by Cara Moser and Barry Moser. 1998. San Diego: Harcourt Brace. Unp. Grades: P–3.

Big Mama has important things to do that fill her day, so it is essential that she know how to tell time. A foldout clock with moveable hands enables young readers to change the time as Big Mama goes about her activities. Her activities include naps, snacks, and climbing into the irresistible new chair just as the sun warms it.

Hullabaloo Time. 1995. Video. New York: Dorling Kindersley. 30 min. Grades: K–2.

Young children enjoy learning to tell time with Buddy the elephant and Pip the mouse. These delightful animated puppets make learning fun. This video helps to reinforce the concepts presented in the classroom.

Llewellyn, Claire. *My First Book of Time*. 1992. New York: Dorling Kindersley. Unp. Grades: K–2.

Color photographs and brief text entries explain how to tell time throughout the day and night, the days of the week, and the seasons. Time is measured in the sequence of events that are part of a child's daily routines. At the end of the book is a foldout clock for telling time and a glossary. This is a book to send home with students for them to share with their parents and older siblings as the students learn to tell time.

Appelt, Kathi. *Bats around the Clock*. Illustrated by Melissa Sweet. 2001. Unp. Grades: K–2.

Click Dark, famous host of American Batstand, keeps the hits spinning and the dancers hopping as the clock spins throughout the twelve-hour dance session. Every hour the dancers switch to a different dance as they twist, swim, and jitterbug their way through the program. Young readers enjoy the rhyming text and the jiving bats, and adult readers enjoy reliving American Bandstand.

TimeLiner 5.0. 1999. Mac/Win. Watertown, Mass.: Tom Snyder. Grades: K–12.

This marvelous software enables students to quickly and imaginatively create timelines. Students simply enter the event with the corresponding date and the software arranges them in chronological order. The software allows students to import graphics, video, and sounds making these multimedia timelines both entertaining and a learning adventure.

Murphy, Stuart J. *Game Time*. Illustrated by Cynthia Jabar. 2000. New York: HarperCollins. 33p. Grades: 2–3.

The Falcons and the Huskies are preparing for the playoff to determine which team will be the league champion. The countdown begins a week before the big game and time is measured throughout the game in hours, minutes, and seconds. This book provides a familiar context for learning about time. At the end of the book are activities for exploring the concept of time. This book is part of the MathStart series.

Chapman, Gillian, and Pam Robson. *Exploring Time*. 1994. Brookfield, Conn.: The Millbrook Press. 32p. Grades: 3–5.

Bright, colorful illustrations, photographs, and diagrams depict changes over time using objects familiar to children. Components of time, such as solar time, historical time, and lunar time are explained in easy-to-read text. Accompanying the text are simple, creative activities enabling students to fully explore the concept. For example, in the section on keeping time, instructions are provided for creating a sand timer. A glossary is provided to further explain vocabulary used in the book.

Mandell, Muriel. *Simple Experiments in Time with Everyday Materials*. Illustrated by Frances Zweifel. 1997. New York: Sterling Publishing. 96p. Grades: 4–6.

These hands-on explorations of time help answer questions children have about shadows that shrink and grow and disappear, and a variety of other time concepts. Information is presented about telling time by the stars, the sun, the moon, and with clocks. Simple experiments enable the students to explore the concepts for deeper understanding, as well as making learning fun.

Darling, David. *Could You Ever Build a Time Machine?* 1991. Minneapolis, Minn.: Dillon Press. 60p. Grades: 4–8.

Time travel is an intriguing concept explored in science fiction. The scientific theories behind time travel are examined and explained in understandable terms with photographs and diagrams. This book explains the theories using concepts and objects familiar to children such as recording the past on camcorders and popular movies such as *Back to the Future*. The captivating question posed by the title of this book insures that it will be widely read and discussed.

EXPLORATIONS

1. Many of the activities provided in *Exploring Time* (Chapman and Robson, 1994) and *Simple Experiments in Time with Everyday Materials* (Mandell, 1997) can be used for independent or small group explorations in classroom centers. Instructions for some of the activities can be sent home for students to complete with siblings or parents, such as the Egyptian shadow clock or a sundial.
2. After reading *Game Time* (Murphy, 2000), have students predict how long it will take them to do things during the school day, such as lining up for lunch or walking to the cafeteria. Then, time the students as they move and compare their predictions with the actual amount of time required.
3. Posting the class schedule near a clock helps students grasp the concept of time passing.
4. Parents and students can work together to create a timeline of the moon's changes during the month.
5. Timelines of historical periods help students place events in relation to one another. TimeLiner software enables students to create their own timelines.

6. Students can create time logs to determine how much time they spend each day watching television, eating, playing with friends, sleeping, and other routine activities. Their results can be compared with a partner. Class averages for each activity can be determined and charted. Prior to keeping the log, students could be asked to estimate how much time they spend at each activity.

7. A class time capsule can be created at the beginning of the year and opened at the end of the year to note the changes occurring during the course of the year. Students can use higher-order thinking skills to make predictions about what they will be learning during the year and place their predictions in the time capsule.

MONEY

Students' interest in money begins at earlier and earlier ages as they are bombarded with advertisements enticing them to obtain the latest in clothes and toys. As cash is replaced by checks, checks by credit cards, and credit cards by online electronic banking, the concrete coins and bills are not as available to help students grasp the concept of money. The use of informational books and other media expand the opportunities for students to comprehend the value of money.

BOOK AND MEDIA CHOICES

Wells, Rosemary. *Bunny Money*. 1997. New York: HarperCollins. 32p. Grades: K–3.

Max and Ruby's excursion to buy a birthday present for their grandmother provides a context for learning about spending money; however, this concept is secondary to the story. Max and Ruby's antics and decisions about how to spend their money entertain both old and young who can easily relate to their adventure. Play money in the back of the book can be photocopied for students to use to keep track of how Max and Ruby spend their money.

Adams, Barbara J. *The Go-Around Dollar*. Illustrated by Joyce Zarins. 1992. New York: Four Winds Press. Unp. Grades: 1–3.

This story of the travels of a dollar bill helps young students understand how money changes hands during the course of a day. Once the story is read, discussed, and related to the students' own lives, they can then revisit the story to examine the facts and comments about money accompanying each event in the story. For example, when Jennifer pulls the dollar out of her just-washed jeans, information about the durability of dollars is provided.

Schwartz, David. M. *If You Made a Million*. Illustrated by Steven Kellogg. 1989. New York: Mulberry Books. Unp. Grades: 2–4.

Marvelosissimo, the mathematical magician, demonstrates for young mathematicians how to earn, invest, and save money in order to end up with a million dollars. Kellogg's enchanting illustrations and Schwartz's simple explanations combine to make this a terrific introduction to money for students. Older students enjoy the author's note that expands on the money concepts presented in the book.

Godfrey, Neale S. *A Money Adventure: Earning, Saving, Spending, Sharing.* Illustrated by Randy Verougstraete. 1996. Parsippany, N.Y.: Silver Press. 32p. Grades: 2–5.

A group of children wanted to find something fun to do for the summer. They decided to open a business and decided to make frozen fruit juice pops they would call "KID Pops." They each invest one dollar to buy the supplies and ingredients they need and open a bank account to deposit their profits. They discover that outside circumstances affect their sales (rain) and they find a way to share their profits by donating to the swimming pool fund in their town. This is a very effective way of sharing economic information with youngsters.

Maestro, Betsy. *The Story of Money.* Illustrated by Giulio Maestro. 1993. New York: Clarion Books. 48p. Grades: 3–5.

The narrative text and detailed illustrations combine to make this an interesting informative book that examines the history of money. An interesting point is made about the fact that paper money was accepted in China because the people believed in their strong government, whereas in Europe people did not trust their governments and so did not believe in the paper money the governments issued.

Godfrey, Neale. *Ultimate Kids' Money Book.* Illustrated by Randy Verougstraete. 1998. New York: Simon and Schuster. 122p. Grades: 3–6.

This comprehensive book examines the history, banking, economics, credit, and investing of money. Colorful illustrations, charts, detailed diagrams, photographs, and posted definitions interspersed through the text make the concepts presented understandable and fun to learn. Friendly cartoon-character students posing questions and making comments throughout the pages keep students reading to find the answers, as well as thinking about what they have read. A Penny for Your Thoughts questions posed in each section require students to use higher-order thinking skills to go beyond the text and connect the material to their own lives.

Leedy, Loreen. *The Monster Money Book.* 1992. New York: Holiday House. 32p. Grades: 4–8.

The Monster Club members have fifty-four dollars in their treasury and are trying to decide what to do with the money. Their activities serve as an introduction to money and finances as students discover how the club members saved their money, set up a budget, and made decisions about spending and giving the money away. This is a good basic book about money for students as it names and pictures the coins and tells how many coins make a dollar. Additionally, checking accounts are explained and a glossary at the end of the book provides definitions of the terms used.

Otfinoski, Steve. *Kid's Guide to Money: Earning It, Saving It, Spending It, Growing It, Sharing It.* 1996. New York: Scholastic. 128p. Grades: 3–8.

This guide provides information on ways to earn money, save money, how to get the most for your money, and how the stock market works. Throughout the book Money Moments provide interesting money trivia such as the fact that a stamp bought in 1847 for five cents sold for a million dollars in 1981. Kids Cents inserts provide tips from kids on great ways to make money grow.

Hot Dog Stand: The Works. 1996. Mac/Win. Pleasantville, N.Y.: Sunburst Communications. Grades: 5 and up.

Students have the opportunity to run a hot dog stand at a sports arena in this challenging simulation. The successful operation of the stand requires them to use their critical-thinking, problem-solving, and communication skills. Students enjoy playing the simulation and may not be aware of all the things they learn as they operate the hot dog stand.

EXPLORATIONS

1. Prior to reading *Bunny Money* (Wells, 1997) students can be asked to relate their experiences buying presents for others. As they listen to the story, older students can be encouraged to write out the number sentences to accompany Max and Ruby's purchases.
2. *Bunny Money* (Wells, 1997) can be extended in the math center where students can be given a set amount of play money to shop from newspaper advertisements and catalogs.
3. Older students enjoy tracking stock prices for familiar brand names using a computer-generated spreadsheet to keep track of their gains and losses. These stock records can then be charted over the course of several weeks.
4. A class pet gives students an opportunity to raise money for the purchase of the pet and necessary pet supplies. Students can do research to determine the best pet for the class and to learn what will be needed to care for the pet.
5. Older students enjoy working with make-believe checking accounts and catalogs to purchase Christmas presents for parents and friends. This real-world learning experience gives students practice budgeting and spending money.
6. Students can be given a hypothetical allowance and then be required to create a budget for spending and investing the money.
7. Students can visit Zillions – Consumer Reports Online for Kids at www.zillions.org to learn about spending their money wisely and viewing toy ratings.

PROBLEM SOLVING

Content standard six reflects the importance of students developing problem-solving skills. Literature provides students with a vast array of math problems to solve. These problems are likely to spark students' interest in solving problems. Young children need early exposures to solving problems, as this is when the thought processes used in problem solving are developed (Shaw and Blake, 1998). Perception and organization abilities are needed for problem solving and these skills can be practiced as students discover how to solve the problems presented in a variety of children's literature. Computer software programs and calculator activities give students opportunities to practice their problem-solving skills.

BOOK AND MEDIA CHOICES

Ledwon, Peter, and Marilyn Mets. *Midnight Math: Twelve Terrific Math Games.* **2000. New York: Holiday House. 32p. Grades: K–3.**

Just as the mice in this book do not realize they are improving their math skills as they play games, students also focus on the games rather than the skills they are practicing. The authors combine photographs with cartoon-like drawings to attract and hold students' attention. Readily available materials and step-by-step directions enable students to play these games on their own.

The Graph Club. **1998. Mac/Win. Watertown, Mass.: Tom Snyder Productions. Grades: K–4.**

Graphing is easy and fun with this terrific software program. Students learn to create and interpret graphs in order to make decisions about the data they have collected. Younger students enjoy making the picture graphs. The program also lets them create bar, circle, table, and line graphs. A teacher's guide is provided with the software. This software won a Technology and Learning Award of Excellence.

Tang, Greg. *The Grapes of Math: Mind-Stretching Math Riddles.* **Illustrated by Harry Briggs. 2001. New York: Scholastic. Unp. Grades: 1–3.**

Festive illustrations and rhyming text make this book a visual and melodic feast for the eyes and ears. Within the pages of the book, Tang illustrates for young and old four important problem-solving techniques: be open-minded, think strategically, use a variety of skills, and organize the information. His focus is on thinking creatively and using common sense rather than memorizing and using formulas. The answers to the questions posed throughout the book and the techniques described are found at the end of the book.

Interactive Math Journey. 1997. Mac/Win. Minneapolis, Minn.: The Learning Company. Grades: 1–3.

This program includes problem-solving activities encompassing patterns and shapes, addition, subtraction, measurement, fractions, and multiplication. It includes four different types of activities: 1) math tales, 2) math explorations, 3) math songs, and 4) math challenges. Colorful graphics, animations, and sounds hold the attention of young students as they explore the math concepts presented in the software. The program includes overhead pattern blocks and a teacher's guide.

Demi. *One Grain of Rice: A Mathematical Folktale*. 1997. New York: Scholastic. Unp. Grades: 2–4.

In long-ago India during a time of famine, a young girl has the Rajah promising to give her one grain of rice on the first day and double the number of grains each day for 30 days. Imagine the shock to the Rajah when the total amount adds up to more than a billion grains of rice. The book provides the instructions for completing this mathematical calculation.

Scieszka, Jon, and Lane Smith. *Math Curse*. 1995. New York: Viking Children's Books. 32p. Grades: 2–8.

In this story a girl discovers that it is impossible to escape math as she goes about her daily activities. By the end of the day she is a "math zombie" and rather than try to figure out what fraction of twenty-four cupcakes twenty-five people will each get, she declares herself allergic to cupcakes.

Nagela, Ann Whitehead, and Cindy Bickel. *Tiger Math: Learning to Graph from a Baby Tiger*. 2000. New York: Henry Holt. 32p. Grades: 3–6.

The growth and development of a Siberian tiger cub in the Denver Zoo is chronicled in pictures, graphs, and text. This book shows students a practical application for graphing and shows them that graphing information makes it more understandable.

Adler, David A. *Calculator Riddles*. Illustrated by Cynthia Fisher. 1995. New York: Holiday House. 32p. Grades: 3–7.

Enter the number 14 on a calculator, then turn it upside down. Can you read the word 'hi?" If your answer is yes, then you're ready to start solving calculator riddles where the answer to the math problem is also the answer to the riddle. This book provides a variety of math calculations that form calculator words. Instructions on using a calculator introduce the concept and the answers are provided at the end of the book.

Anno, Mitsumasa. *Anno's Magic Seed*. 1992. New York: Philomel Books. Unp. Grades: 3–8.

With simple addition and subtraction skills students can solve math problems woven into both the text and illustrations as Jack's two mysterious seeds begin to multiply. Older students delight in discovering and solving the increasingly complex math problems encountered as the story develops. A note from Anno explains that this is more than a math puzzle; there is also a lesson to be learned from the story.

***Puzzle Tanks*. 1992. Mac/Win. Pleasantville, N.Y.: Sunburst Communications. Grades: 3–8.**

Students use their problem-solving skills to transfer liquids between tanks to reach the target level in this engaging software program. Solving these logic puzzles also requires them to use their knowledge of basic math operations. Practicing basic operations while solving puzzles is a great deal more fun than practicing them with drill and practice software. This software is available for the TI-73 calculator and the Windows version is available in Spanish.

***The Factory Deluxe*. 1998. Mac/Win. Pleasantville, N.Y.: Sunburst Communications. Grades: 4–8.**

Once students get started on this program it is hard to convince them to stop. This program is designed to develop their geometry, visual thinking, and problem-solving skills. They do not realize this because they are too busy creating products. The program has different levels of difficulty. Students can work alone or with a partner and can play against each other or the computer.

***Graph Master*. 2000. Mac/Win. Watertown, Mass.: Tom Snyder Productions. Grades: 4–8.**

Collecting data and analyzing it in order to solve problems are skills students use in math, social studies, and science. Graph Master helps them create nine different types of graphs including bar, line, line plot, pictograph, scatter plot, box plot, circle, histogram, and frequency chart. Not only can students use the program to create graphs, there is also an on-screen notebook for recording their interpretation of the data. A teacher's guide is provided with the software.

Adler, David. *Easy Math Puzzles*. 1997. New York: Holiday House. Unp. Grades: 5–8.

This is a collection of mathematical riddles involving common objects such as people, animals, coins, or food. They require students to apply higher-order thinking skills and problem-solving strategies such as making a diagram or looking for a pattern. For example, Janet has eight pets with a total of twenty-six legs. Her pets are either birds or dogs. How many of each animal does she have?

Schwartz, David. *G Is for Googol: A Math Alphabet Book*. Illustrated by Marissa Moss. 1998. Berkeley, Calif.: Tricycle Press. 57p. Grades: 6–8.

This alphabet book for older students defines an extensive collection of math terms, some familiar and some not so familiar. Clever, whimsical drawings and graphs help to explain many of the terms. Included in the text are activities and problems to solve that help students understand the terms. "W" stands for "When are we ever gonna use this stuff, anyway?" which explains when and how the information in the book can be used in everyday life situations.

EXPLORATIONS

1. Beans, grains of rice, or counters can be used by children as they test the *One Grain of Rice* (Demi, 1997) theory or *Anno's Magic Seed* (Anno, 1992).
2. Once students have solved the riddles in *Calculator Riddles* (Adler, 1995), they can create their own to share with their classmates or parents.
3. After working with *Easy Math Puzzles* (Adler, 1997), students can apply higher-order thinking skills to create their own problems requiring higher-order thinking skills and strategies, such as making a diagram or looking for a pattern.
4. Students enjoy working with partners to solve problems found in books. The support of a partner assures that students do not become frustrated as they explore problem solving.
5. Prior to introducing *G Is for Googol: A Math Alphabet Book* (Schwartz, 1998) students can each be assigned a letter of the alphabet and be required to find a math term beginning with that letter. Once students read and share the book, they can compare their terms with the terms in the book.
6. After reading the book with students and sharing answers, teachers will need to help them make connections between the book and their math lessons in the classroom.
7. Students can be given a hypothetical sum of money to plan an outing for themselves and their friends. They then must determine how much the outing will cost and whether or not they have enough money for the outing.

TEACHER RESOURCES

Materials in this section contain useful resources for teaching mathematics concepts across the content area curriculum. One book in this section features a collection of Internet sites reflecting the NCTM standards that teachers find very useful as they incorporate technology into their classrooms.

BOOKS

Smith, Susan Sperry. *Early Childhood Mathematics.* **2001. Boston, Mass.: Allyn and Bacon. 272p. Grades: P–1.**

Teachers of young students find this book has ideas for creating an active learning environment in the classroom as children explore mathematics concepts.

Martinez, Joseph R., and Nancy Martinez. *Math without Fear: A Guide for Preventing Math Anxiety in Children.* **1996. Boston, Mass.: Allyn and Bacon. 167p. Grades: K–6.**

This useful guide contains ideas, activities, and guidelines for preventing math anxiety in elementary students.

Ostrow, Jill. *Making Problems, Creating Solutions.* **1999. York, Maine: Stenhouse. 176p. Grades: K–6.**

Ostrow's process approach to mathematics includes using a workshop approach to enhance student learning.

Whitin, David J., and Sandra Wilde. *Read Any Good Math Lately?: Children's Books for Mathematical Learning, K–6.* **1992. Portsmouth, N. H.: Heinemann. 206p. Grades: K–6.**

Through fiction and nonfiction literature, children explore math in natural everyday occurrences, which assures a meaningful context for learning. The chapters in this book are divided into mathematical topics and each chapter contains information on books and ideas for using the books to extend student learning.

Krulik, Stephen, and Jesse A. Rudnick. *Assessing Reasoning and Problem Solving: A Sourcebook for Elementary School Teachers.* **1998. Boston, Mass.: Allyn and Bacon. 233p. Grades: K–6.**

A variety of ways to assess students' knowledge of math, how they reason, how they solve problems, and how they communicate their knowledge are included in this book.

Ameis, Jerry A. *Mathematics on the Internet: A Resource for K-12 Teachers.* **2000. Upper Saddle River, N. J.: Merrill. 129p. Grade: K–12.**

Teachers who are not familiar with using the Internet in the classroom appreciate the introduction to the Internet and the information on learning mathematics with the Internet in this book. Also included in the book are collections of Web sites reflecting the NCTM standards and professional development sites for teachers. The appendices include electronic journals and a glossary of Internet terms.

Schiro, Michael. *Integrating Children's Literature and Mathematics in the Classroom: Children as Meaning Makers, Problem Solvers, and Literary Critics.* **1997. New York: Teachers College Press, Columbia University. 162p. Grades: 1–4.**

This book provides an in-depth examination of how to use children's literature to make math meaningful to students. Ideas are presented for having children solve mathematical problems presented in books and to critically examine the books from a literary perspective.

Müller, Robert. *The Great Book of Math Teasers.* **1989. New York: Sterling. 96p. Grades: 3–8.**

These mind-boggling math teasers entertain and challenge students to use higher-order thinking skills in order to figure out the problems. The answers to the teasers are at the end of the book.

Salvadori, Mario, and Joseph P. Wright. *Math Games for Middle School: Challenges and Skill Builders for Students at Every Level.* **1998. Chicago: Chicago Review Press. 168p. Grades: 6–8.**

Mario Salvadori loved the beauty and order of math and made it his mission to share his love with children of all ages, which is evident in this book. These challenges and skill builders show students how math can be fun and understandable.

PROFESSIONAL ORGANIZATION

National Council of Teachers of Mathematics
1906 Association Drive
Reston, VA 22091-1593
800-235-7566
www.nctm.org
Journals: *Teaching Children Mathematics, Mathematics Teaching in the Middle School*

INTERNET SITES

Illuminations
http://illuminations.nctm.org/math/index.html
Lesson plans, activities, and Internet links to support the teaching and learning of mathematics can be found on this site. The National Council of Teachers of Mathematics sponsors the site and Illuminations is a partner in the educational program, MarcoPolo. MarcoPolo provides standards-based K-12 Internet content.

The Math Forum
www.forum.swarthmore.edu/
Teachers, parents, librarians, and children all find useful resources on this site. Students

like the "Ask Dr. Math" link where they can pose math questions. This is an extensive site with its own search engine.

REFERENCES

AppleWorks. Version 6. 1998. Cupertino, Calif.: Apple Computer

HyperStudio. Version 4. 2000. Torrance, Calif.: Knowledge Adventure

MicrosoftWorks. 1998. Redmond, Wash.: Microsoft Corporation.

National Council of Teachers of Mathematics. 1999. *Principles and Standards for School Mathematics*. [Online]. Reston, VA: National Council of Teachers of Mathematics. Available: http://standards.nctm.org/ [2001, February 24]

Print Shop Deluxe. Version 11. 1998. El Segundo, Calif.: Mattel Interactive.

Schiro, Michael. 1997. *Integrating Children's Literature and Mathematics in the Classroom: Children as Meaning Makers, Problem Solvers, and Literary Critics*. New York: Teachers College Press.

Shaw, Jean, and Sally Blake. 1998. *Mathematics for Young Children*. Upper Saddle River, N. J.: Merrill.

Sheffield, Linda J., and Douglas E. Cruikshank. 1996. *Teaching and Learning Elementary and Middle School Mathematics*. 3rd ed. Englewood Cliffs, N. J.: Prentice-Hall, Inc.

Storybook Weaver Deluxe. 1999. El Segundo, Calif.: Mattel Interactive.

Tesselmania! Deluxe. 1997. Minneapolis, Minn.: The Learning Company.

Chapter 2

Science

Science informational books for children entice them to explore the wonders of their universe. Children's natural curiosity is piqued as they view the colorful illustrations, detailed diagrams, and breathtaking photographs contained within the pages of these books. Children's literature in the science classroom enhances instruction, motivates children to learn, and excites them about science (Dixey and Baird, 1996). Using informational books, fantasy, and realistic fiction in the science classroom assures that students have a diverse selection of books to read. Additionally, furnishing children with a variety of books on the topic being studied in the science classroom, allowing time for independent exploration, and encouraging students to read, write, reflect, and share what they have read assures that students gain a deeper understanding of the science content. Providing students with opportunities to revisit books facilitates their understanding of the unique aspects of the animals they are studying (Maduram, 2000).

Before reading the science textbook, students can read informational books on the topic to assure they have sufficient background knowledge to comprehend the textbook. To foster comprehension of science concepts presented in textbooks, children must have sufficient prior knowledge of the concept, and the teacher must assist students as they build bridges between their prior knowledge and the science concepts (Walpole, 1999). Science informational books can help to build these bridges by extending and enhancing the science concepts presented in textbooks. These books present the material in different formats and on a variety of reading levels. Colorful illustrations, photographs, diagrams, charts, and shorter blocks of text found in children's literature make science concepts more understandable. Additionally, they offer opportunities for children to develop confidence in their ability to take control of their own learning as they read and find the answers to their own questions (Young and Salley, 1997).

In the pages of these books students discover that science is part of their everyday lives (Stiffler, 1992). Myra Cohn Livingston has collected a book of poems to encourage students to discover that science is all around them and to see science as part of their world. These are poems for reading aloud and sharing with students during breaks in classroom activities.

Livingston, Myra Cohn, comp. *Animal, Vegetable, Mineral: Poems about Small Things*. 1994. New York: HarperCollins. 69p. Grades: 3–8.

Pause a minute and take delight in the small, often overlooked things in life celebrated in this wonderful collection of poems. A variety of poets contributed brief, amusing poems about small, ordinary treasures. The poems cause readers to stop and contemplate small wonders as they recognize that science is all around them, a pervasive part of their lives.

In 1995 the National Research Council (NRC) released the *National Science Education Standards* (NSES). These standards are divided into the following eight categories:

1. Unifying concepts and processes in science
2. Science as inquiry
3. Physical science
4. Life science
5. Earth and space science
6. Science and technology
7. Science in personal and social perspectives
8. History and nature of science

The standards provide teachers insights into teaching science as inquiry where students pose a question and then seek possible answers to their question (Alberts, 2000). Further, Alberts contends science education should include learning science principles and concepts, acquiring scientific reasoning and procedural skills, and understanding the nature of science as a human endeavor. Children's natural curiosity motivates them to question their environment and the science classroom furnishes opportunities for them to find the answers to their questions. Many of the answers they seek can be found in the pages of science information books that encourage them to use the process of inquiry to discover answers to their questions. Reading several books on the same topic furnishes them with opportunities to note consistencies and discrepancies between the books and engages the students in using higher-order thinking skills as they ponder their discoveries.

Science videos are a valuable source of information for students. Videos such as *Science as Inquiry for Children* appeal to them and provide additional information on important concepts in a multimedia format. This particular video provides students with valuable information on the scientific process that can be used throughout their scientific studies.

ized *Science as Inquiry for Children*. 2000. Video. Bala Cynwyd, Penn.: Schlessinger Video Productions-Library Video Company. 23 min. Grades: K–4.

Two young scientists learn about the scientific process with the assistance of Benjamin Franklin, Marie Curie, and George Washington Carver. The program includes a teacher's guide. This video supports the second NSES category, which is Science as Inquiry.

Major sections in this chapter include life science, earth science, space science, physical science, scientists and inventors, and reference books. The life science section includes sub-sections on the human body, animals, plants, and environmental issues and ecology. The earth science section includes information on volcanoes and earthquakes, landforms, soil, and water. In the space science section books and media on stars, planets, and space travel can be found. Physical science includes sections on light, energy, machines, and weather and seasons. There are also sections on scientists and inventors, reference materials, and teacher resources.

LIFE SCIENCE

Science category four focuses on life science that includes the study of organisms, their life cycles, environments, and adaptations. One way to begin students' explorations in life science is by having them explore living things in their own backyard. Have students brainstorm living things that they might find in their backyard. Then, have them spend five minutes quickly writing about living things in their backyard. Share their responses with the class prior to reading *Did You Ever Wonder about Things You Find in Your Backyard?* (Capogna, 2000). When the students go home that evening have them spend fifteen minutes observing and writing down what they saw in their backyard. Students can refer to their written responses throughout their study of living things. Help them to find the lyrical word pictures in the book and help them to realize that the author's words describe rather than tell what is in the backyard. Then, encourage them to create their own lyrical word pictures to describe the things they observe as they study living organisms.

Capogna, Vera Vullo. *Did You Ever Wonder about Things You Find in Your Backyard?* 2000. New York: Marshall Cavendish. 32p. Grades: K–3.

Beautifully illustrated by the author, this book describes in lyrical language the insects, birds, and animals found in backyards. An author's note explains that she and her children have often made explorations into their own backyard. The book closes with a glossary and index.

HUMAN BODY

Peeking inside the human body reveals the marvelous, amazing workings of the body systems. The National Science Education Standard pertaining to life science encompasses the study of body structures used for walking, holding, seeing, and talking. The books in this section engage children in the study of body structures and systems.

BOOK AND MEDIA CHOICES

Barner, Bob. *Dem Bones*. 1996. San Francisco, Calif.: Chronicle Books. Unp. Grades K–3.

A fun way to learn anatomy is by singing along with the words to this popular tune. Cut and torn paper collages depict skeletons playing different instruments as they jive across the pages of the book. Interspersed in the illustrations are text boxes with detailed information on how the bones in the body work. This very informative book is a delight to read and view.

Showers, Paul. *Hear Your Heart*. Illustrated by Holly Keller. 2001. New York: HarperCollins. 33p. Grades: K–4.

Large illustrations and simple descriptions explain how the most important muscle in the body works. Simple experiments such as using a cardboard tube to listen to a friend's heart are interspersed throughout the text. The book concludes with additional ideas for learning about the heart, such as how to measure heart rate. This is one of the Let's-Read-and-Find-Out Science series.

Showers, Paul. *What Happens to a Hamburger?* Illustrated by Edward Miller. 2001. New York: HarperCollins. 33p. Grades: K–4.

This intriguing look at the digestion process follows food as it moves through the body. From beginning to end the book contains simple experiments to help students understand the process of digestion, such as dissolving sugar in water. The book concludes with a diagram of the digestive system and experiments for finding out more about the digestive system. This book is one of the Let's-Read-and-Find-Out Science series.

***All about the Brain*. 2000. Video. Wynnewood, Penn.: Schlessinger Video Productions-Library Video Company. 23 min. Grades: K–4.**

The wondrous workings of the brain and the nervous system are explored in this fascinating video. Children are eager to measure their own reflex reaction time as they try out the simple experiment shown on the video. The program includes a teacher's guide that has a program summary, vocabulary, discussion questions, follow-up activities, Internet resources, and suggested print resources. This is part of the Schlessinger Science Library for Children Collection.

Parker, Steve. *Human Body*. 1994. New York: Dorling Kindersley. 60p. Grades: 1–3.

Rather than just inform students about their bodies Parker encourages them to experiment with their bodies. For example, there is an experiment to discover how the senses of taste and smell work together. There is also information on staying healthy such as why it is important to get sufficient sleep and what to do when leg cramps develop. Color photographs of children, simple labeled diagrams, and cartoon drawings illustrate the text. This is one of the Eyewitness Explorers series.

Sound: A First Look. 2001. Video. Raleigh, N.C.: Rainbow Media. 17 min. Grades: 1–3.

The narrator on this video explains different aspects of sound while children demonstrate the aspects. Sound waves, why objects produce sound, and how to alter sounds are topics covered in the video. Music teachers find the video a useful way to explain pitch and volume.

The Ultimate Human Body. 1996. Mac/Win. New York: DK Multimedia. Grades: 2–4.

Unique glimpses inside the human body are provided in three different sections of this interactive CD: 1) systems scanner, 2) 3D scanner, and 3) x-ray scanner. Sound and video clips enhance the learning experience as students explore the body systems. The Body Quiz Challenge helps students review what they have learned. An online component assures students have access to a variety of resources. Accompanying this CD is a pocket book, *Body Facts*.

The Children's Book of the Body. 1996. Brookfield, Conn.: Copper Beech Books. 128p. Grades: 2–6.

This book deals with questions children ask about their bodies and is in language they can clearly understand. Taking a complex subject and treating it simply with color photographs and drawings make this a wonderful book for the young child. It begins with skin and hair and ends with the brain. There is a section with fascinating facts about the body, such as "you have the same number of bones in your neck as a giraffe—seven." Also included is a glossary written in simple-to-understand language and an easy-to-read index.

Simon, Seymour. The Heart: Our Circulatory System. 1996. New York: Morrow Junior Books. Unp. Grades: 2–6.

Fascinating facts about how long blood cells live and how many times the heart pumps each day are remembered by young scientists and repeated to all who will listen. For example, red blood cells are manufactured at the rate of three million per second and during that time an equal number of red blood cells die. The large colorful photographs taken by a scanning electron microscope (SEM) reveal intriguing details about the blood cells and blood vessels. Under this microscope the walls of the blood vessels appear porous rather than solid and the red blood cells resemble hole-less doughnuts.

Farndon, John. Sound and Hearing. 2001. Tarrytown, N.Y.: Marshall Cavendish. 32p. Grades: 2–7.

Students are intrigued as they conduct an experiment that enables them to "see" sound. This is just one of the experiments in the book that require simple materials and include ideas for extending the experiments for further explorations. The book includes a table of contents, a glossary, and an index. This book is one of the Science Experiments series.

Fornari, Giuliano. *Inside the Body*. 1996. New York: DK. Unp. Grades: 2 and up.

This Lift the Flap Book has over 60 flaps revealing interior portions of the human body. Lifting the skin reveals the bones and muscles. Lifting portions of the skeleton reveals organs such as the brain and the interior of the bones. The digestive system, reproductive system, and respiratory system are described in the text and lifting the flaps on the body provides a visual display of the systems. This book serves as an introduction to the body and students are sure to pursue more detailed books to gain additional information.

Rowan, Pete. *Big Head! A Book about Your Brain and Head*. Illustrated by John Temperton. 1998. New York: Alfred A. Knopf. 44p. Grades: 4 and up.

Peeling off the layers of the head reveals the wonders of the brain and skull. This intimate look at the brain's functions makes fascinating reading. Filled with factoids, little known facts, easy-to-understand descriptions, colorful life-size drawings, and photographs, this book reveals interesting details about the inner workings of the brain. In the top right corner of each double-page spread is a small picture of the author's son's skull showing the location of the area being discussed.

Eyewitness Skeleton. 1994. Video. London, England: Dorling Kindersley. 35 min. Grades: 4 and up.

This video explores the human skeleton and the skeletons of different animals, including some found on the outsides of the bodies.

A.D.A.M. The Inside Story. 1993. Mac/Win. Atlanta, Ga.: A.D.A.M. Software. Grades: 5 and up.

A.D.A.M. stands for Animated Dissection of Anatomy for Medicine that provides an indication of the terrific details about the human body included in this CD. Modesty settings allow the teacher to block out the information about the reproductive system. Animations, video, and sound help students comprehend the complexities of the systems in the human body. A readily accessible dictionary is included.

EXPLORATIONS

1. After reading *Hear Your Heart* (Showers, 2001), introduce the students to the American Heart Web site to learn more about their hearts. The Internet address for this site is www.americanheart.org/Health/Lifestyle/Youth.
2. After reading *What Happens to a Hamburger?* (Showers, 2001), have the students try the simple experiment at the end of the book to determine the length of their small intestine.

3. Prior to reading *Inside the Body* (Fornari, 1996), have students draw a body on a sheet of manila drawing paper. Have the students create flaps over various parts of the body. Under the flaps they are to draw what they think they will see when the skin is peeled away. Then share the book with them to have them see what is really under the skin.

4. Throughout *The Children's Book of the Body* are activities for students to try out as they explore their bodies. As the book is being read to the students, stop to let them try the activities to enhance their understanding of the material. The activities require simple materials, such as a hand mirror to see their breath or simply examining the veins in their wrists.

5. Prior to reading *The Heart: Our Circulatory System* (Simon, 1996), have students quickly draw what they think the inside of their blood vessels looks like. After reading, have them again draw the inside of their blood vessels. Ask them to compare the two drawings as a way to assess what they learned.

6. Many of noted science writer Seymour Simon's books are mentioned in this chapter. Students who are interested in finding out more about this author and writing him can explore his Web site at www.users.nyc.pipeline.com:80/~simonsi/.

7. Before students read *Big Head! A Book about Your Brain and Head* (Rowan, 1998), have them write down everything they think the brain controls. After they read the book have them reexamine their lists to see what they need to add.

SENSES

Humans experience their world through their senses. Children enjoy exploring their senses through a variety of experiments, such as the ones in the books that follow. The science as inquiry category from NSES highlights students having opportunities to ask questions, plan and conduct experiments, gather data, think critically about relationships and alternative solutions, and communicate their findings. These books contain simple experiments that give students opportunities to engage in scientific inquiry.

BOOK AND MEDIA CHOICES

Reiser, Lynn. *My Cat Tuna*. 2001. New York: Greenwillow Books. Unp. Grades: P–2.

This flap book asks questions about what Tuna the cat hears, sees, smells, tastes, and feels on a summer day. The answers to the questions are on the reverse side of the illustrated flaps. Young readers enjoy guessing what is on the other side of the flaps.

Miller, Margaret. *My Five Senses*. 1994. New York: Simon and Schuster Books for Young Readers. Unp. Grades: K–2.

Photographs of five charming young children as they explore the five senses through their surroundings make this an appealing book to young children. The children use their senses to explore things familiar to all children, such as a shadow, the smell of garbage, the taste of medicine, the scream of a baby, and the feel of sand. Large-print text with only a few words on each page assures that young readers can read the book on their own.

All about the Senses. 2001. Video. Bala Cynwyd, Penn.: Schlessinger Video Productions-Library Video Company. 23 min. Grades: K–4.

Real-life adventures show students the importance of their sense organs and senses. Students enjoy the hands-on activities that let them explore their own senses. The program includes a teacher's guide. This is one of the Human Body for Children series.

Ardley, Neil. _The Science Book of the Senses._ 1992. San Diego, Calif.: Harcourt Brace Jovanovich. 29p. Grades: 2–4.

Brief explanations of the five senses begin this book. These explanations are followed by activities that enable students to explore each of the five senses. Simple step-by-step instructions, readily available materials, and photographs of children conducting the experiments allow students to fully explore their mysterious senses.

Hickman, Pamela. _Animal Senses: How Animals See, Hear, Taste, Smell and Feel._ Illustrated by Pat Stephens. 1998. 40p. Buffalo, N.Y.: Kids Can Press. Grades: 2–6.

This beautifully illustrated book explains how the senses of animals work and how they compare to those of human beings. The text about each sense is accompanied by several experiments dealing with that sense. The experiments show comparisons between animals and humans. The book closes with an index.

EXPLORATIONS

1. Prior to reading *My Cat Tuna* (Reiser, 2001) review the five senses with the students. While reading this book, record the students' guesses as to what is on the other side of the flaps. These guesses can then be used to create a class book of the five senses.
2. Working with a partner the students participate in a sensory investigation. One person is blindfolded while their partner leads them around to investigate the room using their other four senses. In order for the blindfolded students to concentrate on their investigations, there should be very little talking. Once all the students have had an opportunity to participate in the sensory investigation, they should write about their feelings of not being able to see and on having to depend on someone else to maneuver them around the room (Smith and Herring, 1996).
3. Using rolls of Lifesavers students can use their sense of taste to investigate the different flavors. First have each student predict what each color will taste like. Then, have them taste the different colors to determine if the Lifesavers taste as they predicted they would.
4. Record a variety of sounds and have the students listen to them to guess what created the sounds.

5. While reading *The Science Book of the Senses* (Ardley, 1992) or *Animal Senses: How Animals See, Hear, Taste, Smell and Feel* (Hickman, 1998) have students try out the experiments and record their results and observations in a log.

ANIMALS

The future of animals depends on children understanding and appreciating them. The more children explore the animal kingdom, the clearer their understanding will be and the more likely they will be to work to preserve animals and their habitats. The NSES life science category requires students to have an understanding of the characteristics of organisms including their structure and function, the life cycles of organisms including reproduction and behavior, and their environments including adaptations and ecosystems. Books in this section have been categorized as follows: birds, mammals, reptiles, insects, fish, adaptations, and habitats.

BIRDS

Birds have existed since the days of dinosaurs and are found in all parts of the world. Children enjoy reading about and observing birds. Birds can usually be found in schoolyards or backyards and readily lend themselves to observations.

Book and Media Choices

Kalman, Bobbie. *What Is a Bird?* 1999. New York: Crabtree Publishing. 32p. Grades: K–2.

This is a basic information book about birds and their world. It includes facts such as why birds fly, why only birds have feathers, birds that cannot fly, eggs and chicks, and bird songs. A combination of photographs and color drawings depict the facts presented in the book. The book closes with a glossary and an index. This book is one of The Science of Living Things series.

Arnosky, Jim. *All about Owls.* 1995. New York: Scholastic. 32p. Grades: K–3.

The detailed illustrations of owl anatomy fascinate young readers. They learn that these nocturnal birds use their superb night vision and acute sense of smell to keep the insect and rodent population under control. Also included are owl calls to practice.

Spinelli, Eileen. *Song for the Whooping Crane.* Illustrated by Elsa Warnick. 2000. Grand Rapids, Mich.: Eerdmans Books for Young Readers. Unp. Grades: K–4.

The migration, behaviors, and habitats of the rare wild whooping crane are described in poetic text and gentle watercolor illustrations. A wealth of information about these rare birds is found in the text and images. Reading the poem and examining the illustrations is such a treat that students may not at first realize how much they have learned by reading the book.

Gibbons, Gail. *Gulls . . . Gulls . . . Gulls . . .* 1997. New York: Holiday House. Unp. Grades: 1–3.

There are forty-three different kinds of gulls in the world and this book focuses on those found in North America. Their life cycle, behavior patterns, and habitats are all examined in this beautifully illustrated book. The book closes with a display of common gulls and interesting facts about gulls.

Gibbons, Gail. *Ducks!* 2001. New York: Holiday House. Unp. Grades: 1–3.

Feeding ducks is a favorite pastime of young children who live near ponds and lakes. Detailed, labeled drawings and brief, interesting text provide children with answers to their questions about these water birds. The book also explains how ducks stay warm and dry when they swim and feed in water.

George, Jean Craighead. *The Moon of the Winter Bird.* Illustrated by Vincent Nasta. 1992. New York: HarperCollins. 48p. Grades: 2–5.

Every year there are thirteen full moons or new moons. Naturalist and author George has assigned an animal to each of our twelve months and when she ran out of months created one, December-January. Each of her stories is beautifully illustrated and each creature is carefully described in words. This book deals with a song sparrow that does not go south for the winter, but stays in Ohio finding food and shelter until the winter is over. An index follows. This is one of the Thirteen Moon series. This book and others in this series are available on audiocassette from Recorded Books, Prince Frederick, Maryland.

Latimer, Jonathan P., and Karen Stray Nolting. *Backyard Birds.* Illustrations by Roger Tory Peterson. 1999. Boston: Houghton Mifflin. 48p. Grades: 2–6.

Using the photographs and artwork from Peterson's Field Guides the authors have written text to appeal to young naturalists. Birds are classified by colors. There is a written description of the birds' characteristics, a list of questions and answers about the birds, and a description of their habitat and food. The book closes with an index. This slim volume is a perfect first book for young bird watchers. This book is part of Peterson Field Guides for Young Naturalists series that also includes *Shorebirds* (Latimer and Nolting, 1999), *Birds of Prey* (Latimer and Nolting, 1999), and *Bizarre Birds* (Latimer and Nolting, 1999).

Patent, Dorothy Hinshaw. *Eagles of America.* Photographs by William Muñoz. 1995. New York: Holiday House. 40p. Grades: 3–6.

Bald and golden eagles are common to North America and these majestic creatures' habits and habitats are examined in this book. Conservation and rehabilitation efforts to protect eagles are described through the story of an injured bald eagle.

Patent, Dorothy Hinshaw. *Looking at Penguins.* **Photographs by Graham Robertson. 1993. New York: Holiday House. 40p. Grades: 3–8.**

Striking photographs show these hardy, "tuxedo-clad" birds in their Antarctic environment. They are also found on the south coasts of Africa and Australia and on the western coast of South America. While their body masses are too heavy and their wings too small to fly, they glide through the water in much the same manner as other birds fly through the air. There are seventeen kinds of penguins, the smallest being the little blue or fairy penguins and the largest being the king and the emperor penguins. The book closes with a glossary.

Birds. **2000. Video. Bala Cynwyd, Penn.: Schlessinger Video Productions-Library Video Company. 23 min. Grades: 5 to 8.**

Students are not surprised to learn that all birds have feathers, however, they may be surprised to learn that not all birds fly. This video look at bird characteristics, how they build nests, and how they migrate. A teacher's guide is available. This video is close-captioned and is part of the Animal Life in Action series.

Explorations

1. After reading *What Is a Bird?* (Kalman, 1999) and *Backyard Birds* (Latimer and Nolting, 1999) set up bird feeders in the schoolyard with different foods. Have students predict which birds will eat at each feeder. Then have them keep a log of their observations detailing which birds ate at which feeders. Ask students to draw conclusions about why the birds ate which food.

2. Using a digital camera take photographs of the birds at the bird feeders over the course of the school year. Have the students create a digital display of the birds using *PowerPoint* or *HyperStudio* to share their observations with other classes in the school.

3. *All about Owls* (Arnosky, 1995) has detailed illustrations of the owl's anatomy. While reading the book pause and have students compare the owl's anatomy to their own.

4. After reading *All about Owls* (Arnosky, 1995) and *Eagles of America* (Patent, 1995), students can create a comparison contrast chart of these two birds of prey.

5. *The Moon of the Winter Bird* (George, 1992) is written in a narrative style whereas *Looking at Penguins* (Patent, 1993) is written in an expository style. Have students examine both books to decide which style they prefer. They should be able to return to the book to locate specific passages to support their views.

6. Prior to reading *Song for the Whooping Crane* (Spinelli, 2000), have the students brainstorm what they know about whooping cranes using Inspiration software. After reading the book, have them add to their Inspiration concept maps and print them out to share with their classmates.

7. In *Gulls . . . Gulls . . . Gulls . . .,* Gibbons (1997) describes how gulls communicate. Prior to reading the book, have students brainstorm all the ways they communicate without speaking. Record their comments on the chalkboard. After reading about how gulls

communicate have students compare their communication strategies with those of the gulls.

MAMMALS

Mammals are found all over the world and come in a variety of shapes and sizes. Some are furry and cuddly, others are ferocious, some are rotund, others are sleek, some are swift, and others are slow. These variations are examined and illustrated in *Mammals* (Jeunesse, 1997). This book can be used as an introduction to the study of mammals or as a reference for further inquiry.

Jeunesse, Gallimard. *Mammals*. 1997. New York: Scholastic. 46p. Grades: 2–5.

This interactive book invites students to touch, feel, lift, and scrutinize as they read about these warm-blooded vertebrates. Detailed, colorful illustrations and photographs show mammals in their natural habitats all over the world. This is one of the Scholastic Voyages of Discovery books.

Book and Media Choices

***Magic School Bus Going Batty*. 1996. Video. Redmond, Wash.: Microsoft Corporation. 30 min. Grades: P–5.**

Hang on for another wild school bus ride as Ms. Frizzle, her students, and their parents explore nocturnal animals. Students learn all about bats as they careen around on a magical school bus. The voice of Lilly Tomlin is featured in this video.

Patent, Dorothy Hinshaw. *Looking at Bears*. Photographs by William Muñoz. 1994. New York: Holiday House. 40p. Grades: 1–3.

Through the pages of this book readers come to appreciate these powerful, intriguing mammals. Well-known bears such as polar bears and grizzlies are discussed, as well as lesser-known bears, such as the sloth bear and the spectacled bear. The evolution of bears, their physical characteristics, habitats, and behaviors, including hibernation, are presented in this book. The colorful, wildlife photographs show bears in their natural habitat. The book concludes with an index.

Gibbons, Gail. *Rabbits, Rabbits, & More Rabbits*. 2000. New York: Holiday House. Unp. Grades: 1–3.

Realizing that rabbits are popular pets for children, this book contains several pages of information on caring for pet rabbits both indoors and outdoors. Fascinating facts, such as rabbits' ability to see in the dark and their ability to see to their front, back, and sides make this book one students will read and remember. The book provides opportunities for vocabulary development with words like nocturnal, vegetarian, warren, and burrow. The text and the illustrations help students understand what these words mean.

Arnold, Caroline. *Fox*. Photographs by Richard Hewett. 1996. New York: Morrow Junior Books. 48p. Grades: 2–5.

With their sharp senses, quick reflexes, and innate cunning, foxes are one of the most successful predators in the world. They are also among the most adaptable — ranging from the arid deserts of North Africa to the frozen tundra of the Arctic Circle. This book follows the tiny kit fox found in the United States as it goes through its day-to-day activities. Readers learn about fox families, their hunting techniques, and how they communicate with one another.

Beavers. 1995. New York: Scholastic. Unp. Grades: 2–5.

This basic book about beavers contains superb color photographs and describes how beavers construct dams and their homes. Each step is shown from the very first day construction begins. There are even a couple of photographs showing the interior of a beaver's domed home. At the end of the book a color drawing is shown with a side view of a beaver lodge, dam, and pond. At the very end is a map of North America showing where beavers live. There is no index, but the information is shared in story style and in only a few pages.

Stuart, Dee. *Bats: Mysterious Flyers of the Night*. 1994. Minneapolis, Minn.: Carolrhoda Books. 47p. Grades: 2–5.

These shy, gentle mammals are vital to our environment because they pollinate flowers, disperse seeds, and control the insect population. Color photographs capture the fascinating variety of ears, noses, and wings found on bats. Their remarkable navigation system, their protective coloring, their benefits to man, and the superstitions surrounding them are all discussed in this informative book.

Bateman, Robert, and Rick Archbold. *Safari*. 1998. Boston: Little, Brown. Unp. Grades: 2 and up.

The magnificent, detailed paintings by Robert Bateman bring to life the brief text about some of the animals found in African jungles and plains. One of the special features of this book is information about the height, weight, food, and habitat of each animal so that the twelve-inch-high dik-dik can be compared to the massive elephant. The book ends with a caution about preserving our wildlife. This book was named an Outstanding Nonfiction book by the 1999 Orbis Pictus Award Committee.

Carwardine, Mark. *Whales, Dolphins, and Porpoises*. Illustrated by Martin Camm. 1992. New York: DK. 64p. Grades: 3–8.

Students are fascinated by the information presented in this book on whales, dolphins, and porpoises. These intelligent creatures are a continuous source of fascination as humans continue to study them and discover their unique qualities. Photographs and illustrations are accompanied by brief, informative text that encourages students to read further to learn more about these denizens of the sea.

Explorations

1. The end of *Looking at Bears* (Patent, 1994) describes problems bears are having trying to survive in today's world. *Backyard Bear* (Murphy, 1993) is a fictional account of a young bear's adventures in an urban setting. Sharing both of these books with students provides them opportunities to see how their lives are intertwined with those of the wild creatures described in Patent's book. Note: The annotation for *Backyard Bear* (Murphy, 1993) can be found in the Understanding Animals section of this chapter.

2. Prior to reading *Fox* (Arnold, 1996) have students brainstorm what they think the fox does during the day. While reading the book have students create a timeline of the fox's day.

3. After reading *Fox* (Arnold, 1996) have students discuss what they learned in small groups. Then have the entire class discuss the book.

4. Prior to reading *Beavers* (*Beavers*, 1995) or *Bats: Mysterious Flyers of the Night* (Stuart, 1994), have students examine the photographs and briefly write down what they learned from them. Then read the story and have the students go back over their notes to determine what they learned from the text. The teacher can also help the students see how the illustrations enhanced their comprehension of the text.

5. *Safari* (Bateman and Archbold, 1998) was named an Outstanding Nonfiction book by the 1999 Orbis Pictus Award Committee. Explain to the students that the Orbis Pictus Award recognizes the illustrations in nonfiction books. Have students compare illustrations in *Safari* with the illustrations in another nonfiction book and speculate as to why *Safari* won the award.

6. Prior to reading *Whales, Dolphins, and Porpoises* (Carwardine, 1992), share the illustrations with the students. Have the students consider what the illustrator, Martin Camm, had to know and do in order to illustrate the book.

7. Students can help support efforts to protect whales by adopting one. The class can collect the money needed to adopt a whale. They are sent information on the whale they adopt and receive periodic updates when the whale is sighted. Information on adopting a whale can be found at www.wdes.org/dan/publishing.nsf/frontpag?readform.

REPTILES

The transformation of a tadpole swimming in water to a frog hopping across the ground fascinates children and motivates them to learn more about these reptiles. The NSES life science category addresses students' need to understand the life cycles of animals. Books in this section help students to understand the life cycles of different reptiles.

Book and Media Choices

Wallace, Karen. *Tale of a Tadpole*. 1998. New York: DK. 32p. Grades: P–1.

Large, colorful photographs accompany this simple story of the life of a tadpole from egg to an adult frog laying eggs of its own. Large easy-to-read print for children who are learning to read make this a book that is returned to again and again. There is an extremely simple picture index.

Hawes, Judy. *Why Are Frogs Wet?* Illustrated by Mary Ann Fraser. 2000. New York: HarperCollins. Unp. Grades: K–3.

This basic introduction to frogs was first published in 1968. It includes information on frog characteristics, kinds of frogs, and frog behavior. A simple experiment at the end of the book provides students with an opportunity to find out what frog eggs feel like. There is also a list of resources for students to pursue in order to learn more about frogs. This is one of the Let's-Read-and-Find-Out-Science series.

Arnosky, Jim. *All about Alligators*. 1994. New York: Scholastic. Unp. Grades: K–3.

Limited text and large, detailed drawings introduce young readers to the fascinating world of alligators. The enticing illustrations invite readers into the swamp for a close-up look at alligators. A cutaway drawing of an egg shows how a ten-inch alligator baby could fit into the egg. A close-up look at an alligator's open mouth shows rows of teeth in frightening detail.

Patent, Dorothy Hinshaw. *Slinky Scaly Slithery Snakes*. Illustrated by Kendahl Jan Jubb. 2000. New York: Walker. 32p. Grades: K–4.

Slinky, scaly, slithery snakes slide across the pages of this book intertwined with intriguing facts about these legless creatures. The realistic pictures cause the reader to cautiously hold the book with only fingertips fearing that these snakes will come to life and strike. The detailed facts presented about snakes make fascinating reading and hold the attention of the squirmiest youngster. At the end of the book are the scientific names of the snakes found in the book.

Gibbons, Gail. *Frogs*. 1993. New York: Holiday House. Unp. Grades: 1–4.

Long before dinosaurs lived on Earth, frogs did. There are now more than 38,000 different types of frogs. With artwork typical of Gail Gibbons, the information about the life cycles of frogs and toads is presented. There are distinct differences between frogs and toads and the emphasis in this book is on frogs beginning with the egg stage through the tadpole stage into the adult frog. This book describes how their bodies change as they grow from tadpoles into frogs, how they make sounds that can mean different things, how they hibernate when it is cold, and how they differ from toads. The book ends with additional interesting facts about frogs.

Souza, Dorothy. *Slinky Snakes*. 1992. Minneapolis, Minn.: Carolrhoda Books. 40p. Grades: 1–4.

The easy-to-read text with bold keywords and definitions accompanied by photographs and illustrations make this a reader-friendly book about snakes. The text is written to be read and understood by young readers as evidenced by the comparison of snakes shedding their skins to pulling off socks. Illustrations of snakes' movements including undulation, sideways, concertina, and rectilinear have students wanting to imitate them.

Arnosky, Jim. *All about Turtles*. 2000. New York: Scholastic. Unp. Grades: 2–4.

Did you know that gopher tortoises room with rattlesnakes? This and many other fascinating facts about turtles are included in this book. Colorful pictures and brief easy-to-read text enable young readers to learn about land-dwelling turtles, freshwater turtles, and sea turtles on their own.

Reptiles. 1999. Video. Bala Cynwyd, Penn.: Schlessinger Video Productions-Library Video Company. 23 min. Grades: 5 to 8.

The characteristics, habitats, and behaviors of turtles, crocodiles, alligators, lizards, and snakes are examined in this video. A teacher's guide is available. This video is close-captioned and is part of the Animal Life in Action series.

Explorations

1. Prior to studying reptiles, have students brainstorm what they know about them. Ask about their encounters with reptiles and have them add to their brainstorming information about the speed of the animals, where they found them, and what they feel like.
2. After reading *Tale of a Tadpole* (Wallace, 1998) or *Frogs* (Gibbons, 1993), have students create a flowchart to illustrate how a tadpole changes into a frog. Older students can write about the changes taking place in each picture.
3. While reading *All about Alligators* (Arnosky, 1994), have students sketch a picture of an alligator and label the parts. A word bank on chart paper will help them spell the words they need to label the parts.
4. After reading *Slinky Scaly Slithery Snakes* (Patent, 2000), children enjoy drawing their own snakes and cutting out the curling, twisting shapes to hang on a bulletin board.

5. Students can do research using books and the Internet to discover the kinds of snakes found in their area. They can use the information to create a booklet to share with the other students.

6. After reading *Slinky Snakes* (Souza, 1992), have students imitate the snake movements illustrated in the book.

7. Reptiles' colorings help them survive by camouflaging them in their environments. Have students color a snake or frog to hide in the classroom. Remind them to color the reptile to match the classroom colorings.

8. After reading several books on reptiles have students refer back to the books to write down their ideas about the benefits of having reptiles in our environment.

DINOSAURS

Young readers delight in things that are bigger than they can fathom. Children find these extinct creatures interesting and they delight in learning to recognize them and learning to pronounce their long, unusual names. Learning to spell the names of the dinosaurs adds to their mysterious charm. The mysteries of dinosaurs are revealed as students read books about these fascinating creatures that lived long ago. Each new generation discovers dinosaurs for the first time and relishes learning about them.

BOOK AND MEDIA CHOICES

Wahl, Jan. *The Field Mouse and the Dinosaur Named Sue*. Illustrated by Bob Doucet. 2000. New York: Scholastic. Unp. Grades: K–4.

The story of the discovery and recovery of the largest and most complete T. rex ever discovered is told from the perspective of a tiny field mouse. When part of the mouse's home, a large bone, is removed to be shipped to Chicago, the mouse hides in a box to try and retrieve his bone. Children delight in the mouse's exploration of various exhibits in The Field Museum.

Zoehfeld, Kathleen Weidner. *Terrible Tyrannosaurus*. Illustrated by Lucia Washburn. 2001. New York: HarperCollins. Unp. Grades: K–4.

Children enjoy learning and reading about this huge, ferocious dinosaur, which at one time stalked the earth eating other dinosaurs. The author explains to students how scientists have used the information gained from studying fossils to learn about Tyrannosaurus. For example, since T. rex's eyes faced forward like those of owls and hawks, scientists believe that like these hunters T. rex would have easily seen his prey and would have been a successful hunter. At the end of the book students can read brief entries about relatives of Tyrannosaurus, such as Siamotyrannus and Nanotyrannus. This is one of the Let's Read-and-Find-Out Science series.

All about Dinosaurs. 1999. Video. Bala Cynwyd, Penn.: Schlessinger Video Productions-Library Video Company. 23 min. Grades: K to 4.

Vivid illustrations and fossils are used to teach students about dinosaurs. They are compared to snakes, lizards, and crocodiles, which helps students make connections between familiar reptiles and their ancestors. A teacher's guide is available. This video is close-captioned and is part of the Animal Life for Children Video series.

Cole, Joanna. *The Magic School Bus in the Time of the Dinosaurs*. Illustrated by Bruce Degen. 1994. New York: Scholastic. Unp. Grades: 1–4.

This delightful part fact, part fantasy book deals with the "time-traveling school bus" of elementary school teacher, Ms. Frizzle. The class takes the bus out West to a dinosaur dig. While the paleontologists search for the duckbilled Maiasaura nests, Ms. Frizzle takes the students back in time to the Triassic, the Jurassic, the Cretaceous, and the Cenozoic Eras.

Dodson, Peter. *An Alphabet of Dinosaurs*. Paintings by Wayne D. Barlowe. 1995. New York: Scholastic. Unp. Grades: 2–6.

While called an alphabet book, this book should not be considered a simple "ABC" book. Twenty-six of the hundreds of dinosaurs are described and illustrated in this book. The paintings are colorful, large, and quite beautiful. The descriptions are brief and interesting and are accompanied by line drawings of the complete skeleton or skull. The book ends with a guide to the dinosaurs listed in the book, detailing the meanings of the names, what they ate, when they lived, where they lived, where their fossils were found, and their length. The book concludes with some theories about what finally happened to the dinosaurs.

Relf, Pat. *A Dinosaur Named Sue: The Story of the Colossal Fossil*. 2000. New York: Scholastic. 64p. Grades: 4–7.

Not long after the wondrous discovery of Sue, the fossil became embroiled in a lawsuit concerning who actually owned her. Once this was settled, scientists began reconstructing and studying the fossil. This detailed examination of this long arduous process affords readers the opportunity to understand the important work of paleontologists. Students marvel at the time, patience, and careful work required to study fossils. An index is included.

Dinosaurs on Earth: Then and Now. 1995. Video. Washington, D.C.: National Geographic Society. 25 min. Grades 4–9.

This animated video shows students what the earth looked like when dinosaurs roamed, it demonstrates the work of paleontologists, and takes students to the San Diego Wild Animal Park to compare present-day animals with dinosaurs.

Holmes, Thom, and Laurie Holmes. *Meat-Eating Dinosaurs: The Theropods.* **Illustrated by Michael William Skrepnick. 2001. Berkeley Heights, N.J.: Enslow. 128p. Grades: 4 and up.**

This book is written by a team of paleontologists and is arranged in a very reader-friendly manner. All of the facts that students find interesting are included such as origins, geographic range, anatomy, feeding habits, and extinction. Included are major Theropod discoveries, currently known Theropods, chapter notes, a glossary, a list for further reading, Internet addresses, and an index. The book is part of the Dinosaur Library series.

Explorations

1. After reading *The Field Mouse* (Wahl, 2000) and *A Dinosaur Named Sue* (Relf, 2000), have students visit The Field Museum online at www.fmnh.org/.

2. While reading *An Alphabet of Dinosaurs* (Dodson, 1995), complete a chart on the blackboard or a sheet of chart paper with two columns, one for familiar dinosaurs and one for unfamiliar dinosaurs (Yopp and Yopp, 2000). After reading about a dinosaur, ask the children if they are familiar or not familiar with that dinosaur. If most of the children are familiar with a dinosaur it goes in the column for familiar dinosaurs or vice versa.

3. In *A Dinosaur Named Sue: The Story of the Colossal Fossil* (Relf, 2000) students learn that Sue and other fossils have recently been sold to the highest bidder, which may be a private individual rather than a museum. Students can carefully study both sides of this issue and debate the issue of selling fossils to the highest bidder, rather than sending them to museums.

4. Some students have a strong fascination with dinosaurs and are experts on them. Ask the dinosaur experts in the classroom to share their dinosaur knowledge and dinosaur collections with their classmates.

INSECTS

Children have a wealth of knowledge about insects as they are readily found in the children's environment. Prior to coming to school, students have spent time observing insects and asking questions about them. Their prior knowledge and experiences with insects can be utilized as they are introduced to using scientific methods to study insects. Observing insects such as ladybugs affords students opportunities to learn to record observations, ask questions, and conduct simple experiments (Hechtman, 1995). The NSES scientific inquiry category requires students to use simple instruments and observations to learn about their environment through scientific investigations. Combining children's literature and hands-on science experiments encourages children to ask questions and motivates them to further explore (Matthews, Gee, and Bell, 1995).

Book and Media Choices

Rockwell, Anne. *Bugs Are Insects*. Illustrated by Steve Jenkins. 2001. New York: HarperCollins. 40p. Grades: P–1.

Brightly colored detailed collages of bugs fill the pages of this book that explains to young children what makes an insect an insect. Children are fascinated by these tiny creatures that they have seen crawling and flying in their back yards. Activities for observing and exploring insects are included in the book. The book concludes with a listing of the insects and animals found in the book and the page numbers on which they are found.

ptitle*Insects*. Illustrated by Eric Robson and Alan Rowe. 1998. New York: Golden Books. 24p. Grades: P–2.

Composed of color photographs, color illustrations, and cartoon illustrations, this book is intended for the very young child. Brief snippets of text accompany each illustration and explain concepts in easy-to-understand words. There is an index in the book.

Holmes, Anita. *Insect Detector*. 2000. Tarrytown, N.Y.: Marshall Cavendish. Grades: 1–3.

Young scientists like to read this book on their own and then to search for insects. Simple words combine with color photographs to help children understand the concepts presented in the book. There is a glossary and an index at the end of the book. This is one of the We Can Read about Nature series.

ptitle*Totally Amazing Spiders*. 1998. New York: Golden Book Publishing. 32p. Grades: 1–4.

This book is a light-hearted approach to the study of spiders. The combination of color photographs and cartoon pictures appeals to the young child. Various types of spiders are depicted with their habitats and eating characteristics. A glossary and index are included. This book is one of the Golden Books Totally Amazing series.

Cole, Joanna. *The Magic School Bus Inside a Beehive*. Illustrated by Bruce Degen. 1996. New York: Scholastic. 48p. Grades: 1–4.

The inner workings of a beehive are explained as the Friz and her students take a fantastic field trip into a beehive. The carefully researched detailed depictions of life in a beehive make this an excellent story and reference source for students. The combination of narrative and facts appeal to children and assures that they comprehend the concepts presented in the book. Notes at the end of the book help students sort the fact from the fiction presented in the book.

Greenaway, Theresa. *The Really Wicked Droning Wasps and Other Things that Bite and Sting.* **1996. New York: DK. Unp. Grades: 1–4.**

These larger-than-life pictures provide an initial look at what many children call scary bugs from bees and wasps to scorpions and fleas. The small bits of text that accompany the pictures are just enough to introduce children to these hideous bugs. Once introduced to these creepy, scary bugs readers want additional books to further their studies of these fascinating creatures. This is one of The Really Horrible Guides series.

Sandved, Kjell B. *The Butterfly Alphabet.* **1996. New York: Scholastic. Unp. Grades: 1–4.**

Over 25 years and across 30 countries the author photographed butterflies and moths. By carefully scrutinizing the enlarged, cropped photographs he discovered all 26 letters of the alphabet. Accompanying each vibrant, colorful cropped photograph is a rhyming couplet and a full picture of the butterfly or moth. The popular name of each is given on the page, and the scientific name and habitat are found at the bottom of the page. After reading this book, readers never see butterflies and moths in the same light.

Bernhard, Emery. *Dragonfly.* **Illustrated by Durga Bernhard. 1993. New York: Holiday House. Unp. Grades: 2–4.**

One hundred million years ago, when dinosaurs roamed the earth, there were insects known as dragonflies. While they were certainly not dragons, neither were they flies, and they were perhaps called dragonflies because of the somewhat frightening markings on their backs. Today the insects have wingspans of from one to seven inches and are considered to be among the most beautiful insects. This illustrated book covers the life cycle, the hatching and mating, and the eating habits of dragonflies. It also discusses how various cultures viewed the insects and how we think of them today. The book also contains a brief but helpful glossary.

Facklam, Margery. *Creepy, Crawly Caterpillars.* **Illustrated by Paul Facklam. 1996. Boston: Little, Brown and Company. 32p. Grades: 2–4.**

Oversized, colorful, detailed drawings portray metamorphosis and show which caterpillars become which moths and butterflies. Caterpillars spend much of their very short lives eating and growing. Their appearance, habits, habitats, and food preferences are discussed in the book.

Parker, Steve. *Insects: How to Watch and Understand the Busy World of Insects.* **1992. New York: Dorling Kindersley. 61p. Grades: 2–5.**

A slim book with short bursts of informative text, illustrations, and photographs is just the thing to tuck into a desk or backpack. Reading this book provides not only information on a variety of insects, but instructions for the safe capture of insects and instructions for creating natural habitats in which to observe them. Readers are reminded throughout the book to safely return the animals to their original habitat once they have been observed. This is one of the Eyewitness Explorers series.

Incredible World of Insects. 2001. Video. Raleigh, N.C.: Rainbow Educational Media. 27 min. Grades: 4–8.

Live action close-ups, models, diagrams, and models are used to teach students about insects. The video explains to students how to determine if a bug is an insect by looking for the three body parts. Students learn which insects are harmful and which ones are helpful. The video ends with a review. This video includes a teacher's guide.

Explorations

1. After reading *Totally Amazing Spiders* (1998), have students record on index cards either in pictures or words the most interesting or weirdest thing they learned about spiders. Have students share their work in small groups.
2. After reading *The Magic School Bus Inside a Beehive* (Cole, 1996), have students create dances to communicate instructions to different areas of the school such as the cafeteria or the gym.
3. Using *Insects: How to Watch and Understand the Busy World of Insects* (Parker, 1992), have students create natural habitats for insect observations. Have the students spend 15 minutes each day observing the insects and recording their observations.
4. *The Butterfly Alphabet* (Sandved, 1996) captures all of the letters in the alphabet on the wings of moths and butterflies. Using a digital camera students can capture the letters of the alphabet in natural or man-made structures around the school and on the playground. They can then create a PowerPoint presentation of their digital pictures.
5. Prior to reading *The Really Wicked Droning Wasps and Other Things that Bite and Sting* (Greenaway, 1996), have students tell about times they were stung by insects and how they felt. Also share with the students about how to treat insect bites and stings.
6. Prior to beginning a unit of study on insects, the teacher can copy intriguing excerpts from the informational books to be used in the study. The cards are given to the students to practice reading. Then all the students gather on the floor and students read their cards aloud. The cards are tacked on the bulletin board for students to refer to as they come across the passages in the books.
7. During their study of insects have students create a large data chart on the wall including an illustration of the insects, their food, habitats, and predators.
8. After reading *Dragonfly* (Bernhard, 1993), have students discuss why they think the dragonfly was considered a symbol of life by Mimbres of the Southwest, who painted dragonflies on pottery as a symbol of life. Then have the students paint pictures of dragonflies to decorate the classroom.
9. Ask students to brainstorm about the impact of insects on their lives. Then have students search books to determine the positive and negative impact of insects.

10. Have students ask their parents about any superstitions they know about insects. For example, in some cultures spiders are thought to bring good luck.

FISH

An aquarium in the classroom or the library provides students opportunities to observe and study fish, as well as opportunities to learn to care for fish. Children take delight in dropping food into the aquarium and watching the fish swim to the surface to eat. Having an aquarium nearby as they learn about fish enables students to make connections between the concepts presented in the book and the fish swimming in the aquarium.

Book and Media Choices

Barner, Bob. *Fish Wish*. 2000. New York: Holiday House. Unp. Grades: P–1.

Large vibrant pictures combine with large print to introduce children to the beautiful creatures found beneath the sea. A child snorkels through a coral reef discovering the sea creatures lurking in the reef. The book closes with a map identifying each creature the child encounters during his undersea swim, additional information on each of the creatures in the book, and notes about the coral reef.

The Cousteau Society. *The Garibaldi: Fish of the Pacific*. 1992. New York: Simon and Schuster Books for Young Readers. Unp. Grades: 2–4.

The garibaldi is an unfriendly, beautiful bright orange fish. The male fish patrols and protects the eggs laid by the female. Stunning underwater photographs show the male protecting the eggs by grasping a hungry starfish by one of its arms and dragging it away from the eggs. He is not even afraid of the large deep-sea divers that photograph him.

Resnick, Jane P. *Fish*. 1993. Chicago: Kidsbooks. 31p. Grades: 2–5.

Illustrated with both color photographs and drawings, this book contains brief facts about freshwater and ocean fish from sharks to eels. A few sea creatures, which are not actual fish such as starfish, jellyfish, and crawfish, are also mentioned. Flying Hatchet fish, sea robins, guitarfish, and other unusual fish are described briefly. This is a good introduction to fish and stimulates students to do additional research on these undersea creatures. This is part of the Eyes on Nature series.

Evans, Mark. *Fish*. 1993. New York: DK. 45p. Grades: 3–6.

Included in this guide are color photographs and step-by-step instructions for setting up an aquarium, caring for the tank, and cleaning the tank. Children interested in setting up their first aquarium find this book a useful resource. The book concludes with instructions for creating a log of the fish in the aquarium and an index. This is one of the ASPCA Pet Care Guides for Kids series.

Maynard, Christopher. *Informania Sharks*. 1997. Cambridge, Mass.: Candlewick Press. 92p. Grades: 3 and up.

Terrifying photographs, detailed line drawings, colorful charts, comic book illustrations and fascinating, informative text assure that students learn a great deal about these creatures of the sea. This book is divided into five sections: 1) shocking shark stories, 2) confidential crime files, 3) database: shark profile, 4) biology notes: reproduction, and 5) ready reference. The format of this book presents the content in a manner sure to appeal to students.

Fish. 1999. Video. Bala Cynwyd, Penn.: Schlessinger Video Productions-Library Video Company. 23 min. Grades: 5 to 8.

This video explores the many different kinds of fish that live in salt water and fresh water. It explains the fishes' adaptations that allow them to survive in water. A teacher's guide is available. This video is close-captioned and is part of the Animal Life in Action series.

Explorations

1. After reading *Fish Wish* (Barner, 2000), have the students turn the classroom into an undersea coral reef by creating their own sea creatures and hanging them from the classroom ceiling.
2. After reading *The Garibaldi: Fish of the Pacific* (The Cousteau Society, 1992), students can write a story about the family and the adventures of the male fish as he cares for the young.
3. Use *Fish* (Resnick, 1993) as an introduction to fish. Have each student in the class select a fish to fully research. The information they gather can be combined in a class book to be placed in the class library.
4. Students can create HyperStudio stacks on the different kinds of sharks found in *Informania Sharks* (Maynard, 1997). Encourage them to go beyond the book to discover additional information about sharks. Prior to creating the stacks, they need to come to a decision about the information to be contained in the stacks.

ANIMAL ADAPTATIONS AND HABITATS

In order to survive in the world, animals have developed disguises to hide from their predators. These disguises are so effective that oftentimes children do not see the animals. Helping students become aware of the animals' presence may be the first step in having them understand the interdependence of humans and animals. The National Science Education Standard pertaining to life science addresses students' knowledge of the interdependence of organisms and their environment. Books in this section build upon students' experiences with animals in their natural environment and encourage students to look carefully to discover other animals hidden in the outdoors.

Book and Media Choices

Rosenberry, Vera. *Who Is in the Garden?* **2001. New York: Holiday House. Unp. Grades: P–1.**

Quiet, careful observations and explorations lead a young boy to discover all the different creatures residing in the garden. Watercolor paintings of a garden brimming with creatures, fruit, flowers, and one curious boy encourage students to carefully examine the pictures so as not to miss any of the creatures waiting to be discovered.

Greenway, Shirley. *Can You See Me?* **Photographs by Oxford Scientific Films. 1992. Nashville, Tenn.: Ideals Children's Books. 31p. Grades: P–2.**

This brief book designed for young children shows the ways animals and insects disguise themselves for protection against predators. Some of them have colorations that make it possible for them to blend into their environment and thus camouflage themselves against harm. Others are able to do this because of their shapes and sizes. This series is sure to capture the attention of young children and familiarize them with various species in nature. Some of the unfamiliar words are spelled phonetically and there is an index. This book is one of the *Animals Q & A* series.

Greenway, Shirley. *Where Do I Live?* **Photographs by Oxford Scientific Films. 1992. Nashville, Tenn.: Ideals Children's Books. 31p. Grades: P–2.**

This book deals with the habitats of various animals and fish. Each page consists of a question and its answer or a color picture. Twelve animals query the reader and there are several two-page photographic spreads. The book closes with a very brief summary and small photograph of each animal selected and an index. This book is one of the *Animals Q & A* series.

Habitats. **2000. Video. El Dorado Hills, Calif.: One Hundred Percent Educational Videos. 15 min. Grades: K–2.**

Habitats such as ponds, deserts, forests, and rainforests are explored to discover how plants and animals adapt to survive. The video includes a teacher's guide and is close-captioned.

Singer, Marilyn. *Tough Beginning: How Baby Animals Survive.* **Illustrated by Anna Vojtech. 2001. New York: Henry Holt. Unp. Grades: 1–3.**

It is a wonder that enough baby animals survive to keep the species alive. This book explains to young readers the different challenges faced by a variety of baby animals. For example, about twenty-four hours after hatching, young wood ducks are expected to leave their cozy nest by plummeting sometimes more than sixty feet to the ground. This is only the first of many dangers they encounter as they make their way to water. An author's note at the end of the book explains that humans intentionally and unintentionally harm baby animals.

Awan, Shaila. *The Burrow Book*. Illustrated by Richard Orr. 1997. New York: DK. 19p. Grades: 1–3.

Foldout pages with cut-out holes enable the reader to look beneath the ground into the habitats of the various creatures. Limited text and copious, colorful illustrations make this a terrific book for young readers. Habitats of common everyday creatures such as cockroaches to the less familiar pangolin are included in this book. Habitats include woodland, arctic, forest, grassland, and desert.

Ganeri, Anita. *Animals in Disguise*. Illustrated by Halli Verrinder. 1995. New York: Simon and Schuster. 24p. Grades: 1–3.

Animals use camouflage to hide from their prey and to hide from their food. Transparent pages with hidden animals painted on them enable students to seek and find the animals as they flip the pages. The small size of the book and the large print make this a book for students to return to on their own again and again as they discover the wonders of animal camouflage.

George, Lindsay Barrett. *Around the Pond: Who's Been Here?* 1996. New York: Greenwillow Books. Unp. Grades: 1–4.

While traveling a deer path around the pond in search of blueberries, Cammy and William encounter clues left behind by a variety of wildlife. They examine the evidence to determine which animals have traveled the path before them. Full-page realistic color illustrations make this a book to share with groups of children who eagerly guess the animal before the page is turned to reveal the answer.

Taylor, Barbara. *Animal Hide and Seek*. Illustrated by John Francis. 1998. New York: DK. 48p. Grades: 2–6.

Student interaction with the book is assured as they search for flora and fauna in different habitats around the world. Brief text introductions are followed by short spurts of text that give information about individual animals with questions for children to answer. The last pages of the book provide a pictorial index that identifies all the animals hidden in the colorful, two-page spread illustrations.

Explorations

1. After reading *Who is in the Garden?* (Rosenberry, 2001) discuss with the students what would have happened if the boy went through the garden in a noisy, hurried fashion. Have them practice quiet walking and observations in the classroom prior to exploring the school playground in search of creatures.

2. In *Can You See Me?* (Greenway, 1992) and *Animals in Disguise* (Ganeri, 1995) students can easily see how animals' disguises save them from their predators. Help them to see that in some instances these disguises also help them capture their prey. For example, the chameleon's camouflage enables it to hide from the insects it eats.

3. After reading *The Burrow Book* (Awan, 1997), have students design an underground house.

4. Divide the class into groups of four. Have them create their own book based on *Around the Pond: Who's Been Here?* (George, 1996). Each student is responsible for the text and pictures for two animals. Appoint one student as the editor who compiles the pictures and creates a map of the pond showing the location of each animal.

5. Have students carefully observe what other students are wearing on the playground or in the cafeteria. Then have them decide what they would wear if they wanted to hide in a crowd on the playground or in the cafeteria.

6. Mount pictures of animals on tag board. Place the pictures in a bag and have the students select a picture and draw a picture of the animal's home or habitat.

7. Younger students enjoy playing animal hide and seek with a stuffed animal hidden in the classroom. Provide students with clues as to where to find the animal.

UNDERSTANDING ANIMALS

The books in this section enable students to make personal connections between what they read and their own lives. They require readers to examine their personal value systems and make decisions about how they will react when faced with similar situations. The books in this section provide insight about a variety of issues dealing with human's impact on animals' lives. These books enable children to think about and discuss what-if scenarios. For example, what if a bear shows up in your backyard?

Book and Media Choices

Manning, Mick. *Supermom*. Illustrated by Brita Granstrom. 2001. Morton Grove, Ill.: Albert Whitman. 31p. Grades: P–2.

Supermoms are everywhere and come in all shapes and sizes. This delightful book is filled with information about how moms take care of their babies. Each two-page spread contains both human and animal moms taking care of their young. The book concludes with a glossary/index of the animals found in the book.

McNulty, Faith. *A Snake in the House.* **Illustrated by Ted Rand. 1994. New York: Scholastic. Unp. Grades: K–3.**

A childhood pastime of catching animals and insects in jars is examined through the eyes of a captured snake and a boy. Longing for freedom, food, and water the snake escapes from the jar and his travels through the boy's house are chronicled. In the end the boy learns a valuable lesson about capturing wild animals.

Goodman, Susan E. *Animal Rescue: The Best Job There Is.* **2000. New York: Aladdin Paperbacks. 48p. Grades: 1–3.**

John Walsh travels around the world, rescuing animals left stranded by floods, wars, earthquakes, and other natural disasters. The book includes three gripping stories of his heroic deeds to save stranded and deserted animals. The book has a table of contents and an address for the World Society for the Protection of Animals. This is one of the Ready-to-Read series.

Kessler, Cristina. *Jubela.* **Illustrated by JoEllen McAllister Stammen. 2001. New York: Simon and Schuster Books for Young Readers. Unp. Grades: 1–4.**

This touching book is based on a true story from Swaziland in Southern Africa. A baby rhino is orphaned when poachers kill his mother. Ordinarily, orphaned babies die without mother's milk and protection. Jubela instinctively seeks protection from other rhinos without success. Barely alive, he finds an old female rhino that adopts him and shows him how to find food and water. She offers him the companionship and protection he needs to survive.

Murphy, Jim. *Backyard Bear.* **Illustrated by Jeffry Greene. 1993. New York: Scholastic. Unp. Grades: 2–4.**

In search of food, a young bear makes his way through a sleeping neighborhood. His scary journey is seen through his eyes and the eyes of the families he awakens. As older bears force younger bears out of their territory, the younger bears show up in backyards across America looking for food.

George, Jean Craighead. *Animals Who Have Won Our Hearts.* **Illustrated by Christine Herman Merrill. 1994. New York: HarperCollins. 56p. Grades: 3–5.**

Each of the animals in the book was included because of their unique interactions with humans. These true stories testify to the animals' bravery and intelligence while offering a glimpse into the interactions between humans and animals. Animals as well known as Smokey the Bear and Koko the gorilla are included as well as lesser-known animals such as Lewis and Clark's dog, Seaman.

Simon, Seymour. *Animals Nobody Loves*. 2001. New York: SeaStar Books. 48p. Grades: 3–5.

Stunning photographs of this collection of fearsome, often misunderstood animals intrigue students who then read the book to find out more about the animals. From the tiny red ant to the huge grizzly, from the Piranha in the water to the vulture in the sky, the animals in this book have bad reputations many of which are not based on fact. The book helps students understand and respect the animals. An introduction and a table of contents are included.

Goodall, Jane. *With Love*. Illustrated by Alan Marks. 1994. New York: North-South Books. Unp. Grades: 3 and up.

These heartwarming, true tales of a life's work and love after nearly 40 years of living with chimpanzees detail the trials and tribulations of their lives. These stories show that not only humans are capable of love, companionship, and altruism. She tells how each chimpanzee has its own distinct personality, some are calm and gentle, and others are wild and adventurous.

Dewey, Jennifer Owings. *Wildlife Rescue: The Work of Dr. Kathleen Ramsey*. Photographs by Don MacCarter. 1994. Honesdale, Penn.: Boyds Mills Press. 63p. Grades: 4–8.

An assortment of sick and injured birds and animals throughout the western United States have been treated by veterinarian, Kathleen Ramsey. Her long days and nights of tirelessly caring for animals delivered to her clinic are chronicled in this inspiring book. She founded the Wildlife Center in New Mexico and developed vital treatments to assure that as many animals as possible are returned to their native habitats. This book received the Orbis Pictus Award.

***Jane Goodall: My Life with Chimpanzees*. 1990. Video. Washington, D.C.: National Geographic. 60 min. Grades: 6 and up.**

Jane Goodall's remarkable life with the chimpanzees is chronicled in this video. Her mission was to observe them and over the course of three decades also became their friend and their ally. This is one of the National Geographic Series.

Explorations

1. Students enjoy talking about their special relationships with their own pets. Have them record their stories and place the tape in a listening center to be shared with their classmates. Students who do not have pets can interview those students with pets and record the interviews.
2. Prior to reading *Backyard Bear* (Murphy, 1993), ask students about encounters they have had with wild animals in their backyards.
3. At the end of *Animals Nobody Loves* (Simon, 2001) the author encourages readers to

reflect on their reading and determine if they feel any differently about the animals after learning more about them. Then he suggests they create their own list of animals they do not love and think about why they are on their list. After creating their lists, students can select one of the animals on their list to research.

4. Prior to reading *Wildlife Rescue: The Work of Dr. Kathleen Ramsey* (Dewey, 1994), elicit information from students about injured animals they have found. After reading the book discuss with students what they should do when they discover an injured animal.

5. Students can debate the issue of why we need to take care of our wildlife and whose responsibility it is to care for them.

6. If there is room in the classroom for housing a pet, have students conduct research to determine the best animal for the classroom and what items are needed for the pet. They should determine a budget to cover the cost of upkeep and then raise money to purchase and care for the pet.

7. After reading *Jubela* (Kessler, 2001), have students brainstorm the reasons why the older female adopted the young rhino. This is a very unusual occurrence.

PLANTS

The cycle of life is readily apparent in the plant world where flowers bloom and die, and leaves sprout, grow, and fall from trees. Growing plants helps students to learn about science and life as they carefully observe and record the plants' growth. The National Science Education Standard pertaining to life science includes an understanding of the study of plants' life cycles. These books provide information about plants to enhance students' understanding of the importance of plants in their world. One way to introduce students to the world of plants is by sharing the video of *The Magic School Bus Gets Planted* with them.

The Magic School Bus Gets Planted. 2001. Redmond, Wash.: Microsoft Corporation. 30 min. Grades: K–5.

What better way to learn about how plants grow than to take a trip inside of one? Mrs. Firzzle and her students are once again on a fantastic voyage to discover all about plants.

BOOK AND MEDIA CHOICES

Carle, Eric. *The Tiny Seed*. 2001. New York: Aladdin Paperbacks. Unp. Grades: P–3.

Carle's unique collage illustrations are used to describe the growth of a plant from a tiny seed. The young child can identify with the stages of plant growth and the roles of sunshine, water, and wind. This simple description of the life cycle of a plant introduces young readers to the miracles that unfold when a seed is planted.

Hubbell, Will. *Pumpkin Jack*. 2000. Morton Grove, Ill.: Albert Whitman. Unp. Grades: K–3.

After Tim enjoys his Halloween jack-o-lantern he puts it in the garden and watches it shrivel and decay. The winter snows cover the garden, but then in the spring a vine begins to grow. By fall there is a glorious pumpkin patch. Tim gives away all of the pumpkins except one, which he carves into a jack-o-lantern. The cycle of life is beautifully depicted in the detailed illustrations.

Stuart, Sarah. *The Gardener*. Illustrated by David Small. 1997. New York: Farrar Straus Giroux. Unp. Grades: K–3.

With her parents out of work a young girl is sent to live temporarily with her silent, dour uncle who resides in the city. She takes with her a love of gardening and her grandmother's gardening wisdom. Before she returns home she has transformed a city rooftop into a magnificent blooming garden. The story is told in a series of letters she writes to her family. This is a Caldecott Honor Book. This book is also available on cassette from Live Oak Media, Pine Plains, New York.

***All about Caring for Plants*. 2000. Video. Wynnewood, Penn.: Schlessinger Video Productions-Library Video Company. 23min. Grades: K–4.**

One of the reasons this video appeals to children is because they see children much like themselves learning about plants and caring for plants. Students not only explore what plants need to grow and thrive they also learn how to assure that the plants get the correct nutrients and care. The program includes a teacher's guide. This is part of the Schlessinger Science Library for Children Collection.

Stevens, Janet. *Tops and Bottoms*. 1995. San Diego: HarcourtBrace. Unp. Grades: 1–4.

Hare uses his wits to trick Bear into choosing whether he wants the tops or the bottoms to the plants Hare will grow on Bear's land. Once Bear makes his choice, Hare plants the appropriate crops. For example, when Bear chooses tops, Hare plants beets and carrots. This book can be used to introduce children to the fact that the foods they eat grow on different parts of the plant—tops, middles, and bottoms. This is a Caldecott Honor Book. This book is also available on video.

Kalman, Bobbie. *How a Plant Grows*. 1997. New York: Crabtree. 32p. Grades: 1–4.

This beautifully illustrated book examines the stages of a seed's development including germination, photosynthesis, and pollination. The importance of plants in the food chain is explained in simple terms that young readers understand. There are activities for growing a bean plant, watching it absorb water, and making an indoor garden. Included in the book are a glossary and an index.

Hickman, Pamela. *Starting with Nature: Tree Book.* **Illustrated by Heather Collins. 1999. Buffalo, New York: Kids Can Press. 32p. Grades: 2–4.**

Most children enjoy climbing, sitting in the shade, or eating the fruit of trees. They possibly have more interactions with trees than with any other plant. This wonderfully illustrated book provides students not only with information on trees but also with ways to study trees. Leaf collecting instructions, an investigation into why leaves change color, and a tree watching check list are just a few of the activities included in the book to enable students to explore trees in greater detail. An index concludes the book.

Talmadge, Ellen. *Unearthing Garden Mysteries: Experiments for Kids.* **2000. Photographs by Bruce Curtis. Fulcrum Press. 90p. Grades: 3–6.**

The author's passion for plants is evident as she leads children on an exploration of the intriguing world of plants. Twenty simple, hands-on experiments are great for classroom learning, at-home extensions of the classroom curriculum, or for science fair projects. Suggestions for making observations and recording them in journals are included. The book includes a glossary, an index, a bibliography, and books for additional reading.

Pascoe, Elaine. *Seeds and Seedlings.* **Photographs by Dwight Kuhn. 1997. Woodbridge, Conn.: Blackbirch Press. 48p. Grades: 3–6.**

Descriptions and photographs of how seeds grow into flowers are found in chapter one. Then, chapters two and three engage readers in explorations to discover how to grow seeds and scientific experiments to learn about seeds. Rather than tell young scientists about seeds and seedlings this book enables students to discover information for themselves. The experiments contain a materials list, instructions for conducting the experiments, information on recording the results, and questions to answer at the conclusion of the experiments. Parents and children enjoy conducting these experiments together.

Kerrod, Robin. *Plant Life.* **Illustrated by Ted Evans. 1994. New York: Marshall Cavendish. 64p. Grades: 3–6.**

To encourage students to think about what they are reading, questions are interspersed throughout the text. The answers to the questions are provided at the end of the book. The book includes chapters on plant biology, plant groups, and plant habitats with investigations to enable students to fully explore these topics. The photographs and drawings are accompanied by detailed captions. The book closes with a timeline, glossary, bibliography, and an index.

Nielsen, Nancy J. *Carnivorous Plants*. 1992. New York: Franklin Watts. 64p. Grades: 3–6.

Plants that eat animals fascinate young and old. How did plants become carnivorous? How do they catch their prey? The answers to these questions and others are found in this intriguing book that includes color photographs of the plants trapping their prey. The book concludes with information on obtaining carnivorous plants, where to go to see them growing, reference sources for additional information, and an index.

Burton, Jane, and Kim Taylor. *The Nature and Science of Flowers*. 1998. Milwaukee, Wis.: Gareth Stevens. 32p. Grades: 4–6.

Beginning with why plants have flowers, this book captures students' attention and holds it as they learn about the parts of the flowers, how flowers are pollinated, how seeds are made, and how they are dispersed. Boldface type alerts readers to words found in the glossary. Each page has color photographs of the flowers in their natural habitats. Activities for studying flowers are included. The book ends with a glossary, scientific names of the flowers, a list of additional books to read, videos and Web sites on flowers, and an index.

Tesar, Jenny. *Fungi*. Illustrated by Wendy Smith-Griswold. 1994. Woodbridge, Conn.: Blackbirch Press. 64p. Grades: 5–7.

Fungi include mushrooms growing in the backyard, the mold growing on bread, and the athlete's foot growing on people's feet. Some fungi live in soil, some on dead organisms, and some on living organisms. This in-depth examination of fungi reveals that they are found in foods and medicines. Color photographs and diagrams accompany this fascinating text. At the end of the book are a classification chart, a glossary, a list of books for further reading, and an index.

***Botanical Gardens*. 1993. Mac/Win. Pleasantville, N.Y.: Sunburst Communications. Grades: 5–8.**

Changing a plant's environment impacts its growth and students discover this very quickly when they manipulate the environmental variables in this software program. Students experiment with different plants and growing conditions as they attempt to find the optimal conditions for plant growth. The results of their experiments are reported on graphs that help the students make decisions about what conditions are needed for optimal plant growth.

EXPLORATIONS

1. After reading *The Tiny Seed* (Carle, 2001) provide students with a bag containing a collection of different kinds of seeds. Then, have them decide on different ways to sort and classify the seeds.
2. After reading *Tops and Bottoms* (Stevens, 1995) have students work in groups to create lists of vegetables that grow on the top, middle, and bottom of the plant.

3. After reading *Tops and Bottoms* (Stevens, 1995) students can see vegetables such as carrots, onions, and radishes growing underground with a Root-Vue Farm that enables them to see the roots as plants grow. A Root-Vue Farm is available at www.insectlore.com.

4. After reading *How a Plant Grows* (Kalman, 1997) have the students work in small groups to create a list of questions about plants. Invite a gardener in to answer the students' questions.

5. After reading *Seeds and Seedlings* (Pascoe, 1997) have the students predict which seeds will germinate first in different media such as wet sawdust, between damp paper towels, and in peat pots.

6. After reading *Carnivorous Plants* (Nielsen, 1992) have the students order plants to grow in the classroom. Prior to ordering the plants have the students research to determine what they need to grow them in, decide on the best place in the classroom to place the plants, and how they will feed them.

7. Using *Plant Life* (Kerrod, 1994), *Starting with Nature: Tree Book* (Hickman, 1999), and *The Nature and Science of Flowers* (Burton and Taylor, 1998) have the students create a guide to the plants in the schoolyard using a desktop publishing program and a digital camera.

8. After reading *Starting with Nature: Tree Book* (Hickman, 1999) have the students create a tree log and record the changes in a tree in the schoolyard over the course of the school year. A digital camera allows students to easily record the changes in the tree.

9. Prior to reading *Fungi* (Tesar, 1994) have the students examine mushrooms brought in from the grocery store.

ENVIRONMENTAL ISSUES AND ECOLOGY

The conflict between humans and nature requires students to stop and consider how humans' actions impact nature, because nature and the world are entrusted to their care and their actions have profound effects. Animals and plants depend on humans to keep them safe and insure that their habitats are secure. Making decisions about what is good for humans and good for the earth requires students to research and think about the consequences of their actions. The NSES category pertaining to life science requires that students understand that humans' impact on their environment can be either beneficial or detrimental to humans and other organisms.

Literature enables students to gain information and make decisions about universal problems faced by the inhabitants of this planet. Books in this section present authentic situations for students to learn about their environment and to use higher-order thinking skills to contemplate problems and to use scientific inquiry as they seek solutions to problems facing the environment. Goforth (1998) describes this as a cyclical learning process: students read about a problem, ask questions, research to find answers from a variety of sources, reflect on the information they have gathered, and offer a possible solution.

BOOK AND MEDIA CHOICES

Ryder, Joanne. *Little Panda: The World Welcomes Hua Mei at the San Diego Zoo*. 2001. New York: Simon and Schuster Books for Young Readers. Unp. Grades: K–2.

Through photographs and large-print text, the story of the birth of the first giant panda cub to ever survive in captivity in the Western Hemisphere is shared with readers. The excitement of the baby panda's birth and development is captured in the exclusive photographs provided by the zoo. The book tells not only of the giant panda's first year, but also of the plight of the endangered giant pandas.

Gibbons, Gail. *Recycle!: A Handbook for Kids*. 1992. Boston: Little, Brown. Unp. Grades: K–3.

The recycling process is presented in easy-to-understand text with colorful illustrations to help explain what happens to recycled garbage. It concludes with fascinating facts about the amount of garbage produced each day, as well as things everyone can do to recycle. The book itself is printed on recycled paper. This book has been recognized as an Outstanding Science Trade Book for Children and a Notable Children's Trade Book in the Field of Social Studies.

***This Pretty Planet: Tom Chapin Live in Concert*. 1993. Video. New York: Sony. 50 min. Grades: K–4.**

Tom Chapin sings thirty of his earthy, friendly songs such as *Year 3000* and *Good Garbage*. This recording is also available in audiocassette.

***Here's My Question: Where Does My Garbage Go?* 2000. Video. London, England: Middlemarch Productions. 26 min. Grades: K–5.**

Lively, catchy tunes and camera tricks highlight this lively video that shows children where the garbage they throw away goes. Garbage is followed as it makes its way to either a landfill or to a recycling plant.

Joslin, Mary. *The Tale of the Heaven Tree*. Illustrated by Meilo So. 1999. Grand Rapids, Mich.: Eerdmans Books for Young Readers. Unp. Grades: K and up.

This is a tale of the creation, the destruction, and the renewal of the earth's natural resources. A weeping young girl desolate about the destruction hears the voice of the Great Maker who directs her to plant and nurture a seed. The earth's renewal begins as a tree grows from the seed whose branches provide a haven for plants and animals. Watercolor illustrations capture the earth's changes using both movement and mood.

Schimmel, Schim. *Dear Children of the Earth: A Letter from Home.* **1994. Minnetonka, Minn.: NorthWord Press. Unp. Grades: K and up.**

A letter to each of us from Mother Earth accompanies the astonishing paintings in this book. She explains that all living things on the planet are connected. She appeals to the "children" of the earth to love and protect her from pollution and lack of care and concern. Each painting contains a small or large representation of the Earth as seen from outer space. As children are "natural" environmentalists, they should enjoy and be inspired by both the pictures and the text. The Izaak Walton League of America named this book the Children's Book of the Year.

Schimmel, Schim. *Children of the Earth . . . Remember.* **1997. Minnetonka, Minn.: NorthWord Press. 31p. Grades: K and up.**

While this book was created with children in mind, most adults find it appealing. The environmental message is not overly sentimental and yet makes a point. The artwork is magnificent and one is almost convinced some of the pictures are photographs. As in his previous book the author/artist has included a representation of the planet Earth in each painting. This book was given the Benjamin Franklin Award by the Publishers Marketing Association.

Totally Amazing Rain Forests. **1998. New York: Golden Book. 32p. Grades: 1–4.**

This lighthearted, brief discussion of tropical rain forests combines color photographs, cartoon-like drawings, and limited text to attract and hold the attention of the young child. The authors assign conversational comments to the animals and objects and include a glossary and index. This is one of the Totally Amazing series.

Van Allsburg, Chris. *Just a Dream.* **1990. Boston: Houghton Mifflin. Unp. Grades: 2–4.**

Walter is unconcerned about recycling, until he falls asleep one night and gets a magical ride into the future. He discovers that smog has covered the Grand Canyon, ducks cannot find lakes, and belching smokestacks make his eyes burn and water. He awakens determined to do his part to save the earth.

Chandler, Gary, and Kevin Graham. *Guardians of Wildlife.* **1996. New York: Henry Holt. 64p. Grades: 4–8.**

Each of the four chapters in this book includes stories about many of the individuals and organizations that are working to preserve and protect wildlife across the world. Of interest to students are the names and addresses of the different agencies that are willing to share information with school children. The organizations are working to protect the wildlife in diverse ways. For example in Indonesia, wild elephants were trampling farms and villages. At the Way Kambas National Park Training Center wild elephants have been captured, trained to respond to human commands, and returned to the wild. These trained elephants help to keep the elephant herds away from settlements. Should the elephants get too close to the village, villagers issue commands to the trained elephants that shepherd the entire herd away from the village.

Pringle, Laurence. *Global Warming: The Threat of Earth's Changing Climate*. 2001. New York: SeaStar Books. 48p. Grades: 4–8.

The brief chapters, each with their own short introduction, hold readers' attention as they learn about global warming and its effect on the earth. Pringle discusses various causes of global warming including the use of aerosols, the burning of fossil fuels, and deforestation. The book challenges readers to be proactive in order to avert a global disaster. The book concludes with a glossary, a list of further readings, and an index.

EXPLORATIONS

1. Reading *Little Panda: The World Welcomes Hua Mei at the San Diego Zoo* (Ryder, 2001) prior to a trip to the zoo enables students to see that zoos are important breeding grounds for a variety of endangered animals.
2. After reading *Recycle!: A Handbook for Kids* (Gibbons, 1992) have students draw a flowchart to show what happens to items that are recycled.
3. Create a bulletin board for posting newspaper and magazine articles about local recycling and preservation. Have students briefly tell about the article before it is posted on the bulletin board.
4. Have students brainstorm a list of ways to protect the earth. Then, have them decide on one way the class will work together to help protect the earth.
5. *Dear Children of the Earth: A Letter from Home* (Schimmel, 1994) and *Children of the Earth . . . Remember* (Schimmel, 1997) speak of the interrelationships between people and animals and the earth. Help students make the connections between the stories and their own lives.
6. After reading *Just a Dream* (Van Allsburg, 1990) have students create a list of facts that they learned in the book.
7. Children like to imagine the future. Have them paint pictures to show how their town or neighborhood will look when they have children.
8. After reading *Global Warming: The Threat of Earth's Changing Climate* (Pringle, 2001), have students brainstorm ideas for things they can do to protect Earth's atmosphere.

EARTH SCIENCE

The study of earth science includes investigations into volcanoes, earthquakes, landforms, soil, and water. Children are aware of the destructive forces of volcanoes and earthquakes and naturally have questions about them. Wetlands and deserts are very different landforms and are homes to unique plants and animals that have adapted to the environment each provides. NSES category five focuses on earth science, including the structure of the earth and the history of the earth. Children have a wealth of personal experiences to draw upon as they study soil and water and the books on these topics extend and enhance these experiences to deepen children's understanding. Sharing *Our Planet Earth* (Llewellyn, 1997) with students is one way to introduce the study of the earth.

Llewellyn, Claire. *Our Planet Earth*. 1997. New York: Scholastic. 77p. Grades: 2–4.

As students begin their study of the earth, this book provides them with brief, informative text, illustrations, and photographs. The book includes a short introduction to the earth followed by three sections: Earth's surface, the changing planet, and life on Earth. Included in the book are snippets of interesting information in "Did you know?" text boxes. Bold text is used to indicate words included in the glossary.

VOLCANOES AND EARTHQUAKES

The violent forces of volcanoes and earthquakes and the destruction they cause fascinate readers of all ages who eagerly turn the pages of these books to learn more about these natural disasters. The NSES category on earth science recognizes that students need an understanding of the changes in the earth due to natural disasters such as volcanoes and earthquakes. The books below are starting points for further exploration of these intriguing phenomena.

BOOK AND MEDIA CHOICES

Arnold, Eric. *Volcanoes!: Mountains of Fire*. Illustrated by Doug Knutson. 1997. New York: Random House. 48p. Grades: 2–3.

This book focuses primarily on the eruption of Mount St. Helens in Washington state. It includes information on the work of volcanologists, ancient volcanoes, and myths told to explain why they erupt. In the last chapter of the book, readers learn about the renewal of the land after an eruption. This is one of the Step into Reading books designed specifically for second and third graders to be able to read independently.

Branley, Franklyn M. *Earthquakes*. Illustrated by Richard Rosenblum. 1990. New York: HarperCollins. 32p. Grades: 2–5.

This is a very basic book describing the causes of earthquakes, a natural phenomenon in nature. The movement of the earth beneath us, in different strengths, causes all things on the earth both natural and manmade to be affected in some way. The origin of the Richter Scale and the definition of seismos are given. This book is one of the Let's-Read-and-Find-Out Science series.

Griffey, Harriet. *Volcanoes and Other Natural Disasters*. Illustrated by Peter Dennis. 1998. New York: DK. 48p. Grades: 3–5.

This well-illustrated and photographed short book describes two volcanic eruptions, two earthquakes, a flood, a hurricane, a fire, and an avalanche in terms youngsters can readily comprehend. The entries are four to six pages in length with plenty of illustrations. This book is part of the Eyewitness Readers series.

Earthquakes. 2000. Video. Bala Cynwyd, Penn.: Schlessinger Video Productions-Library Video Company. 23 min. Grades: 5 to 8.

Students learn how the earth's underground movements and stresses cause the tremors felt on the surface. The video explores the most destructive earthquakes of the twentieth century and explains how scientists predict them. A teacher's guide is available. This video is close-captioned and is part of the Earth Science in Action series.

Volcanoes. 2000. Video. Bala Cynwyd, Penn.: Schlessinger Video Productions-Library Video Company. 23 min. Grades: 5 to 8.

Close-up shots of a volcano erupting provide a fascinating look at these destructive natural phenomena. Students learn what causes volcanoes to form and why they erupt. A teacher's guide is available. This video is close-captioned and is part of the Earth Science in Action series.

EXPLORATIONS

1. Have students who have experienced a natural disaster such as a hurricane or earthquake share their experiences with the class. Encourage them to describe their experience using their five senses.
2. Interesting facts about volcanoes and current information about volcano eruptions can be found at http://volcano.und.nodak.edu/.
3. Have students research and create a timeline of natural disasters that have occurred in their state. Tom Snyder's *TimeLiner* can be used to create the timeline.
4. After studying about a natural disaster, have students create a pamphlet of things to do to be prepared for a natural disaster. For example, students who live along the coast can create a hurricane preparation booklet.
5. Students can work with their parents to create a disaster preparation checklist that may include evacuation plans and lists of supplies to have on hand.

LANDFORMS

By studying the earth's landforms students gain a deeper understanding of the importance of protecting and preserving them for future generations. The NSES category for earth science acknowledges the need for students to understand that the earth furnishes humans many of the materials they need to exist. Colorful pictures and informative text in the following books cause readers to stop and reflect on the importance of the different landforms found on planet Earth.

Book and Media Choices

Luenn, Nancy. *Squish!: A Wetland Walk.* Illustrated by Ronald Himler. 1994. New York: Atheneum Books for Young Readers. Unp. Grades: K–3.

Lyrical language and attractive watercolor pictures identify and explore an area of wetlands. The flora and fauna are pictured and discussed. Children delight in watching a grandfather and grandson explore this water meadow.

All about Land Formations. 2000. Video. Bala Cynwyd, Penn.: Schlessinger Video Productions-Library Video Company. 23 min. Grades: K–4.

From the peaks of mountains to the bottoms of canyons this video teaches students about the magnificent land formations found on the earth. Additionally, the video examines the forces that create and shape land formations. The program includes a teacher's guide. This is part of the Earth Science for Children Video series.

Levinson, Nancy Smiler. *Death Valley: A Day in the Desert.* Illustrated by Diane Dawson Hearn. 2001. New York: Holiday House. 32p. Grades: 1–3.

The book presents very basic information about deserts in an easy-to-read format. The desert plants and animals depicted in the illustrations are labeled to assist young readers as they learn about desert life. At the end of the book silhouettes of the common plants and animals found in Death Valley are displayed. The book concludes with additional information about Death Valley.

Siebert, Diane. *Mississippi.* Illustrated by Greg Harlin. 2001. New York: HarperCollins. Unp. Grades: 1 and up.

This lyrical tribute to the Mississippi describes how the river has flowed throughout the history of the United States. The force and power of the river, its magic and mystery unfold in evocative illustrations and eloquent text.

Gibbons, Gail. *Planet Earth/ Inside Out.* 1995. New York: Morrow Junior Books. Unp. Grades: 2–4.

Young earth scientists enjoy examining the diagrams depicting the inside of planet Earth. From seething molten lava to plates that bump and slide, the earth is constantly moving. The third planet from the sun is the only one hospitable to plants and animals. Much damage has been done to the earth by the human beings living on the planet and much needs to be done to save the environment.

Dewey, Jennifer Owings. *Antarctic Journal: Four Months at the Bottom of the World.* 2001. New York: HarperCollins. 64p. Grades: 2–4.

A grant from the National Science Foundation provided Dewey the opportunity to live in the Antarctic to sketch and photograph this mysterious, frozen environment. Her sketches and photographs are interspersed with text from her journal entries and the letters she wrote home. This first-person account of her experiences furnishes a very personal look at this world often described in factual, scientific terms.

Garrett, Ann. *Keeper of the Swamp.* Illustrated by Karen Chandler. 1999. New York: Turtle Books. Unp. Grades: 2 and up.

A young boy and his grandfather pole through the lush, eerie, muddy swamp in search of an alligator that the grandfather has protected over the years. The grandfather is dying and wants to make sure the boy will be able to take his place as protector of the alligator. The boy questions his courage and strength for the task as he confronts the alligator.

George, Jean Craighead. *Everglades.* Paintings by Wendell Minor. 1995. New York: HarperCollins. Unp. Grades: 3–5.

A guide tells the story of the Florida Everglades as he takes a boatload of children on a tour. The story is poignant without being maudlin, factual without being fanciful, and appeals to children because they are the potential saviors of the everglades. The Florida Everglades is the only ecosystem of its kind in the world. Beautiful paintings of this lush paradise entice the students to read and learn about this wondrous ecosystem. At the end of the book readers find symbols of the plants and animals found in the vanishing everglades.

Simon, Seymour. *Deserts.* 1990. New York: Mulberry Books. Unp. Grades: 3–5.

The wonders and mysteries of deserts are depicted in gorgeous color photographs and lyrical text that invite readers to learn about deserts. Maps show where deserts are found throughout the world. The book focuses on hot deserts, but does mention that there are "polar deserts." This book is a wonderful introduction to deserts.

Malam, John. *Highest Longest Deepest: A Fold-Out Guide to the World's Record Breakers.* **Illustrated by Gary Hincks. 1996. New York: Simon & Schuster Books for Young Readers. 41p. Grades: 3–6.**

Pages that fold up, out, and down visually display the length of rivers, the height of mountains, and the depth of oceans. Colorful diagrams depict the inner core of the earth, how mountains are made, and other phenomena of the earth's landforms. The brief, engaging descriptions and the colorful illustrations are just enough to cause curious students to want to find other books to explore the topics in greater depth.

Wallace, Marianne D. *America's Mountains: A Guide to Plants and Animals.* **2000. Golden, Colo.: Fulcrum. 48p. Grades: 3–8.**

America's six mountain regions and the plants and animals that inhabit them are described in this book. Illustrations and maps are interspersed throughout the text. Information is provided on identifying animal tracks and making animal and plant observations. A glossary, eco-history, and pronunciation guide conclude the book. The author has written a companion book about the four desert regions in North America.

Geographical Features: Landforms. **2000. Video. El Dorado Hills, Calif.: One Hundred Percent Educational Videos. 15 min. Grades: 3–8.**

NASA footage, live footage, and animation are used to show Earth's physical features in this entertaining, educational video.

Blue Planet. **2001. DVD. Aurora, Ill.: Time Warner. 41 min. Grades: 3 and up.**

From two hundred miles above the earth viewers see how mankind, volcanoes, earthquakes, and hurricanes have shaped the earth's surface. This IMAX movie is in both English and French and includes subtitles in English, French, Spanish, and Portuguese.

Fisher, Leonard Everett. *Niagara Falls: Nature's Wonder.* **1996. New York: Holiday House. 63p. Grades: 4–8.**

Beginning with the discovery of the falls by the Native American tribes to the delivery of electric power far beyond Niagara Falls, this book contains a wealth of information on this natural wonder. Fascinating facts and anecdotal reports combine to provide a comprehensive history of the falls. Samuel Clemens complained about the hordes of tourists who tainted the magnificent view. The exploits of various daredevils who have attempted to go across Niagara Falls or who have attempted to go over the falls are included in this book and make fascinating reading.

Markle, Sandra. *Pioneering Frozen Worlds*. 1996. New York: Atheneum Books for Young Readers. 48p. Grades: 4 and up.

Questions throughout the book and simple experiments to conduct actively engage readers as they learn about frozen worlds. Striking color photographs reveal areas of the world few people ever see. The author spent the 1995-1996 season in Antarctica researching the information presented in the book. The book concludes with an index.

Sayre, April Pulley. *Wetland*. 1996. New York: Twenty-First Century Books. 78p. Grades: 6 and up.

Included in wetland biomes are Michigan's bogs, the Amazon's flooded forests, and South Carolina's swamps. These diverse watery places are home to equally diverse plants and animals. Color photographs, drawings, interesting text, and text boxes of interesting facts provide a wealth of easy-to-understand material about wetlands. The book includes a table of contents, a collection of resources, glossary, and an index.

EXPLORATIONS

1. After reading *Squish!: A Wetland Walk* (Luenn, 1994), help students create a list of why wetlands are important to the environment.
2. Prior to reading *Death Valley: A Day in the Desert* (Levinson, 2001), bring in cactus plants for the students to examine. Have the students record what they know about cacti and what is required for their growth.
3. After learning about the different environments, divide the students into groups and assign each group a different environment. Have them reflect on what they know about each environment and compile a list of the items they will need to camp out in their environment. Request that they write down the reasons why they have put each item on their list. Post the lists in the classroom.
4. Prior to reading *Keeper of the Swamp* (Garrett, 1999), have students share what they know about animal conservation in their own neighborhood.
5. After reading *Keeper of the Swamp* (Garrett, 1999), have students share what they have learned about nature from their grandparents or other relatives. Some children in the class may have been introduced to gardening or bird watching by a relative.
6. After reading *Deserts* (Simon, 1990), students can form groups to select a particular desert to study. Using HyperStudio the students create a multimedia presentation about their particular desert to share with the class.
7. Ask students to work in small groups to discuss what they think the inside of the earth is like and provide reasons for their responses. Have one student in the group briefly record their discussion. Read *Planet Earth/Inside Out* (Gibbons, 1995) to the students. Have the groups meet to discuss the book and compare their original comments to what they learned about the inside of the earth.
8. Included in the book *Wetland* (Sayre, 1996) is a simple colored pencil drawing of a salt

marsh. Have the students work in small groups to complete drawings of the other wetland biomes described in the book.

SOIL

Many students have fond recollections of creating mud pies, digging to China, building sand castles, or planting gardens. Playing and working in dirt has provided them opportunities for explorations and observations. Teaching children about soil using fiction and informational books helps them to create bridges between what they learn in school and their own personal lives. Additionally, combining fiction and informational books has reciprocal effects on students' understanding of the content (Yopp and Yopp, 2000). The NSES category for earth science addresses students' understanding of soil's properties and the vital role it has in supporting plant growth.

BOOK AND MEDIA CHOICES

Jeunesse, Gallimard. *Under the Ground*. Illustrated by Daniele Bour. 1995. New York: Scholastic. Unp. Grades: K–2.

This book has slick, colorful pages with several transparencies that overlay other pages to reveal something new. Young children are enchanted with this method of "discovery." The book challenges readers to think about what is going on beneath the ground when they look at the soil. It includes worms, eggs, and larva as well as beetles, roots, rocks, stones, and pebbles. Larger creatures are also shown and discussed briefly. This book is one of the First Discovery series.

O'Malley, Kevin. *Bud*. 2000. New York: Walker. Unp. Grades: 1–3.

This delightful rhinoceros family, the Sweet-Williams, includes the very fastidious, organized Mr. and Mrs. Sweet-William and their son Bud, who is anything but fastidious and organized. He loves dirt, gardening, and disorganized, jungle-like greenery. Understanding how important gardening is to their son, they graciously support his messy hobby. When Grandfather Sweet-William comes to visit, he sets about showing Bud how to organize his crayons by size and color and then to label them before placing them in the box. The parents worry about Grandfather's reaction to Bud's disorganized, out-door jubilance, but following a storm they discover that Grandfather's love for his grandson overcomes his own propensity for cleanliness and organization as he joins Bud in rebuilding his garden.

Gans, Roma. *Let's Go Rock Collecting*. Illustrated by Holly Keller. 1997. New York: HarperCollins. 32p. Grades: K–3.

A combination of cartoon-like drawings, photographs, and diagrams illustrate this basic book on beginning rock collecting. Two young rock hounds lead students on a rock collecting adventure and share information on identifying rocks and starting a rock collection. Young readers enjoy reading this book on their own. This is one of the Let's-Read-and-Find-Out Science series.

Hurst, Carol Otis. *Rocks in His Head.* Illustrated by James Stevenson. 2001. New York: Greenwillow. Unp. Grades: K and up.

This loving tribute to the author's father has a powerful message to readers of all ages to follow their passion and see where it leads. Her father's passion was rocks. During the Depression on days when he could not find work, he spent his day looking at the rocks in a local museum. With rocks in his pockets and rocks in his head, he became the museum janitor and eventually became the museum director.

Bial, Raymond. *A Handful of Dirt.* 2000. New York: Walker. 32p. Grades: 3–6.

Bial's words lyrically describe the mundane activities involved in working with soil and colorful photographs enhance the text. Animals and organisms that live in dirt and their importance to soil are explored in great depth in this book. This author's love for dirt derived from his grandfather's love of gardening, which he shares with his grandson. Raymond Bial's fond memories of his grandfather are rekindled each time he uses his grandfather's tools in his own garden as he works with his own grandchildren. The book closes with a brief index.

Science Court: Soil. 1998. Mac/Win. Watertown, Maine: Tom Snyder Productions. Grades: 4–6.

Working in cooperative groups, students become involved in a series of science demonstrations and make predictions based on the evidence presented in the courtroom trial taking place on the computer screen. This trial is to determine which of the competing machines can best fix the soil at The Old Dust Field. During the trial students learn what plants need to grow, the components of soil, how soil aids plant growth, and the role of worms in plant growth. This is one of the Science Court series of interactive group software.

Ricciuti, Edward, and Margaret W. Carruthers. *National Audubon Society First Field Guide to Rocks and Minerals.* 1998. New York: Scholastic. 159p. Grades: 5 and up.

This handy, pocket-size guide to rocks and minerals includes four major sections: the world of rocks and minerals, how to look at rocks and minerals, the field guide, and references. Young rock hunters appreciate the brief text and color photographs as they begin their exploration of rocks in their neighborhoods.

EXPLORATIONS

1. Reading *Bud* (O'Malley, 2000) may lead to questions about the soil and gardening that could be answered in *Under the Ground* (Jeunesse, 1995) for younger students or *A Handful of Dirt* (Bial, 2000) for older students.
2. Encourage students to share their personal experiences with planting gardens and growing plants.

3. Potted plants in the classroom or a container garden outside the classroom furnish students with opportunities to experience gardening including the work involved in growing healthy plants and the pleasure derived from seeing them grow.

4. Have students work with a parent, partner, or sibling to discover the insects living beneath rocks and decaying branches in their yard or a local park or the schoolyard. Have them record the insects that they see under the rocks and branches. Remind them that they will have to be fast, as the insects will quickly scurry away.

5. After introducing students to *National Audubon Society First Field Guide to Rocks and Minerals* (Ricciuti and Carruthers, 1998) place the book in the science center with a collection of rocks and minerals for students to identify.

WATER

Students have daily personal experiences with water; however, they may not have stopped to think about the importance of water in their lives. A diverse selection of books on water assures that students gain a full understanding of the properties of water. Additionally, providing students opportunities to explore different books on the same topic enables them to make comparisons on the style, illustrations, and techniques used by the authors to present the content (Duthie, 1994). Critically examining books and recording their findings helps students develop higher-order thinking skills.

Book and Media Choices

Seuling, Barbara. *Drip! Drop! How Water Gets to Your Tap.* Illustrated by Nancy Tobin. 2000. New York: Holiday House. Unp. Grades: P–3.

Many youngsters do not think about where the water that flows from their faucets comes from or how it gets to their homes. A young girl and her dog explain the water purification process and the water cycle. The cartoon-style illustrations and the dog's humorous comments make this a fun book to read. Experiments at the end of the book show young scientists how to make water evaporate, how to filter water, and how to make raindrops.

Chase, Edith Newlin. *Waters.* Illustrated by Ron Broda. 1996. N.Y.: Firefly Books. 25p. Grades: K–2.

Starting high in the mountains where the snow is melting all the way to the large, green ocean, as water moves from trickling stream to rolling ocean it nourishes creatures all along the way. Readers delight in hearing the language used to describe the water as it flows. Paper sculpture and watercolors give a three-dimensional look to the illustrations of the various creatures who depend on the water. The creatures on each page are identified at the end of the book and the importance of water to the creatures is explained.

Gibbons, Gail. *Exploring the Deep, Dark Sea*. 1999. Boston: Little, Brown. Unp. Grades: 2–4.

Gibbons has gathered a wealth of information about exploring the ocean that both fascinates and informs the reader. The simple drawings are colorful and detailed, and the text is brief yet informative. Different depths of the ocean are examined and the creatures found in each layer are described. Readers delight in learning about the mysterious world found under the sea. They are introduced to a variety of strange, unusual creatures that inhabit the depths of the sea.

Farndon, John. *Water*. 2001. Tarrytown, N.Y.: Marshall Cavendish. 32p. Grades: 2–7.

Students explore water through a series of experiments using easily obtainable materials and simple instructions. One such experiment has students constructing hydrometers with poster putty, straws, and a marker. Using their hydrometers, students then test the density of a variety of liquids. The book includes a table of contents, a glossary, and an index. This book is one of the Science Experiments series.

Markle, Sandra. *Down, Down, Down in the Ocean*. Illustrated by Bob Marstall. 1999. New York: Walker. 32p. Grades: 3–6.

Mysterious creatures of the deep, dark Pacific Ocean swim across the pages of this book. As readers turn the pages, they are taken deeper into the ocean to explore this watery ecosystem. The cycle of life is shown through the birth of a shark pup and its eventual death. At each level of the ocean the creatures' adaptations to the growing darkness and increasingly colder temperatures are described. Geysers warm some portions of the sea floor and the creatures near them have adapted to the warmer temperatures. An author's note and glossary/index are found at the end of the book.

Science Court: *Water Cycle*. 1997. Mac/Win. Watertown, Maine: Tom Snyder Productions. Grades: 4–6.

Students become actively involved as a courtroom drama unfolds on the computer screen. As the trial proceeds, students learn all about the water cycle by working in cooperative groups and participating in a series of demonstrations that they explain to their classmates. This is one of the Science Court series of interactive group software.

MacQuitty, Miranda. *Ocean*. Photographed by Frank Greenaway. 1995. New York: Alfred A. Knopf. 64p. Grades: 4 and up.

This book includes photographs, as well as drawings, of different depths of the ocean, sea creatures, plants, and machinery used to explore the ocean. The text is brief yet detailed. A great deal of material is presented on each page in small text boxes. Detailed drawings depict processes and activities occurring in the farthest depths of the ocean. Material presented in *Exploring the Deep, Dark Sea* (Gibbons, 1999) is expanded on, hence providing answers to questions raised by Gibbons's book. This book is part of the Eyewitness series.

Eyewitness II: Seashore. 1996. Video. London, England: Dorling Kindersley. 28 min. Grades: 4 and up.

From thunderous, crashing waves to calm tide pools, this video explores the seacoast and the wildlife that live along the shores. This is one of the Eyewitness video series.

Wick, Walter. *A Drop of Water.* 1997. New York: Scholastic. 40p. Grades: 4 and up.

Clear, elegant photographs, accompanied by informative, concise text, illustrate and explain complex properties of water, such as surface tension and capillary action. The photographs entice readers to replicate the activities in order to see for themselves how water behaves in its different forms. The photographs capture the action and magnify the water providing incredible, fascinating shots. At the end of the book observations, experiments, and precautions are noted for each of the pictures. Readers are encouraged to devise additional experiments based on questions raised as they complete the experiments.

Science Seekers: Safe Water. 1997. Mac/Win. Watertown, Maine: Tom Snyder Productions. Grades: 5–8.

Using this interactive software program, students determine what is polluting the water in the new well. Students learn about aquifers, water tables, and ground water. This is one of the Science Seekers series of software that teaches science content as students work through real-world problems.

Water as a Liquid. 1999. Video. Jacksonville, Ill.: New Dimension Media. 10 min. Grades: 5–8.

The spherical property of water and surface tension are demonstrated using slow-motion videography. A simple experiment is also used to show students the properties of water and its uses. This is one of the Water Properties and Uses series.

EXPLORATIONS

1. After reading *Drip! Drop! How Water Gets to Your Tap* (Seuling, 2000), provide students with the materials needed to filter water in a science center in the classroom.
2. Divide the class into groups of six and have them create a folded paper cube about what they have learned about the ocean. One person in each group is responsible for

completing the information on one side of the cube. The sides of the cube should contain the following information: a description of the ocean; comparison of the ocean to something else; an association of the ocean to something else; tell what the ocean is composed of; information on how the ocean is used; and reasons why the ocean should be protected (Tompkins, 1998).

3. While reading *Exploring the Deep, Dark Sea* (Gibbons, 1999) students can make charts depicting the animals to be found at each depth and the ones that are found at several depths.

4. Have students compare and contrast the presentation styles of *Down, Down, Down in the Ocean* (Markle, 1999) and *Ocean* (MacQuitty, 1995).

5. Using material from several books on ocean creatures, have students create a collage of an underwater scene.

6. To assess students' knowledge of the depths at which various animals are found, have them create a mobile of sea creatures that reflects the depths where they are found.

7. Have students investigate to discover the source of water for their community and create a plan for protecting the source for the future.

8. Working in groups, students can create a list of animals and the adaptations the animals have made for living at the different levels of the sea.

9. After completing the experiments in *A Drop of Water* (Wick, 1997) have students reflect on the results and discuss questions they have based on their results. Then, have the students write down the procedures they will use for follow-up experiments to answer their questions.

SPACE SCIENCE

Dark skies sparkle with light and the twinkling stars and planets capture children's imagination. Children have wished on stars and wondered about the moon's changing shapes. Accounts of astronauts' journeys into space are on the television, in the newspaper, and on the Internet. Science information books enable librarians and teachers to capitalize on this natural curiosity and furnish children with the information they need to answer their questions and to extend their knowledge of space. NSES category five focuses on space science, including understanding the objects in the sky and the changes taking place in the sky.

STARS AND PLANETS

According to the NSES category for earth and space science students need to understand the patterns of movement of objects in the sky. Children have personal recollections of space expeditions witnessed on television and many have read other books on space. Allowing them to share their knowledge and expertise on the topic enhances their understanding and that of their classmates. Interactive teacher-led read-alouds of informational books involves encouraging children to interrupt and respond to a book by making connections with the book being read and one previously read on the same topic or with a personal experience (Oyler and Barry, 1996).

The teacher's role is to recognize the social significance of the students' contributions and acknowledge the intertextual connection.

BOOK AND MEDIA CHOICES

Branley, Franklyn M. *What the Moon Is Like*. Illustrated by True Kelley. 2000. New York: HarperCollins. 32p. Grades: K–4.

The wonder and beauty of the moon is examined with simple, descriptive text highlighted by photographs and drawings. One of the illustrations is a map of the moon showing where the Apollo astronauts landed. Comparisons of the moon and earth help young readers make connections between the two and aid in understanding the material. At the end of the book is a section of resources for finding out more about the moon and includes Internet Web sites. This book is one of the Let's-Read-and-Find-Out Science series.

All about the Planets. 1999. Video. Bala Cynwyd, Penn.: Schlessinger Video Productions-Library Video Company. 23 min. Grades: K–4.

Spectacular NASA footage and animation hold students' attention as they learn the basics about the planets. The program includes a teacher's guide. This is one of the Space Science for Children series.

Earth: A First Look. 2000. Video. Raleigh, N.C.: Rainbow Educational Media. 17 min. Grades: 1–3.

This video opens with a shot of Earth taken from the space shuttle. Graphic illustrations and scenic shots are used to show students Earth's bodies of water and layers.

Simon, Seymour. *Destination: Jupiter*. 1998. New York: HarperCollins. Unp. Grades: 1–5.

Travel to Jupiter, the largest planet in our solar system, through the magnificent photographs sent back to Earth by Voyager, in 1979, and by Galileo, in 1996. Jupiter's many moons are as fascinating as the planet. The excitement of exploration and the mysteries of this planet and its moons unfold in the pages of this book.

The Magic School Bus Gets Lost in Space. 1999. Video. New York: Kid Vision. 30 min. Grades: 1–5.

The indomitable Ms. Frizzle and her students tour the solar system in this animated video, which is also available on DVD. Only the Friz could take students to the planetarium and from there launch into outer space to visit the nine planets. This video is based on the book by Joanna Cole and Bruce Degen.

Gibbons, Gail. *Stargazers*. 1992. New York: Holiday House. Unp. Grades: 2–4.

Gazing into the twinkling sky on a dark, clear night causes young stargazers to wonder and ask questions about the heavens above. They are intrigued to learn that stars have names and form constellations. This book provides an introduction to the study of stars and explains how telescopes work. Colorful illustrations and brief text encourage young readers to read this book on their own. Also included is a history of stargazing.

***Exploring Space*. 1993. New York: Scholastic. 48p. Grades: 3–5.**

This glossy and colorful book introduces children to space and the planetary system by showing the night skies and stars, the moon, the sun, and secrets of our galaxy. The book includes many activities for students to try as they read. There are three-dimensional glasses to examine the star patterns, as well as information on extended readings and a time line. This is one of the Scholastic Voyages of Discovery series.

Simon, Seymour. *Comets, Meteors, and Asteroids*. 1994. New York: Mulberry Books. Unp. Grades: 3–5.

Comets, meteors, and asteroids are defined on the first page of the book as a way to set the stage for the information presented in the book. Then, each of these celestial bodies is described in great detail. They are all similar, as well as distinctively different, and all date back to the beginning of our solar system—4.6 billion years ago. Full-page illustrations and photographs facilitate understanding the text.

Branley, Franklyn M. *Neptune: Voyager's Final Target*. 1992. New York: HarperCollins. 56p. Grades: 3–6.

After 12 long years, Voyager 2 flew by the mysterious planet, Neptune, and its four rings. Voyager 2 captured photographs of Jupiter and Saturn and few believed its cameras would still be working when it reached Neptune. The sense of awe and excitement the scientists felt when data was first transmitted from Neptune fills this fascinating book. The breathtaking photographs of the planet's surface and Neptune's rings add to the sense of wonder.

***Flumpa's World: Out of this World*. 2000. Audiocassette. Nashville, Tenn.: Imagination Entertainment. Grades: 3–6.**

The planets, constellations, and outer space are introduced in 13 original songs. Conversations with the Apollo 11 astronauts and excerpts from John Kennedy's address to Congress are included on this recording. The song lyrics are also included.

Fradin, Dennis Brindell. *The Planet Hunters: The Search for Other Worlds.* **1997. New York: Simon and Schuster. 147p. Grades: 4 and up.**

Beginning with the Greek astronomers Aristarchus and Ptolemy over 1,900 years ago, this book tells in a very readable fashion of the never-ending search through the skies. Planets were the first searched-for things, followed by comets, asteroids, and stars. The squabbling among astronomers is described in a very frank manner and the differences among discoverers are left to the reader to decide. One of the chapters deals with the unanswered question "Is there anyone else out there?" Both black-and-white and color photographs enhance the text and make it all the more understandable. The book includes a bibliography and an index.

Wunsch, Susi Trautmann. *The Adventures of Sojourner: The Mission to Mars That Thrilled the World.* **1998. New York: Mikaya Press. 63p. Grades: 6 and up.**

Awe-inspiring photographs, color illustrations, detailed diagrams, and explicit captions draw the reader into the text to discover more about this fascinating mission. The small rover, Sojourner, sent back scenes of Mars never before viewed that provided waiting scientists with stunning photographs of the surface of Mars. The detailed, painstaking work that went on prior to the launch provides a glimpse into the years of work that occurs before a space launch. The book concludes with a picture of the rover team and Sojourner, a time line of Mars voyages that stretches to 2018, and a comparison of Mars and Earth.

EXPLORATIONS

1. After reading *Stargazers* (Gibbons 1992) and *Exploring Space* (*Exploring Space*, 1993), have students create their own constellations by punching holes in a piece of black construction paper. Cut holes in both ends of a shoebox. Place the flashlight in one hole and cover the other hole with the piece of black construction paper. Have students project their constellations for their classmates.

2. Prior to reading *Comets, Meteors, and Asteroids* (Simon, 1994), create an anticipation guide with four statements about comets, meteors, and asteroids. Have students work in small groups to decide if the statements are true or false. As a group have the class discuss their responses. After reading the book, revisit the anticipation guide and have students locate the information in the book that supports their position.

3. After reading and discussing *Neptune: Voyager's Final Target* (Branley, 1992) and *The Adventures of Sojourner: The Mission to Mars That Thrilled the World* (Wunsch, 1998), have students create a planet. They need to write down a description of their planet's environment and determine if it will support life. If it will support life, they will need to indicate what types of life.

4. *The Planet Hunters: The Search for Other Worlds* (Fradin, 1997) explores many unanswered questions and provides valuable insights into the lives of astronomers and the relationships between astronomers. Students can role-play the different astronomers and have them debate their findings. Additional research may have to be done on some of the astronomers to support their views.

5. In order to help students understand the complexities of navigating Sojourner from Earth as she traveled over the surface of Mars, bring in a remote control car for them to practice navigating. Then have them navigate the car when it is blocked from their view.

6. Students can create a row-and-column table to compare the climate and weather of Mars, Neptune, and Earth.

SPACE TRAVEL

Journeys into space are made by dreamers and adventurers who persist until they accomplish their goals. One such dreamer and adventurer was Neil Armstrong, who as a small boy often dreamed of hovering above the ground. The wonder and excitement of space exploration is celebrated in the books in this section.

Brown, Don. *One Giant Leap: The Story of Neil Armstrong*. 1998. Boston: Houghton Mifflin. Unp. Grades: 1–4.

This inspiring story of one of America's heroes is told in lyrical language with great reader appeal. The simple description of Neil's love of flying and his determination to become a pilot resulted in his earning a pilot's license before he could drive an automobile. On July 20, 1969 he became the first man to set foot on the moon. The simplistic, pastel, child-like illustrations appeal to readers of all ages. This is a book that is read again and again.

BOOK AND MEDIA CHOICES

Branley, Franklyn M. *The International Space Station*. Illustrated by True Kelley. 2000. New York: HarperCollins. 32p. Grades: K–4.

The book begins with an introduction by Mercury astronaut Scott Carpenter. Fascinating facts about the space station are presented in an interesting, easy-to-read format with detailed illustrations. Working, eating, and sleeping aboard the space station and working outside of the space station are described in just enough detail for young readers. The book concludes with a recipe for growing crystals and additional resources, including Internet Web sites, for learning more about the space station. This book is one of the Let's-Read-and-Find-Out Science series.

Langille, Jacqueline, and Bobbie Kalman. *The Space Shuttle*. 1998. New York: Crabtree Publishing. 32p. Grades: 1–3.

Color photographs of the space shuttle on the ground and in the sky accompany this brief text about the space shuttle. Information is included on the preparations prior to liftoff, life on the shuttle, and landing the shuttle. Readers enjoy learning about how the astronauts complete everyday tasks, such as eating and bathing. The book concludes with a glossary and an index.

Berger, Melvin, and Gilda Berger. *Can You Hear a Shout in Space? Questions and Answers about Space Exploration.* Illustrated by Vincent Di Fate. 2000. New York: Scholastic. 48p. Grades: 3–6.

Moving from place to place in a spacecraft requires floating and using handgrips to pull yourself along the walls. This and other fascinating facts are presented through brief answers to a variety of questions. Dramatic, color illustrations set the stage for the intriguing facts revealed about life in space. The book concludes with an index. This book is one of the Scholastic Question and Answer series.

Agle, D. C. *Heroes of Space: A Three-Dimensional Tribute to 40 Years of Space Exploration.* 1999. Santa Monica, Calif.: Intervisual Books. Unp. Grades: 3 and up.

Pressing on the picture of an astronaut on the front cover of the book activates a sound bite that includes the voice of John F. Kennedy as the nation embarks on its goal of landing a man on the moon. From establishing NASA in 1958 to the proposed completion of the space station in 2004, the United States' journey into space is chronicled in over 100 stunning NASA photographs, pop-up scenes, quotes from the astronauts, statistics on the spacecrafts, lift-up flaps, tiny fact booklets, and interesting, informative text. At the bottom of each two-page spread is a timeline of text and photographs that places the space adventures in the context of world history. For example, in 1975 the Vietnam War ended and the first US-USSR joint space mission occurred.

The Dream Is Alive. 2001. DVD. Aurora, Ill.: Time Warner. 35 min. Grades: 3 and up.

Viewers travel into space with space shuttle astronauts and see the earth from this unique perspective. Included in the film is a thrilling satellite capture and the first spacewalk by an American woman.

Scott, Elaine. *Adventure in Space: The Flight to Fix the Hubble.* Photographs by Margaret Miller. 1995. New York: Hyperion Paperbacks for Children. 64p. Grades: 4–7.

In 1993, the crew of the Endeavor flew into space to repair the Hubble telescope. Behind-the-scenes preparations for the mission and the actual mission itself furnish fascinating reading. Much of this story is told through the eyes of astronaut and mission specialist, Kathryn Thornton. Information about the astronauts' families provides an intimate glimpse into their private lives. This book has won awards including the School Library Journal Best Book of the Year 1995, Booklist Editors' Choice 1995, and VOYA's 1995 Nonfiction Honor List.

Stott, Carole. *Moon Landing*. Illustrated by Richard Bonson. 1999. New York: DK. 48p. Grades: 4 and up.

Colorful illustrations and photographs are used to tell the story of our race to the moon. The real impetus for rocketing the U.S. into a viable space program was the launch of Sputnik by the Russians in the late 1950s. Prior to that time, Wernher von Braun and other scientists had ploddingly worked on rocketry, but Sputnik spurred them on to rapidly putting a man into space and ultimately landing on the moon. The book concludes with data on the moon obtained through the exploration of the moon by astronauts. Also included is a description of all of the moon missions from Apollo 11 through Apollo 17.

The Space Race. 1996. Win. London, England: Flagtower Multimedia. Grades: 5 and up.

This software program is an interactive documentary of America's space race with film clips and still shots.

EXPLORATIONS

1. Prior to reading *The Space Shuttle* (Langille and Kalman, 1998), have students draw a cross-section of the space shuttle to reveal what they think the inside looks like. After reading the book, have students compare their drawings with the drawings in the book.
2. Prior to reading *Can You Hear a Shout in Space? Questions and Answers about Space Exploration* (Berger and Berger, 2000), provide students a mini-lesson in small groups on how to use the index to find specific information, rather than having to read the entire book.
3. Using TimeLiner, create a time line of Neil Armstrong's life. Intersperse in the timeline historical events that occurred during his lifetime. Students may want to refer to the timeline in *Heroes of Space: A Three-Dimensional Tribute to 40 Years of Space Exploration* (Agle, 1999) to find world events to include in the timeline.
4. The NASA Web site is an excellent place to research space exploration. It is located at www.nasa.gov/.

PHYSICAL SCIENCE

Quality children's literature integrated into the science curriculum motivates children to examine science concepts and make connections between what they learn and their life experiences (Dixey and Baird, 1996). Category three from the NSES pertains to the properties of objects and materials. This includes an understanding of motion, force, energy, and how materials can exist in different states, which is one of the science concepts presented in Vicki Cobb's book.

Cobb, Vicki. *Why Can't You Unscramble an Egg? And Other Not Such Dumb Questions about Matter*. Illustrations by Ted Enik. 1990. New York: Lodestar Books. 40p. Grades: 3–5.

Nine questions ranging from why an ice cube floats to why eggs cannot be unscrambled are examined in this intriguing book. Each of the questions has an answer in physical science that both informs and entertains students. This book challenges readers to think deeply and question ordinary occurrences. Once they have read the answers, students want to try the experiments on their own. The text is easy-to-read and the charming cartoons expand and explain the material presented in the book.

LIGHT

Students enjoy experimenting and playing with light. The books in this section provide opportunities for a variety of explorations, many of which the students can do on their own. Conducting experiments on their own allows them to take control of their own learning, which makes it more meaningful.

BOOK AND MEDIA CHOICES

***All about Solids, Liquids & Gases*. 1999. Video. Bala Cynwyd, Penn.: Schlessinger Video Productions-Library Video Company. 23 min. Grades: K–4.**

Real-life examples of how matter changes states help students make connections between what they know and what they learn in this video about the states of matter. A teacher's guide is included. This video supports the National Science Education Standard for Physical Science.

Ardley, Neil. *The Science Book of Light*. 1991. San Diego, Calif.: Harcourt Brace Jovanovich. 29p. Grades: 2–5.

This very basic book is comprised of a little text and a lot of photographs of experiments. Step-by-step directions and photographs assure that young readers successfully complete the experiments. Some of them require adult supervision and Ardley identifies those experiments.

Farndon, John. *Light and Optics*. 2001. Tarrytown, N.Y.: Marshall Cavendish. 32p. Grades: 2–7.

In the pages of this book students have the opportunity for hands-on explorations of light. Included with the experiments in the book are step-by-step photographs to help students as they recreate the experiments on their own or with the help of adults. The book includes a table of contents, a glossary, and an index. This book is one of the Science Experiments series that includes books on color, electricity, water, sound and hearing, and weather.

Farndon, John. *Color*. 2001. Tarrytown, N.Y.: Marshall Cavendish. 32p. Grades: 2–7.

Students enjoy learning about color by experimenting. This book provides them opportunities to create a spectrum and a color wheel as they explore the fascinating world of color. The book includes a table of contents, a glossary, and an index. This book is one of the Science Experiments series that includes books on color, electricity, water, sound and hearing, and weather.

Robson, Pam. *Light Color and Lenses*. 1993. New York: Shooting Star Press. 32p. Grades: 3–6.

In this book students explore the intricacies of light by first reading the brief text excerpts, and then by completing the simple science experiments included in each section. Directions are included for making a simple microscope, a box camera, a periscope, and other devices for exploring the properties of light. After reading the brief text and conducting the experiments, students understand and retain what they have discovered.

Taylor, Barbara. *Bouncing and Bending Light*. Photographs by Peter Millard. 1990. New York: Franklin Watts. 32p. Grades: 3-6.

Divided into five sections identified by different colored triangles, this book is about reflection and refraction of light. It includes sections on the movement of light, shadows, bouncing light, and bending of light, among others. Color photographs enhance the text and aid students as they complete the experiments. At the end of the book is a list of more things to try, questions and answers, a glossary, and an index. This is part of the Science Starters series.

***Light*. 1999. Video. Bala Cynwyd, Penn.: Schlessinger Video Productions-Library Video Company. 23 min. Grades: 5 to 8.**

Light waves, reflection, absorption, and refraction are all explored in this illuminating video. Real-life examples are used to clearly demonstrate the principles. A teacher's guide is available. This video is close-captioned and is part of the Physical Science in Action series.

EXPLORATIONS

1. Scrambling an egg in the classroom helps students understand the concepts presented in *Why Can't You Unscramble an Egg? And Other Not Such Dumb Questions about Matter* (Cobb, 1990). After scrambling the egg, have students brainstorm why you cannot unscramble an egg prior to reading the book.
2. Prior to reading *The Science Book of Light* (Ardley, 1991), have students tell one thing they already know about light before reading the book.
3. After reading *Light Color and Lenses* (Robson, 1993), have students cut out paper to create shadow puppets.
4. After reading *Bouncing and Bending Light* (Taylor, 1990), have students work in groups

to create a rainbow with a mirror propped in a pan of water. Shining the flashlight down into the water at an angle causes it to reflect off the mirror to create a rainbow. As students write up their procedure for doing this experiment remind them to record the colors in the spectrum.

5. Have students trace each other's shadows on the playground in the morning. In the afternoon have them return to the playground and redraw their shadows.

ENERGY

Students see the sun in the sky and know that when it is shining, the sun warms them. However, they may not realize that the sun is the source of most of our energy. They know that when they push or pull an object, they cause it to move, but they may not understand that they are expending energy to move the object. Through simple experiments young scientists come to understand the transfer of energy from one object to another. The physical science category from NSES addresses students' understanding of force and motion; specifically that pushing and pulling can change the position and motion of objects. Books in this section encourage young scientists to explore and discover how energy impacts their daily lives.

BOOK AND MEDIA CHOICES

Gibson, Gary. *Science for Fun: Making Things Float and Sink.* Illustrated by Tony Kenyon. Photographs by Roger Vlitos. 1995. Brookfield, Conn.: Copper Beech. 32p. Grades: 2–4.

Why some things float and others sink provides for intriguing science investigations. Common household materials are used to explore this phenomenon and to create craft items, such as colorful marbleized paper. Some experiments require adult supervision, but many are simple enough for students to complete on their own. The book includes a table of contents and an index.

ics Court Explorations: Magnets. 1997. Mac/Win. Watertown, Maine: Tom Snyder Productions. Grades: 2–4.

An animated story on the CD-ROM sets the stage for students' hands-on explorations of magnets. Working in cooperative groups students form hypotheses and then test them using the manipulatives included with the software. This is one of the Science Court Exploration series. It received a Technology & Learning Award of Excellence.

Ardley, Neil. *The Science Book of Energy.* 1992. San Diego: Harcourt Brace Jovanovich. 29p. Grades: 2–5.

Color photography and simple step-by-step instructions make this book on basic energy very easy for youngsters to follow and understand. The experiments are very simple and easy to do, requiring materials found around the house. There is a cautionary symbol for activities that need adult supervision. Connections are made between the experiments and everyday activities. For example, young scientists explore energy transfer using string, an orange, and a grapefruit. The principle of energy transfer is described by circus acrobats who transfer energy from one to the other.

Farndon, John. *Electricity*. 2001. Tarrytown, N.Y.: Marshall Cavendish. 32p. Grades: 2–7.

This exploration of electricity cautions young scientists that others, who have tried Benjamin Franklin's experiment involving flying a kite in a thunderstorm, have been electrocuted. Children conduct a series of experiments using easily obtainable materials and make connections between their experiments and real-world applications of the principles they have studied. The book includes a table of contents, a glossary, and an index. This book is one of the Science Experiments series.

Burton, Jane, and Kim Taylor. *The Nature and Science of Energy*. 1998. Milwaukee, Wis.: Gareth Stevens. 32p. Grades: 3–5.

There are many color photographs depicting the types of energy seen in nature. The book discusses natural, kinetic, and noisy energy, and how energy cannot be destroyed, but it can be stored, saved, and burned. There are two pages of activities for the readers to try, a glossary, bibliography, and an index. This book is part of the Exploring the Science of Nature series.

White, Larry. *Energy: Simple Experiments for Young Scientists*. Illustrated by Laurie Hamilton. 1995. Brookfield, Conn.: Millbrook Press. 48p. Grades: 3–5.

A brief discussion of the source of all energy, the sun, opens this delightful book filled with simple experiments for scientists to try. Each experiment begins with a short explanation about what the experiment intends to show and a list of things needed to perform the experiment. Excellent illustrations accompany each activity and show students what is intended. Fossil fuels are mentioned, as is kinetic and potential energy. The common forms of energy are named with a mnemonic device, SCREAM, to help remember them. The book closes with a glossary and an index.

DiSpezio, Michael. *Awesome Experiments in Force and Motion*. Illustrated by Catherine Leary. 1998. New York: Sterling Publishing Company. 160p. Grades: 3–8.

What better way to learn about force and motion than through a series of experiments? Each experiment has a list of materials found in most households. The cautionary instructions offer tips to help students, such as not to worry about adding too much salt when making a salt float. Students are queried about their results, and the science behind the experiment is explained. Simple line drawings clarify the directions. The book concludes with an index.

Exploring Energy. 1995. New York: Scholastic. 46p. Grades: 4–8.

Transparent pages, cut-away diagrams, photographs, and illustrations, combined with interactive diagrams to rub and a feather used to explore static electricity, enable students to discover for themselves the properties of energy. Students learn that science fiction writer Jules Verne first imagined many of the things that are part of their lives such as televisions, airplanes, submarines, and space satellites. Included at the end of the book are a glossary, an index, a timeline, people to know, and suggestions for further reading. This is one of the titles in the Scholastic Voyages of Discovery series.

Bartholomew, Alan. *Electric Gadgets and Gizmos: Battery-Powered Buildable Gadgets That Go!* **Illustrated by Lynn Bartholomew. 1998. New York: Kids Can Press. 48p. Grades: 4 and up.**

Wires, batteries, scissors, tubes, cork, tape, clothespins, and glue can be turned into gadgets that move and light up. Detailed illustrations and simple instructions make this a book for young inventors, or perhaps students who do not like to read, but like to take things apart and put them back together. A remote control boat, a warning sign, a communication buzzer, and a squirt finger are just a few of the gadgets in this book.

EXPLORATIONS

1. Participating in partner questioning sessions requires each student to ask a question that must be answered with a question. For example: Is the sun a source of energy? Where does energy come from? Does all energy come from one source? Guide students in the direction they need to go to obtain answers from the material that they have read.

2. Students can be encouraged to prepare index cards describing the materials needed and the necessary steps for an experiment. These can be placed in a science center with materials for students to try the experiments on their own.

3. Pop one-fourth cup popcorn without placing the lid on the pot. Have students measure how far the popcorn shoots. What was the farthest distance the popcorn went? Prior to beginning this activity students could estimate how far they think the popcorn will go.

4. Ask the students to write down all the sources of energy they encountered from waking up in the morning until they arrived at school.

5. Create teams of students in the classroom to work together to record all the sources of energy in the classroom. Determine which team found the most sources of energy and which one found the most unique source of energy.

6. Many of the experiments in *Awesome Experiments in Force and Motion* (DiSpezio, 1998) are ones that students can do at home with their siblings and/or parents. Encourage them to try the experiments at home and write down their procedures and their results. They can then compare their results with other students in the class.

7. Create a center in the classroom equipped with wires, batteries, scissors, tubes, cork, tape, clothespins, and glue for students to make their own battery-powered gadgets. Encourage them to create some unlike any in the book, *Electric Gadgets and Gizmos: Battery-Powered Buildable Gadgets That Go!* (Bartholomew, 1998).

8. Share with students how gadgets are invented to solve problems. Have them brainstorm things that would make their lives easier and discuss possible inventions that would solve their problems.

MACHINES

Young readers are aware that machines are a routine part of their lives. Many find it hard to believe that they have not always existed, simply because they have always been a part of their lives. The NSES includes a category for science and technology. This category focuses on students' understanding of how science helps to drive technology and that technological solutions may have unexpected benefits and consequences. The books in this section help students understand that machines they take for granted have not always existed. These machines were invented by people who saw a problem and developed a solution. The inner workings of machines are examined in some of the books in this section, as well as how things are made.

BOOK AND MEDIA CHOICES

Humphrey, Paul. *What Was It Like Before the Telephone?* Illustrated by Lynda Stevens. 1995. Austin, Tex.: Steck-Vaughn. 32p. Grades: K–2.

From drums and smoke signals to telephones and fax machines, humans have communicated throughout the years. In this book three young students learn about the history of communication when they visit a science museum. The large print and simple, easy-to-read text make the information easily accessible to young readers. At the end of the book are four review questions and a brief index. This is one of the Read All about It series, a collection of first information books on science and social studies.

Hunter, R. A. *Take Off!* 2000. New York: Holiday House. Unp. Grades: 1–3.

From the "Icarus" type wings of Monk Eilmer in 1060 to the U.S. spyplane "Blackbird" in 2000, the story of flight is covered in sparse wording and with large colorful drawings. Of great appeal to the young child, this book explains the differences in travel time from New York to Paris, from the first solo transatlantic flight to the "Blackbird," from thirty-three hours to two hours. There are also instructions on making paper airplanes.

***Simple Machines: A First Look.* 2001. Video. Raleigh, N.C.: Rainbow Media. 17 min. Grades: 1–3.**

The six simple machines are clearly and concisely explained to students. Playground equipment is used to show students how simple machines are used in everyday life. This video includes a teacher's guide.

Farndon, John. *What Happens When . . . ?* Illustrated by Steve Fricker and Mike Harnden. 1996. New York: Scholastic. 45p. Grades: 2–4.

Bright cartoon-like illustrations and brief step-by-step descriptions across two- and four-page spreads explain 13 common everyday processes such as how the telephone works, how flowers are delivered, and how sewage is processed. Children's natural curiosity about their immediate world means they have questions that are often difficult for adults to answer. This behind-the-scenes look provides answers to many of their questions. The book concludes with a glossary and an index.

Llewellyn, Claire. *How Things Work.* 1995. New York: Scholastic. 93p. Grades: 2–5.

This is one of a series of Scholastic First Encyclopedias and it is designed to give basic and brief information to young readers on how things operate from airplanes to wheels. The photographs and illustrations are very colorful and are used to enhance and expand on the text. Cross-reference terms for each subject are shown at the top of the page. Important words appear in bold print and difficult words have pronunciation guides following them. While the book can be used for ready reference, it is written so well that it could be read for pleasure. The book concludes with a glossary and a very good index.

Jones, George. *My First Book of How Things Are Made: Crayons, Jeans, Peanut Butter, Guitars, and More.* 1995. New York: Scholastic. 64p. Grades: 2–5.

The manufacturing processes involved in creating crayons, peanut butter, guitars, blue jeans, orange juice, grape jelly, footballs, and books are all described in this book. The author illustrates with colorful photographs how these familiar products are manufactured from raw materials. The text is complete, but brief enough to hold children's interest.

Bikes, Cars, Trucks, and Trains. 1995. New York: Scholastic. 46p. Grades: 3–6.

From feet to wheels, humans are on the move using a variety of transportation modes to cross land. From simple foot-powered bicycles to powerful motors, readers can learn about humans' fascination with getting from here to there. This interactive book encourages students to read and explore with pull-out pages of trains and stickers to place. Like other books in the Scholastic Voyages of Discovery series there is a glossary, an index, a timeline, and suggestions for further reading.

Butterfield, Moira. *Look Inside Cross-Sections Record Breakers.* Illustrated by Chris Grigg and Keith Harmer. 1995. New York: Dorling Kindersley. 32p. Grades: 3–6.

Elaborate illustrations with detailed labels of these speed machines capture readers' interest. Brief text boxes interspersed throughout the two-page spread provide fascinating details about the record breakers. The book concludes with a "speedline" rather than a timeline, a glossary, and an index.

Stein, R. Conrad. *Chuck Yeager Breaks the Sound Barrier.* 1997. New York: Children's Press. 32p. Grades: 3–6.

At the age of nineteen, Chuck Yeager was recognized by superiors as a natural aviator. He intuitively knew things that could not be taught. He served in World War II as a bomber pilot and was shot down over German-occupied France, where the French underground spirited him to neutral Spain. Young aviation enthusiasts learn that some believe that Yeager's breaking the sound barrier made space travel possible. This book is one of the Cornerstones of Freedom series that includes books on famous American battles and the Underground Railroad.

Pollard, Michael. *The Light Bulb and How It Changed the World.* 1995. New York: Facts on File. 46p. Grades: 3–8.

Beginning with the light that glowed, invented by Thomas Edison, and ending with the potential of renewable resources to create electricity, this book provides an extensive examination of how electricity impacted the world. Photographs and drawings colorfully depict the first light bulb and original versions of appliances such as the washing machine, refrigerator, toaster, and dishwasher. The book ends with a glossary, index, and books for further reading. This is one of the History and Invention series that also includes books on how the wheel and clock changed the world.

Baker, David. *Scientific American Inventions from Outer Space: Everyday Uses for NASA Technology.* 2000. New York: Random House. 128p. Grades: 3–8.

NASA technology has benefited both reentering spacecrafts and dolphins by creating audible beacons that send out signals from deep-water locations for several days. The beacons enable NASA to find submerged spacecrafts and they help dolphins avoid gillnets. Dolphins who become entangled in gillnets cannot surface for air; hence, they drown. Human ingenuity has found solutions for a myriad of challenges encountered during space exploration and these ingenious ideas have found their way into our lives. The money spent on space exploration has had a far-reaching impact throughout the universe. An index is included in the book.

Gifford, Clive. *How the Future Began: Machines.* 1999. New York: Kingfisher. 64p. Grades: 4–8.

This intriguing title sets the stage for learning how machines have changed the world and sets the stage for future changes. Illustrations and diagrams depict machines of the future. Students are always interested in reading about the domestic robots that in the future can assist them with their chores. The book includes a glossary, Web sites, museums, and an index.

Hagadorn, Dan. *The Story of Flight*. 1995. New York: Scholastic. 46p. Grades: 4–8.

Readers can learn the history of flight through color photographs and illustrations accompanied by brief, interesting text. A variety of techniques such as reusable vinyl stickers and a tracing paper page encourage students to become actively involved in learning about flight as they read this book. The mechanics of flight, balloons, dirigibles, early fliers, and planes of the future are all covered in this book. To expand students' thinking at the end of the book is a section titled, Extending Your Reading. In addition to a glossary, an index, and a list of People to Know, this section contains a timeline. The timeline goes from antiquity to the twentieth century covering these topics: flight, science and nature, visual arts, music and theater, literature, and history. This book is one of the Voyages of Discovery interactive series.

Holden, Henry M. *Air Force Aircraft*. 2001. Berkeley Heights, N.J.: Enslow. 48p. Grades: 4 and up.

Intriguing color photographs and detailed descriptions of Air Force aircraft leave the reader ready to head for an air show to see some of these planes. Students are amazed to read about the accommodations on Air Force One. The book includes a table of contents, a list of active USAF aircraft, chapter notes, a glossary, books and Internet sites for further reading, and an index. This is one of the Aircraft series that includes books on the Black Hawk helicopters, air show pilots and planes, hurricane hunters, agricultural aircraft, and stealth fighters and bombers.

Rubin, Susan Goldman. *Toilets, Toasters & Telephones*. Illustrated by Elsa Warnick. 1998. San Diego, Calif.: Harcourt Brace. 132p. Grades: 4 and up.

Did you ever wonder about how everyday household appliances and fixtures came to be? This book describes the invention of everything from toilets to telephones, from toasters to typewriters, from stoves to vacuum cleaners. The book is filled with drawings and photographs and the language is both entertaining and informative. The author spends a great deal of time on the origin of industrial design and explains its impact on household appliances and fixtures.

Spangenburg, Ray, and Diane K. Moser. *Science and Invention*. 1997. New York: Facts on File. 158p. Grades: 4 and up.

This book looks at historic sites associated with scientific inventions such as the original laboratory of Thomas Edison and George Washington Carver's birthplace. Each chapter ends with books for additional reading and related places to visit. Since each of these sites is open to visitors, this book can be used as a guidebook to plan vacation travels. This book is part of the American Historic Places series that focuses on the study of historic places that changed the lives of the American people.

Ash, Russell. *Fantastic Book of 1001 Lists.* 1999. New York: DK. 208p. Grades: 5 and up.

The author has done extensive research to compile this book of over a thousand lists. Youngsters, and many oldsters as well, are fascinated with knowing the biggest, the fastest, the firsts, and the lasts. His information comes from libraries, the Internet, publications, and individuals. While little of this information can be used for actual research, it is high on entertainment value.

EXPLORATIONS

1. Have students brainstorm all of the reasons they use telephones. Next to each reason write down some way to communicate the same information without using a telephone. For example, walking to a friend's house to talk rather than calling. Then, share with them *What Was It Like Before the Telephone?* (Humphrey, 1995).

2. After examining the paper airplanes in *Take Off!* (Hunter, 2000), organize a paper airplane contest. Certificates can be awarded for the airplane with the most unique design and the one that flew the farthest.

3. Using *Bikes, Cars, Trucks, and Trains* (*Bikes, Cars, Trucks, and Trains*, 1995) have the students create a flowchart of the evolution of the bicycle, the automobile, or the train.

4. Prior to reading *The Light Bulb and How It Changed the World* (Pollard, 1995), have students share their experiences about a recent power outage. Ask them to talk about accommodations they made until the power was restored.

5. Prior to reading *Scientific American Inventions from Outer Space: Everyday Uses for NASA Technology* (Baker, 2000), share some of the NASA technology with the students by showing them pictures in the book. Have them form groups to brainstorm how the technology is being used in their everyday lives.

6. After reading *How the Future Began: Machines* (Gifford, 1999), have students draw pictures of machines they would like to see invented to do their chores. Then have them write up what the machines will do for them.

7. After reading *Toilets, Toasters & Telephones* (Rubin, 1998), have students select an invention and create a slogan and advertisement for the invention.

8. After reading *Science and Invention* (Spangenburg and Moser, 1997), have students create a headline and write a news story about one of the places in the book.

WEATHER AND SEASONS

Children are aware of the impact of weather on their lives. They know that rain can cancel a trip to the zoo or the beach. They realize that when the temperature drops and the wind blows they need a warm coat to play outdoors. Studying weather helps them to see that seemingly random changes in the weather have causes and can be predicted. The earth and space science category from NSES acknowledges that students need an understanding of the changes in weather and the seasons. By studying weather and conducting experiments students learn that weather can be described in measurable quantities. Viewing the video, *The Magic School Bus Kicks Up a Storm,* is one way to activate students' prior knowledge about weather and to get them enthusiastic about learning what makes the weather.

***The Magic School Bus Kicks Up a Storm.* 1995. Redmond, Wash.: Microsoft Corporation. 30 min. Grades: K–5.**

In this animated video, the Magic School Bus becomes a weathermobile that transports the students on a wild journey to discover all about weather. This video features the voice of Lily Tomlin.

BOOK AND MEDIA CHOICES

Hall, Zoe. *Fall Leaves Fall!* Illustrated by Shari Halpern. 2000. New York: Scholastic. Unp. Grades: P–1.

Beginning with the green leaves of summer, two brothers watch for their favorite season, fall. As the leaves turn bright red, orange, and yellow, the boys rake them into piles and jump into them. They collect leaves, identify them, and make pictures with them. At the end of the book the life cycle of trees is explained, as well as how some leaves remain green all year long.

Updike, John. *A Child's Calendar.* Illustrations by Trina Schart Hyman. 1999. New York: Scholastic. Unp. Grades: P–2.

The calendar year is celebrated in poems that highlight the unique characteristics and celebrations of each month. Richly painted, detailed illustrations capture the joy and wonder found in the poems. These are poems for sharing with young readers at the start of each month in anticipation of things to come.

Carr, Jan. *Splish, Splash, Spring.* Illustrated by Dorothy Donohue. 2001. New York: Holiday House. Unp. Grades: P–2.

The three-dimensional collage is so detailed as to make the illustrations appear to be raised on the pages. Carr's poem describes a rainy spring day being celebrated by three children and a dog. Just as spring is a combination of sprinkling rain, blowing wind, blooming flowers, and flying kites, so too is this poem.

Carlstrom, Nancy. *What Does the Sky Say?* Illustrated by Tim Ladwig. 2001. Grand Rapids, Mich.: Eerdmans Books for Young Readers. Unp. Grades: K–2.

One way to learn about the weather is to study the sky, which is what the young girl does in this book. Stunning, pastel illustrations depict the weather, the seasons of the year, and the expressions on the young girl's face as she learns to appreciate the changing weather.

Barasch, Lynne. *A Winter Walk.* 1993. New York: Ticknor and Fields. Unp. Grades: K–3.

On a cold, dreary, colorless winter day, this book will have young readers out searching for the colors of winter. Sophie is pleasantly surprised when her mother takes her for a walk and shows her the color in berries, in grasses, and in a flowing stream. Rich watercolor paintings showcase the colors of winter.

All about Climate and Seasons. 2001. Video. Bala Cynwyd, Penn.: Schlessinger Video Productions-Library Video Company. 23 min. Grades: K–4.

The changing of the seasons is always a time of wonder and excitement. Why the seasons change and what causes different climates are explained in easy-to-understand language with engaging examples. The program includes a teacher's guide. This is one of the Weather for Children series.

Scheer, Julian. *By the Light of the Captured Moon*. Illustrated by Ronald Himler. 2001. New York: Holiday House. Unp. Grades: 1–3.

On the last night of summer, a young boy captures the full moon so that he can bring it out whenever he wants to relive summer evenings with friends capturing fireflies. Unfortunately, once he pulls the moon into his bedroom, he cannot seem to find a good place to hide the brightly glowing orb. Young readers will relate to the boy's mother wanting him to turn out the light, so he can get a good night's sleep and be rested for school in the morning.

Owens, Mary Beth. *Be Blest: A Celebration of Seasons*. 1999. New York: Simon and Schuster. Unp. Grades: 1–3.

These poems celebrate the natural world and humans' connections to that world. They were inspired by *Canticle of Brother Sun* by Saint Francis of Assisi, which recognizes the relationships between people and animals in addition to God's presence in nature. These poems remind us to give praise and rejoice each month of the year as the world around us unfolds with new and wondrous sights. The short verses are contained in wreaths of nature's bounty, and the opposite page is a full-color illustration of the month of the year. It concludes with the music to the poem *Be Blest* written by the author.

Casey, Denise. *Weather Everywhere*. Photographs by Jackie Gilmore. 1995. New York: Macmillan Books for Young Readers. 36p. Grades: 1–4.

Color photographs of nature and children enjoying nature combined with brief interesting text, make this a basic introduction to weather. It explains the elements of weather such as humidity, wind sources, clouds, and fog in easy-to-understand language. Two simple experiments explain weather phenomena, and children can be challenged to create their own weather experiments based on what is shown in the color photographs throughout the book. A glossary concludes the book.

All about Wind and Clouds. 2001. Video. Wynnewood, Penn.: Schlessinger Media; Library Video. 23 min. Grades: 1–6.

Students participate in a lively exploration to learn how scientists use winds and clouds to predict the weather. A hands-on demonstration shows students how to build their own weather vane to monitor the wind. This video includes a teacher's guide. This is part of the Weather for Children series.

Simon, Seymour. *Weather.* 1993. New York: Morrow Junior Books. Unp. Grades: 2–5.

One topic that is discussed daily is the weather. Simon's book uses economical language to describe weather patterns. He discusses insolation, the process of sunlight passing through the atmosphere, and the greenhouse effect, which traps heat and prevents its escaping into space. The balance between insolation and the greenhouse effect make our planet livable. Types of clouds, fog, frost, and dew are all discussed. He also explains the danger of smog, a combination of smoke and fog. The full-page color photographs and colorful diagrams encourage even reluctant readers to read the book to learn more about this topic of daily discussion.

Berger, Melvin, and Gilda Berger. *Do Tornadoes Really Twist?: Questions and Answers about Tornadoes and Hurricanes.* Illustrated by Higgins Bond. 2000. New York: Scholastic. Unp. Grades: 2–5.

Written in a question-and-answer format, this book gives students a great deal of information and little known facts about these horrifying natural events. The back of the book suggests that students memorize the facts and amaze their friends with them. The photographs of destruction capture the readers' interest and cause them to pay close attention to the information on what to do when a tornado is spotted. Detailed explanations and diagrams show young scientists how tornadoes and hurricanes form. An index concludes the book. This book is one of the Scholastic Question and Answer series.

Farndon, John. *Weather.* 2001. Tarrytown, N.Y.: Marshall Cavendish. 32p. Grades: 2–7.

Students conduct experiments by making a sundial, a mobile, and a hygrometer. Each of these helps students understand how weather can be forecast. Throughout the book are text boxes that provide a focus for the experiments, fascinating facts, and explanations of what is happening. The book includes a table of contents, a glossary, and an index. This book is one of the Science Experiments series.

Busch, Phyllis S. *Autumn.* Illustrated by Megan Halsey. 2000. Tarrytown, N.Y.: Marshall Cavendish. 47p. Grades: 2 and up.

This book is filled with a variety of activities for exploring the changes in the world indoors and out-of-doors during autumn. Indoor activities include making a leaf wreath, gathering seeds, and growing an indoor garden. Outdoor activities include listening for the sounds of autumn, collecting leaves, and observing animals as they prepare for winter. The book contains a table of contents, suggestions for further reading, and an index. This is one of the Nature Projects for Every Season series that includes books on summer, winter, and spring.

Benton, George. *Wind and Weather: Climates, Clouds, Snow, Tornadoes, and How Weather Is Predicted.* 1995. New York: Scholastic. 46p. Grades: 4–8.

Clever devices such as transparent pages, double fold-ups, reusable vinyl stickers, and 3-D glasses are used to entice readers young and old to explore the book. The topics in this book include: air, the sky, precipitation, wind, climate, and storms. These are described in brief passages accompanied by color photographs and illustrations. At the end of the book there is an Extending Your Reading section that includes an index, glossary, bibliography, and addresses of museums to visit. This is one of the Voyages of Discovery books.

Morris, Neil. *Hurricanes and Tornadoes.* 1999. Hauppauge, N.Y.: Barron's Educational Series. 33p. Grades: 4–8.

Pictures, illustrations, graphs, and charts help to explain these complex weather occurrences. Short descriptions of popular movies depicting hurricanes and tornadoes along with actual photographs and news excerpts of the destruction caused by them appeal to readers as they explore these phenomena. An index is included at the end of the book.

EXPLORATIONS

1. After reading a poem in *A Child's Calendar* (Updike, 1999), help the children connect the words in the poem to the illustrations. For example, in "March," the poet speaks of a lost mitten and in the illustration on the ground is a lost mitten.
2. Reading *By the Light of the Captured Moon* (Scheer, 2001) on the first day of school is one way to have students share what they did during the summer as they get to know their classmates. Students could then create a chart showing their favorite things to do during the other seasons of the year.
3. Prior to reading *By the Light of the Captured Moon* (Scheer, 2001), talk to the students about how the book combines events that could happen and events that could not happen. As the story is being read, ask students to complete a two-column chart listing the events in the story that could happen and those that could not happen. After reading the story have students discuss the reasons why they placed the events in each column.
4. Since students will memorize many of the facts about these natural events, they could form groups and decide which natural event they will become. Their classmates use yes/no questions to quiz them to determine which natural event they are representing. *Weather Everywhere* (Casey, 1995), *Do Tornadoes Really Twist?: Questions and Answers about Tornadoes and Hurricanes* (Berger and Berger, 2000), and *Hurricanes and Tornadoes* (Morris, 1999) provide students with the background information they need on these natural events.
5. Have students look up wind currents in an encyclopedia and in *Wind and Weather: Climates, Clouds, Snow, Tornadoes, and How Weather Is Predicted* (Benton, 1995). Then have them draw the predominate wind currents on a map.

6. When students finish studying about weather and reading informational books about weather, have them locate their favorite passage about weather in one of the books to use in a read-around (Tompkins, 1998). Have them practice reading their passage. Begin the read-around by asking one student to read a favorite passage. As that student finishes, another student spontaneously begins their passage. The read-around continues until everyone has had a chance to read a passage.

7. Create a concept map of the four seasons using Inspiration software. Then have students brainstorm a list of chores that have to be done for each season to add to the concept map. After reading about seasons, see if there are any chores to be added to the concept map.

8. After reading about tornadoes have students draw a flowchart of how a tornado forms.

9. In tornado-prone areas of the country, schoolchildren participate in tornado drills at school. Have them devise a plan for what to do if they are at home when a tornado threatens.

10. Invite students to share experiences of living through natural disasters prior to reading about natural disasters.

11. Have students create a personal weather chart to record the daily weather. Each afternoon have them make predictions about what the weather will be like in the morning and to write down the basis for their prediction. Upon arriving at school in the morning, have them determine if their prediction was correct.

SCIENTISTS AND INVENTORS

Evans (1992), concerned about his students' stereotypical portrayal of scientists as adult males wearing white coats in laboratories, set out to determine if these images came from children's books. He discovered that some, but not all of the twenty-five books he examined contained these stereotypes. One way to assure that students see scientists from a variety of perspectives is to share with them biographies about scientists. The books in this section include information about the scientists and their personal lives that give students a balanced view of scientists. NSES category eight includes the study of the history and nature of science and science as a human endeavor.

BOOK AND MEDIA CHOICES

Birch, Beverly. *Marconi's Battle for Radio*. Illustrated by Robin Bell Corfield. 1995. Hauppauge, N.Y.: Barron's Educational Series. Unp. Grades: 3–4.

The title helps to tell the story of Marconi's struggle to make a successful radio. His hard work, triumphs, and challenges are chronicled here. Pastel illustrations convey the sense of despair and discouragement that he encountered. Marconi was not the only inventor working on the radio and it took the efforts of many before today's radios were invented.

Galileo: On the Shoulders of Giants. **2001. Video/DVD. Toronto, Ontario: Devine Entertainment. 56 min. Grades: 3–8.**

Filmed on location in Italy, with authentic costumes made in Italy, the stage is set for this stunning production that won two Emmy awards. Galileo's discoveries and his struggle for acceptance of his findings is chronicled as he teaches one of the young boys of the Medici family. The options on this DVD include three different languages and interviews with the actors. This title is also available on videocassette and is part of The Inventors' Specials series. Other scientists profiled in this award-winning series include Leonardo, Newton, Marie Curie, Edison, and Einstein. Additional information about these scientists can be found at www.devinetime.com.

Parker, Steve. *Galileo and the Universe*. 1992. New York: HarperCollins. 32p. Grades: 3–8.

This is a brief introduction to the life and work of Galileo. His discoveries in physics and astronomy were considered heretical and he spent the last years of his life under house arrest. Many years later Isaac Newton based much of his work on Galileo's discoveries and writings. The book concludes with a timeline, a glossary, and an index. This is part of the Science Discoveries series.

Sandler, Martin W. *Inventors*. 1996. New York: HarperCollins Children's Books. 93p. Grades: 3 and up.

Americans have an inventive spirit that is celebrated in over one hundred photographs and illustrations. Inventions changed the world and made it a better place. Inventors' early failures and later successes show their tenacity. The book includes information on the Library of Congress and an index. This book is one of the series A Library of Congress Book.

Parker, Steve. *Marie Curie and Radium*. 1992. New York: HarperCollins. 32p. Grades: 4–6.

Throughout her life Marie Curie was denied recognition for her work and denied teaching positions solely because she was a female. This renowned scientist was eventually recognized for her outstanding work for which she gave her life when she died of radiation poisoning. The book is filled with photographs depicting her personal and professional life. It includes a timeline, glossary, and index. In the timeline, her accomplishments are placed in the context of events occurring in science, western expansion and exploration, politics, and arts. This is one of the Science Discoveries series.

Parker, Steve. *Thomas Edison and Electricity*. 1992. New York: HarperCollins. 32p. Grades: 4–6.

Whereas Edison is remembered for the invention of the light bulb and the phonograph, he actually shares the honors with other scientists who were working on similar projects at the same time. He specialized in improving on others' inventions. Students relate to Edison, a problem student, who was labeled retarded by the school. His mother took him home and schooled him. On his own he taught himself philosophy, chemistry, and physics. This is one of the Science Discoveries series that includes books on Galileo and Charles Darwin.

McKissack, Patricia, and Fredrick McKissack. *African-American Scientists*. 1994. Brookfield, Conn.: The Millbrook Press. 96p. Grades: 4 and up.

Both well-known and lesser-known African American scientists are profiled in this book. The focus of the book is on the things that interested each scientist and how they developed into the scientists that they became. This book illustrates how scientists of different ethnic backgrounds contributed to each discovery often working along similar paths at the same time. This book is part of A Proud Heritage series.

Freedman, Russell. *The Wright Brothers: How They Invented the Airplane*. 1991. New York: Holiday House. 129p. Grades: 6 and up.

The inseparable Wright brothers worked together in their bicycle shop. Without formal training in science or engineering they invented the airplane. Their years of work, their failures, and success are all chronicled. Included in the book are original photographs by Wilbur and Orville. The book concludes with places to visit, books for further reading, and an index. This book is a Newbery Honor book.

EXPLORATIONS

1. Students can create an open-mind portrait (Tompkins, 1998) of one of the inventors. The face of the inventor is drawn on one sheet of paper, cut out, and attached to the top of another sheet of paper. Students lift the face drawing and write about the inventor's thoughts while creating an invention. Once completed, students can share their open-mind portraits in small groups and display them in the classroom.
2. Students can conduct additional research on a scientist and then have their classmates interview them as that scientist.
3. The discoveries of African American scientists profoundly impacted society. Explore the impact of some of their discoveries on the world today.
4. During much of her lifetime Marie Curie suffered from radiation sickness. Lead students in a discussion of the hazards of radiation and have them create a list of ways to protect themselves from excessive radiation exposure.
5. After reading books on inventions, have students create a timeline of the inventions using TimeLiner.

REFERENCE BOOKS

Within the pages of science reference books students find specific information on topics of interest to them. These books present a broad overview of one topic or provide small amounts of information on a variety of topics. Placing these books in the classroom library furnishes students a ready reference when questions arise during their studies. Students benefit from direct instruction on how to use the reference sources with opportunities to use them to independently explore answers to their questions.

BOOK AND MEDIA CHOICES

Jeunesse, Gallimard, and Claude Delafose. *Atlas of Animals*. Illustrated by Rene Metttler. 1994. New York: Scholastic. Unp. Grades: K–2.

Small-size, colorful pictures, and limited text make this book one that children want to peruse on their own after it has been shared with them by an adult. Animals drawn on celluloid pages show different perspectives of each animal. Small globes indicate the continents the animals inhabit. This book is one of the series, A First Discovery Book.

Corbeil, Jean-Claude, and Arian Archambault. *Scholastic Visual Dictionary*. 2000. New York: Scholastic. 224p. Grades: K–2.

This visual dictionary consists of pages and pages of detailed, labeled illustrations for the youngest readers. The dictionary is divided by themes and subjects that are found in the table of contents. An index enables teachers and librarians to find specific pictures in the dictionary.

Eyewitness Encyclopedia of Science. 1997. Mac/Win. New York: DK Multimedia. Grades: 2–4.

Sections on this CD include mathematics, physics, chemistry, life sciences, and biographies of noted scientists. Scrolling text boxes, animated graphics, sounds, and links to additional information assure students have access to in-depth information on the science principles they are studying. Also included is a link to Internet resources and a quiz to take alone or with a partner. A *Science Facts* pocket book is included.

One Small Square: Backyard. 1995. Mac/Win. Los Angeles, Calif.: Virgin Sound and Vision. Grades: 3-7.

This CD provides students an extensive database of information on plants, soil, rocks, and creatures they can find in their backyard. It also includes several games and outdoor experiments.

Simon, Seymour. *Science Dictionary*. Illustrations by Oxford Illustrators Ltd. 1994. New York: HarperCollins. 256p. Grades: 3–8.

Noted science author Seymour Simon defines science terms in easy-to-understand text. For words that have both a scientific and an everyday meaning only the scientific meaning is included in this reference book. Science surrounds us, and it explains things that do not seem to make sense. Simon's definitions help to explain these things.

Rubel, David. *Science*. 1995. New York: Scholastic. 192p. Grades: 3–8.

This Scholastic Kid's Encyclopedia has colorful artwork and illustrations. The book provides information on all fields of science from Astronomy, to Physics, to Chemistry. Brief definitions and explanations are written in everyday language that children can read and understand on their own. Suggestions for further reading on the topic are included on each two-page spread. The book's content is arranged alphabetically, however, the table of contents is grouped according to the branches of science. In the table of contents the blue bullets indicate the easiest topics to understand. An index at the back of the book enables the reader to look up a specific subject and a glossary provides definitions of unfamiliar terms.

Treasures of the Museum of Natural History. 1997. Mac/Win. New York: Voyager CD-ROMs. Grades: 3 and up.

Fifty treasures from the American Museum of Natural History are recorded on this interactive CD. Artwork, video, text, photographs, animation, maps, and audio excerpts enable students to fully experience the museum's collections. Included on the CD is a notebook for students to record their own expeditions and a glossary hyperlinked to the text.

Vogel, Carole G. *Nature's Fury: Eyewitness Reports of Natural Disasters*. 2000. New York: Scholastic. 127p. Grades: 4–8.

Black-and-white photographs depict the destruction caused by earthquakes, volcano eruptions, hurricanes, blizzards, flood, droughts, and fires in this science reference book. Survivors' personal recollections of the natural disasters add to the stark realism of the photographs. At the end of the book is a list of magazine articles, books, and Web sites for further explorations. The book also contains an index.

Parker, Steve. *Natural World*. 1994. New York: Dorling Kindersley. 192p. Grades: 4 and up.

Abundant, engrossing photographs and drawings accompanied by succinct text assure that even reluctant readers find it difficult to put this book down. The natural world is presented in chapters that include animal body structures, hunting and eating, the cycle of life, the fight for survival, evolution and extinction, and animal classification. Readers want to share the book with their classmates and discuss what they have found in their own backyards. This book is one of DK's Eyewitness series. An extensive glossary and index are included.

TEACHER RESOURCES

This section contains books and Internet sites to enhance the science curriculum. One of the books listed is a catalog of free science resources for teachers. This book is updated yearly and can be found in many school, public, and university libraries. Contact information is also given for the National Science Teachers Association.

BOOKS

Kneidel, Sally. *Creepy Crawlies, and the Scientific Method: More than 100 Hands-On Science Experiments for Children*. 1993. Golden, Colo.: Fulcrum Resources. 224p. Grades: K–6.

A fun way to study nature is by observing the bugs, worms, and insects that abound there. Instructions for the safe capture and maintenance of the critters, as well as experiments and instructions for observing them, make this book a useful classroom resource.

Shaw, Donna Gail, and Claudia S. Dybdahl. *Integrating Science and Language Arts: A Sourcebook for K–6 Teachers*. 1996. Boston: Allyn and Bacon. 320p. Grades: K–6.

This resource is organized into teaching units and contains a variety of science activities that integrate the language arts.

***Educator's Guide to FREE Science Materials*. 2000-2001. Randolph, Wis.: Educator's Progress Service. 233p. Grades: K and up.**

In this guide, teachers will find free videos, films, filmstrips, lesson plans, print resources, and Web resources. To assist teachers in locating items in the book there are title, subject, source, and what's new indexes. There is also a sample letter to use to request the materials.

Johmann, Carol A., and Elizabeth J. Rieth. *Gobble Up Nature: Fun Activities to Complete and Eat for Kids in Grades 1–4*. Illustrated by Kelly Kennedy. 1996. Santa Barbara, Calif.: The Learning Works. 136p. Grades: 1–4.

Children enjoy eating and enjoy being outdoors. This book combines these two favorite things with clever hands-on activities for children to complete with their teachers, librarians, or parents. The Pizza Plant Safari has children mapping the plants in their backyard and then creating a pizza with a variety of toppings to represent the different plants.

Levine, Shar, and Leslie Johnstone. *The Magnet Book*. Illustrated by Jason Coons. Photographs by Jeff Connery. 1998. New York: Sterling. 80p. Grades: 1–8.

There are 39 games, tricks, and experiments in this book designed for students to discover the wonder of magnets and electricity. Each activity has a list of required materials, a procedure section with questions for students to answer as they work, and an explanation of what happened. Also included are tricks to perform for friends.

Farndon, John. *How the Earth Works*. Photographs by Michael Dunning. 1992. Pleasantville, N.Y.: The Reader's Digest Association. 192p. Grades: 1 and up.

Step-by-step directions accompanied by photographs of children discovering how the earth works and three-dimensional models combine to make this a book to include in every classroom. Teachers, parents, librarians, and students all learn together as they explore the earth while conducting these fascinating experiments.

Moje, Steven W. *Cool Chemistry: Great Experiments with Simple Stuff*. 1999. New York: Sterling. 96p. Grades: 3–6.

After a brief introduction and a listing of safety procedures, this book launches into a variety of simple chemistry experiments students can do either at home or in the classroom with adult supervision. The experiments require easily obtainable materials and they make chemistry fun.

Abruscato, Joseph. *Whizbangers and Wonderments: Science Activities for Children*. 2000. Boston: Allyn and Bacon. 312p. Grades: 3–6.

This book takes an interdisciplinary approach to science integrating it into the language arts, math, and arts curriculums.

PROFESSIONAL ORGANIZATION

National Science Teachers Association
1840 Wilson Boulevard
Arlington, VA 22201-3000
703-243-7100
http://nsta.org
Journal: *Science and Children, Science Scope*

INTERNET SITES

Carolina Biological Supply Company
www.carolina.com/

> This site includes a Teacher's World that features information on lab safety, downloads, grant-writing resources, links to other science sites, product booklets, and other resources for science teachers.

Cool Science for Curious Kids

www.hhmi.org/coolscience

> The Howard Hughes Medical Institute sponsors this site. Children click on illustrated questions to discover information about their world such as "Why are snakes like lizards, and monkeys like moose?"

The Exploratorium

www.exploratorium.edu/learning_studio/index.html

> This electronic magazine teaches students how science is everywhere and helps them see the impact of science on their lives. The Exploratorium is located in the San Francisco Palace of Fine Arts.

Insect Lore

www.insectlore.com

> A wonderful collection of books, videos, living kits, manipulatives, and other resources for learning about insects can be found on this site.

Ranger Rick

www.nwf.org/rrick

> This is the Web site for *Ranger Rick Magazine*, a popular science magazine for children. The site is sponsored by the publisher of the magazine, the National Wildlife Federation.

Savage Earth Online

www.pbs.org/wnet/savageearth/

> Learn the science behind volcanoes, earthquakes, and tsunamis through articles and animations. This is a companion Web site to the PBS series.

Science Learning Network

www.sln.org www.sln.org

> Through a partnership between science museums around the globe, their combined resources are linked on this Web page sponsored by the National Science Foundation and Unisys Corporation. The Web site is a model of how inquiry-based learning can be supported on the Internet.

Science NetLinks

www.sciencenetlinks.com/index.html

> Reviewed Web sites and lesson plans for K–12 science teachers can be found here. The American Association for the Advancement of Science sponsors this site. Science NetLinks is a partner in the educational program, MarcoPolo.

Stennis Space Center Educator Resource Center
http://education.ssc.nasa.gov/htmls/trc/trc.htm
> Free services to educators provided by this center include videotapes, software, slides, lesson plans, and other educational resources.

REFERENCES

Alberts, Bruce. 2000. Preface. *Inquiry and the National Science Education Standards: A Guide for Teaching and Learning*. Washington, D.C.: National Academy.

Dixey, Brenda P., and Kate A. Baird. 1996. "Students' Entry into Science through Literature." Paper Presented at the Global Summit on Science and Science Education, San Francisco, Calif., December. ERIC, ED 408159.

Duthie, Christine. 1994. "Nonfiction: A Genre Study for the Primary Classroom." *Language Arts* 71, no. 8 (December): 588-595.

Evans, Allen. 1992. "A Look at the Scientist as Portrayed in Children's Literature." *Science and Children* 29, no. 6 (March): 35-37.

Goforth, Frances S. 1998. *Literature and the Learner.* Belmont, Calif.: Wadsworth Publishing.

Hechtman, Judi. 1995. "Ladybug, Ladybug, Come to Class." *Science and Children* 32, no. 6 (March): 33-35.

HyperStudio. Version 4. 2000. Knowledge Adventure, Torrance, Calif.

Inspiration. Version 6. 1999. Inspiration Software, Portland, Ore.

Latimer, Jonathan P., and Karen Stray Nolting. 1999. *Birds of Prey*. Peterson Field Guides for Young Naturalists. Boston: Houghton Mifflin.

——————. 1999. *Bizarre Birds*. Peterson Field Guides for Young Naturalists. Boston: Houghton Mifflin.

——————. 1999. *Shorebirds*. Peterson Field Guides for Young Naturalists. Boston: Houghton Mifflin.

Maduram, Ida. 2000. "'Playing Possum': A Young Child's Responses to Information Books." *Language Arts* 77, no. 5 (May): 391-397.

Matthews, Marian, Donna Gee, and Elwanda Bell. 1995. "Science Learning with a Multicultural Emphasis." *Science and Children* 32, no. 6 (March): 20-23, 54.

Microsoft PowerPoint. 2000. Microsoft Corporation, Redmond, Wash.

National Research Council. 1995. *National Science Education Standards*. [Online] Available: www.nap.edu/readingroom/books/nses/html/ [cited 30 October 2000]

Oyler, Celia, and Anne Barry. 1996. "Intertextual Connections in Read-Alouds of Information Books." *Language Arts* 73, no. 5 (September): 324-329.

Smith, J. Lea, and J. Daniel Herring. 1996. "Literature Alive: Connecting to Story through the Arts." *Reading Horizons* 37, no. 2 (January): 102-115.

Stiffler, Lee Anne. 1992. "A Solution in the Shelves." *Science and Children* 29, no. 6 (March):17, 46.

TimeLiner. 1999. Watertown, Mass.: Tom Snyder Productions.

Tompkins, Gail E. 1998. *Fifty Literacy Strategies: Step by Step*. Upper Saddle River, N. J.: Prentice-Hall.

Walpole, S. 1999. "Changing Texts, Changing Thinking: Comprehension Demands of New Science Textbooks." *The Reading Teacher* 52, no. 4 (January): 358-369.

Yopp, Ruth Helen, and Hallie Kay Yopp. 2000. "Sharing Informational Text with Young Children." *The Reading Teacher* 53, no. 5 (February): 410-423.

Young, Terrence E. Jr., and Coleen Salley. 1997. "Meeting Standards with K-8 Science Tradebooks." *Science Books and Films* 33, no. 6 (August/September): 161-163, 185.

Chapter 3

English Language Arts

The English language arts involve more than just learning rules and how to apply them. Students use language for thought and communication. Communication occurs through writing, speaking, and listening, which are interconnected and learned simultaneously. Offering students opportunities to communicate in a warm, supportive environment where they can explore and play with language assures that they develop the needed language skills. Children's literature serves as a model for student writing and, when read aloud, it serves as a model for speaking and listening.

The interconnectedness of reading and writing is evidenced in the *Standards for English Language Arts* jointly prepared by the National Council of Teachers of English (NCTE) and the International Reading Association (IRA). These two organizations recognize that students need both opportunities and resources to learn to effectively use language. Additionally, they note the importance of building on the emerging literacy skills that children bring to school. The *Standards for English Language Arts* are guides for the development of curriculum rather than prescriptions to be followed. Teachers are encouraged to apply the standards with creativity and innovation cognizant of the needs and abilities of their students. The standards are as follows:

1. Students read a wide range of print and nonprint texts to build an understanding of texts, of themselves, and of the cultures of the United States and the world; to acquire new information; to respond to the needs and demands of society and the workplace; and for personal fulfillment. Among these texts are fiction and nonfiction, classic, and contemporary works.
2. Students read a wide range of literature from many periods in many genres to build an understanding of the many dimensions (e.g., philosophical, ethical, aesthetic) of human experience.
3. Students apply a wide range of strategies to comprehend, interpret, evaluate, and appreciate texts. They draw on their prior experience, their interactions with other readers and writers, their knowledge of word meaning and of other texts, their word

      identification strategies, and their understanding of textual features (e.g., sound-letter correspondence, sentence structure, context, and graphics).

4. Students adjust their use of spoken, written, and visual language (e.g., conventions, style, and vocabulary) to communicate effectively with a variety of audiences and for different purposes.

5. Students employ a wide range of strategies as they write and use different writing process elements appropriately to communicate with different audiences for a variety of purposes.

6. Students apply knowledge of language structure, language conventions (e.g., spelling and punctuation), media techniques, figurative language, and genre to create, critique, and discuss print and nonprint texts.

7. Students conduct research on issues and interests generating ideas and questions, and by posing problems. They gather, evaluate, and synthesize data from a variety of sources (e.g., print and nonprint texts, artifacts, and people) to communicate their discoveries in ways that suit their purpose and audience.

8. Students use a variety of technological and information resources (e.g., libraries, databases, computer networks, and video) to gather and synthesize information and to create and communicate knowledge.

9. Students develop an understanding of and respect for diversity in language use, patterns, and dialects across cultures, ethnic groups, geographic regions, and social roles.

10. Students whose first language is not English make use of their first language to develop competency in the English language arts and to develop understanding of content across the curriculum.

11. Students participate as knowledgeable, reflective, creative, and critical members of a variety of literacy communities.

12. Students use spoken, written, and visual language to accomplish their own purposes (e.g., for learning, enjoyment, persuasion, and the exchange of information).

As teachers and librarians integrate children's literature throughout the curriculum they address many of these standards. The activities they use to extend the literature selections assure that these standards are met, as well as the appropriate content area standards.

      One need that students from diverse backgrounds have is to find children like themselves in the books they read. These students need to know that others face similar challenges as they move between different cultures. Janet Wong a Korean, Chinese, American speaks to these children through her poetry.

Wong, Janet S. *A Suitcase of Seaweed and Other Poems*. 1996. New York: Margaret K. McElderry Books. 42p. Grades: 5 and up.

Divided into three chapters, this book has a chapter of poems about each of her heritages. Her grandmother comes from Korea for a visit with a suitcase of seaweed and squid, hence the title of the book. In "Manners" she speaks of the differences between the Korean and Chinese etiquette for eating with chopsticks and ponders that it might be better to just eat with a fork and knife. These short poems help students begin to understand what it is like to live between different cultures.

Children's literature in the English language arts classroom motivates students to learn to write, speak, and listen in ways that textbooks cannot. Informational trade books that look like narrative picture books facilitate children's transition to learning from textbooks (Headley and Dunston, 2000). Further, students soon learn that the informational books' style of writing is different than the narrative found in picture books and they discover that informational books do not have to be read from beginning to end. Instead students can read just the parts that are of interest. Books and media in this chapter stimulate children to think, to play, and to respond as they explore and experiment with the alphabet, parts of speech, word play, writing, speaking, and poetry. The chapter concludes with reference materials for the English language arts classroom and teacher resources.

THE ALPHABET

Alphabet books and songs introduce young readers to the letters of the alphabet and their sounds. They also provide for many children their first introduction to reading and teach children about the fundamentals of reading. Young readers learn about the placement of words and pictures in books and come to learn the relationship between the two. Readers both young and old derive hours of pleasure from alphabet books such as the ones in this section. Books and media in this section address content standard three regarding students' understanding of letter and word identification. Books, such as *Alphabet Fiesta: An English/Spanish Alphabet Story* (Miranda, 2001), that are written in both English and Spanish help to address content standard ten regarding helping English as a Second Language students to develop competency in the English language.

BOOK AND MEDIA CHOICES

Rose, Deborah Lee. *Into the A, B, Sea: An Ocean Alphabet*. Illustrated by Steve Jenkins. 2000. New York: Scholastic. Unp. Grades: P–1.

Paper collage is used to illustrate this beautiful introduction to the ABCs. The theme of the sea is used to acquaint students to creatures from insects, to angelfish, from sharks, to zooplankton. Told in poetry form, the book delights Abecedarians of all ages. The book ends with further information about the creatures swimming across the pages.

***Jazzles: A to Z Clever Songs*. 2000. Audiocassette. Salinas, Calif.: Clever Show. Grades: P–2.**

This audiocassette contains 30 clever songs for learning the alphabet. The lyrics for the songs are included.

Scillian, Devin. *A Is for America: An American Alphabet Book.* Illustrated by Pam Carroll. 2001. Chelsea, Mich.: Sleeping Bear Press. 56p. Grades: P–3.

This unique alphabet book focuses on symbols that represent America. Large full-page color illustrations accompany the brief text. The book is visually appealing and is a good one for students to read and share with a partner.

Lester, Mike. *A Is for Salad.* Illustrated by Jane O'Connor. 2000. New York: Putnam. Unp. Grades: P–3.

This rather twisted alphabet book delights youngsters as they guess what it is in the illustrations that really begins with the letter on the page. For example, on the first page an alligator is holding a salad. Young readers who know their alphabet realize that salad does not start with "A," but alligator does. The correct answers are found at the end of the book.

Dr. Seuss's ABC. 1995. Mac/Win. Novato, Calif.: Living Books. Grades: P–3.

Animation, music, songs, and sound effects make this interactive CD a favorite with students. Students enjoy singing along with the computer as they learn their ABCs. Clicking on hot spots on the screen starts an amazing array of animations.

Miranda, Anne. *Alphabet Fiesta: An English/Spanish Alphabet Story.* Illustrated by young schoolchildren in Spain. 2001. New York: Turtle. Unp. Grades: K–2.

Zelda the zebra's mother has sent out invitations for a surprise birthday party for Zelda. This is the alphabetical story written in both English and Spanish. Both upper and lower case letters are written in the top corners of the pages. An author's note at the end of the book explains how she and her husband examined English and Spanish dictionaries to find key words with the same first letters in both languages to include in the poems. Schoolchildren in Spain, the author's own children, and friends' children were enlisted to create the artwork for the book.

Cassie, Bryan, and Jerry Pallotta. *The Butterfly Alphabet Book.* Illustrated by Mark Atrella. 1995. New York: Scholastic. Unp. Grades: K–2.

Each letter of the alphabet introduces butterflies, their habitats, and other information about them. These delicate fragile creatures are illustrated in vibrant colors. Jerry Pallotta has written numerous alphabet books on other animals and creatures that inhabit the earth. All of the books contain a great deal of information about the animals and creatures.

Bryan, Ashley. *Ashley Bryan's ABC of African American Poetry.* 2001. New York: Aladdin Paperbacks. Unp. Grades: K–4.

This unique ABC book showcases the work of African American poets as they describe the African American experience. Ashley Bryan carefully selected lines of poetry based on the images that came to his mind as he read the words. The letter of the alphabet that each represents is capitalized wherever it appears in the lines, hence the letter of the alphabet is usually not the first word in the lines. The letter of the alphabet appears in the top right corner of each page and the poets' names appear across the bottom of the page. The lines of the poem are found near the bottom of the page superimposed over the vibrant illustrations. An acknowledgements page at the end of the book contains information on where the poems can be found. This book won a Coretta Scott King award.

Rosen, Michael J. *Avalanche*. Illustrated by David Butler. 1998. Cambridge, Mass.: Candlewick Press. Unp. Grades: 1–3.

An errant snowball becomes a raging avalanche that picks up a variety of objects as it travels. Fortunately, the objects are all picked up in alphabetical order. This clever rhyming text tells a story of Bobby and his dog Zippy and their snowball.

EXPLORATIONS

1. Students enjoy singing along to the alphabet songs on *Jazzles: A to Z Clever Songs.* This audiocassette can also be placed in a listening center for students to enjoy.
2. Prior to reading *Alphabet Fiesta: An English/Spanish Alphabet Story* (Miranda, 2001), have students talk about what they do to get ready to go to a birthday party.
3. After reading *A Is for Salad* (Lester, 2000), have the students create their very own twisted alphabet book.
4. Prior to reading *Ashley Bryan's ABC of African American Poetry* (Bryan, 2001), locate some of the original sources of the poems and share the complete poems with the students. These poems can then be put in the class writing center for students to select other lines of the poems to illustrate.
5. After reading *Avalanche* (Rosen, 1998), older students can create their own snowball alphabet book by finding things in their neighborhood that could be picked up as the snowball rolls along. It may take the entire class working on this project to find objects in the neighborhood to represent each letter of the alphabet.

PARTS OF SPEECH

Learning the parts of speech is fun with this collection of interesting, intriguing books. Vibrant, colorful illustrations, rhyming text, humor, and nonsense encourage students to read these books again and again. These books contain a great deal of information about the parts of speech, and the information is presented in such a way that students learn and remember what they read. Kane (1997) advocates collecting sentences while reading children's literature and using the sentences to teach grammar and punctuation skills. The *Grammar Rock* computer CD is another fun way to learn about the parts of speech.

Grammar Rock. 1996. Mac/Win. Minneapolis: The Learning Company. Grades: K–5.

Short videos introduce the different parts of speech and then students can play a variety of games designed to reinforce the concepts presented in the video. A teacher's guide accompanies the software program. The lyrics and music can also be found on the Internet at http://genxtvland.simplenet.com/SchoolHouseRock/.

Learning the parts of speech addresses content standards three, six, and twelve. Content standard three addresses students developing their knowledge of word meaning and understanding of textual features, such as sentence structure. Content standard six concerns students' ability to apply their knowledge of the conventions and structure of language. In content standard twelve the focus is on students being able to use language for their own purposes.

BOOK AND MEDIA CHOICES

Appelt, Kathi. *Elephants Aloft*. Illustrated by Keith Baker. 1993. San Diego, Calif.: Harcourt Brace. Unp. Grades: P–2.

Having readers ride along with a pair of elephant children on their hot air balloon voyage to visit their aunt is a clever way to teach prepositions. Bright colorful illustrations with lots of action make the story especially appealing to young readers. There is only one word per two-page spread, assuring that young readers can read it on their own.

Cleary, Brian P. *To Root, To Toot, To Parachute: What Is a Verb?* Illustrated by Jenya Prosmitsky. 2001. Minneapolis, Minn.: Carolrhoda Books. Unp. Grades: 1–4.

This lesson on verbs includes rhyming text and silly cats that show what verbs are all about. Printing the verbs in a different color text assures that readers know which ones are verbs. This is part of the Words Are Categorical series.

Cleary, Brian P. *A Mink, a Fink, a Skating Rink: What Is a Noun?* Illustrated by Jenya Prosmitsky. 1999. Minneapolis, Minn.: Carolrhoda Books. Unp. Grades: 1–4.

Rhyming text and colorful cartoon-like illustrations make reading this book a fun way to learn nouns. The opening page of the book defines a noun and then the readers embark on a joyous exploration of nouns. Just to make sure readers pick out the nouns, they are written in colored text. This is part of the Words Are Categorical series.

Cleary, Brian P. *Hairy, Scary, Ordinary: What Is an Adjective?* Illustrated by Jenya Prosmitsky. 1999. Minneapolis, Minn.: Carolrhoda Books. Unp. Grades: 1–4.

Festive, humorous illustrations of cute, round cats and offbeat humans, bright colored pages, and colorful, bouncy text make learning about adjectives fun. Descriptive sentences demonstrate the importance of adjectives in the English language and the adjectives are written in contrasting colors. This is part of the Words Are Categorical series.

Heller, Ruth. *Kites Sail High: A Book about Verbs.* **1988. New York: Scholastic. Unp. Grades: 2–5.**

Colorful, festive paintings of familiar objects explode across the pages and show readers active verbs, passive verbs, linking verbs, indicative verbs, irregular verbs, and imperative verbs. Each of the verbs is in upper case letters to distinguish them from other words in the rhyming text. The creative illustrations help anchor the different kinds of verbs in the students' minds. This book is available in both video and audiocassette from Spoken Arts, New Rochelle, New York.

Heller, Ruth. *Many Luscious Lollipops: A Book about Adjectives.* **1989. New York: Grosset and Dunlap. Unp. Grades: 2–5.**

Heller's appealing rhymes enchant readers while teaching the rules of adjective usage. After seeing a plain ice cream cone change to a waffle cone and then change to a banana split, who could forget the irregular adjectives of good, better, and best. Adjectives come in many forms and can be confusing, so writers are cajoled to check a dictionary when in doubt. This book is available in both video and audiocassette from Spoken Arts, New Rochelle, New York.

Heller, Ruth. *Merry-Go-Round: A Book about Nouns.* **1990. New York: Scholastic. Unp. Grades: 2–5.**

Throughout this rhyming enchanting text, nouns are defined, discovered, and explored. Colorful, realistic illustrations capture the eye and assure that the content is retained after the book is closed. Adding "s" to nouns to make plurals is easy, but readers are warned that it is not always that easy. Then all the exceptions are explained on pages that explode with color. This book is available in both video and audiocassette from Spoken Arts, New Rochelle, New York.

Heller, Ruth. *A Cache of Jewels and Other Collective Nouns.* **1998. New York: Putnam and Grosset. Unp. Grades: 2–5.**

Lush, imaginative illustrations and informative, engaging text help children learn this collection of collective nouns, such as herd, school, and fleet. Children delight in stumping adults as they demonstrate their knowledge of collective nouns. This book is available in both video and audiocassette from Spoken Arts, New Rochelle, New York.

Heller, Ruth. *Up, Up and Away: A Book about Adverbs.* **1991. New York: Scholastic. Unp. Grades: 2–5.**

Lively, festive illustrations include decently dressed penguins, a recently painted house, and a rather corpulent cat. Adverbs are needed to answer questions, such as how, how often, when, and where. Not only does the book teach students to identify adverbs, it also teaches the correct placement of adverbs when answering when and where. For example, to tell when a ship will sail it is "away today" rather than "today away."

Heller, Ruth. *Behind the Mask: A Book about Prepositions.* 1995. New York: Putnam and Grosset. Unp. Grades: 2–5.

Heller's carefully chosen words assure that the rules of grammar are not only understandable, they are memorable. Fanciful illustrations of far away and long ago place images in the readers' minds that assure the rules for using prepositions are retained and considered when writing and speaking.

Heller, Ruth. *Mine All Mine: A Book about Pronouns.* 1997. New York: Putnam and Grosset. Unp. Grades: 2–5.

To assist readers as they learn pronouns, they are written in bold, blue text throughout the book. This assures that readers focus on the words being described in the text. Everyday childhood experiences and pleasures are used to illustrate the rhyming text. The importance of pronouns in our language is demonstrated by rewriting the nursery rhyme, Old King Cole, without pronouns. The wordy, awkward, text destroys the rhythm of the rhyme and has the reader repeating the rhyme with the pronouns.

Heller, Ruth. *Fantastic! Wow! and Unreal!: A Book about Interjections and Conjunctions.* 1998. New York: Putnam. Unp. Grades: 2–5.

Interjections are lively action-packed words, but conjunctions are rather bland. However, Heller manages to make learning about both interjections and conjunctions a lively endeavor. Rhyming text and vibrant illustrations hold readers' attention as they learn all about these parts of speech and how to properly use them.

EXPLORATIONS

1. After sharing *Elephants Aloft* (Appelt, 1993) with the students, have them demonstrate the prepositions. For example, they could put their books "in" their desk or they could walk "out" the door.
2. After reading *A Mink, a Fink, a Skating Rink: What Is a Noun?* (Cleary, 1999), have students name nouns in the room in alphabetical order. For example, A is the right angle formed by the corners of the blackboard, B is the blackboard. When they come to a letter they cannot find a noun to represent, they ask two students next to them for help. If all three cannot find a noun that begins with that letter, they go on to the next letter in the alphabet.
3. Prior to reading *Hairy, Scary, Ordinary: What Is an Adjective?* (Cleary, 1999), provide children with an assortment of fresh fruits and vegetables to nibble, such as celery, apple, carrot, grape, and banana. As they eat the fruits and vegetables have them write down what they hear, see, smell, and taste. Read the book and have the children listen to hear if any of the words they wrote down are in the book. Help them to see that the words they wrote down to describe the fruits and vegetables are adjectives. Then have

them write phrases or sentences to describe what they tasted using descriptive adjectives.

4. Prior to reading *Kites Sail High: A Book about Verbs* (Heller, 1988), have students observe the classroom pet or their own pet and make a list of the pet's actions. For example, our classroom gerbil eats, runs, and tears paper.

5. After reading *Kites Sail High: A Book about Verbs* (Heller, 1988), have students pantomime the active verbs mentioned in the book. Then have them pantomime other active verbs and have their classmates guess what they are doing.

6. Prior to reading *Many Luscious Lollipops: A Book about Adjectives* (Heller, 1989), have students close their eyes and visualize a plain sugar cookie. Tell them to add pink icing to the cookie they have visualized. Then tell them to make the cookie larger. Have them open their eyes and write on the board "large, pink, sugar cookie." Continue this with other nouns and adjectives to help the students understand how adjectives describe nouns.

7. After reading *Many Luscious Lollipops: A Book about Adjectives* (Heller, 1989), have students work with a partner to find adjectives in trade books in the classroom. Tell the students to write down the adjectives and the nouns they describe on a sheet of paper. At the end of the lesson ask the students to share the most descriptive phrases they found.

8. After reading *Merry-Go-Round: A Book about Nouns* (Heller, 1990), have students brainstorm a lists of nouns. Write the nouns down in two columns on the blackboard or the overhead projector. Then, ask the students to select one noun from each column and compare them using similes.

9. Prior to reading *Up, Up and Away: A Book about Adverbs* (Heller, 1991), divide the class into small groups and give each group a list of adverbs. Then have the students think of synonyms and antonyms of the words. For example, a synonym for "quickly" could be "fast" and an antonym could be "slowly."

10. After reading *Up, Up and Away: A Book about Adverbs* (Heller, 1991), divide the class into two groups and line them up side by side. One group is the adverbs and the other group is the verbs. The first person in the verb group says a verb and the first person in the adverb group qualifies the verb with an adverb. For example, the verb is "smiles" and the adverb could be "sweetly." If a student gets stuck thinking of a verb or adverb, they can get assistance from a student next to them.

11. After reading *Behind the Mask: A Book about Prepositions* (Heller, 1995) aloud to the students, have them use the text to participate in choral readings. Provide pairs of students with copies of the words from a two-page spread in the book. Have one student read only the prepositions and the other student read the other text.

12. After reading *Behind the Mask: A Book about Prepositions* (Heller, 1995), have students work in groups and examine books in the classroom to find sentences containing prepositions. Have the students write the sentences on poster board to display in the classroom.

13. After reading *Mine All Mine: A Book about Pronouns* (Heller, 1997), have the students rewrite familiar nursery rhymes replacing the pronouns with the correct nouns. Besides Old King Cole, students can rewrite Little Bo Peep, Little Tommy Tucker, Old Mother Hubbard, and I'm a Little Teapot. Once they have the nursery rhymes rewritten, allow them to recite them for their classmates. Then have their classmates recite them with the pronouns. Challenge students to find other nursery rhymes to rewrite and recite.

14. Read *Fantastic! Wow! and Unreal!: A Book about Interjections and Conjunctions* (Heller, 1998) aloud to the students. Discuss the interjections and conjunctions found in the book. Read the book again and give the students a blue card to hold up when they hear an interjection and a yellow card to hold up when they hear a conjunction.

15. After reading *Fantastic! Wow! and Unreal!: A Book about Interjections and Conjunctions* (Heller, 1998), have students search books in the classroom library to find interjections and conjunctions. Hang chart paper on the wall for them to write down the interjections and conjunctions they find.

WORD PLAY

Word play furnishes students opportunities to play and explore the English language in order to understand how language works. The knowledge of words gained from word play enables students to enhance their writing and speaking skills. Word play shows students that words can have more than one meaning and hence, how sentences can have more than one meaning. The fun, playful books in this section offer students opportunities to play with words. Once they become familiar with these books students want to share them with everyone they know.

To fully comprehend what they read, students need to know both the literal and figurative definitions of words. To understand idioms they need to know the figurative meanings of the words. Exploring figurative language helps students to master it, so they can use it in their writing and speaking. Using metaphors and similes in their writing enables students to expand their thought processes and makes their writing more interesting. Metaphors and similes afford students a means to communicate and express abstract thoughts and feelings.

As students participate in the explorations of the books in this section they are developing the language skills addressed in content standards five and six. Content standard five focuses on the development of a range of strategies for written communication. Content standard six has students applying their knowledge of figurative language to create, critique, and discuss a variety of texts.

BOOK AND MEDIA CHOICES

Capucilli, Alyssa Satin. *Inside a Barn in the Country: A Rebus Read-Along Story*. Illustrated by Tedd Arnold. 1995. New York: Scholastic. Unp. Grades: P–1.

This cumulative tale uses both words and pictures to tell of the experiences of barnyard animals, one night in the country, when the cat is awakened by a mouse's squeak. The left side of each two-page spread uses both words and pictures for the cumulative refrain and the right side uses just words to introduce the new idea.

Degen, Bruce. *Sailaway Home*. 2000. New York: HarperFestival/HarperCollins. Unp. Grades: P–1.

The whimsical, lyrical text tells of the adventures of a fantasizing young pig as he sails, runs, skips, and flies, always returning home. Young children delight in the playful language and want to join in to recite the book with the teacher or librarian.

Yoon, Jung-Huyn. *Popposites: A Lift, Pull, and Pop Book of Opposites*. 1996. New York: DK. Unp. Grades: P–1.

Learning opposites is great fun as young readers lift, pull, and flip to discover what lies beneath and inside. This interactive book actively involves the readers in their learning. Colorful photographs of young children and everyday objects assures that readers make connections between the concepts presented in the book and their everyday experiences.

Swinburne, Stephen R. *What's Opposite?* 2000. Honesdale, PA. Boyds Mill Press. Unp. Grades: P–1.

After a definition and explanation of opposites, bright, colorful pictures of a multicultural collection of children and familiar objects show exactly what is meant by opposites. For example, there is a photograph of whole, round, ripe red tomatoes and a photograph of flat, smashed tomatoes.

McMillan, Bruce. *Play Day: A Book of Terse Verse*. 1991. New York: Holiday House. Unp. Grades: P–1.

Fourteen two-word rhymes are shown with 14 color photographs of two-year-olds acting out the rhymes. The rhymes are fun combinations such as "brown crown" and "goat boat." The writer/photographer used friends as subjects of his photographs and took the pictures in the backyard of a neighbor. He explains the concept of this photographic essay in comments at the end of the book.

Schwartz, Alvin. *Busy Buzzing Bumblebees and Other Tongue Twisters*. Illustrated by Paul Meisel. 1992. New York: HarperTrophy/HarperCollins. 64p. Grades: P–1.

Forty-six tangling tongue twisters are included in this fun-to-share book. These silly tongue twisters are accompanied by equally silly cartoon-like illustrations. This I Can Read Book is a hit with young readers, who delight in twisting their tongues.

Ziefert, Harriet. *What Rhymes with Eel?* Illustrated by Rick Brown. 1996. New York: Penguin Books. Unp. Grades: P–1.

Young children delight in word play with rhyming words and this is a fun book to share with them. Each page features two flaps; one reveals a picture and the other a word. Lift the "c" from the word carrot to reveal the word parrot. Lifting the flap with the illustration of the carrot reveals a parrot. Observant readers notice that the end of the carrot extends over the edge of the flap and helps to form the tail of the parrot. Readers delight in guessing what is under the flap and what part of the objects are shared between the two illustrations.

Edwards, Pamela Duncan. *Clara Caterpillar.* Illustrated by Henry Cole. 2001. New York: HarperCollins. Unp. Grades: P–1.

This alliterative adventure follows a caterpillar from egg to butterfly. In this clever look at the life of a caterpillar students learn not only about the life cycle, but the importance of camouflage, and most importantly about the bonds of friendship.

Edwards, Pamela Duncan. *Some Smug Slug.* Illustrated by Henry Cole. 1996. New York: HarperCollins. 32p. Grades: P–3.

A rather smug, unsuspecting slug slithers up a suspicious slope in the garden. Oblivious to the warnings from other animals in the garden, he continues to climb leaving behind a slimy trail. Young readers enjoy guessing what the slug is climbing and how the book will end. This witty garden adventure is a fun way to explore alliteration.

Steig, William. *CDB!* 2000. New York: Simon & Schuster. Unp. Grades: P–3.

This updated version of a favorite classic has larger pages and the black-and-white illustrations have been enhanced with watercolor splashes. The pictures help readers decipher the letter codes; however, if all else fails the answers are in the back of the book.

***Rhythm in My Shoes.* 2000. CD. Cambridge, Mass.: Rounder Records. Grades: P–4.**

Word play, tongue twisters, and chants combine with lively rhythms to make this a rollicking CD. Students enjoy listening to this one over and over again as they try out the tongue twisters and chants.

Collins, Beverly, and Stephanie Calmenson, compilers. *Six Sick Sheep: One Hundred One Tongue Twisters.* Illustrated by Alan Tiegreen. 1993. New York: William Morrow. 64p. Grades: K–2.

This hilarious collection of tongue twisters includes some that are only one sentence and others that tell an entire story. Some of them repeat the same word several times and what makes them fun is that the repeated words have more than one meaning. The comical black line illustrations add to the fun. The book includes suggestions for finding more tongue twisters and an index of key phrases.

Most, Bernard. *Pets in Trumpets and Other Word-Play Riddles.* 1991. San Diego, Calif.: Harcourt Brace Jovanovich. Unp. Grades: K–2.

Large-print, colorful illustrations, and clever riddles assure that this book is one students want to read on their own again and again. The answer to the riddle is hidden in the word written in large, bold text. Students want to carefully examine the word to find the hidden answer prior to turning the page and having the answer revealed.

Capucilli, Alyssa Satin. *Inside a Zoo in the City: A Rebus Read-Along Story.* Illustrated by Tedd Arnold. 2000. New York: Scholastic. Unp. Grades: K–2.

This cumulative, rhyming tale contains rebuses that encourage young readers to read along. As the animals wake in the morning they make their way to the zoo and wake the zookeeper, so they can return to their cages before their visitors arrive.

Hoban, Tana. *Exactly the Opposite.* 1990. New York: Mulberry Books/William Morrow. Unp. Grades: K–3.

This wordless picture book of opposites lets children supply the words. Many pictures represent more than one opposite. For example, on the left-hand page a sheep is facing the reader and lying down on the ground. On the right-hand page the sheep is facing away from the reader and standing up.

Christensen, Bonnie. *Rebus Riot.* 1997. New York: Dial Books for Young Readers. Unp. Grades: K–3.

Some of the words in this collection of rhymes have been replaced by pictures forming a rebus. The pictures and the words they represent are at the bottom of the page or on the opposite page. Figuring out what words some of the illustrations represent can be a little tricky, so it is handy to have the answers nearby. Young and old enjoy reading and listening to the rhymes.

***Kid Works Deluxe.* 1999. Mac/Win. Torrance, Calif.: Davidson and Associates. Grades: K–6.**

Students enjoy writing their stories using this software program because when they finish, the computer reads their story back to them. They can select from several different voices. With a microphone attached to the computer, students can record their own voice. Also with the click of the mouse they can turn a word in the story into a graphic icon.

Imagination Express, Destination: Neighborhood. 1995. Mac/Win. Redmond, Wash.: Edmark. Grades: K–6.

Students enjoy using this creative software to write stories about their neighborhood. They can write multimedia stories about their neighborhood and include narration and music. This is one of the Imagination Express series.

Laden, Nina. *Bad Dog*. 2000. New York: Walker and Company. Unp. Grades: K and up.

Children of all ages delight in this story of a dog's misadventures as he sets out to find free-range chicken. Young children enjoy the silly story. Older readers appreciate the homage paid to Jack Kerouac and Jack London. Elementary and middle school readers delight in finding the puns properly peppered throughout the story.

Nikola-Lisa, W. *Tangletalk*. Illustrated by Jessica Clerk. 1997. New York: Dutton Children's Books. Unp. Grades: 1–3.

This delightfully convoluted tale is told in rhyme. From the city of May to the month of Boston, every tangled couplet brings forth giggles. Students delight in finding the mixed-up words and pictures and discussing how to correct them. The illustrations of a time long ago make the nonsensical tale believable.

Terban, Marvin. *Punching the Clock: Funny Action Idioms*. Illustrated by Tom Huffman. 1990. New York: Clarion Books. 64p. Grades: 2–5.

Terban takes everyday English language terms and makes them both fascinating and humorous. Action idioms such as "Kick the habit," "Hit the road," and "Tackle the job" show how certain words used together have a special meaning. The illustrations are comical in their interpretation of the action. Idioms are particularly difficult for students who speak English as a second language to understand, because they cannot be taken literally. These students particularly appreciate books that help them learn American idioms. The book ends with a list of the idioms and a bibliography.

Terban, Marvin. *Funny You Should Ask: How to Make Up Jokes with Word Play*. Illustrated by John O'Brien. 1992. New York: Clarion Books. 64p. Grades: 2–5.

Children love to read jokes, tell jokes, and make up jokes. Terban shows them how to turn homographs, homophones, homonyms, and idioms into jokes and riddles. He provides information on what makes a good joke or riddle. O'Brien's illustrations are humorous and appropriate.

Lester, Julius. *Ackamarackus: Julius Lester's Sumptuously Silly Fantastically Funny Fables*. Illustrated by Emilie Chollat. 2001. New York: Scholastic. Unp. Grades: 2–5.

Alliteration and word play make these six original fables fun to read aloud again and again. In the midst of the fun students learn important lessons about accepting others and respecting individuality. Lester challenges readers to look at their world from a different perspective, to think about the fact that an ant in their shoe might actually be trying it on for size.

Frasier, Debra. *Miss Alaineus: A Vocabulary Disaster*. 2000. San Diego, Calif.: Harcourt Brace. Unp. Grades: 3–5.

Being homesick and having to obtain vocabulary words over the telephone from a classmate leads to a comical misunderstanding of the spelling and definition of "miscellaneous." However, Sage manages to turn the disaster into an opportunity to poke fun at herself and shows readers how to gracefully turn a mistake into a learning experience when she shows up for the Vocabulary Parade as "Miss Alaineus, Queen of all Miscellaneous Things." The book is filled with ideas for learning vocabulary words and the endpapers have a word-find puzzle.

Agee, Jon. *Elvis Lives!: And Other Anagrams*. 2000. New York: Farrar Straus Giroux. Unp. Grades: 4 and up.

Take a word, a phrase, or a sentence and use the letters to write another word, phrase or a sentence and that is an anagram. Students chuckle as they read the witty letter combinations and illustrations found within the pages of this book. The book concludes with information about the origins of some of the anagrams and a bibliography.

Agee, Jon. *So Many Dynamos! and Other Palindromes*. 1994. New York: Farrar Straus Giroux. Unp. Grades: 4 and up.

Cartoon black-and-white drawings illustrate this collection of marvelous, amusing reversible phrases and sentences. Carefully examining the drawings reveals clever, funny details just waiting to be discovered.

Agee, Jon. *Sit on a Potato Pan, Otis! More Palindromes*. 1999. New York: Farrar Straus Giroux. Unp. Grades: 4 and up.

Weird, wacky cartoon drawings illustrate these amazing phrases and sentences. Students find themselves reading the phrases and sentences backwards because it is hard to believe they read the same in both directions.

Agee, Jon. *Who Ordered the Jumbo Shrimp? and Other Oxymorons*. 1998. New York: HarperCollins. Unp. Grades: 4 and up.

Clever line drawings deftly portray the juxtaposition of the words and their meanings. This collection of oxymorons pokes fun at the English language and makes readers wonder why the oxymorons were not noticed before. Smiles and chuckles escape from readers as they explore the pages of the book.

Lederer, Richard. *Pun and Games: Jokes, Riddles, Daffynitions, Tairy Fales, Rhymes, and More Wordplay for Kids.* Illustrated by Dave Morice. 1996. Chicago: Chicago Review Press. 101p. Grades: 5 and up.

Students enjoy sharing the silly wordplay found in this book with friends, teachers, parents, and anyone else who will listen. The chapters contain examples of the wordplay, answers, and ideas for students to write their own to stump their friends.

EXPLORATIONS

1. After reading *Inside a Barn in the Country: A Rebus Read-Along Story* (Capucilli, 1995), have students work in small groups to retell the story using Popsicle stick puppets.

2. After sharing *Popposites: A Lift, Pull, and Pop Book of Opposites* (Yoon, 1996) or *Exactly the Opposite* (Hoban, 1990) with the students, place the book in a center with manipulatives for students to explore opposites on their own. For example, a box of blocks could be used for in and out and if the box has a lid it could also be used for open and closed.

3. *Busy Buzzing Bumblebees and Other Tongue Twisters* (Schwartz, 1992) is just the book for using in a tongue twister bee. Students can see who can say the verses the fastest without making a mistake.

4. After reading *Play Day: A Book of Terse Verse* (McMillan, 1991) and showing the children the pictures, have them look around the room to find pairs of rhymes. For example, a wooden block and a sock would be block/sock.

5. Reading aloud books such as *What Rhymes with Eel?* (Ziefert, 1996) shows children not only what words rhyme, but that rhyming words can be fun. After reading the book aloud, have the students come up with their own rhyming words. At first be willing to accept non-words that rhyme with real words.

6. After reading *CDB!* (Steig, 2000), provide children an opportunity to work with a partner to create their own letter codes to stump their classmates.

7. While reading *Pets in Trumpets and Other Word-Play Riddles* (Most, 1991), demonstrate how the small words are part of the large words. One way to do this is to write the word in large letters on tagboard. Then cut the word into parts, so that the small word can be held up by itself.

8. Reading aloud books like *Pets in Trumpets and Other Word-Play Riddles* (Most, 1991) helps develop students' vocabularies as they discover the humor and word play in the riddles. Students can work in small groups to create their own word play riddles to share with their classmates.

9. After reading *Inside a Zoo in the City: A Rebus Read-Along Story* (Capucilli, 2000), have students retell the story using zoo animal puppets or stuffed animals.

10. After reading *Rebus Riot* (Christensen, 1997) to the students, have them use KidWorks Deluxe software to write their own rebus stories. This software changes words to pictures with the click of the mouse. Have the students print out two versions of the story—one with the words and one with the pictures. These books can also be saved on the

computer to share with their classmates. KidWorks Deluxe also reads aloud the words the students write.

11. While reading aloud *Bad Dog* (Laden, 2000), have students jot down the puns they hear. When finished reading, go back through the book and see if they discovered all of the puns.

12. Students can correct the mixed-up words and pictures in *Tangletalk* (Nikola-Lisa, 1997) by writing their corrections on sticky notes and placing them over the mixed-up words and pictures.

13. Students can create their own version of tangled talk using familiar nursery rhymes. For example, Old Mother Cupboard went to the hubbard, to fetch her poor bone a dog.

14. After reading *Punching the Clock: Funny Action Idioms* (Terban, 1990), have students create their own illustrations for the idioms. Give each child a piece of drawing paper and have them fold it in half. At the top of the paper, they write the idiom they have decided to illustrate. On the left side of the paper they draw the literal interpretation of the idiom and on the right side of the paper they draw the actual interpretation of the idiom.

15. Joke and riddle books are among the most circulated books in a library. Students enjoy reading the books and sharing the jokes and riddles with anyone who will listen. *Funny You Should Ask: How to Make Up Jokes with Word Play* (Terban, 1992) includes instructions for creating jokes and riddles. Students can write and illustrate jokes and riddles to share with their classmates.

16. Prior to reading *Ackamarackus: Julius Lester's Sumptuously Silly Fantastically Funny Fables* (Lester, 2001), tell the students to listen for the alliteration and wordplay found throughout the fables. After reading a fable discuss the alliteration and wordplay in the fable.

17. After reading *Ackamarackus: Julius Lester's Sumptuously Silly Fantastically Funny Fables* (Lester, 2001), challenge students to look at everyday things with a slightly different perspective and to imagine what would happen if things were different.

18. At the end of *Elvis Lives!: And Other Anagrams* (Agee, 2000) the author gives thanks to the people who have shared anagrams with him. Have the students share some of the anagrams with their parents and friends and then see if they know or can think of some other anagrams. Create an anagram wall in the classroom for students to write down ones they collect or create.

19. After reading *So Many Dynamos! and Other Palindromes* (Agee, 1994) and *Sit on a Potato Pan, Otis! More Palindromes* (Agee, 1999) children want to try to write their own palindromes. Usually they quickly discover that this is a difficult task. They may want to create original drawings to illustrate the palindromes.

20. Whereas creating palindromes is somewhat difficult, students find thinking up oxymorons somewhat easier. Sharing *Who Ordered the Jumbo Shrimp? and Other Oxymorons* (Agee, 1998) with students starts them thinking about oxymorons and soon

they are creating their own. Have them write their oxymorons on drawing paper and illustrate them to hang in the classroom. Students may want to work on this project with a partner.

21. After reading *Pun and Games: Jokes, Riddles, Daffynitions, Tairy Fales, Rhymes, and More Wordplay for Kids* (Lederer, 1996), provide students space on a classroom wall to post their own wordplay creations with space beneath for their classmates to make comments and provide answers.

WRITING

Books and media in this section look at writing from different perspectives, but all focus on writing for authentic purposes. In these materials are ideas for writing and models to show students how to write. Students may dread writing, but books, videos, and software programs make writing fun. Having their writing published and placed in the class library gives students both a purpose and an audience for their writing. Teachers who save student-created books from year to year find that these books continue to be favorites with each new class of students. Having a writing center in the classroom near a reading center encourages young authors to write and to model their writing after the writing of their favorite authors.

As students develop their writing skills they meet content standards four, five, seven, eight, and twelve. Standards four and five address using the writing process for effective communication to a variety of audiences for a variety of purposes. Standards seven and eight concern using both print and electronic formats for research and communicating their findings to an audience. Standard twelve involves using language for learning and the exchange of information.

BOOK AND MEDIA CHOICES

Selway, Martina. *Don't Forget to Write*. 1992. Nashville, Tenn.: Ideals Children's Books. Unp. Grades: P–2.

While visiting her grandfather, Rosie starts a letter home telling her mother that she wants to go home. She adds to the letter each day as she describes her activities. On each page of her letter she seems less and less anxious to return home and by the end of the week she begs to stay longer. Pastel-colored illustrations depict her daily adventures with her grandfather.

Day, Alexandra, and Cooper Edens. *Special Deliveries*. Illustrated by Alexandra Day. 2001. New York: HarperCollins. Unp. Grades: P–2.

Lavish, detailed pictures with sparse text tell the story of a mother, her daughters, and their farm pets who all take over a rural mail route when the mailman retires. When they realize that some of the people on their route receive little mail, the family writes letters to deliver to them. Not only are the mother and daughters involved in the mail delivery and letter writing, so are their farm pets.

Rylant, Cynthia. *The Wonderful Happens*. Illustrated by Coco Dowley. 2000. New York: Simon and Schuster Books for Young Readers. Unp. Grades: P–3.

The simple things in life can bring us the most pleasure and fill our lives with wonder. Flying birds, blooming flowers, sleeping squirrels, and growing children are just a few of the many things celebrated in the pages of this book. Large-print text makes this a book children return to again and again to read on their own.

Poydar, Nancy. *Mailbox Magic*. 2000. New York: Holiday House. Unp. Grades: P–3.

Letters and packages seem to magically appear in Will's mailbox; however, none of them are for him. One morning he notices on his cereal box that if he sends in three box labels he can get his very own personalized cereal bowl. He enlists the help of his family, friends, and even the mailman to get the cereal eaten as he saves his box labels. He drops the labels in the mail and eventually the bowl arrives. At the end of the book is a brief description of how to address and mail an envelope.

Cronin, Doreen. *Click, Clack, Moo: Cows That Type*. Illustrated by Betsy Lewin. 2000. New York: Simon and Schuster Books for Young Readers. Unp. Grades: K–2.

The power of the written word and the art of negotiation are demonstrated in this hilarious book. Farmer Brown's cows and chickens type up their demands for electric blankets and then go on strike when their requests are ignored. A neutral party, one of Farmer Brown's ducks, steps into resolve the standoff. Bold, watercolor washes and brushed black lines are used to illustrate this clever tale. This book won a Caldecott Honor Award.

Kidspiration. 2000. Mac/Win. Portland, Ore.: Inspiration Software. Grades: K–3.

This amazing concept-mapping software allows students to easily organize information and re-organize the information as they learn more on a topic. Adding colors and graphics to the concept maps aids retention of the material. This software is part of the Inspiration Products series.

Ahlberg, Janet, and Allan Ahlberg. *The Jolly Pocket Postman*. 1995. Boston: Little, Brown. Unp. Grades: K–3.

The Jolly Postman's travels continue as he delivers letters to storybook characters. Children who are familiar with *The Jolly Postman or Other People's Letters* (Ahlberg and Ahlberg, 1986) and *The Jolly Christmas Postman* (Ahlberg and Ahlberg, 1991) enjoy trying to figure out where they have previously met this collection of characters. In this adventure, a series of mishaps befall the postman and leave him wondering if it was all just a dream. The rhyming verse adds to the fun of reading this story aloud.

Leedy, Loreen. *Messages in the Mailbox: How to Write a Letter*. 1991. New York: Holiday House. Unp. Grades: K–4.

A class of friendly critters discovers that one way to receive letters is to send them. This book goes beyond the friendly letter and the business letter to include a thank you note, a fan letter, a letter of complaint, a note of apology, a sympathy note, and others. Simple, easy-to-emulate models of the different types of letters are included. The parts of the letter and the return address are labeled to assure students learn the correct terminology.

Leedy, Loreen. *The Furry News: How to Make a Newspaper*. 1990. New York: Holiday House. Unp. Grades: 1–4.

Realizing that their news is not in the local newspaper, a charming group of animals decide to start their own newspaper. The very basics of newspaper reporting, editorial chores, and the different sections of the newspaper are explained as the animals receive their assignments. At the end of the book are instructions for creating a newspaper and a glossary of newspaper terms. The cartoon-like illustrations are popular with young children.

Burkholder, Kelly. *Diaries and Journals*. 2001. Vero Beach, Fla.: Rourke Press. 24p. Grades: 1–4.

Beginning with a definition of a diary, this book quickly moves on to describe different types of diaries and how to get started keeping one. For example, it explains how to keep a travel diary about a trip. It also suggests using a diary to collect creative ideas and writing down feelings. At the end of the book is a glossary, an index, and a list of Web sites. This is one of the Artistic Adventures series.

etStorybook Weaver Deluxe. 1997. Mac/Win. Minneapolis, Minn.: The Learning Company. Grades: 1–6.

This open-ended program encourages students to write and illustrate stories to share with their classmates. The program includes a dictionary, a thesaurus, graphic images, a paint program, and a text-to-speech option. Even reluctant writers are willing to write when they have the opportunity to do so with this program.

Stevens, Janet. *From Pictures to Words: A Book About Making a Book.* 1995. New York: Holiday House. Unp. Grades: 2–4.

This clever book illustrated with both black-and-white, as well as color illustrations, describes how to make a book from scratch. Aided by a bothersome collection of imaginary animals, each wanting to be included in the book, the author chooses characters, selects a setting, decides on a plot, and prepares a dummy book with illustration ideas. Polishing and making changes in the book is the last thing the author does before submitting the book to a publisher. Children respond positively to this simple how-to book helped by Stevens' imaginary animals.

Dragonwagon, Crescent. *Home Place.* Illustrated by Jerry Pinkney. 1990. New York: Macmillan. Unp. Grades: 2–5.

On a walk through the woods a family comes upon an abandoned homestead. They comb the yard to look for clues about the family who once lived there. They listen for the voices of the departed family and hear their conversations. Jerry Pinkney's rich, evocative drawings bring to life the family who might have lived in the abandoned homestead. Readers see how the author and illustrator used their imaginations to create a portrait of a family. This provides students with a model for their own creative writing endeavors based on a stimulus from their experiences.

Terban, Marvin. *It Figures!: Fun Figures of Speech.* Illustrated by Giulio Maestro. 1993. New York: Clarion Books. 63p. Grades: 2–6.

Figures of speech furnish writers with words that paint pictures in the minds of their readers. Simile, metaphor, onomatopoeia, alliteration, hyperbole, and personification are all defined and explained in this slim book. Examples of each are given, as well as instructions on how students can create their own. Information is also presented on how to use figures of speech effectively in writing.

***Write, Camera, Action!* 1996. Mac/Win. Novato, Calif.: Brøderbund Software. Grades: 3–6.**

With this program students write a film script and then see it acted out on the computer screen. Once the film is completed students are then responsible for creating press releases, news stories, and posters to publicize their films. This is one of the Active Mind series of software programs.

Bowen, Gary. *Stranded at Plimoth Plantation 1626.* 1994. New York: HarperCollins. 82p. Grades: 3–6.

In this journal, thirteen-year-old orphan Christopher Sears recounts his year at Plimoth Plantation. After thorough research and numerous visits to Plimoth Plantation Gary Bowen created this narrative of life in the New World. Poignant, brief entries provide fascinating reading and furnish intimate details of day-to-day living. Strong, colorful, detailed woodcuts are interspersed throughout the journal entries.

Parts of a Story. 2000. Video. Chicago: CLEARVUE/eau. 20 min. Grades: 4–6.

This video compares story writing to building a house. It introduces the parts of a story using movie clips with voiceovers. It describes character, setting, plot, and theme to writers and encourages them to use higher-order thinking skills.

Microsoft Publisher. 2000. Mac/Win. Redmond, Wash.: Microsoft Corporation. Grades: 4 and up.

This software program has a collection of templates for creating newspapers. Students simply click and type to add their stories. A selection of clip art is available and it is easy to import pictures into the templates. Students also enjoy creating flyers and brochures using this program.

Ringgold, Faith, Linda Freeman, and Nancy Roucher. *Talking to Faith Ringgold*. 1996. New York: Crown. 48p. Grades: 4 and up.

Questions interspersed throughout this autobiography encourage readers to reflect on their own life experiences and respond to those reflections as they read. Encouraging students to reflect and discuss, then write as they read this book, assures that they gain a deep understanding of the life of this noted African American and of their own lives.

Diary Maker. 1997. Mac/Win. New York: Scholastic. Grades: 4 and up.

Included in this software is a wonderful presentation of Anne Frank's Diary. Students use this software to write their own diary entries selecting from a variety of backgrounds for the pages of their diary. This software easily lends itself to a variety of creative writing projects.

EXPLORATIONS

1. After reading *Don't Forget to Write* (Selway, 1992), look back in the letters with the students to determine which phrases and words show that the main character is gradually becoming accustomed to being away from home.
2. *Don't Forget to Write* (Selway, 1992) can also be used to teach children sequence of events. The teacher can write down the events in the story and display them in a pocket chart in mixed-up order. As the story is read, the teacher stops and has the students put the sentence strips in order.

3. After reading *The Wonderful Happens* (Rylant, 2000), have students create their own celebrations of wonder by reflecting on important things in their lives. They may need a few minutes to quietly look around and to think about wondrous things in their lives.

4. After students read *Messages in the Mailbox: How to Write a Letter* (Leedy, 1991), have them write fan letters to a musician or movie star asking for an autographed picture. As the pictures begin arriving in the classroom, provide space to display them.

5. Prior to reading *The Jolly Postman or Other People's Letters* (Ahlberg and Ahlberg, 1986), *The Jolly Christmas Postman* (Ahlberg and Ahlberg, 1991), or *The Jolly Pocket Postman* (Ahlberg and Ahlberg, 1995), ask the children about the nursery rhymes mentioned in each book.

6. After reading *The Jolly Pocket Postman* (Ahlberg and Ahlberg, 1995), have the students go back to the book to look for cause-and-effect relationships.

7. After reading *The Jolly Pocket Postman* (Ahlberg and Ahlberg, 1995), students can create their own versions with other nursery rhymes. Or have the students create a holiday version based on *The Jolly Christmas Postman* (Ahlberg and Ahlberg, 1991).

8. After reading *The Furry News: How to Make a Newspaper* (Leedy, 1990), have students follow the instructions at the end of the book for creating a newspaper. If there is a computer available, software programs such as Classroom Newspaper Workshop or Microsoft Publisher simplify the process of making a newspaper. Students can create a classroom newspaper to tell their parents about what they learned in school. A feature story in the newspaper could focus on one child in the classroom each week.

9. In *Diaries and Journals* (Burkholder, 2001), the author suggests students keep a diary for collecting creative ideas and writing down feelings. These ideas and notes can be used as students write (Apol and Harris, 1999). Word-processing programs such as AppleWorks simplify the writing process and motivate children to write.

10. *Diaries and Journals* (Burkholder, 2001) explains to students how to keep a diary or a journal. Diary Maker software adds to the fun of keeping journals and students can save their journal entries on the computer or print them out.

11. Prior to reading *From Pictures to Words: A Book about Making a Book* (Stevens, 1995), have students bring in their stuffed animals. Create a space in the room to display them. Read the book aloud to the students and return to the book for writing instructions and ideas as the students begin writing their own stories selecting from the collection of stuffed animals in the room. Students can make electronic books using Imagination Express, Destination: Neighborhood that includes options for adding sounds and animation.

12. After reading *Home Place* (Dragonwagon, 1990), have students discuss how the author and illustrator used their imaginations to make up a family who might have lived in the abandoned homestead. On chart paper write down the characters who appear in the story. Read the book again showing the students the pictures of the characters. After reading about each character, have the students take turns recording information about the character on the chart paper. Then using the notes on the chart paper, write a class

story about the family. Modeling the writing process facilitates children writing stories on their own.

13. After reading *Home Place* (Dragonwagon, 1990), discuss the importance of setting in stories. The setting provides a location in time and place, as well as a geographical and historical background for the story. Have the students examine the illustrations in the book and describe the setting.

14. After reading each chapter in *It Figures!: Fun Figures of Speech* (Terban, 1993), have students think up their own figures of speech. Have them write and illustrate their figures of speech on drawing paper. Or have the students write and illustrate their figures of speech in a class HyperStudio stack.

15. Share diary entries from *Stranded at Plimoth Plantation 1626* (Bowen, 1994) with the students. Help them to search the entries for interesting ideas that they can use as models as they write in their own diaries.

16. *Stranded at Plimoth Plantation 1626* (Bowen, 1994) furnishes a model for students to use as they create their own journal entries. Students can prepare weekly journal entries about classroom activities for a classroom journal. At the end of the year students can read the journal to reflect on what they learned. At the beginning of the next year the teacher's new students will enjoy reading the journal as a preview of things to come.

17. While reading *Talking to Faith Ringgold* (Ringgold, Freeman, and Roucher, 1996), have students respond to the questions written throughout the book. Compile their artwork and written reflections into binders to create a personal recollection of their own lives. Students enjoy writing their reflections using Diary Maker software.

SPEAKING

Speaking and listening take up a large part of each day in classrooms; however, not much time is devoted to practicing speaking and listening. Students need direct instruction, guided practice, and independent practice to fully develop these skills. Discussions, readers' theater, puppet shows, storytelling, choral reading, oral reports, and dramatic readings are all ways to practice speaking and listening. This practice assures students develop their listening and speaking vocabularies. The materials in this section contain practical ideas and suggestions for developing speaking and listening skills.

Providing students opportunities to develop their speaking and listening skills assures that they are working towards the guidelines established by content standards four and twelve. These standards encompass using spoken language for effective communication with a variety of audiences for different purposes.

BOOK AND MEDIA CHOICES

Ross, Dave. *A Book of Hugs*. Illustrated by Laura Rader. 1999. New York: Harper Trophy. Unp. Grades: P–1.

Hugs are a very special form of communication. This book describes all sorts of different hugs and what they communicate. The charming animal characters with their unique hugs bring smiles to readers' faces. Ice cube hugs, hurt hugs, and one-arm hugs are just a few of the wonderful hugs included in the book.

Bruss, Deborah. *Book! Book! Book!* Illustrated by Tiphanie Beeke. 2001. New York: Arthur A. Levine Books. Unp. Grades: P–2.

What do farm animals do when they get bored? Well, the ones in this book head to town to check books out of the library. One by one the animals fail to get the librarian to understand what they want. Then the chicken clucks "Book! Book!" and the librarian lends her some books. The animals parade back to the farm and spend the rest of the afternoon reading their books. The story ends with a twist about why the frog did not read the books.

Crotty, K. M. *Dinosongs: Poems to Celebrate a T. Rex Named Sue*. Illustrated by Kurt Vargo. 2000. New York: Scholastic. Unp. Grades: K–2.

Sue is the largest and most complete Tyrannosaurus Rex fossil found to date. These delightful poems introduce young readers to her life and the world of dinosaurs. The book comes with a CD that features Susan Sarandon reading the poems with an accompanying musical score. Her expressive reading serves as a model for teaching students to read poems aloud for enjoyment.

Aliki. *Hello! Goodbye!* 1996. New York: Greenwillow Books. Unp. Grades: K–3.

"Hello" and "goodbye" are greetings that can be said in different words or with no words at all. For example, "howdy" and "yoo-hoo" can both mean "hello"; "farewell" and "so long" can both mean "goodbye." Additionally, waving or hugging someone can mean either hello or goodbye. Aliki tells young readers that sometimes "good-bye" means that someone is moving or has died and that those are difficult to say "goodbyes."

Aliki. *Communication*. 1999. New York: Mulberry Books. Unp. Grades: 1–3.

Communication involves telling, listening, and responding. We communicate through words, symbols, pictures, dancing, body language, and other methods. The book stresses the importance of communicating, even when things are difficult to say. The cartoon-like illustrations and the simple text make this a book children can read and understand on their own; however, it is also a book for adults to read and discuss with children.

Jenkins, Steve. *Slap, Squeak, and Scatter: How Animals Communicate*. 2001. Boston: HoughtonMifflin. Unp. Grades: 2–5.

Beautiful paper collage illustrations and brief, engaging text combine to create an intriguing book about how animals communicate. The text is organized by types of messages that animals send, such as mating signals, warning signals, and signals sent to locate their young.

Badt, Karin Luisa. *Greetings!* 1994. New York: Children's Press. 32p. Grades: 3–5.

Greetings are used around the world as people come and go. However, greetings are oftentimes culturally specific and a greeting that is considered polite in one culture might be considered impolite in another culture. For example, in the United States waving a hand is a friendly greeting meaning either "hello" or "goodbye," but in Scotland it is considered an insult. This book is a fascinating look at greetings in cultures around the world and contains photographs of people from different countries. The book concludes with a glossary and an index. It is part of the series, A World of Difference.

Otfinoski, Steven. *Speaking Up, Speaking Out: A Kid's Guide to Making Speeches, Oral Reports, and Conversations*. Illustrated by Carol Nicklaus. 1996. Brookfield, Conn.: The Millbrook Press. 79p. Grades: 5 and up.

Included in this book are chapters on speaking in social situations, reading aloud, overcoming stage fright, giving oral reports, and making speeches for different occasions. The introduction tells readers how speech is used to communicate and helps them understand how important it will be throughout their lives. Interspersed are thoughtful quotes from children on speaking. Black-and-white drawings accompany the text. The book concludes with a glossary, books for further reading, and an index.

EXPLORATIONS

1. Listening to the CD that accompanies *Dinosongs: Poems to Celebrate a T. Rex Named Sue* (Crotty, 2000) students hear the dramatic reading of the poems accompanied by music and sound effects. This serves as a model for students to use as they learn to read and recite poems with expression. Have students work with a partner to select one of the poems and practice reading it with expression.
2. *Hello! Goodbye!* (Aliki, 1996) contains a variety of words and phrases to convey hello and goodbye. This book introduces children to a variety of words that help to build their vocabulary. After reading the book, discuss social situations for using the different words as greetings.
3. After reading *Hello! Goodbye!* (Aliki, 1996), students can think up other words for which there are a variety of synonyms. For example, "eat" can be "chow down" and "look out" can be "heads up." Have students discuss situations where they would use one synonym rather than the other.

4. *Communication* (Aliki, 1999) encourages children to communicate even when it is difficult and words are hard to find. The book contains examples of situations when it is hard to communicate. One way to make communicating difficult things easier is to role-play the situations. Have two student volunteers role-play a communication situation, such as admitting a mistake was made.

5. *Communication* (Aliki, 1999) impresses on children the importance of good listening skills. Students spend a great deal of time in school listening and need to practice this important skill. One way to do this is to have the teacher read a paragraph from a storybook while the students write down what they heard. Then they can compare what they each wrote down.

6. To practice listening, the teacher can read a short story to the students and have them listen for certain words and hold up an index card when they hear them.

7. As evidenced in the book *Greetings!* (Badt, 1994), being able to appropriately greet people is a necessary social skill. Students need opportunities to role-play and practice using greetings in different social situations such as on the playground, in school, and in a store. Additionally, they may need help understanding that greetings they use with friends may not be appropriate for greeting adults.

8. After reading *Speaking Up, Speaking Out: A Kid's Guide to Making Speeches, Oral Reports, and Conversations* (Otfinoski, 1996), have students discuss how advertisers use persuasion. Then have them create a presentation to persuade their classmates to buy a popular game or toy.

9. Many schools begin the day with announcements over a central public address system. These announcements often go unheard. However, using a classroom crier (Norton and Norton, 1994) to make announcements would be more effective. Being the classroom crier gives students opportunities to practice public speaking and listening skills.

POETRY

Poetry activates senses as the words draw images, rekindle smells, create sounds, trigger the sense of touch, and make readers feel. The figurative language in poetry evokes the senses and causes readers to stop and feel the words. Imagery, personification, metaphor, rhyme, rhythm, repetition, alliteration, consonance, assonance, and onomatopoeia provide the lyrical, musical nature of poetry. Poetry creates a mood; a feeling that evokes responses in the reader in ways that prose does not. The language play of poetry can be shared through choral readings, dramatizations, and read-alouds.

Poetry is affirming; it connects to students' lives, and hence they are motivated to read and enjoy poetry (Grimes, 2000). Further, Grimes contends that poetry is portable. It can be memorized and carried with children in their minds. Sharing poetry with children helps them learn to look beyond the obvious to the possibilities that abound in their world (McClure et al., 1999). Students need exposure to a wide variety of poetry, so that they learn that it does not all rhyme, it is not all humorous, but that it can all be enjoyed. Students need opportunities to experience poetry prior to writing their own poems (Apol and Harris, 1999). Siemens (1996) starts her elementary students writing poetry on the first day of school and it is an activity that continues throughout the year.

Hulme, Joy N., and Donna W. Guthrie. *How to Write, Recite, and Delight In All Kinds of Poetry*. 1996. Brookfield, Conn.: The Millbrook Press. 96p. Grades: 4 and up.

Poetry writing is one way to express feelings and creativity. To help writers explore their feeling and express their creativity, these authors have provided a book rich with examples, ideas, and instructions for writing poetry. The book is filled with poetry and many are accompanied by paintings by noted artists. Included are chapters on poets' tools, poetry forms, figures of speech, finding the poet inside, and ideas for sharing poems. Ways to share poems include memorizing, reciting, poetry parties, and gifts of poems. Books for further reading and an index are included.

Studying poetry helps students develop the skill necessary to address content standards one, four, nine, eleven, and twelve. Standards one and nine have students reading a variety of print texts to gain an understanding of themselves and the diversity found in their world. Poetry introduces children to themselves and their world in ways not possible with other types of literature. Standards four and twelve encompass using spoken language for effective communication with a variety of audiences for different purposes. Reading and understanding poetry requires reflective, critical thinking, which is the focus of standard eleven.

BOOK AND MEDIA CHOICES

Lear, Edward. *The Owl and the Pussycat*. Illustrated by Jan Brett. 1991. New York: G. P. Putnam's. Unp. Grades: P–2.

Delightful, bold, colorful illustrations capture young readers' attention and this is a book they want to hear again and again. This brief, popular poem from noted poet Edward Lear tells the tale of a love-struck owl and pussycat that decide to marry. A clever twist discovered in the illustrations is the tale of two love-struck fish painted across the bottom of the page. This visual subplot can be pointed out to the students during subsequent readings.

Opie, Iona, editor. *My Very First Mother Goose*. Illustrated by Rosemary Wells. 1996. Cambridge, Mass.: Candlewick. 107p. Grades: Grades: P–2.

Both the editor's and the illustrator's love for Mother Goose is evident in the pages of this marvelous book. The large text and illustrations are just the size for sharing with small groups of children who quickly begin to chime in as their favorite rhymes are read. The book includes an introduction, a table of contents, and index of first lines.

Opie, Iona, editor. *Here Comes Mother Goose*. Illustrated by Rosemary Wells. 1999. Cambridge, Mass.: Candlewick Press. 107p. Grades: P–2.

Charming, bright, colorful illustrations, large print, and the generous size of this book make it one for sharing with large groups of young children. This delightful feast for the eyes and ears quickly becomes a favorite book for reading again and again. The short, simple nursery rhymes are ones the teachers, librarians, and parents will hear again and again as youngsters quickly and easily memorize them. The nursery rhymes are filled with familiar characters and a few delightful new characters, such as Dusty Bill from Vinegar Hill. The book has won numerous awards.

Jones, Ivan, and Mal Jones. *Good Night, Sleep Tight: A Poem for Every Night of the Year!* 2000. New York: Scholastic. 256p. Grades: P–3.

These clever, creative, and funny poems are to be read aloud at bedtime, but there is no reason not to share them with students in the classroom or library. However, reading only one might be a problem, as young readers want to hear more than one and want to hear their favorites over and over again. This collection of poems, by a variety of poets, appeals not only to children, but also to adults who do not mind repeatedly reading them.

Grimes, Nikki. *Come Sunday*. Illustrated by Michael Bryant. 1996. Grand Rapids, Mich.: Eerdmans Books for Young Readers. Unp. Grades: P–4.

This collection of poems describes LaTasha's Sunday spent at church. The poems cover the day from her mother braiding her hair in the morning to saying a prayer of thanks before going to sleep that night. The poems and the watercolor illustrations celebrate ladies in church with hats and white gloves, Sunday school, a woman preacher, and other parts of the daylong service.

Hopkins, Lee Bennett, editor. *It's about Time*. Illustrated by Matt Novak. 1993. New York: Simon and Schuster. Unp. Grades: K–2.

A clock in the top corner of the page reflects the passage of time throughout the day as the young children in the illustrations get up, get dressed, head to school, learn, play, eat, and head for bed. Young children often have trouble understanding the passage of time; however, the combination of the easy-to-read clock and familiar daily activities helps them comprehend this concept. The colorful illustrations depict children from different ethnic backgrounds assuring that children see themselves reflected in the illustrations and the poems.

Manson, Christopher. *A Farmyard Song: An Old Rhyme with New Pictures*. 1992. New York: North-South Books. Unp. Grades: K–3.

Young children enjoy making animal sounds and this nursery rhyme gives them a chance. A young farm boy introduces the animals and their sounds as he feeds them. Inspiration for the charming woodcut illustrations came from early children's books. The text and illustrations are framed with stamped borders that make the pages of the book a feast for the eyes.

Marks, Alan. *Ring-a-Ring O' Roses and a Ding, Dong, Bell: A Book of Nursery Rhymes*. 1991. Saxonville, Mass.: Picture Book Studio. 96p. Grades: K–3.

What makes this collection special is the watercolor illustrations and the silhouette montages that accompany the nursery rhymes. Additionally, the book is just the right size to hold up to share the pictures with children. The large text and familiar rhymes encourage beginning readers to read the book on their own. Extra verses that may not be familiar to the reader are included.

Livingston, Myra Cohn, compiler. *If You Ever Meet a Whale*. Illustrated by Leonard Everett Fisher. 1992. New York: Holiday House. 32p. Grades: K–3.

This anthology of whale poems of every length from very brief to moderately long describe chirping Belugas, migrating Humpbacks, breaching Orcas, and other wondrous whales. The rich, deep illustrations celebrate these giant mammals and remind readers to care for and to protect these treasures from the deep.

Miranda, Anne. *To Market, To Market*. Illustrated by Janet Stevens. 1997. San Diego, Calif.: Harcourt Brace. Unp. Grades: K–3.

This favorite nursery rhyme is updated with a cast of zany animals who create havoc in the woman's house as she makes trips to the grocery store to buy food for lunch. Young and old are delighted to find that in the end vegetable soup is served for lunch rather than one of the animals. The rhyming, repetitious verses have students chiming in as the tale progresses. The hilarious illustrations set young and old to chuckling.

Florian, Douglas. *Beast Feast*. 1994. New York: Scholastic. Unp. Grades: K–4.

Whimsical paintings accompany these poems in celebration of beasts that inhabit the earth. The lyrical verses describe the animals, their habitats, and their behaviors. The book truly provides a beast feast for the eyes and ears. These poems could also be used in the science class to introduce the animals to students. This book won the Lee Bennett Hopkins Poetry Award.

Beast Feast. 1998. New Rochelle, N.Y.: Spoken Arts. 12min. Grades: K–4.

Students delight in watching this short video and listening to the humorous poems. This book is available in both video and audiocassette.

Whitehead, Jenny. *Lunch Box Mail and Other Poems*. 2001. New York: Henry Holt. 48p. Grades: K and up.

Students appreciate the wide variety of poetry found in this book, all reflecting common childhood experiences. Whimsical illustrations are interwoven through the text. The poems are divided into four categories: 1) Training Wheels, 2) In Full Swing, 3) Appeteasers, and 4) Winding Down. The book includes a table of contents.

Harrison, David L. *The Purchase of Small Secrets*. Illustrated by Meryl Harrison. 1998. Honesdale, Pa.: Wordsong Boyds Mills Press. 48p. Grades: 1–4.

The pleasures and treasures of everyday country life are explored in verse interwoven with detailed black-and-white drawings. These poems range from humorous, to introspective, to sad. An encounter with a bull, reflections on a boyhood fight, and gazing at a rabbit killed by a car are all topics of this eclectic collection of poems.

Emerson, Ralph Waldo. *Father, We Thank You*. Illustrated by Mark Graham. 2001. New York: SeaStar. Unp. Grades: 1 and up.

Breathtaking illustrations dominate the pages of this book. A family hiking through the mountains uncovers the beauty of nature around every bend in the path. This book is a wonderful introduction to the work of Ralph Waldo Emerson.

Janeczko, Paul B. *Very Best (almost) Friends: Poems of Friendship*. Illustrated by Christine Davenier. 1999. Cambridge, Mass.: Candlewick. 37p. Grades: 2 and up.

Young and old find themselves and their friends in this collection of poems by contemporary poets including Kalli Dakos, Nikki Grimes, Walter Dean Myers, and Judith Viorst. The poems reveal the ups and downs of friendship and almost friendship.

Smith, Jr., Charles R. *Short Takes: Fast-Break Basketball Poetry*. 2001. New York: Dutton Children's Books. Unp. Grades: 2 and up.

These short bursts of poetry are accompanied by small photographs that capture the words reflected in each line. The grace and excitement of a basketball game are depicted in both words and photographs. Athletes who disdain poetry can appreciate these poems and perhaps be encouraged to create their own. The book includes a table of contents and ends with an author's note on his inspirations for the poems and a glossary.

Feelings, Tom, editor. *Soul Looks Back in Wonder*. 1993. New York: Dial Books. Unp. Grades: 3–5.

Moving, flowing poetry written by African American poets fills the pages of this book. Exquisite artwork accompanies each poem in double-spread pages. The artwork was completed and then the poets were asked to write poems to accompany the paintings. Poems range from ancient to contemporary and address every heartfelt emotion of the readers. This book received a Coretta Scott King award.

Venokur, Ross. *Haiku! Gesundheit: An Illustrated Collection of Ridiculous Haiku Poetry*. Illustrated by Kenny Scharf. 2001. New York: Simon and Schuster. Unp. Grades: 3–5.

This collection of preposterous haiku brings smiles and giggles to readers, who then want to create their own equally outrageous verses. Included in this collection are a boy with a television for a head, a beetle protesting he is not an ant to a hungry anteater, and a poet tree.

Prelutsky, Jack. *The New Kid on the Block*. 1990. New York: Greenwillow Books. 159p. Grades: 3–6.

Line drawings, rhythm, nonsense, and wordplay combine to form hilarious poems that appeal to children. The title poem of the book is about a young boy talking about the new kid on the block. The new kid is faster, stronger, and cleverer than the boy who decides he does not like HER one bit. Children respond to the spontaneous humor in the book and quickly make connections between their lives and the children in the poems. There is also a CD-ROM version of this book with animated characters.

***The New Kid on the Block*. 1994. Mac/Win. Novato, Calif.: Living Books. Grades: 3–6.**

This interactive multimedia version of the book is a favorite with children because when they click on some of the words the animated characters act out the words. For instance, when Tillie eats the chili she begins to wheeze, by clicking on the word "wheeze" in the poem students see an animated Tillie begin to wheeze.

Silverstein, Shel. *Falling Up*. 1996. New York: HarperCollins. 176p. Grades: 3–6.

Irreverent humor and clever pen-and-ink drawings are hallmarks of Silverstein's poetry. Children enjoy hearing, reciting, and dramatizing his poems. The wordplay and silliness he incorporates into his poems endear them to children. Companion books to this one are *Where the Sidewalk Ends* (Silverstein, 1974) and *A Light in the Attic* (Silverstein, 1981).

Silverstein, Shel. *Where the Sidewalk Ends, 25ᵗʰ Anniversary Edition*. 2000. Audiocassette. New York: Sony Music Entertainment. Grades: 3–6.

Listening to Shel Silverstein perform his works is truly a delight. Some of his other works are also available on audiocassette. This audiocassette is a Grammy Winning Classic.

Nye, Naomi Shihab. *Salting the Ocean: Poems by Young Poets*. Illustrated by Ashley Bryan. 2000. New York: Greenwillow Books. 112p. Grades: 3 and up.

This book of 100 poems was written by 100 students from first to twelfth grade. The poems are different in meter and style, most of them do not rhyme, but each comes from the heart and has a powerful message. The book has four sections including: the self and the inner world, where we live, anybody's family, and the wide imagination. Suggestions for further reading, an author's note, an index of poems, an index of poets, and poignant vignettes about writing poetry conclude the book.

Stevenson, James. *Just Around the Corner*. 2001. New York: Greenwillow Books. 56p. Grades: 3 and up.

Ordinary things such as a collection of junk on a windowsill, worn shoes, and frozen chunks of slush in the wheel wells of a car become objects of delight and reflection in these amusing thought-provoking poems. Ink and watercolor illustrations remind the readers of their own similar experiences and encourage them to stop and appreciate the ordinary things in their own lives.

Carroll, Joyce Armstrong, and Edward E. Wilson, compilers. *Poetry After Lunch: Poems to Read Aloud*. 1997. Spring, Tex.: Absey. 164p. Grades: 5 and up.

Students' feelings and reactions to the dreaded assignment of writing a poem are described in one of the verses. Throughout the book students encounter poems they can relate to that are reflective of life in their school. The compilers contend that students learn to delight in poetry by simply listening to poems. Hearing a poem read aloud furnishes the listener with an opportunity to savor and relish the sounds of the words. The poems are arranged in categories having to do with dining, such as beverages, appetizers, entrees, and desserts. There is even a children's menu.

EXPLORATIONS

1. *The Owl and the Pussycat* (Lear, 1991) is not only delightful to listen to, it is filled with words to explore as young students develop their vocabulary. Unfamiliar words from the poem can be written in large letters and their definitions explained to the students. They can also be placed on the classroom word wall. One way to facilitate vocabulary development is to have the students use the words in speaking and writing; however,

"runcible spoon" may be difficult for them to use in everyday language. This phrase can be found in an unabridged dictionary and is thought to be one Lear made up.

2. *Here Comes Mother Goose* (Opie, 1999) and *Ring-a-Ring O' Roses and a Ding, Dong, Bell: A Book of Nursery Rhymes* (Marks, 1991) are for reading aloud again and again. Copying the nursery rhymes on transparencies or projecting them on a large screen from a computer provides students an opportunity to follow along as the words are read. After several readings some students have the confidence to read the rhymes on their own. They can be provided with individual copies of their favorite nursery rhymes to keep in their desk to read on their own or to take home and read to adults or siblings.

3. Prior to reading *Some Smug Slug* (Edwards, 1996), review with students the term alliteration. Then have them brainstorm a list of words that begin with the letter "s."

4. After reading *Some Smug Slug* (Edwards, 1996), work with students to help them create a class book describing another alliterative adventure.

5. Provide students with a paper desktop clock with moveable hands while reading *It's about Time* (Hopkins, 1993). As the poems are read, the students move the hands of their clocks to match the clock in the top corner of the page. As the hands of the clock are moved, have the students check with a neighbor to be sure everyone has the correct time on their clock.

6. *A Farmyard Song: An Old Rhyme with New Pictures* (Manson, 1992) is a cumulative tale about feeding nine farmyard animals. Divide the students into nine groups and give each an animal sound to make. While reading, the teacher pauses and nods to the groups to indicate when they are to make their sounds.

7. *If You Ever Meet a Whale* (Livingston, 1992) celebrates the wonder and beauty of whales. Students can do research to locate information about another type of mammal, such as bears, and write a collection of poems to describe them.

8. *To Market, To Market* (Miranda, 1997) is a variation of a familiar nursery rhyme that students can use as a model to create a variation of their favorite nursery rhyme. For example with Wee Willie Winkie, students can brainstorm all sorts of silly things that would happen if someone ran through town in a nightgown rapping at windows.

9. The poems in *Beast Feast* (Florian, 1994) are filled with tongue twisting word play and clever made-up words. Students can use these short, silly poems as models for their own. First, the class could brainstorm ideas for the poems and create one together as a class. Then, the students could be given the option of working alone or with a partner to create their own poems. Once they have their poem written they may want to draw an illustration for their poem.

10. After reading *Lunch Box Mail and Other Poems* (Whitehead, 2001), have students pick out their favorite poem and create their own poem based on the pattern used by the author. Since many of the poems are short descriptions, students can easily find a poem to use as a basis for creating their very own.

11. *The Purchase of Small Secrets* (Harrison, 1998) is a collection of poems for reading aloud and for engaging in thought-provoking discussions as the layers of the poems are re-

vealed. Questions such as "How did the poet create the mood?" and "What feelings are evoked as the poem is read?" encourage students to reflect and think deeply about the poem.

12. After reading *Short Takes: Fast-Break Basketball Poetry* (Smith, 2001), encourage students to write their own short bursts of poetry and to illustrate each line with a digital photograph taken with a digital camera or found on the Internet.

13. In *Soul Looks Back in Wonder* (Feelings, 1993) the paintings were completed before the poems were written. A collection of photographs and art reproductions placed in a corner of the room can serve as an art center and as a poetry center. As students examine and reflect on the artwork, their thoughts can be written down as poems.

14. After reading *Haiku! Gesundheit* (Venokur, 2001), project one of the haiku from the overhead projector and have the students work together to count the syllables in each line before writing their own verses.

15. *The New Kid on the Block* (Prelutsky, 1990) and *Falling Up* (Silverstein, 1996) are collections of poems that children enjoy reciting, memorizing, and staging. Working in small groups, children select the poem that they want to stage. They gather simple props, memorize the poem, and decide how to act it out. They rehearse the poem in front of their classmates and then travel to other classrooms in the school to perform.

16. Prior to listening to *Where the Sidewalk Ends, 25ᵗʰ Anniversary Edition* (Silverstein, 2000), ask students to listen carefully to the inflections in Silverstein's voice as he performs his poetry. Then have students practice performing their favorite poems.

17. After reading *Salting the Ocean: Poems by Young Poets* (Nye, 2000), the young poets in the classroom want to write and publish their own poems. Collect their poems and reproduce them to create a book of the collection for each student. The poems can be typed in a word processing software program to facilitate the collection and reproduction of the poems.

18. The poems in *Poetry After Lunch: Poems to Read Aloud* (Carroll and Wilson, 1997) easily lend themselves to choral reading. They could be read in a cumulative fashion where one voice starts and as each line begins another voice chimes in.

REFERENCE BOOKS

The materials in this section range from a visual encyclopedia, to books on the history of libraries and book making, to books on writing. These books are filled with fascinating information that is helpful, interesting, and entertaining. Students find the books on writing invaluable references as they research and write. These books are written for children and contain practical, helpful ideas.

BOOK AND MEDIA CHOICES

***The Dorling Kindersley Visual Encyclopedia.* 1995. New York: Dorling Kindersley. 456p. Grades: 1 and up.**

Detailed illustrations, charts, diagrams, and color photographs fill this encyclopedia and cause the reader to stop on every page and read the brief text entries that further explain the visuals. Detailed search efforts will require other resources; however, this is a great book for beginning a search.

Knowlton, John. *Books and Libraries.* Illustrated by Harriett Barton. 1991. New York: HarperCollins. 36p. Grades: 3–5.

Here is a fascinating look at the development of writing, the creation of books, and the building of libraries. Ancient Roman libraries had pigeonhole cupboards for storing scrolls and in the old West they had "Library in a Box" that was shipped from a New York publisher. These little-known facts make for very interesting reading. Colorful, simplistic drawings depict the development of libraries from 30,000 years ago to the computerized present. The history is very briefly told, but includes important events, such as Melvil Dewey's decimal system.

Appelt, Kathi, and Jeanne Cannella Schmitzer. *Down Cut Shin Creek: The Pack Horse Librarians of Kentucky.* 2001. New York: HarperCollins. 58p. Grades: 3–6.

One of the programs started by the Works Progress Administration was the Pack Horse Library Project of Eastern Kentucky. This innovative program employed "book women" who took books, magazines, newspapers, church bulletins, and pamphlets to rural, remote families and schools by horseback. These tenacious women rode over treacherous terrain through harsh, unforgiving weather to deliver reading materials. In their saddlebags they carried materials that brought news of the world and of their neighbors. The book concludes with a bibliography of resources.

Jeunesse, Gallimard. *The History of Making Books.* 1995. New York: Scholastic. 46p. Grades: 3–6.

Ancient writing, papermaking, printing presses, bookbinding, censorship, and the art of picture books are all discussed in these pages. This interactive book encourages students to read and explore the partial pages that fold out to reveal gorgeous color photographs. An embossed foil page contains lines of type to feel and use to create rubbings with paper and pencil. The book ends with suggestions to extend the reading and includes books to read, addresses for requesting additional information, people to know, a glossary, an index, and a timeline. This is one of the Scholastic Voyages of Discovery series.

Young, Sue. *Writing with Style.* **1997. New York: Scholastic. 143p. Grades: 4–8.**

Intended to help students become polished writers, this book explains the four steps of the writing process: planning, producing, polishing, and presenting. Samples of good and poor writing styles are given with suggestions toward making the text more readable. The author directly addresses student writers as she explains the four steps in the writing process, hence the students feel as if the book was written directly for them. This is one of the Scholastic Guides series.

Heiligman, Deborah. *The New York Public Library Kid's Guide to Research.* **1998. New York: Scholastic. 134p. Grades: 5 and up.**

Heiligman has written a friendly, informative guide for students that does not talk down to them even though she reminds them of seemingly commonsense things to do, such as have the topic approved by the teacher prior to beginning the research. She cautions them to check the library's hours before having their parents drop them off, so that they can be picked up before the library closes. A checklist of things to take to the library includes items such as a library card, note cards, pencil, and change for the copy machine. This step-by-step guide to research includes information on conducting Internet searches. The skills taught in this book are ones that children will be able to use throughout their lifetimes.

TEACHER RESOURCES

Many of the teacher resources in this section can be used throughout the curriculum as teachers and librarians seek a variety of ways to extend the books they use with children. The professional organizations and Web sites contain resources that teachers can easily adapt to use in their own classrooms.

BOOKS

Coody, Betty. *Using Literature with Young Children.* **5th edition. 1997. Madison, Wis.: Brown and Benchmark. 310p. Grades: P–3.**

Different ways of responding to literature is the focus of this book. Cross-curricular activities for using dramatization, poetry, writing, art, cooking, and storytelling to extend books are described and books are suggested for each activity.

Cullinan, Bernice E. *Read to Me: Raising Kids Who Love to Read.* **2000. New York: Scholastic. 151p. Grades: P–6.**

Parents who are interested in sharing with their children a love of reading appreciate the ideas and resources in this book. The book ends with Surefire Hits Booklists for children from birth to twelve and a list of magazines for children.

Short, Kathy, editor. *Research and Professional Resources in Children's Literature: Piecing a Patchwork Quilt.* **1995. Newark, Del.: International Reading Association. 272p. Grades: P–8.**

This book contains an annotated bibliography of resources for teachers including strategies for using children's literature in the classroom. Sections in this book include research on children's literature, professional journals, and professional books on children's literature.

Tannenbaum, Judith. *Teeth, Wiggly as Earthquakes.* **2000. York, Maine: Stenhouse. 88p. Grades: K–3.**

Easy-to-follow lessons with examples of children's work provide teachers the information they need to engage their students in writing poetry.

Hindley, Joanne. *Inside Reading and Writing Workshops.* **1998. Video. York, Maine: Stenhouse. 20 min. (each). Grades: K–6.**

This collection of four videos includes Reading Conferences, Reading Mini-Lessons, Writing Conferences, and Writing Mini-Lessons.

Peterson, Ralph, and Maryann Eeds. *Grand Conversations: Literature Groups in Action.* **1990. New York: Scholastic. 79p. Grades: K–6.**

Teaching reading with trade books and engaging children in grand conversations is the focus of this book. A list of references and book lists of grade-appropriate books are included.

Bromley, Karen D'Angelo. *Webbing with Literature: Creating Story Maps with Children's Books.* **2d ed. 1996. Boston: Allyn and Bacon. 307p. Grades: K–8.**

Not only does this book contain information on webbing, it also contains chapters on literary elements and sharing and responding to literature. A wide variety of webbing activities are described and many include examples of students' work.

Burke, Eileen M., and Susan Mandel Glazer. *Using Nonfiction in the Classroom.* **1994. New York: Scholastic Professional Books. 96p. Grades: K–8.**

Practical suggestions for selecting and using nonfiction books are given in this short easy-to-read book. Examples of students' work and responses to nonfiction books are included.

Cullinan, Bernice E., editor. *Fact and Fiction: Literature across the Curriculum*. 1993. Newark, Del.: International Reading Association. 92p. Grades: K–8.

The short, readable chapters in this book contain a great deal of helpful information for teachers who want to use literature in their classrooms. Chapters are included on using literature in social studies, math, science, and for teaching about cultures.

Norton, Donna E., and Saundra E. Norton. *Language Arts Activities for Children*. 4th edition. 1999. Upper Saddle River, N. J.: Merrill. 432p. Grades: K–8.

While the activities in this book focus on one or several books, the activities can be adapted for use with a variety of books. Book summaries and detailed instructions help teachers quickly and easily include these activities in their teaching.

Tompkins, Gail E. *50 Literacy Strategies: Step-by-Step*. 1998. Upper Saddle River, N. J.: Merrill. 124p. Grades: K–8.

Not only does this book have step-by-step instructions for strategies to extend reading; a grid showing appropriate usage, grade levels, and grouping accompanies each strategy. Examples of student work are included.

Yopp, Ruth Helen, and Hallie Kay Yopp. *Literature-Based Reading Activities*. 3d edition. 2001. Boston: Allyn and Bacon. 70p. Grades: K and up.

This book is brimming with activities for extending literature. Instructions are given for each of the activities and several examples are given using the activity with a variety of books. This book is a wonderful resource when planning literature extension activities for students.

Jackson, Norma R., and Paula L. Pillow. *The Reading-Writing Workshop: Getting Started*. 1992. New York: Scholastic Professional Books. 136p. Grades: 1–6.

For teachers interested in starting a reading-writing workshop in their classroom this is an easy-to-use guide. It contains directions, flowcharts, reproducible checklists, lessons, and other helpful items for teachers just starting out with the reading-writing workshop.

Carter, David A., and James Diaz. *The Elements of Pop-Up: A Pop-Up Book for Aspiring Paper Engineers*. 1999. New York: Little Simon. Unp. Grades: 3–6.

Students enjoy reading and creating pop-up books. This book provides them with clear instructions and examples of a variety of techniques for creating their very own pop-up books. The templates for the book are also available on a Web site.

Moss, Joy F. _Using Literature in the Middle Grades: A Thematic Approach_. 1994. Norwood, Mass.: Christopher-Gordon Publishers. 248p. Grades: 4–8.

The book begins with an introduction to using literature in thematic units. Each chapter focuses on a different thematic unit that includes activities and a variety of books for possible inclusion in the unit.

PROFESSIONAL ORGANIZATIONS

International Reading Association
P. O. Box 8139
Newark, DE 19714-8139
800-628-8508
www.ira.org
Journals: _The Reading Teacher, Journal of Adolescent & Adult Reading Research Quarterly, Reading Online_

National Council of Teachers of English
1111 West Kenyon Road
Urbana, IL 61801-1096
217-328-3870
800-369-6283
www.ncte.org
Journals: _Language Arts, English Journal, Research in the Teaching of English, Primary Voices, Voices from the Middle, Talking Points_

National Reading Conference
11 East Hubbard St., Suite 5A
Chicago, IL 60611
312-431-0013
http://nrc.oakland.edu/
Journal: _Journal of Literacy Research_

Teachers of English to Speakers of Other Languages
700 South Street, Suite 200
Alexandria, VA 22314
703-836-0774
www.tesol.edu/
Journals: _TESOL Matters, TESOL Quarterly, TESOL Journal,_

INTERNET SITES

A to Z Teacher Stuff

http://atozteacherstuff.com/stuff/

The teacher stuff on this site includes a variety of resources and lesson plans. Resources include links to education sites for teachers, a discussion forum, articles, and units. The site is easy to navigate and includes a search engine.

Between the Lions

www.pbs.org/wgbh/lions/

This site features games, stories, and songs to promote the literacy growth and development of students ages four to seven. The site won the 2001 Notable Children's Web Site Award from the American Library Association. This a companion site to the Emmy Award-winning PBS program.

Children's Literature Association of Utah

www.clau.org/index.html

The literature links on this site are varied and plentiful. There are links to award-winning books, sites for children, sites for teachers, sites for librarians, and sites for parents. There are also links to sites to find information to help children learn to read and books for them to read online.

The Children's Literature Web Guide: Internet Resources Related to Books for Children and Young Adults

www.ucalgary.ca/~dkbrown/index.html

It seems as though anything you would expect to find on a children's literature Web site is on this one. There are links to lists of award-winning books, to authors, to discussion groups, and to journals. Resources for teachers, parents, storytellers, writers, and illustrators are all found here.

EDSITEment

http://edsitement.neh.gov/lessonplans/oregon.html

The National Endowment for the Humanities sponsors this site and provides links to the best humanities sites, lesson plans, at-home activities, and other learning projects. The categories on this site include literature and language arts, foreign language, art and culture, and history and social studies. EDSITEment is a partner in the educational program, MarcoPolo.

REFERENCES

Ahlberg, Janet, and Allan Ahlberg.1986. *The Jolly Postman or Other People's Letters.* Boston: Little, Brown.

————. 1991. *The Jolly Christmas Postman.* Boston: Little, Brown.

Apol, Laura, and Jodi Harris. 1999. "Joyful Noises: Creating Poems for Voices and Ears." *Language Arts* 76, no. 4 (March): 314-322.

AppleWorks. Version 6. 2000. Cuppertino, Calif.: Apple Computer.

Grimes, Nikki. 2000. "The Power of Poetry." *Book Links* 9, no. 4 (March): 32-37.

Headley, Kathy N., and Pamela J. Dunston. 2000. "Teachers' Choices Books and Comprehension Strategies as Transaction Tools." *The Reading Teacher* 54, no. 3 (November): 260-268.

HyperStudio. Version 4. 2000. Torrance, Calif.: Knowledge Adventure.

Kane, Sharon. 1997. "Favorite Sentences: Grammar in Action." *The Reading Teacher* 51, no. 1 (September): 70-72.

McClure, Amy A., Joan Bownas, Lisa Dapoz, Karen Hildebrand, Peggy Oxley, Lillian Webb, and Lynda Weston. 1999. "To See the World Afresh: Talking about Poetry." *Language Arts* 76, no. 4 (March): 341-348.

National Council of Teachers of English. 1996. *Standards for English Language Arts.* [Online]. Urbana, Ill.: National Council of Teachers of English. Available: www.ncte.org/standards/ [cited 30 November 2000]

Norton, Donna E., and Saundra E. Norton. 1994. *Language Arts Activities for Children.* Upper Saddle River, N. J.: Prentice-Hall.

Siemens, Lisa. 1996. "'Walking through the Time of Kids': Going Places with Poetry." *Language Arts* 73, no. 4 (April): 234-240.

Silverstein, Shel. 1974. *Where the Sidewalk Ends.* New York: Harper and Row.

————. 1981. *A Light in the Attic.* New York: HarperCollins.

Chapter 4

Social Studies

Children's literature exposes students to details, passion, and interesting stories not possible in a social studies textbook (Edgington, 1998). Using children's literature in the social studies classroom engenders enthusiasm, motivates children to learn, and addresses students' different reading abilities (Davis and Palmer, 1992). These books turn social studies into good stories. Stories that children want to hear again and again, as well as to read on their own. They are read not only for the information they contain, but also for the pleasure of reading. Books selected for sharing with students should appeal to their interests, be on their ability levels, and stretch their knowledge about the topic (Goforth, 1998). Books and media give life to the men and women who made history. These materials motivate children to learn history by presenting information in interesting, meaningful ways through stories, charts, documents, and maps. Students take pleasure in learning social studies as they read books, view videos, and work on computer programs that are written for them about times long ago and times not so long ago.

The National Council for the Social Studies developed *Curriculum Standards for Social Studies* (NCSS, 1994) that establish guidelines for curriculum development. The social studies standards are divided into thematic strands based on what should be in social studies programs. Social studies programs should include experiences that provide for the study of:

1. Culture and cultural diversity
2. Time, continuity, and change
3. People, places, and environments
4. Individual development and identity
5. Interaction among individuals, groups, and institutions
6. How people create and change structures of power, authority, and governance
7. How people organize for the production, distribution, and consumption of goods and services
8. Relationships among science, technology, and society
9. Global connections and interdependence
10. Ideals, principles, and practices of citizenship in a democratic republic

Some of the books included in this chapter are historical fiction. As children are introduced to this genre, they should be encouraged to contrast and compare it to both historical books and fiction books. Historical fiction provides information about the period, as well as an emotional connection to the time by creating characters to which readers can relate (Lott and Wasta, 1999). According to historical fiction author Karen Hess, readers relate to the characters because they share certain needs: good health, sustenance, survival, approval, and security (Beck, Nelson-Faulkner, and Pierce, 2000). Characters in historical fiction may be the same age as the children reading the stories that provide them with a familiar perspective from which to learn about faraway places and times. Social studies trade books facilitate students making strong connections between the people and events in history and the characters and events in the pages of the books (Seda, Liguori, and Seda, 1999).

Learning history reading trade books, viewing video, and listening to audio makes the pain, danger, excitement, and mystery of past events very real to students. They evoke an emotional response in them. The words, pictures, and sounds capture the readers' attention and imagination as the horrors of war are revealed. The hardships encountered during voyages and explorations and the courage and tenacity of early settlers is lived through media. Included in this chapter are trade books and media to use when teaching American history, people and places, geography, government, and biography. The chapter closes with reference books and teacher resources.

The study of social studies includes numerous wars and the impact of war on peoples' lives. Robb's collection of poems is an excellent way to introduce wars and helps students realize that real people much like themselves fight and suffer during wars.

Robb, Laura, editor. *Music and Drum: Voices of War and Peace, Hope and Dreams*. Illustrated by Debra Hill. 1997. New York: Philomel Books. 32p. Grades: 5–8.

This powerful collection of poems by famous poets, survivors of wars, and children tell of the horrors of war and the poets' longing for peace. Not only are children the victims of war, they are also the hope for a peaceful tomorrow. These moving poems are printed on top of photographic illustrations composed of two or more photographs most of which include children. These poems encourage students to reflect and think deeply about the impact of war on society. They motivate students to become involved and participate in learning about history.

AMERICAN HISTORY

This section of the chapter is divided into important time periods in American history. These time periods include: The New World 1530-1760, Struggle for Freedom 1760-1790, A New Nation 1790-1840, A Nation Divided 1840-1865, A Changing Nation 1865-1914, Troubled Times 1914-1945, and A World Power 1945-2000. Each time period begins with a brief introduction. The second social studies strand includes time, continuity, and change. This includes the study of history to enable students to learn about the past and to understand why and how things change and develop. Throughout the course of studying American history, students are introduced to all the social studies thematic strands.

The text and illustrations in informational trade books offer fascinating details and glimpses into the lives of the people and how their lives were impacted by the times in which they lived. These books offer more than the survey of the time periods as found in many social studies textbooks. Additionally, there are software programs, videos, CDs, and audiocassettes to enhance the teaching and learning of American history.

THE NEW WORLD 1530-1760

During this time Spain, France, and England explored and established colonies in the Americas. It was during this time period that the thirteen original colonies were founded and colonists settled in the New World for economic and religious reasons. The original settlers gave thanks to the Native Americans by preparing a feast for them. Today this holiday remains a time of giving thanks for one's blessings and is celebrated with family and friends as described in Carlstrom's poems.

Carlstrom, Nancy White. *Thanksgiving Day at Our House: Thanksgiving Poems for the Very Young.* Illustrated by R. W. Alley. 1999. New York: Simon and Schuster Books for Young Readers. 32p. Grades: P–2.

This is the story of one family's joyful Thanksgiving celebration in which they give thanks for the pilgrims and give thanks for their blessings. These delightful, brief poems accompanied by colorful, cartoon-like illustrations captivate young readers. They are poems to read aloud again and again with a youthful chorus chiming in to add emphasis.

BOOK AND MEDIA CHOICES

Waters, Kate. *On the Mayflower: Voyage of the Ship's Apprentice and a Passenger Girl.* Photographs by Russ Kendall. 1996. New York: Scholastic. 40p. Grades: 2–4.

The voyage of the Mayflower is told through the eyes of a fictional ship's apprentice. This story was photographed on the Mayflower II, a reproduction of the original ship, with the characters dressed in period costumes. The color photographs vividly depict this important event in American history and show details of the ship and people in ways not seen in drawings. Key words are defined in a glossary at the end of the book.

Moss, Marissa. *Emma's Journal: The Story of a Colonial Girl.* 1999. New York: Scholastic. Unp. Grades: 2–4.

Like a true diary, drawings and notes are found on the borders of the pages and bits of postcards and maps are included in the pages. In order to maintain the look of a journal the author printed this book by hand. This is the story of a ten-year old serving girl, Emma, who lived in the country outside of Boston. When a British general moves into the ground floor of the house, Emma listens to the general's conversations through a knothole in the floor. Using a code her father taught her she sends messages hidden in buttons sewed to garments. This fascinating diary includes information about the Battle of Bunker Hill and its aftermath. The front-end flaps contain a map of the area. Another book in the Young American Voices series is *Rachel's Journal: The Story of a Pioneer Girl* (Moss, 1998).

McGovern, Ann. . . . *If You Sailed on the Mayflower*. Illustrated by Anna DiVito. 1991. New York: Scholastic. 80p. Grades: 2–4.

The first things the Pilgrim children did when they reached shore was to run and play games after being cooped up on the Mayflower for many months. The first thing the women did was wash clothes, and the first thing the men did was repair a small boat. Throughout the book readers learn of the daily life of the pilgrims who came to America on the Mayflower. One reading strategy students learn to help them remember what they read is to look at the pictures and ask themselves questions about the book prior to reading. In this book series, the questions are there for the students at the beginning of each section. These questions help set the stage for the informative text that is written in a simplistic, conversational style. This is one of the books in the . . . If You series.

Lauber, Patricia. *Who Discovered America?: Mysteries and Puzzles of the New World*. Illustrated by Mike Eagle. 1992. New York: HarperCollins. 79p. Grades: 2–6.

At the end of the book Patricia Lauber asks, "Who discovered America?" The question may be easier to answer before reading the book than after reading the book. Many explorers landed on the shores of the Americas and the mysteries of who they were and where they came from are explored in this fascinating book. A list of books for further reading and an index are included.

Plimoth Plantation. 1998. Video. Bala Cynwyd, Penn.: Schlessinger Video Productions-Library Video Company. 23 min. Grades: 3–7.

The daily lives and culture of the original settlers at Plimoth Plantation are portrayed in this video. Pilgrim men and women had very different roles, none of them easy, and students see this portrayed as they follow the pilgrims throughout their daily chores. A Wampanoag Indian tells the students about the daily lives of the Native Americans living in the region during this time. A brief teacher's guide accompanies the videos and includes recommended resources for teachers and students. This is one of the Colonial Life for Children Video Series that includes visits to nine colonial settlements.

Fritz, Jean. *Around the World in a Hundred Years: From Henry the Navigator to Magellan.* **Illustrated by Anthony Bacon Venti. 1994. New York: G. P. Putnam's Sons. 128p. Grades: 3 and up.**

More than just information about the explorers and their explorations in the fifteenth century, this is a masterful story of the explorers who changed the world map. Each explorer's story is presented in a separate chapter, but the chapters are interwoven just as their stories are. The book concludes with an index, bibliography, and endnotes.

Kent, Zachary. *Jacques Marquette and Louis Jolliet.* **1994. Chicago: Children's Press. 128p. Grades: 4 and up.**

Lyrical language, color photographs, black-and-white photographs, and maps are used to describe the expedition of two Frenchmen, a Catholic priest and an adventurer, who set out to explore the Mississippi River in the seventeenth century. The book concludes with a timeline, a bibliography, and an index. This book is part of The World's Great Explorers series.

Masoff, Joy. *Colonial Times: 1600-1700.* **2000. New York: Scholastic. 48p. Grades: 5–8.**

Short text boxes interspersed with color photographs of actors in authentic costumes and settings guarantee that this book is read and recommended to others. The day-to-day lives of the colonists are described. "Surprising History" text boxes contain unusual information, such as the fact that most of our major roads and cities are located on Native American villages and trails. Other text boxes have instructions for making household items just like the settlers did. For example, directions are given for making a quill pen. At the end of the book readers find a short bibliography, Web sites to visit, and an index. This is one of the books in the Chronicle of America series.

West, Delno C., and Jean M. West. *Braving the North Atlantic: The Vikings, the Cabots, and Jacques Cartier Voyage to America.* **1996. New York: Atheneum Books for Young Readers. 86p. Grades: 5–8.**

This fascinating account of the discovery and early attempts at settling North America is enjoyed and appreciated by readers of any age. Thanks to the habit of the Norsemen of keeping good records (sometimes called sagas), there are accounts of the first Viking travels west. There is also a brief discussion of the very first travelers to North America, Eurasians who crossed the Bering Sea from Russia. Accounts of the Cabots and Jacques Cartier are also included in this volume.

Decisions Decisions: Colonization. 1997. Mac/Win. Watertown, Mass.: Tom Snyder Productions. Grades: 5–10.

In this simulation students become involved in the colonization of space. They discuss the problems of the space colonists and the government's role in establishing a colony, and make decisions based on the knowledge gained from studying the colonization of the United States.

Early American History. 1998. Mac/Win. Santa Barbara, Calif.: ABC-CLIO. Grades: 7 and up.

Once students have finished exploring this CD they create their own presentation to show what they have learned. Photographs, documents, biographies, and maps are just some of the materials on this CD. This is part of the American History series.

EXPLORATIONS

1. Prior to reading *On the Mayflower: Voyage of the Ship's Apprentice and a Passenger Girl* (Waters, 1996), have students spend five minutes writing about what they think life was like on the Mayflower. After reading the book, ask students what they found out about life on the Mayflower that was not included in their original writing.

2. Prior to viewing the video, *Plimoth Plantation*, provide the students with a list of unfamiliar vocabulary words found in the Teacher's Guide. Briefly define the words to the students and have them listen for the words as they watch the video. After viewing the video, have the students discuss when in the video they heard the unfamiliar words.

3. While reading aloud *Around the World in a Hundred Years: From Henry the Navigator to Magellan* (Fritz, 1994), assist the students as they create a concept map showing how the explorers' travels are interconnected.

4. After reading *Jacques Marquette and Louis Jolliet* (Kent, 1994), have students print a map of the United States in 1673 from Mapmakers Toolkit software. Have them fill in the map as they think it appears today. Then have them print out a current map of the United States and compare it to the one they just completed.

5. After reading both *On the Mayflower: Voyage of the Ship's Apprentice and a Passenger Girl* (Waters, 1996) and *. . . If You Sailed on the Mayflower* (McGovern, 1991), ask the students to compare the two accounts. One thing they notice is that the people in the photographs in Waters's book look healthy and clean, whereas in McGovern's book they learn that many of the pilgrims were ill and had not bathed in months.

6. Prior to reading about the discovery of America, have students write down on a slip of paper who they think discovered America. Count and record the number of responses for each explorer. Midway through reading *Who Discovered America?: Mysteries and Puzzles of the New World* (Lauber, 1992) or *Braving the North Atlantic: The Vikings, the Cabots, and Jacques Cartier Voyage to America* (West and West, 1996), ask the students to again write down who they think discovered America and record the responses. After finishing the book, once again survey the class about who they think discovered

America. Ask the students to support their final response to the question with evidence from one of the books.

7. Prior to reading *Colonial Times: 1600-1700* (Masoff, 2000), ask students about natural remedies or medicines that they have heard about or taken. After reading about illnesses during Colonial Times have students research to determine what garlic, horseradish, licorice, mustard, mint, nutmeg, prickly pears, violets, swamp lilies, and sassafras were used to treat. The research may be done in books, on the Internet, or through conversations with adult relatives and friends. They may also discover that some of these remedies are still used today.

8. After reading *Colonial Times: 1600-1700* (Masoff, 2000), students enjoy following the directions given for creating everyday items, such as quill pens, bandages, and bracelets.

9. After studying the New World, students can participate in a simulation using Decisions Decisions: Colonization software. Place students in small groups to role-play the colonization of space.

STRUGGLE FOR FREEDOM 1760-1790

Around the world, Spain, France, and England were competing for land during the 1700s. As the traders and settlers from the thirteen American colonies moved westward they began to encroach on the Indians' lands and on land claimed by the French. In 1754, skirmishes between France and Britain broke out in the Ohio River Valley. These skirmishes marked the beginning of the French and Indian War that lasted for nine years. At the end of the war England needed to raise money to repay the money borrowed to finance the war. England looked to the thirteen American colonies and began imposing taxes. The colonists did not believe that the British had the right to tax them and began protesting. As part of this protest the colonists drafted the Declaration of Independence declaring themselves free of English rule. However, England was not willing to give up the colonies without a fight and so England and the colonies were soon embroiled in the Revolutionary War.

BOOK AND MEDIA CHOICES

Marzollo, Jean. *In 1776.* Illustrated by Steve Bjorkman. 1994. New York: Scholastic. Unp. Grades: K–2.

What better way to introduce this eventful year in American history to very young students than through rhyming narrative accompanied by colorful, playful illustrations. This book explains the origin of the American Revolution and the Declaration of Independence. It begins with information for adults to share with young children to help them understand this time in American history.

Kirkpatrick, Katherine. *Redcoats and Petticoats*. Illustrated by Ronald Himler. 1999. New York: Holiday House. Unp. Grades: 1–4.

A seemingly ordinary family living in Long Island was actually part of the Setauket Spy Ring, who kept George Washington informed as to the whereabouts of the Redcoats during the Revolutionary War. Petticoats and handkerchiefs were hung on the clothesline to signal the location of the whaleboat used to ferry messages to Washington. This story was based on the real adventures of the Strong family.

Waters, Kate. *Mary Geddy's Day: A Colonial Girl in Williamsburg*. Photographs by Russ Kendall. 1999. New York: Scholastic. 40p. Grades: 1–4.

On May 15, 1776, the colonists were voting either for or against separating from Great Britain. Mary Geddy can feel the excitement in the air, as well as sadness. If the vote is for separation her best friend, Anne, will return to England. Beautiful color photographs shot in Williamsburg help tell the story of daily life in 1776. The child in the photographs who represents Mary Geddy is Emily Smith, who is now an interpreter and speaks to visitors about children's life in colonial Williamsburg. The book concludes with notes on Williamsburg, the prelude to Independence, slavery, Native Americans, the Geddy family, girlhood in Williamsburg, directions for making lavender sachet bags, an apple pie recipe, and a glossary. The Colonial Williamsburg Web site at www.history.org/ contains additional information about the Geddy Family.

Haskins, James, and Kathleen Benson. *Building a New Land: African Americans in Colonial America*. Illustrated by James Ransome. 2001. New York: HarperCollins. 44p. Grades: 2–4.

This story of the beginnings of slavery during the colonization of America is wonderfully illustrated by James Ransome. The colors are bright and vivid. The chapters are well written and brief enough to hold young readers' attention. Readers may be surprised to learn that the proportion of blacks to whites in America was higher in the eighteenth century than it ever has been. This is an introduction to a shameful part of history in the United States. The book concludes with a list of milestones, a selected bibliography, and an index. This is part of the African Beginnings series.

Community Construction Kit. 1998. Mac/Win. Watertown, Mass.: Tom Snyder Productions. Grades: 2–6.

This fun easy-to-use software enables students to design and print buildings to create three-dimensional communities. Students select from a variety of options as they construct historical or contemporary communities.

Moore, Robin. *My Life with the Indians: The Story of Mary Jemison.* **Illustrated by Victor Ambrus. 1997. New York: Franklin Watts. 32p. Grades: 3–6.**

When she was 15 years old, Mary Jemison was kidnapped by a Shawnee war party that killed the other members of her family. This mesmerizing first-person narrative of her life depicts both the savage and admirable aspects of the Seneca Indians who adopted her and with whom she lived for 76 years. When given an opportunity to leave the Indians, she chose to stay and raise her children. This thought-provoking account raises questions and sparks debates as to why Mary Jemison chose to live the life she did.

Enslow, Anne, and Ridley Enslow. *Music of the American Colonies.* **Audio CD. 2001. Berkeley Heights, N.J.: Enslow Publishers. Grades: 3 and up.**

Students studying the colonies enjoy listening to these recordings of early American music including dances and songs about daily life and political satire. The music is performed on period instruments, such as a bass lute and a glass armonica. Two primary source readings and a teacher's guide are included. This CD was named a Notable Children's Recording by the Association for Library Services to Children.

Masoff, Joy. *American Revolution, 1700-1800.* **2000. New York: Scholastic. 48p. Grades: 5–8.**

Readers step back into the time of the American Revolution as they experience the colonists' lives in brief text boxes and colorful, detailed pictures. The intimate details of the colonists' lives, such as the fact that most people in the 1700s kept journals, enable readers to understand life during these trying times. The book includes a list of places to visit, a bibliography, Web sites, and an index.

Zell, Fran. *A Multicultural Portrait of the American Revolution.* **1996. Tarrytown, N.Y.: Marshall Cavendish. 80p. Grades: 6 and up.**

Usually the focus of study of the American Revolution is on the white males who made the decisions, but this book also includes African Americans, Native Americans, poor European colonists, and women. The impact of war is examined from these diverse perspectives and their contributions to the war are discussed. Looking at the war from a variety of perspectives furnishes a comprehensive look at a complex time in American history. The book includes a chronology, a glossary, books for further reading, and an index. This book is one of the Perspectives series.

Bober, Natalie, S. *Countdown to Independence: A Revolution of Ideas in England and Her American Colonies: 1760-1776.* **2001. New York: Atheneum Books for Young Readers. 342p. Grades: 6 and up.**

The story of America's countdown to independence is told through the eyes of the heroes and rebels involved in this turbulent time in American history. From letters and diaries the author reveals the very human side of the politicians and patriots active in this struggle. History is not dry or boring when revealed through the eyes of the people with conviction to stand up for their beliefs.

EXPLORATIONS

1. As students listen to stories or read on their own about America's struggle for freedom have them write about what they learn each day in a journal. They can share their journal entries with a partner to compare thoughts and clarify their understanding of what they learned.

2. Prior to studying the American Revolution, read *In 1776* (Marzollo, 1994) to activate students' prior knowledge of this crucial time in American history. After reading the book, have students work in small groups to create an *Inspiration* concept map showing what they know about the Revolution. Then have them add questions to the map that they would like to have answered as they study this time period.

3. Prior to reading *Redcoats and Petticoats* (Kirkpatrick, 1999), have students share any family signals they may have or talk about signals the teacher uses in the classroom. Tell them to pay close attention as you read the story aloud to figure out what signals were used in the story and what the signals meant.

4. After reading *Mary Geddy's Day: A Colonial Girl in Williamsburg* (Waters, 1999), have students visit www.history.org/places/geddy/geddyhdr.html to learn more about the daily life of the Geddy family.

5. Read the first eight pages of *My Life with the Indians: The Story of Mary Jemison* (Moore, 1997). At this point in the story Mary realizes that she will never see her natural family again. She chooses to spend her life with the Indians even though when she is older she has a chance to leave. Have the students brainstorm a list of reasons why they think she made this choice. After reading the book, review the list of reasons and delete or add to the list. Students should be able to support the reasons with information in the text.

6. After reading *My Life with the Indians: The Story of Mary Jemison* (Moore, 1997), have students create a three-dimensional Indian village using Community Construction Kit. Before constructing the village have students brainstorm and discuss what needs to go in the village. Students might start the activity by constructing some of the Ready-Made models and then progress to designing and constructing their own buildings.

7. After reading *American Revolution, 1700-1800* (Masoff, 2000), have students work in groups to list the contributions of African Americans, Native Americans, poor Euro-

pean colonists, and women. They may need to refer back to the book to complete their lists. Then have the students read *A Multicultural Portrait of the American Revolution* (Zell, 1996) and as they read the book, add to their lists of the contributions of each group.

A NEW NATION 1790-1840

In 1789, George Washington was sworn in as the first president of the United States. He faced the monumental task of establishing a strong government to lead the new nation. His leadership established precedents for governing the nation that are followed to this day. For example, Washington established the precedent of each president serving only two terms in office. This period in American history was characterized by westward expansion and before it ended, America extended from the Atlantic Ocean to the Pacific Ocean. It was also during this period that northern states developed industry and established trade routes, and southern states developed large farms.

BOOK AND MEDIA CHOICES

Ammon, Richard. *Conestoga Wagons*. Illustrated by Bill Farnsworth. 2000. New York: Holiday House. Unp. Grades: 1–4.

Children are fascinated by this book about the Conestoga wagons, named for a valley in Pennsylvania. The wagons were instrumental in the movement of people and their belongings from the east to the west in the late 1700s and early 1800s. Although these wagons have long been relegated to museums, their heritage lives on in our language. Today's teamsters union is named for the men who drove the horse teams that pulled the Conestoga wagons. The drivers frequently stayed at roadside inns where tabs were kept for their beer. The innkeeper wrote "p" for pint and "q" for quart. Near the end of the evening the drivers would be reminded to "Mind their p's and q's," hence the origin of that familiar rejoinder.

Wright, Courtni C. *Jumping the Broom*. Illustrated by Gershom Griffith. 1994. New York: Holiday House. Unp. Grades: 1–4.

Described through the eyes of an eight-year-old slave, this wedding in the slave quarters is cause for celebration. After long hard days of working in the Big House and in the fields, many long nights are spent crafting furniture and bedding for the newlyweds. The highlight of the wedding ceremony is when the happy couple jumps over a broom to symbolize sweeping away their past and evil spirits.

***Follow the Drinking Gourd: A Story of the Underground Railroad.* 1993. Video. Lancaster, Penn: Rabbit Ears Productions/Microleague Multimedia. 30 min. Grades: 2–4.**

Morgan Freeman narrates this animated video of the Prentices, a slave family that follows the Drinking Gourd north to freedom. This video won a special festival award for the Elevation of the Technique of Motion Graphics at the Tenth Annual Chicago International Children's Film Festival in 1994.

Kroll, Steven. *Lewis and Clark: Explorers of the American West.* Illustrated by Richard Williams. 1994. New York: Holiday House. 32p. Grades: 2–4.

This beautifully illustrated book tells the story of the famous Lewis and Clark expedition to discover a water route to the Pacific. Beginning at the Mississippi River in St. Louis, Meriwether Lewis and William Clark began their journey with fourteen soldiers, nine volunteers, a slave, two French river men, an interpreter, and Lewis's Newfoundland dog. During their difficult trip they met Indians from various tribes and encountered many animals they had never seen before such as jackrabbits, coyotes, antelopes, and prairie dogs. They did not discover a water route, but they did eventually reach the Pacific with only one life lost, a sergeant who died of a burst appendix.

Minahan, John A. *Abigail's Drum.* 1995. New York: Pippin. 64p. Grades: 2–5.

Thirty years after the American Revolution, America, still young and struggling, was once again besieged by the British. In a small coastal town in Massachusetts, a family with two daughters were lighthouse keepers. The two young girls played a fife and a drum, and because of this they were able to save their father and their village from the British. This story is based on an actual event in American history and has real appeal to youngsters. An afterword gives further information about the incident.

Wright, Courtni C. *Journey to Freedom: A Story of the Underground Railroad.* Illustrated by Gershom Griffith. 1994. New York: Holiday House. Unp. Grades: 3–5.

This fictionalized account of a family's harrowing journey with Harriet Tubman on the Underground Railroad helps students understand what it was like to travel on this railroad without tracks and trains. The book introduces students to the Underground Railroad and to this famous African American who gave unselfishly of herself to help others become free. Beautiful artwork provides the backdrop for the story of this journey to freedom.

Lester, Julius. *From Slave Ship to Freedom Road*. Paintings by Rod Brown. 1998. New York: Dial Books. 40p. Grades: 3–5.

Thought-provoking, vivid paintings illustrate the journey from slavery to freedom. The paintings are accompanied by meditations that challenge readers to look deeply into the paintings and place themselves in the paintings in order to feel the grief, terror, humiliation, and spirit of the slaves. Some of the meditations are directed at Caucasians, some at African Americans, and others are written for both. The paintings in this book have been displayed in museums and many are held in private collections.

McKissack, Patricia C., and Fredrick L. McKissack. *Christmas in the Big House, Christmas in the Quarters*. Illustrated by John Thompson. 1994. New York: Scholastic. 68p. Grades: 3–6.

In the big house, there is an abundance of food and decorations. In the quarters, food and decorations are scarce; however, the slaves make the best of what they have. The stark contrast between the lives of the masters and the lives of the slaves is portrayed in beautiful, realistic illustrations. Working from sunup to sundown months before Christmas, the slaves prepare the big house and the plantation for the "Big Times." When they return to the slave quarters, they work in the dark to prepare for their own holiday celebrations.

Kroll, Steven. *Pony Express!* Illustrated by Dan Andreasen. 1996. New York: Scholastic. Unp. Grades: 3–6.

Prior to the Pony Express, mail traveled from coast-to-coast on ships and took six months to arrive. Dashing, fearless Pony Express riders delivered mail across the country in an astonishing ten days. This story chronicles the first ride from coast-to-coast. Information at the beginning and end of the story provides additional information about the Pony Express. An author's note briefly details the history of mail delivery and is followed by a mini-photo museum. A map of the Pony Express route, a bibliography, and an index are included.

Lavender, David. *Snowbound: The Tragic Story of the Donner Party*. 1996. New York: Holiday House. 87p. Grades: 4 and up.

In the 1840s during the Westward movement to California, the Donner brothers led a group of settlers from St. Louis to California. They read about a new shortcut that would make the trip easier. Unfortunately, the shortcut turned out to be a disaster. Hostile Indians, a devastating winter, a lack of food and supplies, and sickness led to the deaths of 40 of the 88 people in the Donner party. Only two families were spared any losses. This tragic story depicts the hardships that settlers faced as they traveled westward in search of a better life.

Blumberg, Rhoda. *What's the Deal? Jefferson, Napoleon, and the Louisiana Purchase*. 1998. Washington, D.C.: National Geographic Society. 144p. Grades: 4 and up.

In 1682, the French explorer LaSalle discovered the land the Mississippi River flowed through and claimed it for his king, Louis XIV. The king had no interest whatever in "Louisiana." Following the French Revolution, Napoleon Bonaparte ruled France and thought at first to take over Louisiana to gain control of North America. He finally decided to sell it to the United States and use the money to gain control of Europe. This purchase included much of the land west of the Mississippi River and reached from Canada to the Gulf of Mexico. Included in this book are a cast of characters, a timeline, a bibliography and an index.

American Paradox: Slavery in the Northeast. 2000. Video. Chappaqua, N.Y.: Lucerne Media. 26 min. Grades: 5–8.

Period paintings, ink sketches, and video clips from a living history museum portray the role and economic impact of slavery in the Northeast and Middle Colonies. This is part of the American Paradox series.

Thomas, Velma. *Lest We Forget: The Passage from Africa to Slavery and Emancipation*. 1997. New York: Crown. 32p. Grades: 7 and up.

Documents and photographs from the Black Holocaust Exhibit were carefully chosen for this book by the creator and curator of the exhibit. They document the brutal treatment and the determined spirit of the slaves. The subject is not sensationalized; rather it is presented in a factual manner that portrays the horror of slavery. Unique to this book are artifacts such as a realistic hand-written note that unfolds from the page, a three-dimensional container holding a manumission document, and a ribbon-tied envelope holding ship's papers.

EXPLORATIONS

1. After reading *Conestoga Wagons* (Ammon, 2000), mark off the length and width of a Conestoga wagon in the classroom or on the playground. Have the students determine what they would think essential to take west with them and how much of it would fit in the wagon.
2. Read and discuss with students the differences in the two Christmas celebrations portrayed in *Christmas in the Big House, Christmas in the Quarters* (McKissack and McKissack, 1994). Then read *Jumping the Broom* (Wright, 1994) and have the students write their descriptions of what they think a wedding in the Big House would be like.
3. After reading *Lewis and Clark: Explorers of the American West* (Kroll, 1994), students can lead their own expedition called Into the Unknown at www.pbs.org/lewisandclark/into/. This simulation is based on the Lewis and Clark expedition.
4. After reading *Journey to Freedom: A Story of the Underground Railroad* (Wright, 1994), have students visit the National Geographic's Underground Railroad site where they

have to decide if they will follow Harriet Tubman to freedom. The journey begins at www.nationalgeographic.com/features/99/railroad/.

5. *From Slave Ship to Freedom Road* (Lester, 1998) is a book for reading aloud as the pictures are shared with the students followed by a discussion of the book. Thoughtful, meaningful discussions of books such as this offer students opportunities to link their lives to the lives of the people in the book (Freeman, Lehman, and Scharer, 1999). Then the students need time to contemplate the meditations in the book. They may not want to share their thoughts with the class, but should be given the opportunity to discuss the meditations if they choose.

6. Prior to reading *Pony Express!* (Kroll, 1996), ask students how they think mail went from the East coast to the West coast prior to the railroads, trucks, and airplanes. Then have them estimate how long it took the mail to travel on the routes they suggest. Read the story to determine if their predictions are correct. Ask them to estimate how long it takes mail to travel from their town to another town where they have friends or relatives. Have them mail postcards to their friends or relatives requesting to be notified when the mail arrives. They can check their predictions against the actual length of time it takes the postcard to arrive.

7. Prior to reading *Snowbound: The Tragic Story of the Donner Party* (Lavender, 1996), students can visit The Donner Party Internet site at www.pbs.org/wgbh/amex/donner/abprogram.htm to prepare them to learn about this gripping tale. There is information on the site about the westward expansion and an interactive map of the route of the Donner Party. Additionally, at this site there is information about purchasing a Public Broadcasting Service (PBS) video about the Donner Party.

8. At the beginning of *What's the Deal? Jefferson, Napoleon, and the Louisiana Purchase* (Blumberg, 1998) is a list of the cast of characters who were involved in the Louisiana Purchase. Prior to reading the book, assign each student a character. As the book is read they are to make notes on their character's role in the Purchase. After reading the book, students compare their notes with the notes on the characters at the beginning of the book.

9. Divide the class into groups and assign each group one of the sections from *Lest We Forget: The Passage from Africa to Slavery and Emancipation* (Thomas, 1997). The students are to read their section of the book and design an interactive presentation to present their section of the book to their classmates. For example, in the section titled To Make a Slave, steps are outlined to make the slaves fearful of their masters. The students in the class could be asked to brainstorm ways they think masters made slaves fearful. Then the group presenting this section could share the ways discussed in the book.

A NATION DIVIDED 1840-1865

This time period in American history was one of great unrest as Americans fought for equal rights for its citizens. In America, abolitionists worked to free slaves, women sought basic rights, and reformers tried to improve schools and prisons. There was also unrest in Texas as Texans fought Mexico for their independence. In 1860, the Civil War began and for five long years Northern states and Southern states were locked in a bitter battle over slavery.

BOOK AND MEDIA CHOICES

In the Hollow of Your Hand: Slave Lullabies. 2000. CD. Boston: Houghton Mifflin. Grades: P and up.

Slaves sang songs to give themselves hope for better lives. The love of parents for their children is reflected in these songs. This CD includes a book with the lyrics to the songs.

Turner, Ann. *Drummer Boy: Marching to the Civil War.* Illustrated by Mark Hess. 1998. New York: HarperCollins. Unp. Grades: 1–3.

Approximately forty thousand drummer boys joined the Union Army. These young boys beat their drums to relay officers' orders to their men and to give them spirit. This is the story of a young boy struck by Mr. Lincoln's words who runs away and lies about his age in order to join the Union Army. The striking, historically accurate illustrations give testimony to the hours Mark Hess spent studying actual Civil War photographs.

Krensky, Stephen. *Striking It Rich: The Story of the California Gold Rush.* Illustrated by Anna DiVito. 1996. New York: Simon and Schuster Books for Young Readers. 48p. Grades: 1–3.

On January 24, 1848, gold was discovered in California by James Marshall, who himself never became rich from the discovery. Eventually, news of gold brought people from around the world to seek their fortune in California. Many dreamed of making their fortunes, but few actually did. In easy-to-read text and colorful illustrations the story of the gold rush and its impact on the settlement of California is explained to young readers. This is one of the Ready to Read series.

Winnick, Karen. *Mr. Lincoln's Whiskers.* 1996. Honesdale, Penn.: Boyds Mills Press. Unp. Grades: 1–3.

This book is based on the true story of eleven-year old Grace Bedell who wrote to Abraham Lincoln suggesting that he grow a beard. He took her advice and when he made a campaign stop in her town, he visited with her to find out what she thought of his whiskers. Copies of the letters the two shared are displayed at the end of the book.

Garland, Sherry. *Voices of the Alamo.* **Illustrated by Ronald Himler. 2000. New York: Scholastic. Unp. Grades: 2–5.**

Starting in the 1500s, this book chronicles the events leading up to and including the 13-day siege of the Alamo. The story is told through the voices of a wide range of participants from a conquistador, a Texan farmer, Sarah Seely DeWitt, Davy Crockett, a drummer, and Sam Houston. Their brief, poetic narratives are filled with interesting information about this historic event. At the end of the book readers find a historical note, glossary, bibliography, and ideas for additional reading.

Polacco, Patricia. *Pink and Say.* **1994. New York: Scholastic. Unp. Grades: 2 and up**

This powerful, moving story depicts the common bond of brotherhood in the midst of hatred. Two young boys of different races fighting in the Civil War meet after they are separated from their combat units. One boy is injured and the other boy, a slave, takes him home to his mother's slave cabin. She cares for the injured boy and when he is healed both boys set out to rejoin their units. Readers cannot help but be moved by this story of love and respect.

Pink and Say. **1996. Video. New Rochelle, N.Y.: Spoken Arts. 30 min. Grades: 1–5.**

The author, Patricia Polacco, narrates this animated tale of brotherhood set in the Civil War. This is one of the Patricia Polacco series. This book is available in both video and audiocassette format.

Haskins, Jim. *The Day Fort Sumter Was Fired On: A Photo History of the Civil War.* **1995. New York: Scholastic. 96p. Grades: 3–7.**

The firing on Fort Sumter by the Confederate army marked the start of the Civil War. Dramatic black-and-white photographs tell the story of this historic battle. The accompanying text has a conversational tone that makes the book easy to read and understand. Some soldiers brought their families with them when they enlisted and one portion of the book deals with the role of children and families in the Civil War. Children were members of the fife and drum corps, served as officers' aides, assisted in hospitals, and retrieved wounded soldiers.

Civil War: America's Epic Struggle. **1995. Mac/Win. New Rochelle, N.Y.: MultiEducator. Grades: 4 and up.**

What part did hot air balloons play in the Civil War? Find answers to questions such as this one in these information-packed CDs. Biographies, major battles, a chronology, timelines, narrations, and an extensive photo archive are just some of the materials available to enhance the study of the Civil War.

Sandler, Martin. W. *Civil War*. 1996. New York: HarperCollins. 91p. Grades: 4 and up.

During the Civil War reporters, photographers, and artists followed the soldiers into battle. Their documentation of the war combined with excerpts from songs, speeches, and letters vividly portray the horrors of war. This documentation also depicts the soldiers' attempts to create a life for themselves away from the battlefields, as they eat, gamble, and clown around for the photographers. An index concludes the book. This is a Library of Congress Book.

***A Few Appropriate Remarks: Lincoln at Gettysburg*. 2000. Video. Shawnee Mission, Kans.: Kaw Valley Films. 34 min. Grades: 4 and up.**

Lincoln thought little of his famous Gettysburg Address. He was so overcome with emotion at seeing this battleground that he felt his words were inadequate to describe the carnage there. Yet this address is one of the most quoted in world history.

January, Brendan. *Reconstruction*. 1999. New York: Children's Press. 32p. Grades: 5–8.

The book begins with a brief summary of the Civil War and then focuses on the tumultuous years after the Civil War. The south was decimated after the war, farms were destroyed, and many people were out of work. Information on the Freedmen's Bureau, the Black Codes, the Civil Rights Act, and the Carpetbaggers is included. The strife between African Americans and Caucasians continues as the United States' government works to provide freedom and equality for all Americans. The book concludes with a glossary, a timeline, and an index. This is one of the Cornerstones of Freedom series.

Beller, Susan Provost. *Never Were Men So Brave: The Irish Brigade During the Civil War*. 1998. New York: Margaret K. McElderry Books. 98p. Grades: 5 and up.

Many black-and-white photographs and drawings accompany the text and depict the story of a famous, though small, group's involvement in the Civil War. This group, known as the Irish Brigade, fought fearlessly for the Union forces at the battle at Antietam where 535 members of the Brigade lost their lives. This book begins in Ireland in the early 1800s where Catholics lived under oppressive English Penal Laws. This story is told through the words of those who were there. The book contains a bibliography and an index.

***American History Inspirer: The Civil War*. 1997. Mac/Win. Watertown, Mass.: Tom Snyder Productions. Grades: 5–12.**

With this software program students travel back in time and use historical maps as they plan routes across the United States. In their travels they learn about developments that lead up to the Civil War including the westward expansion, the industrial revolution, and the antislavery movement. This is part of the Inspirer Geography Series 4.0 series.

Haskins, Jim. *Black, Blue & Gray: African Americans in the Civil War*. 1998. New York: Simon and Schuster Books for Young Readers. 154p. Grades: 5 and up.

When the Civil War began in 1861 few African Americans were allowed to enlist. It was not until the noted abolitionist Frederick Douglass made a public request for their involvement that such enlistments began. Primarily placed in roles of cooks and laborers, they rarely saw combat duty until after the battle at Fort Sumter. The Louisiana Native Guards, the Pennsylvania Hannibal Guards, and a group of African Americans in Boston, Massachusetts, were among the first Negroes to enlist. Haskins has illustrated the book with black-and-white photographs and ends with important dates, a list of African American Medal of Honor recipients, a bibliography, and an index.

EXPLORATIONS

1. *Pink and Say* (Polacco, 1994), *The Day Fort Sumter Was Fired On: A Photo History of the Civil War* (Haskins, 1995), and *Drummer Boy: Marching to the Civil War* (Turner, 1998) contain information about the impact of the Civil War on the lives of children and their roles in the war. Around the globe children's lives are impacted by wars in their countries as evidenced by newspapers and news reports. After reading these three books, sharing and discussing newspaper clippings of present-day children involved in war enables the students to make connections between the past and the present.

2. After reading *Striking It Rich: The Story of the California Gold Rush* (Krensky, 1996), have the students brainstorm ways that people today strike it rich. Using the ideas they brainstorm have them write stories about how they could strike it rich.

3. The Web site California's Untold Stories of the Gold Rush at www.museumca.org/ goldrush has additional resources including art of the gold rush and extensive curriculum materials for teachers.

4. Have students select one of the poetic narratives from *Voices of the Alamo* (Garland, 2000) and do an oral reading of the character's poetic narrative. After they practice reading the piece several times, have them perform for the class.

5. After reading *Pink and Say* (Polacco, 1994), have students discuss the boys' friendship.

6. After reading *The Day Fort Sumter Was Fired On: A Photo History of the Civil War* (Haskins, 1995), have students focus on the chapter about women's roles in the war. Then have them research to compare the women's roles to the roles of women in today's military.

7. After reading *Reconstruction* (January, 1999), have students take the role of either a former slave, a plantation owner, or a member of the Freedmen's Bureau. Working in small groups have them discuss reconstruction from their character's position. They should be able to justify their character's reaction to reconstruction.

8. *Never Were Men So Brave: The Irish Brigade During the Civil War* (Beller, 1998) and *Black, Blue & Gray: African Americans in the Civil War* (Haskins, 1998) are both about minority groups who fought in the Civil War. Have the students compare and contrast the groups' roles during the Civil War. Then have them determine what happen to both groups of soldiers after the war.

A CHANGING NATION 1865-1914

After the Civil War, Americans began moving westward in great numbers. Indians were forced onto reservations and homesteaders carved the Indians' land into farms. Industries grew rapidly and workers faced harsh conditions. As Americans moved west, immigrants from other lands arrived and settled in eastern cities. To better understand historical events students should be aware of the context in which they happened and effective teachers help them make these connections (Nelson and Nelson, 1999).

BOOK AND MEDIA CHOICES

Houston, Gloria. *My Great-Aunt Arizona*. Illustrated by Susan Condie Lamb. 1992. New York: HarperCollins. Unp. Grades: 1–3.

Relive the days of the one-room schoolhouse and relish this beloved teacher who hugged her students and knew that they would see things she only read about in books. She lovingly taught several generations of the same families. The author shares memories of her great-aunt, a dedicated teacher, and at the same time makes readers stop and think about their favorite teacher.

Bartone, Elisa. *Peppe the Lamplighter*. Illustrated by Ted Lewin. 1993. New York: Mulberry Books. Unp. Grades: 1–3.

Peppe and his family are Italian immigrants who live in New York City. His mother has died and his father is sick. In an attempt to help support his father and his eight sisters, young Peppe finds a job as a lamplighter. His father objects to the job considering it beneath Peppe's dignity to be walking the streets lighting lamps. The struggles and hardships of immigrant families who came to America seeking a better life, are portrayed in this touching story of a father and son coming to terms with life in America. This is a Caldecott Honor Book. This book is also available in video and audiocassette editions.

Van Leeuwen, Jean. *Going West*. Illustrated by Thomas B. Allen. 1992. New York: Dial Books for Young Readers. Unp. Grades: 1–4.

Dark, somber, primitive artwork sets the stage for this narrative of one family's journey westward in search of a better life. Leaving behind family, friends, and the treasured family piano, they gather a few belongings and begin their journey. The hardships, despair, loneliness, and homesickness overcome the family members as they struggle to survive in their new home on the prairie.

McCully, Emily Arnold. *The Ballot Box Battle*. 1996. New York: Alfred A. Knopf. Unp. Grades: 1–4.

This beautifully illustrated book studies the childhood and adulthood of Elizabeth Cady Stanton, an author and scholar who led the movement to give women the right to vote. Cordelia, a fictitious character, questions Mrs. Stanton on why she feels so strongly about women's rights. Mrs. Stanton tells Cordelia the story of her brother who died young and was mourned by her father. After the death of her brother, her father wished that Elizabeth was a boy. She learned Greek and horsemanship so that her father would tell her that she was as good as a boy; however, her father never recognized her accomplishments.

Thomas, Joyce Carol. *I Have Heard of a Land*. Illustrated by Floyd Cooper. 1995. New York: Joanna Cotler Books. Unp. Grades: 1–4.

In the 1880s, the Oklahoma territory offered free land to courageous pioneers, including African Americans and women. Based on her own family's history, the author writes about a single Black woman who staked her claim and settled in Oklahoma. This book was awarded the 1999 Coretta Scott King Honor Book for Illustration and was named a Notable 1999 Children's Trade Book in Social Studies.

Rounds, Glenn. *Sod Houses on the Great Plains*. 1995. New York: Holiday House. Unp. Grades: 2–4.

Anyone who has ever seen pictures of sod houses built on the Great Plains and wanted to know more about them has their questions answered in this book. Details about how the houses were built and the hazards of living in a sod house, such as cows stepping through the roof or snakes dropping from the ceiling, are all included in this interesting easy-to-read book. The author, born in a sod house in South Dakota, writes from personal experience.

Wright, Courtni C. *Wagon Train: A Family Goes West in 1865*. Illustrated by Gershom Griffith. 1995. New York: Holiday House. Unp. Grades: 3–5.

At the end of the Civil War, freed slaves left the South in search of better lives for their families. This is a fictionalized account of one African American family's journey west on the Oregon Trail told through the eyes of a young girl, Ginny. Realistic paintings, many of which are full page, hold students' attention and motivate them to read the text to find out more about these courageous pioneers. An author note at the beginning of the book provides background information on westward migration.

Collins, Mary. *The Industrial Revolution*. 2000. New York: Children's Press. 32p. Grades: 3–6.

The Industrial Revolution began in England and manufactured goods were shipped to America. During the War of 1812 these goods were no longer shipped to American shores. Americans began to manufacture the textile products they could no longer import from England. The construction of railroads in America during the mid-1800s enabled raw and manufactured goods to move across the country and thus manufacturing thrived. Prior to the Industrial Revolution, manufactured goods were made in homes, and the book ends with the Computer Age revolution that allows people to once again work at home. Included in the book are a glossary, timeline, and an index. This is one of the Cornerstones of Freedom series.

Cobb, Mary. *The Quilt-Block History of Pioneer Days with Projects Kids Can Make*. Illustrated by Jan Davey Ellis. 1995. Brookfield, Conn.: Millbrook Press. 64p. Grades: 3–6.

Many do not realize that quilt blocks tell the story of the settling of the American frontier. Reading the stories behind quilt block patterns is a unique way to learn American history. As students read they are encouraged to recreate the quilt patterns using magazine pictures, crayons, paper, and scissors. The book concludes with books for further reading and an index.

Worcester, Don. *Cowboy with a Camera, Erwin E. Smith: Cowboy Photographer*. Photographs by Erwin E. Smith. 1998. Fort Worth, Tex.: Ammon Carter Museum. 48p. Grades: 3–6.

From 1905 to 1912, Erwin E. Smith worked as a cowboy on ranches in Texas, New Mexico, and Arizona. During this time he took pictures as a way to preserve the cowboy way of life. Worcester uses Smith's voice to tell the story of cowboys in the West. Their work, play, and daily life events are portrayed in pictures and words. Little-known, interesting details are included, such as the fact that at the end of the day the chuck wagon was parked with the tongue pointing north. In the morning the trail boss used it as a compass before he rode out in the morning.

Murphy, Jim. *Blizzard! The Storm that Changed America*. 2000. New York: Scholastic. 136p. Grades: 4–8.

Prepare to bundle up in a blanket to read this book. The illustrations and the text send chills up the readers' spines as the bone-chilling cold grips the coast from Virginia to Maine. Since the weather bureaus were closed on weekends, the nation was unaware of the looming, immense blizzard. This fascinating account of the Blizzard of 1888 includes a wealth of information on American life and society during the nineteenth century. The book concludes with notes on sources and additional reading material, as well as an index.

Gourley, Catherine. *Good Girl Work: Factories, Sweatshops, and How Women Changed Their Role in the American Workforce.* **1999. Brookfield, Conn.: The Millbrook Press. 96p. Grades: 4 and up.**

In the late 1800s and early 1900s, women factory workers were called "girls," and some were as young as ten years old. These "girls" worked 12 hours a day and were paid less than their male counterparts. Their own words are used to tell of their revolt against their working conditions. Upper-class ladies, who were sympathetic to the "girls'" plight, joined them on the picket lines. Their revolts brought about changes in their working conditions, the hours they worked, and in their pay. The power of this story is in the women's own words about their lives. The book includes an index.

Conrad, Pam. *Prairie Visions: The Life and Times of Solomon Butcher.* **1991. New York: HarperCollins. 85p. Grades: 4 and up.**

Solomon Butcher spent his life photographing pioneers in Custer County, Nebraska, with the vision of creating a history book of his photographs and the stories he collected of the families in the portraits. There is the snowbound farmer who, having had enough of his wife, went outside and lay in the snow to freeze to death. After a bit, he had his nephews bring him his buffalo robe. When they later reported his wife was laughing at him, he gave up the suicide idea. This is a companion book to *Prairie Songs* (Conrad, 1987).

Stanley, Jerry. *Big Annie of Calumet: A True Story of the Industrial Revolution.* **1996. New York: Crown. 104p. Grades: 5 and up.**

Between 1860 and 1920 America changed from a largely agrarian society to an industrial one as the Industrial Revolution changed the way many worked and lived. Thirty-three million immigrants from all over the world came to the United States seeking opportunity and a better way of life. Many of them found their way to Calumet in Northern Michigan where they worked in copper mines. Few of the immigrants spoke English and so they banded together with others from their homelands and struggled to make a living. They had low wages, no benefits, and unsavory working conditions. Annie Clemenc, the wife of a miner, decided to make the world aware of the plight of the miners and this is the story of her inspiring struggle. The book closes with a bibliography and an index.

EXPLORATIONS

1. Using Mapmakers Toolkit software have students create maps showing the westward expansion that occurred after the Civil War. With this software program students can convert the maps into a slide show to depict the changes overtime.
2. Prior to reading *My Great-Aunt Arizona* (Houston, 1992) have students brainstorm a list of reasons why teachers teach. After reading the story ask the students if they have any other ideas about why teachers teach.

3. After reading *Peppe the Lamplighter* (Bartone, 1993), ask students to brainstorm other jobs that have to be done daily. Then ask them to speculate on what would happen if those jobs were not done each day.

4. Prior to reading about the westward movement, ask the students about moves they have made. Then record a list of reasons why they moved. In a second column ask them to brainstorm why they think American settlers decided to move west. After reading *Going West* (Van Leeuwen, 1992), *I Have Heard of a Land* (Thomas, 1995), and *Wagon Train: A Family Goes West in 1865* (Wright, 1995), have students look back in the books to verify why these families moved west and record the reasons in a third column. Then have students compare their brainstormed list of reasons (second column) why the families moved to the actual reasons the families moved. Lastly, have them compare their reasons for moving (first column) with the reasons why the families in the stories moved.

5. After reading *I Have Heard of a Land* (Thomas, 1995), have students offer suggestions as to why women and African Americans were allowed to own land in Oklahoma and not in other states. Then have them work in groups to find support for their answers.

6. *The Ballot Box Battle* (McCully, 1996) is more than just about voting rights. It also focuses on society's different expectations for males and females. Have students discuss the different gender-related expectations they have experienced.

7. After reading *The Quilt-Block History of Pioneer Days with Projects Kids Can Make* (Cobb, 1995), help students see the relationship between the shapes in the quilt block and what they have just read. Then have students create a quilt block to tell about a time in their own lives.

8. Prior to reading *Sod Houses on the Great Plains* (Rounds, 1995), have students write down a description of their house or apartment. While reading the book have them make notes about the sod houses. After they have finished reading have them share their notes in small groups to make sure they have not left out any details. Then have them create a comparison contrast chart between their house and a sod house.

9. *The Industrial Revolution* (Collins, 2000), *Big Annie of Calumet: A True Story of the Industrial Revolution* (Stanley, 1996), and *Good Girl Work: Factories, Sweatshops, and How Women Changed Their Role in the American Workforce* (Gourley, 1999)—using these books have students create a chart recording women's impact on the Industrial Revolution.

10. *Cowboy with a Camera, Erwin E. Smith: Cowboy Photographer* (Worcester, 1998) and *Prairie Visions: The Life and Times of Solomon Butcher* (Conrad, 1991) are both about photographers who used their photographs to preserve American history. Have the students work with a partner to select several photographs to carefully study. Ask them to write down details about items in each quadrant of the picture. Then have them share their observations of the details discovered in the pictures. Additional information on having students examine pictures can be found on the Library of Congress Web site at http://lcweb2.loc.gov/ammem/ndlpedu/webwork/discover/yousee.html.

11. While reading *Blizzard! The Storm that Changed America* (Murphy, 2000), have stu-

dents record information about everyday life in 1888. After reading the book ask them to share their notes and compare their lives and the lives of children in 1888.

TROUBLED TIMES 1914-1945

This period in history was marked by two world wars and the Great Depression. In 1917 Americans were brought into World War I and following the war Americans' lives began to change. Prohibition made it illegal to make or sell liquor. Women gained the right to vote. Movies and jazz became part of the culture of the nation. Then the nation's prosperity began to falter and in the summer of 1929 the stock market crashed and the nation was plunged into the Great Depression. These hard times were followed by World War II, which America joined in 1941 after the bombing of Pearl Harbor. The books in this section provide opportunities for students to learn about this time in American history from multiple sources. However, it is important that the teacher mediate their learning in order to assure that they understand the different viewpoints presented in these historical writings (Nelson and Nelson, 1999). Additional information on using primary and secondary sources for studying history can be found in *First World War* (Clare, 1995).

BOOK AND MEDIA CHOICES

Littlesugar, Amy. *Tree of Hope*. Illustrated by Floyd Cooper. 1999. New York: Philomel Books. Unp. Grades: 1–4.

The bleakness of the Great Depression is contrasted with the hope for better times through the eyes of a young girl living in Harlem. With the Lafayette Theatre closed, the girl's actor father works in a bakery. The father and daughter return to the theater to rub the Tree of Hope and wish for better times. As part of the Federal Theater Project, Orson Wells comes to Harlem to direct Macbeth. The theater reopens and the young girl's father once again has the opportunity to act. One of the tree's roots is on the stage of the Apollo Theater in New York. Before appearing on stage, performers rub the Tree of Hope.

Mochizuki, Ken. *Baseball Saved Us*. Illustrated by Dom Lee. 1993. New York: Scholastic. Unp. Grades: 2–4.

Life in a Japanese internment camp during World War II is told through the eyes of a young boy. He questions his parents about why they had to leave their homes in California to stay first in a horse stall and then in communal barracks. His father shakes his head sadly and replies that other Americans feel they cannot be trusted. Discouraged at the lack of respect the children are showing their elders, the fathers build a baseball field and the mothers sew uniforms. The baseball field and the teams provide the camp children (as well as the elders) with something to strive for and to achieve—something that helps them when they finally return to their homes. The pictures are colorful in a muted way and convey the somberness of this painful experience.

Ray, Deborah Kogan. *My Daddy Was a Soldier: A World War II Story*. 1990. New York: Holiday House. Unp. Grades: 2–4.

War separates families and the impact of this separation on the children is examined in this story. With a father who is miles away fighting a war, a mother who joins the work force, and food shortages, a small girl's life undergoes profound changes during the war. This book presents war from the perspective of a child and is based on the stories of those who grew up during World War II. Charcoal illustrations portray this time of loneliness and sadness.

Coombs, Karen Mueller. *Children of the Dust Days*. 2000. Minneapolis, Minn.: Carolrhoda Books. 48p. Grades: 2–5.

From 1931 to 1937, drought and dust storms swept the plains of the United States and Canada. The stories of children and their parents are portrayed in photographs and text. An afterword explains how farmers plowed up the prairie grass that originally held the soil in place. With modern methods this does not have to happen again. The end of the book includes instructions on making a burlap shirt, ideas for class discussions, and activities based on the book. The book concludes with resources for additional information, a brief glossary, and an index. Resources for additional information on the dustbowl era of American history can be found at www.pbs.wgbh/pages/amex/dustbowl/.

***Diamonds in the Rough: The Legacy of Japanese-American Baseball*. 2000. Video. Derry, N.H.: Chip Taylor Communications. 35 min. Grades: 3 and up.**

Narrated by Noriyuki "Pat" Morita, this is the story of how baseball saved many Japanese Americans detained in internment camps in America during World War II. Baseball enabled them to overcome bigotry and to maintain their pride and self-respect. This documentary pays tribute to the Father of Japanese American baseball, Kenichi Zenimura.

O'Connor, Barbara. *The Soldiers' Voice: The Story of Ernie Pyle*. 1996. Minneapolis, Minn.: Carolrhoda Books. 80p. Grades: 4 and up.

A young man born and reared on a farm near Dana, Indiana, could not have imagined living the kind of life that was his destiny. Ernie Pyle was not sure what he wanted to do with his life, but he did know that he did not want to be a farmer. Ernie went into journalism at the suggestion of a friend even though he had not tried writing as a child. Overcome by wanderlust, he dreamed of seeing all of the places out in "the world." Ernie Pyle became a roving reporter, went to Europe during World War II and sent home columns about the day-to-day life of the soldiers. He became "their voice" and endeared himself to them and to all Americans.

Clare, John D., editor. *First World War*. 1995. San Diego, Calif.: Harcourt Brace. 64p. Grades: 4 and up.

Incidents leading up to World War I are introduced at the beginning of the book. Then the events of the war are discussed in chapters. One chapter focuses on the innovative warfare of the Germans that included poisonous gases. This chapter includes pictures of soldiers in early gas masks and a dog in a gas mask. Dogs were used as sentries, to carry messages, and to search for wounded. The last chapter in the book is How Do We Know? This intriguing chapter tells about the material available to historians studying the war including primary and secondary sources and photographs. Cautions are issued about relying totally on newspaper accounts and memoirs when writing historical accounts. The book ends with an index. This is one of the Living History series.

Stein, R. Conrad. *The Great Depression*. 1993. Chicago: Children's Press. 32p. Grades: 5–8.

The book begins by stating that the depression hit the middle-class and the poor the hardest, but that not everyone suffered, in fact some prospered from the depression. Photographs portray the harsh degrading conditions through which most of the population suffered. One in four Americans was unemployed by 1932. The author states that the roots of the depression can be traced to the stock market collapse of 1929. Franklin Roosevelt and his New Deal are discussed, as well as his wife Eleanor, who worked to make sure that African Americans received the benefits of the New Deal. The book also describes how the Works Progress Administration gave jobs to approximately two million American workers. This is one of the Cornerstones of Freedom series.

Kuhn, Betsy. *Angels of Mercy: The Army Nurses of World War II*. 1999. New York: Atheneum Books for Young Readers. 114p. Grades: 5 and up.

Less pay, fewer privileges, and a lack of recognition for their efforts did not stop fifty-nine thousand courageous women from serving their country during World War II. Many Army nurses worked in hospitals on the front lines tending the wounded soldiers and some became prisoners of war. This book recounts not only their courage, but also the care, kindness, and humanity they gave the soldiers. Black-and-white photographs portray these Angels of Mercy at work and play. Endnotes and an index are included.

Durrett, Deanne. *Unsung Heroes of World War II: The Story of the Navajo Code Talkers*. 1998. New York: Facts on File. 122p. Grades: 5 and up.

One of the most important battles in World War II was the Battle of Iwo Jima. American forces won this battle by using the only code the Japanese could not decipher. The code was based on the Navajo language and developed by a group of specialized Navajo Marines, called the Code

Talkers. Included are books for further reading and an extensive index. This is a part of the Library of American Indian History series.

Gay, Kathlyn, and Martin Gay. *World War I*. 1995. New York: Henry Holt. 64p. Grades: 5 and up.

The "war to end all wars" is described through the voices of those who fought in the war. Their personal accounts make this war personal and real as they describe their experiences on the front lines. During World War I, women enlisted in the service and took the places of men who had left to fight the war. One veteran comments at the end of the book that we do not learn from our experiences, war will never end, and it never solves a thing. At the end of the book are source notes, books for additional reading, and an index. This is one of the Voices from the Past series.

Ambrose, Stephen E. *The Good Fight: How World War II Was Won*. 2001. New York: Atheneum. 96p. Grades: 6 and up.

The concise, informative chapters cover the most important aspects of the war and include maps, photographs, and "Quick Facts" about the war. World War II veterans' personal accounts make this a compelling book. The impact on the lives of the soldiers, their families, the women workers, and the victims is described in vivid details that assure readers come away with a sense of how war impacts everyone.

EXPLORATIONS

1. After reading *Tree of Hope* (Littlesugar, 1999), ask students to share any good luck rituals they may have, such as knocking on wood or wishing on a star.

2. *The Great Depression* (Stein, 1993) is a factual account of this bleak time in American history and *Tree of Hope* (Littlesugar, 1999) is historical fiction about the same time period. After reading *The Great Depression* have students write down their thoughts on the impact of the depression on families. Then read aloud *Tree of Hope* and ask them to once again write down their thoughts on the impact of the depression on families. Discuss their reflections to determine if one book had a larger impact than the other on their thoughts about the depression.

3. *Baseball Saved Us* (Mochizuki, 1993) and *My Daddy Was a Soldier: A World War II Story* (Ray, 1990) look at World War II through the eyes of children. How do the two children's concerns about the war differ and how are they the same?

4. *Children of the Dust Days* (Coombs, 2000) tells about government programs that offered assistance to the victims of the dustbowl. Students can conduct research to find out what organizations in their neighborhood help in times of disaster. Then have the students decide how they can help one of the organizations—for example, by holding a food or clothing drive.

5. After reading *The Soldiers' Voice: The Story of Ernie Pyle* (O'Connor, 1996), have students write newspaper articles based on one of the events in the story. These articles can be placed in a newsletter using one of the templates in Microsoft Publisher.

6. Prior to reading *Angels of Mercy: The Army Nurses of World War II* (Kuhn, 1999), ask the students why fifty-nine thousand women became Army nurses even though they received less pay and fewer privileges than males who went to war. Record their thoughts on chart paper to hang in the room. Encourage the students to add to the list as they read the book.

7. Students find similarities between the roles of women in World War II as discussed in *Angels of Mercy: The Army Nurses of World War II* (Kuhn, 1999) and the roles of women during the Civil War as discussed in *The Day Fort Sumter Was Fired On: A Photo History of the Civil War* (Haskins, 1995). Students can use this information to create a Venn diagram to illustrate their comparisons.

8. While reading *Unsung Heroes of World War II: The Story of the Navajo Code Talkers* (Durrett, 1998), have students take notes on Navajo customs and characteristics that caused them problems and those that benefited them during the war. For example, the Navajo believe that after death the spirit lingers near the body and poses a threat to anyone who comes near. During battle the Navajo frequently encountered dead bodies and this was frightening to them.

9. After reading *World War I* (Gay and Gay, 1995), have students create a web of important points in the book. Then, after reading *First World War* (Clare, 1995), have students add to the web. Engage students in a discussion of the authors' different styles of writing and how their styles impacted the material in the books.

A WORLD POWER 1945-2001

This time period was marked by growth in the American economy and conflict with foreign nations. By 1947, the peaceful coexistence between nations ended as communism spread throughout Eastern Europe and the Cold War began. Americans fought in the Korean Conflict, the Vietnam War, and the Persian Gulf War. Also, during this time Americans were in conflict with one another as the Civil Rights movement swept the land. Students' relatives and family friends who lived through this time in American history can provide information from their unique perspective and should be invited into the classroom to share their recollections.

BOOK AND MEDIA CHOICES

Wiles, Deborah. *Freedom Summer*. Illustrated by Jerome Lagarrigue. 2001. New York: Atheneum Books for Young Readers. Unp. Grades: K–3.

In the South during the summer of 1964 after the passage of the Civil Rights Act, two young boys, one Caucasian and one African American, learn that not everyone is colorblind like they are. The boys swim together in the local creek because African Americans are not allowed to swim in the public pool. Then one evening at dinner, Joe's father announces that because of the new law, the town pool will be open in the morning to everyone. The boys arrive at the pool the next morning only to find that it has been filled in with hot, black tar.

Williams, Sherley Anne. *Working Cotton*. Illustrated by Carole Byard. 1992. New York: Harcourt Brace. Unp. Grades: K–4.

Drawing on personal life experiences the author shares the story of a migrant worker family as they pick cotton from dawn until dark. Evocative illustrations capture this life of hardship. An author's note at the beginning of the book reminds readers that it is up to this country to provide other options for the young children in the fields picking crops. This book has been named a Caldecott Honor Book, a Coretta Scott King Honor Book for Illustrations, and an ALA Notable Book.

Bunting, Eve. *Smoky Night*. Illustrated by David Diaz. 1994. San Diego, Calif.: Harcourt Brace. Unp. Grades: 1–4.

During the Los Angeles riots, people hid in their homes and this story tells of neighbors who meet each other in the darkness. When fires break out in their building a young boy and his mother cannot find their cat. They rush to safety with others from their building and discover a neighbor's cat is also missing. When it is safe to return home they find the cats are together. From a night of strife a new friendship between neighbors is formed. This book received the 1995 Caldecott Medal.

Hoyt-Goldsmith, Diane. *Buffalo Days*. Photographs by Lawrence Migdale. 1997. New York: Holiday House. 32p. Grades: 1–4.

The decimation of the buffalo herds in North America from thirty million to a few thousand in nine years is vividly portrayed by a photograph of a mountain of buffalo skulls. This photo essay of the Crow Indians' culture shows how important the buffalo were to their daily lives. Presently the Crows are working to replenish their buffalo herd. Each year a fair and rodeo are held to celebrate and experience life as it was during Buffalo Days. This story is told through the eyes of a ten-year old Crow Indian. The book concludes with a glossary and an index.

Hoyt-Goldsmith, Diane. *Arctic Hunters*. Photographs by Lawrence Migdale. 1992. New York: Holiday House. 32p. Grades: 1–4.

Amidst the conveniences of modern Alaska, arctic hunters exist who hunt as their ancestors did. This is the story of an Alaskan family living in a house with modern conveniences. However, in the summer when the ice begins to melt the family moves to their summer home to hunt and fish in order to have food for the winter. This story is told through the eyes of a ten-year-old Inupiat boy. The book concludes with a glossary and an index.

Ringgold, Faith. *If a Bus Could Talk: The Story of Rosa Parks.* **1999. New York: Simon and Schuster. Unp. Grades: 1–4.**

Once a year, on Rosa Parks's birthday, a special bus takes riders on a historical journey through the life of Rosa Parks. When the bus pulls up to her bus stop, Marcie climbs aboard and soon discovers that the other passengers on the bus are important people in Mrs. Parks's life. The bus begins to speak to her and tells of Rosa Parks's experiences with unjust segregation laws, the horrendous activities of the Klu Klux Klan, and her struggle to get a good education. After a hard day at work Mrs. Parks refused to give up her seat on the bus to a white male. This simple act had a profound impact on the Civil Rights movement in America.

Bunting, Eve. *The Blue and the Gray.* **Illustrated by Ned Bittinger. 1996. New York: Scholastic. Unp. Grades: 2–4.**

A Civil War battleground now the location of an interracial neighborhood is the setting for this story. A father shares with his son and his son's friend the reasons for the Civil War and how it destroyed families. These interracial friends vow to remember the lessons learned on this battlefield as they sled and play ball. Suggestions for further reading are included at the end of the book.

Bunting, Eve. *The Wall.* **Illustrated by Ronald Himler. 1990. New York: Clarion Books. Unp. Grades: 2–4.**

The death of a loved one in battle leaves a space in the family that is felt for generations. This moving story of a young boy and his father finding the boy's grandfather's name on the Vietnam Veterans Memorial depicts the sadness and anguish mixed with pride felt by families who have lost loved ones during battle. This is an ALA Notable Book and a Reading Rainbow selection.

Levine, Ellen. *... If You Lived at the Time of Martin Luther King.* **Illustrated by Anna Rich. 1990. New York: Scholastic. 80p. Grades: 2–5.**

This conversational book begins by asking, "What was segregation?" It describes life before the Civil Rights movement and how the movement began. It talks about songs of the movement, children's involvement, and voting rights. Martin Luther King's place in the Civil Rights movement is explained and the effect of his death. The book ends with the question, "What's left to be done?" On the last page of the book is the musical score and words to *We Shall Overcome.* This is one of the . . . If You series.

Duncan, Alice Faye. *The National Civil Rights Museum Celebrates Everyday People*. Photographs by J. Gerard Smith. 1995. Mahwah, N. J.: BridgeWater Books. 64p. Grades: 2–5.

The motel where Martin Luther King, Jr. was assassinated was transformed into a museum honoring everyday people who fought for civil rights. The room where King stayed has been furnished to look as it did on the evening he was assassinated. The interactive exhibits in the museum allow students to relive the days of the Civil Rights movement. On a bus like the one Rosa Parks rode, students encounter a life-size statue of the bus driver turned around yelling at Mrs. Parks to move and they can touch and feel the life-size statue of Mrs. Parks resolutely sitting in her seat.

Sneve, Virginia Driving Hawk. *The Cherokees*. Illustrated by Ronald Himler. 1996. New York: Holiday House. 32p. Grades: 3–5.

Beginning with the Cherokee creation myth, this book describes the tribe's history from its earliest beginnings through the 1990s. As treaties were signed in America the Cherokees lost more and more of their land. At one time their nation covered six states; today the Cherokee are relegated to fourteen counties in northeastern Oklahoma. This is one of the First American series.

Bridges, Ruby. *Through My Eyes*. 1999. New York: Scholastic. 64p. Grades: 3 and up.

On November 14, 1960, Ruby Bridges walked through the door of previously all-white William Franz Public School in New Orleans. She tells her own story of the remarkable year she spent all alone in a classroom with her teacher, Mrs. Henry. Photographs, newspaper and magazine excerpts, and comments from her teacher are intertwined with Ruby Bridges's own story. At the end of the book she brings the reader up to date on her life and her reunion with Mrs. Henry. A brief timeline of the Civil Rights movement is included.

Feinstein, Stephen. *The 1960s: From the Vietnam War to Flower Power*. 2000. Berkeley Heights, N.J.: Enslow. 64p. Grades: 3 and up.

What do Jackie Kennedy, hippies, and Muhammad Ali have in common? They are all products of the sixties, a time of enormous change in our country. The Vietnam War was raging and young people were clamoring for freedom. This book highlights events such as lifestyles, arts and entertainment, sports, politics, environmental issues, and science, technology, and medicine. The book concludes with a timeline, a further reading list, and an index. It is part of the Decades of the 20th Century series.

Myers, Walter Dean. *One More River to Cross: An African American Photograph Album.* 1995. New York: Harcourt Brace. 166p. Grades: 4 and up.

Black-and-white photographs and brief, elegant narrative portray the lives of African Americans in the United States during the past 150 years. The spirit and courage of their lives is seen in the faces in the photographs, many taken from family albums. Rather than focusing on great accomplishments, their lives are portrayed in everyday activities. Their participation in and contributions to American life are evident in this evocative collection of large photographs. Obstacles in their lives are referred to as rivers to cross. So as not to detract from the narrative, captions for the photographs are included at the end of the book.

Monroe, Judy. *The Rosenberg Cold War Spy Trial.* 2001. Berkeley Heights, N.J.: Enslow. 128p. Grades: 4 and up.

This is a fascinating story that ends with unanswered questions and readers are challenged to form their own opinions. The last chapter of the book addresses the controversy of whether or not the Rosenbergs were spies. The book includes a table of contents, discussion questions, chapter notes, a glossary, books for further reading, related Internet sites, and an index. This is one of the Headline Court Case series that also includes books on the Andersonville Prison Civil War crimes trial, the John Brown Slavery trial, the Salem witchcraft trials, the Scopes Monkey trial, and the Teapot Dome Scandal trial.

Hampton, Wilborn. *Kennedy Assassinated!: The World Mourns: A Reporter's Story.* 1997. Cambridge, Mass.: Candlewick Press. 96p. Grades: 4 and up.

Two months after Wilborn Hampton obtained his first job as a reporter in the Dallas U.P.I. office, Kennedy was assassinated. Suddenly he was in the middle of a tragic news story that rocked the world. His first-person account as a reporter covering the story is fascinating reading. Gripping black-and-white photographs accompany this narrative. As the story of the assassination unfolds, the readers learn about the life of a reporter.

Sherrow, Victoria. *The Oklahoma City Bombing: Terror in the Heartland.* 1998. Berkeley Heights, N.J.: Enslow. 48p. Grades: 4 and up.

Moving color photographs, quotes, and stories from the rescuers, survivors, and family members of victims tell the story of this disaster. Words are defined in context helping to make the text very understandable. The book includes a table of contents, a chart of related disasters, chapter notes, a glossary, books and Internet sites for further reading, and an index. This is one of the American Disasters series that also includes books on the Exxon Valdez, Hurricane Andrew, Plains tornadoes, the San Francisco earthquake, and the World Trade Center bombing.

Foster, Leila M. *The Story of the Great Society.* **1991. New York: Children's Press. 32p. Grades: 4–8.**

With the assassination of President John F. Kennedy, Lyndon Johnson became president of the United States. He quickly announced his Great Society program that involved the federal government in many aspects of Americans' social and economic lives. He concentrated on domestic policy by working for social reform in this country including poverty, medical care for the elderly, conservation of natural resources, housing shortages, and civil rights. The book provides a brief interesting look at the work of this president, who is remembered for his work to improve the lives of Americans. This is one of the Cornerstones of Freedom series.

Gay, Kathlyn, and Martin Gay. *Korean War.* **1996. New York: Henry Holt. 64p. Grades: 5 and up.**

For many years Korea had been under the domination of Japan. The allied nations promised Korea that at the end of World War II they would be released from Japanese bondage. However, Russia, connected to Korea by a short, common border, had other plans. They had long desired a strong foothold in Korea and they declared war on Japan to achieve that end. This book covers the involvement of the United States in Korea. The reasons behind the war, the action, and the effects on the country are covered in this book, one of the Voices from the Past series.

Gay, Kathlyn, and Martin Gay. *Persian Gulf War.* **1996. New York: Henry Holt. 64p. Grades: 5 and up.**

In January of 1991, a CNN (Cable Network News) news team reported from their hotel room in Baghdad of the American bombing of Iraq's capital city. Iraq, under the orders of its ruler Saddam Hussein, had invaded neighboring Kuwait several months before, and the United States, protesting this invasion, retaliated. In this part of the Voices from the Past series, the history of the involvement of the U.S., the actions of the war, and how three countries (Iraq, Kuwait, the United States) were affected, are all described.

EXPLORATIONS

1. Prior to reading *Working Cotton* (Williams, 1992), show the students the pictures and ask them to describe what they see. After reading the book to older students, share the author's note with them and discuss the book.
2. Reading aloud both *Working Cotton* (Williams, 1992) and *Going Home* (Bunting, 1996) furnishes students a more complete look at children who work as migrant labors. After reading the books, allow students to share their thoughts and to draw their own conclusions on the ethics of having these children working in the fields.
3. After reading *Smoky Night* (Bunting, 1994), have students discuss what happened that changed the neighbors feelings toward each other. Why did it take a smoky night to change their feelings?

4. Prior to reading *Buffalo Days* (Hoyt-Goldsmith, 1997), have students brainstorm what they know about buffalo and rodeos. Ask them what they think the two have in common. Record their responses using Inspiration software to show the connections between buffalo and rodeos. Then read them the quote from Joe Medicine Crow on the last page of the book before reading the book aloud. After reading the book, discuss it with the students and return to the Inspiration concept map to decide if they want to include additional information or change any information.

5. As *Arctic Hunters* (Hoyt-Goldsmith, 1992) is read call students' attention to the contrast between their modern home and their summer home. After reading the story have students discuss reasons why Reggie and his family hunt for food instead of buying it at the grocery store.

6. *Pink and Say* (Polacco, 1994) and *The Blue and the Gray* (Bunting, 1996) both contain an African American boy and a Caucasian boy who are friends. After reading both stories have students put themselves in either Pink's or Say's character and have them reflect on the boys' friendship in *The Blue and the Gray.*

7. One way to help students make connections between events in history and their own lives is to have them record an interview with a relative or neighbor who lived through the event. For example, after reading *The Wall* (Bunting, 1990) students can interview a family friend or relative who is a Vietnam veteran. Prior to the interview students can visit www.pbs.org/battlefieldvietnam. They need guidance as to the questions they should ask in the interview.

8. The books . . . *If You Lived at the Time of Martin Luther King* (Levine, 1990), *The National Civil Rights Museum Celebrates Everyday People* (Duncan, 1995), and *If a Bus Could Talk: The Story of Rosa Parks* (Ringgold, 1999) all are about the Civil Rights movement. Each book presents the material in a different way. After reading all three books have students talk about the different styles of writing in them. Divide the students into small groups to answer the question, "What's left to be done?" Then have the groups present their ideas to their classmates. The teacher can circulate around the room as the groups are working to listen to the discussions. Then the teacher uses the comments heard during the discussions to guide a whole class discussion of the topic (Gravelek and Raphael, 1996).

9. While reading *The Cherokees* (Sneve, 1996), have students record notes of key years and events in the book. Using TimeLiner have the students work in groups to create a timeline of the events. Then have them research to add to the timeline other events that were taking place in American history during the same time. This activity helps provide a context for remembering the material they learned about the Cherokees.

10. As the story of Ruby Bridges unfolds in *Through My Eyes* (Bridges, 1999), have students keep a character journal (Yopp and Yopp, 2001). While reading the book, the teacher stops at intervals for the students to record the events from Ruby Bridges's perspective and then record their own personal reflections on the events.

11. Before reading *One More River to Cross: An African American Photograph Album*

(Myers, 1995), have students bring in family photographs to share with the class. Then place the photographs on a bulletin board. After reading the book, have students make comparisons between their family photographs and the ones in the book.

12. While reading *Korean War* (Gay and Gay, 1996) and *Persian Gulf War* (Gay and Gay, 1996), have students use Mapmakers Toolkit software to create maps depicting the major battles of the wars.

13. After reading *The Soldiers' Voice: The Story of Ernie Pyle* (O'Connor, 1996) and *Kennedy Assassinated!: The World Mourns: A Reporter's Story* (Hampton, 1997), have students discuss the differences in the lives of the reporters and their reporting.

14. In *The Great Depression* (Stein, 1993) President Roosevelt's New Deal is explained and in *The Story of the Great Society* (Foster, 1991) President Johnson's Great Society is explained. Both of these programs focused on domestic problems in the United States. Ask students to record key components of the programs and look for similarities in them.

PEOPLE AND PLACES

Books and media about children from different cultures and ethnic backgrounds enable children to learn about others, but also enable them to see things from others' perspectives. Seeing the world through the eyes of children of a different culture helps them to build empathy and acceptance for those of different cultures. Learning about diverse groups through literature enables students to move beyond their stereotyped ideas of the groups (Athanases, 1998). While studying about the lives of other children, students discover similarities and differences between their lives. These discoveries help students appreciate their own lives, as well as the lives of the children.

Sharing books about other cultures encourages children to move beyond their own world as they come to understand cultures that are different from their own. Through literature students come to understand how culture shapes people's lives (Goforth, 1998). Using picture books in upper-elementary and middle-school classrooms has the potential to stimulate students to learn about their world (Farris and Fuhler, 1994). Readers must interact with the text and illustrations to fully comprehend the concepts presented in the book (Kincade and Pruitt, 1996). Discussions about the text and careful examinations of the illustrations help children comprehend the concepts. During discussions, teachers can encourage children to share information about their own cultures that fosters understanding and acceptance from their classmates.

Studying about people and places encompasses four social studies thematic strands. Strand one focuses on culture and by studying cultures students are able to understand social studies concepts from different perspectives. Strand three deals with students' understanding of the relationships between people and their environments. Strand four addresses how individual development and identity are influenced by culture, groups, and institutional influences. Strand nine requires an understanding of global connections among societies. Materials in this section help students to understand different cultures and provide students with multiple perspectives for viewing their world.

BOOK AND MEDIA CHOICES

Bunting, Eve. *Going Home*. Illustrated by David Diaz. 1996. New York: HarperCollins. Unp. Grades: P–3.

This is the story of a migrant farmer worker family returning to Mexico to celebrate Christmas with their relatives, who are proud of the children because they are bilingual. The parents bring their children to the United States each year to assure the children have opportunities to go to school. Diaz's bright, festive illustrations set the tone for the joyous family celebration.

May, Kathy L. *Molasses Man*. Illustrated by Felicia Marshall. 2000. New York: Holiday House. Unp. Grades: K–3.

Come fall in the rural south the sorghum is harvested and brought to the Molasses Man for processing. This is a time where families, friends, and neighbors all work together to assist the local Molasses Man, who continues the time-honored tradition of making molasses outdoors over an open fire. This book chronicles a passing piece of American culture.

McBrier, Page. *Beatrice's Goat*. Illustrated by Lori Lohstoeter. 2001. New York: Atheneum Books for Young Readers. Unp. Grades: K–4.

Inspired by a true story from the Heifer Project International this book tells how the gift of a goat dramatically changed the lives of a family in Uganda. The Heifer Project International provides poor families around the world with farm animals donated by churches, schools, and individuals. The gift of a goat provided Beatrice's family with milk and cheese to eat and sell. The money made from the sales enabled Beatrice to attend school.

Lipp, Fredrick. *The Caged Birds of Phnom Penh*. Illustrated by Ronald Himler. 2001. New York: Holiday House. Unp. Grades: K–4.

Ary wishes for better lives for the members of her poor family. She has heard that if she releases a caged bird and it flies to freedom her wishes will be granted. She saves her money to purchase a caged bird and wishes for better lives for her family and for herself, knowledge, as she longs to go to the university.

***African-American Heritage*. 1997. Video. Bala Cynwyd, Penn.: Schlessinger Video Productions-Library Video Company. 23min. Grades: K–4.**

Hosted by Phylicia Rashad this video introduces students to West Africa's geography, languages, and cultures. On-site video footage, animation, songs, and graphics make this an entertaining learning experience. This is one of the American Cultures for Children Video series.

***Families of Japan.* 1998. Video. Wilmington, Del.: Families of the World. 29 min. Grades: K–5.**

In this video students step into the lives of two families and follow them throughout the day as they go to school and work. The video is composed of two short segments that follow a family with a farm and a family with their own business in the city. A child who simply describes what the family members are doing as they go about their daily lives narrates each segment of the video. This is one of the Families of the World series. These videos provide intriguing examples of the homes and lives of families of different cultures without making comparisons or judgements about the culture.

Berger, Melvin, and Gilda Berger. *Where Did Your Family Come From?: A Book About Immigrants.* Illustrated by Robert Quackenbush. 1993. Nashville, Tenn.: Ideals. 48p. Grades: 1–3.

General information about immigrants is provided at the beginning of the book in a simple format that young readers easily comprehend. Then four simple, short stories of immigrant children from different countries provide details on the children's lives in their native countries and why they came to America. The book explains that all Americans, except the Native Americans, are immigrants. The book contains an index. This book is one of the Discovery Reader series that children can read on their own.

Rosen, Michael J. *Our Eight Nights of Hanukkah.* 2000. New York: Holiday House. Unp. Grades: 1– 4.

Not only do students learn about Hanukkah in this holiday book, they also learn about the importance of family, sharing what they have with others, and celebrating holidays with people of other religions. During the holidays the focus is often on presents, and this book reminds young and old that the holidays are a time to focus on others, to take time to celebrate, and to visit with family and friends.

Bertrand, Diane Gonzales. *Family, Familia.* Illustrated by Pauline Rodriguez Howard. 1999. Houston, Tex.: Piñata Books/Arte Publico Press. Unp. Grades: 1 and up.

A young Texas boy, Daniel, dreads having to attend a family reunion of relatives from across the United States and Mexico. Daniel does not look forward to spending the day listening to old people tell stories. He meets Brian, a cousin his age, and plays with him while Mexican music fills the air. They become good friends and promise to write to each other. The story is told in both English and Spanish with the English text on the top half of the page and the Spanish text on the bottom half of the page.

Dooley, Norah. *Everybody Bakes Bread.* **Illustrated by Peter J. Thornton. 1996. Minne-apolis, Minn.: Carolrhoda Books. Unp. Grades: 2–4.**

To end a sibling quarrel during a bread-making session the mother sends her daughter off to find a three-handed rolling pin. As she scours her multiethnic neighborhood, each of the neighbors she visits gives her a sample of the bread they are baking. The book closes with recipes for the seven different types of bread she samples. A companion book to this one is *Everybody Cooks Rice* (Dooley, 1991). These books facilitate children finding similarities between their lives and the lives of people from other countries.

Kroll, Steven. *Ellis Island: Doorway to Freedom.* **Illustrated by Karen Ritz. 1995. New York: Holiday House. 32p. Grades: 2–5.**

Ellis Island's history is chronicled in this picture book along with the experiences of the immigrants as they made their way through the grueling immigration process. The skillful blending of sepia and color illustrations portray in a way more powerful than words the obstacles that had to be overcome to enter America. Today the Ellis Island Immigration Museum serves to remind all Americans that they are immigrants. At the end of the book is a glossary of unfamiliar terms and an index.

Say, Allen. *Grandfather's Journey.* **1993. Boston: Houghton Mifflin. 32p. Grades: 2 and up.**

This delightfully illustrated book covers the history of the author's grandfather who journeyed from Japan to the United States. He was torn by his love for both countries. These are feelings that immigrant children can relate to as they reflect on their own lives. The drawings have an almost photographic quality and the readers feel as though they are looking at a family photo album. This book won the Caldecott Award in 1994.

Knight, Margy Burns. *Talking Walls.* **Illustrated by Anne Sibley O'Brien. 1992. Gardiner, Maine: Tilbury House. Unp. Grades: 3–7.**

An unusual way to examine the cultures of the world is through the writings on their walls. From ancient caves to the Berlin Wall, walls tell of the people who built them. Examining the walls in this book provides students opportunities for exploring the similarities and differences between the people who built them. Geography skills can be practiced as students find the location of the walls on a world map. Students can be encouraged to do additional research on the walls in the book. *Talking Walls: The Stories Continue* (Knight, 1996) is the sequel to this book.

***Talking Walls.* 1996. Mac/Win. Redmond, Wash.: Edmark. Grades: 3–7.**

This CD companion to the book includes links to Web sites and videos. The multimedia format appeals to students and provides them additional information about the cultures and countries presented in the book. *Talking Walls: The Stories Continue* (Knight, 1996) is also available in CD-ROM format.

Chavarria-Chairez, Becky. *Magda's Tortillas.* 2000. Houston, Tex.: Arte Publico Press. Unp. Grades: 3–8.

In both English and Spanish text on each page this book tells the story of a young Hispanic girl and her grandmother. Magda loves to watch her grandmother make tortillas and on her seventh birthday her grandmother gives her her first tortilla-making lesson. Through much trial and error, Madga rather impatiently learns finally to make tortillas. She is embarrassed because her tortillas do not come out round like her grandmother's. However, her family accepts Magda's tortillas with their unusual shapes and declares her a tortilla artist. Her grandmother assures her that on her eighth birthday she can learn to mix the dough.

Yale, Strom. *Quilted Landscape.* 1996. New York: Simon and Schuster Books for Young Readers. 80p. Grades: 3–8.

Twenty-six young immigrants were interviewed about leaving their countries and living in America. As they move from childhood to adulthood they traverse different cultures and speak different languages sometimes alone, sometimes with only some of their immediate family members, and sometimes with all of their family members. They tell their stories of moving to America and adapting to American customs with words, photographs, poems, and illustrations. Their courage, pride, and resolve to get an education inspire readers.

Sandler, Martin W. *Immigrants.* 1995. New York: HarperCollins. 92p. Grades: 3 and up.

An abundance of photographs, illustrations, brief text boxes, and short quotes from immigrants tell the stories of these brave people in search of a better life as they passed through Ellis Island and adjusted to their new lives. The courage of the immigrants and their profound impact on America are depicted in this book. It is one of the books in the series, A Library of Congress Book that displays the vast collection of visual and text materials available in the Library of Congress.

Press, Petra. *Puerto Ricans.* 1996. Tarrytown, N. Y.: Benchmark Books, Marshall Cavendish. 80p. Grades: 4 and up.

This book has a clear and interesting writing style that encourages students to read to learn about these immigrants. Information is included on why the immigrants left their countries, their lives in America, their family and community, their religions and celebrations, their customs, and their contributions to American culture. The book has text boxes throughout with interesting facts, such as the value of an individual, personal shrines, and migrant farm workers. The book ends with a chronology, glossary, books for further reading, and an index. This is one of the Cultures of America series. Other books in this series include: *Japanese Americans* (Lee, 1996), *Greek Americans* (Phillips and Ferry, 1996), and *Lebanese Americans* (Whitehead, 1996).

Blumberg, Rhoda. *Shipwrecked! The True Adventures of a Japanese Boy.* 2001. New York: HarperCollins. 80p. Grades: 4 and up.

This is the fascinating, true account of a fourteen-year-old Japanese fisherman, Manjiro, who was shipwrecked with four other fishermen during the 1800s. At this time Japan was closed to foreigners and Japanese who came into contact with foreigners were not allowed to return. So when American whalers rescued the stranded fishermen, they were not allowed to return to their homeland. Manjiro was the first Japanese person to come to America. Many years later he was able to return to Japan where he became a samurai and was instrumental in opening Japan to the world. The book ends with an author's note including a bibliography and Web site for additional information.

Ashabranner, Brent. *To Seek a Better World: The Haitian Minority in America.* Photographs by Paul Conklin. 1997. New York: Cobblehill/Dutton. 88p. Grades: 5–8.

Accompanied by stunning black-and-white photographs, this book presents the story of the Haitian immigrants in America. While people today are well aware of the thousands of "boat people" who try to reach South Florida in unseaworthy craft, many do not remember the fifties when thousands tried to escape Haiti and its dictator known as "Papa Doc." The author tells the story of many accomplished Haitians who live in America today.

Greenberg, Judith E. *Newcomers to America: Stories of Today's Young Immigrants.* 1996. Danbury, Conn.: Franklin Watts. 128p. Grades: 5–8.

Much has been written about adult immigrants entering our country, but this book is about young people entering the United States with or without their families. Fourteen young faces and voices are introduced to the reader from fourteen different cultures. Some of their problems are similar and some are quite different. They left their homelands for different reasons: to find a better way of life, to escape religious or political persecution, to avoid starvation and poor health. Some of them had relatives already here; many of them did not know anyone in America. Rather than devoting a chapter to each youngster, each chapter asks certain questions and each immigrant responds to the questions. This is one of the In Their Own Words series.

The Ellis Island Experience. 2000. Mac/Win. Cary, N.C.: SouthPeak Interactive. Grades: 5 and up.

This compelling CD was made in conjunction with The History Channel and The Statue of Liberty-Ellis Island Foundation. It includes Internet links, oral histories, quotes, photographs, and other resources, such as documents that enable students to understand what it was like for immigrants who passed through Ellis Island.

EXPLORATIONS

1. Prior to reading *Going Home* (Bunting, 1996), have students share their memories of going to relatives' houses for Christmas. After reading the book, have them make connections between their Christmas visits and the visit of the family in the book.

2. Prior to reading *Molasses Man* (May, 2000), provide children with an opportunity to taste molasses. After reading the book, share gingerbread or gingersnaps with them.

3. After reading *Beatrice's Goat* (McBrier, 2001), have the children taste goat's milk and share with them the different items that can be made from goat's milk.

4. Prior to reading *The Caged Birds of Phnom Penh* (Lipp, 2001), ask the students if they wish for things before they blow out their birthday candles. Then have the students share things that they have wished for in the past.

5. Prior to watching the video *Families of Japan* (1998), tell the students that as they watch the video they are to look for similarities and differences in their lives and the lives of the children in the video. After watching the video, students work with partners to compare their lives to the lives of the children in Japan.

6. Read the first part of the book, *Where Did Your Family Come From?: A Book About Immigrants* (Berger and Berger, 1993). Before reading the stories of the immigrant children, tell the students the immigrants' names and list the names on the board in a four-column chart. Have the students guess what the immigrant children want for their futures. After reading about each of the immigrant children, compare what they want for the future with what the students guessed.

7. Prior to reading *Family, Familia* (Bertrand, 1999), ask students about attending family reunions. Have them recall what takes place at a family reunion. Then have them share what they like or dislike about family reunions.

8. After reading *Family, Familia* (Bertrand, 1999), allow students with a Mexican American heritage to share their culture with their classmates. Invite their parents to class to discuss their family histories or experiences. Reading books reflective of the students' heritages provides them with positive role models and helps them develop pride in their heritage (Murray and Velazquez, 1999).

9. Read aloud *Talking Walls* (Knight, 1992) and have the students reflect on some of the questions at the end of the book. These questions require students to determine if they build walls and if walls are needed. Students may need guidance as they think about and respond to these higher-order thinking questions.

10. After reading *Talking Walls* (Knight, 1992), have the students determine which walls were built to keep people in and which walls were built to keep people out.

11. Prior to reading *Everybody Bakes Bread* (Dooley, 1996), ask the students what they think they have in common with people from Barbados, India, and the Middle East. Ask the students who ate bread yesterday. Tell them that is one thing they have in common with people from other countries. Read the book aloud to the students. After discussing the different types of bread in the book share bread from one of the countries with students.

12. After reading *Ellis Island: Doorway to Freedom* (Kroll, 1995) or *Immigrants* (Sandler, 1995), students can learn more about Ellis Island or research their family's arrival via Ellis Island using The Ellis Island Experience software.

13. Prior to reading *Grandfather's Journey* (Say, 1993), show the children a picture from the book and ask them to write down questions they have about the picture. After reading the book have them work in small groups to determine if they learned the answers to their questions. Then have the whole class suggest answers to the questions that were not answered in the book.

14. After reading *Magda's Tortillas* (Chavarria-Chairez, 2000), have students use clay to create their own versions of Magda's tortillas. Parent volunteers could be enlisted to assist in the classroom as children create real tortillas and discover for themselves the challenges faced by Magda as she tried to create round, flat tortillas like her grandmother's.

15. In *Quilted Landscape* (Yale, 1996), the courage, pride, and resolve of the young immigrants to get an education is inspiring. Have students discuss these characteristics and tell how they relate to themselves.

16. After reading *Immigrants* (Sandler, 1995), students can create a timeline using TimeLiner to depict when different groups of immigrants arrived in America.

17. After reading *Puerto Ricans* (Press, 1996) and *To Seek a Better World: The Haitian Minority in America* (Ashabranner, 1997), have students create a Microsoft PowerPoint presentation showing the contributions of these two groups to America.

18. In *Newcomers to America: Stories of Today's Young Immigrants* (Greenberg, 1996), following each chapter introduction are questions the young immigrants were asked. Prior to reading the immigrants' responses, have the students predict the immigrants' responses.

19. Books encourage students to reflect on what it means to be human. After studying about immigrants have students reflect on this question: How was the human dignity of people of different cultures impacted when they moved to this country?

GEOGRAPHY

Social studies content strands three, eight, and nine help students understand the importance of geography as they learn about their world. Strand three deals with students' understanding of the relationships between people and their environments. Strand eight introduces students to the impact of technology on their lives. Strand nine requires an understanding of global connections among societies.

Geography teaches children about the world in spatial terms. They learn about places, regions, ecosystems, the environment, and how to use geography to examine the past and plan for the future (National Council for Geographic Education, 1994). In children's literature, maps not only complement the text, they help children make sense of the text (Ranson, 1996). For example, comparing a map of America prior to the Louisiana Purchase to a map after the purchase shows children the dramatic increase in the size of America. One way to introduce students to geography themes is through the following video.

Five Themes of Geography. 1993. Video. El Dorado, Calif.: One Hundred Percent Educational Videos. 15 min. Grades: 3–5.

This brief video introduces students to the four geography themes: location and place; human/environment interactions; movement of people, goods, and ideas; and regions. Five student characters in the video learn the themes along with the students watching the video.

BOOK AND MEDIA CHOICES

Walters, Virginia. *Are We There Yet Daddy?* 1999. Illustrated by S. D. Schindler. New York: Viking Children's Books. Unp. Grades: K–3.

In this familiar story a boy, his father, and the family dog set out to visit the boy's grandmother who lives one hundred miles away. As they travel they count down the miles by tens and children can follow along on a map as the story is read. This book was based on map reading activities the author, a classroom teacher, uses with her students.

Leedy, Loreen. *Mapping Penny's World.* 2000. New York: Henry Holt and Company. Unp. Grades: 1-3.

After learning about maps at school, Lisa creates a map of her bedroom. Then she decides to create maps of her dog, Penny's world. She creates a series of maps including one of Penny's favorite places to hide things and one of Penny's favorite places to spend time. This later map she creates as a three-dimensional map using construction paper and clay.

Barner, Bob. *Which Way to the Revolution?: A Book About Maps.* 1998. New York: Holiday House. Unp. Grades: 1–3.

Young students learn and practice map-reading skills as they scamper along with a band of mice that keep Paul Revere on course on his famous ride. Bold, simple, colored illustrations, large text, and an easy-to-read map key assure that students grasp simple map-reading skills. The book includes a picture glossary that explains the map terms used in the book. The last page of the book includes a very brief biography of Paul Revere.

Berger, Melvin, and Gilda Berger. *The Whole World in Your Hands.* **Illustrated by Robert Quackenbush. 1993. Nashville, Tenn.: Ideals. 48p. Grades: 1–3.**

In one small book the Bergers have packed an enormous amount of information about maps. Starting with a house floor plan, the maps in the book progress to a neighborhood map, to a city map, to a state map, to a United States map, and finally end with a map of the world. As each colorful map is introduced, students are asked questions about the map that are answered by reading the map. The questions encourage the students to interact with the maps, which aids in retention of the material. An index concludes the book. This book is one of the Discovery Readers series.

Hopkinson, Deborah. *Sweet Clara and the Freedom Quilt.* **Paintings by James Ransome. 1993. New York: Alfred A. Knopf. Unp. Grades: 1–4.**

Clara overhears other slaves talking about how they could escape to freedom if only they had a map to show them the way north. Clara, a seamstress, realizes that a map north can easily be disguised in a patchwork quilt. Other slaves share their knowledge of the way north and Clara pieces together a quilt to show the way. When the quilt is complete, Clara and her husband escape north leaving the quilt behind for others to follow the path to freedom. This book is based on a little-known fact of African American history.

Neighborhood Map Machine. **1997. Mac/Win. Watertown, Mass.: Tom Snyder Productions. Grades: 1–6.**

Students have an opportunity to refine and practice their map-making skills as they create maps of their neighborhood. The slide-show feature enables students to create presentations of their maps. The program includes a teacher's guide. This program won the Technology and Learning Software Award of Excellence.

Chapman, Gillian, and Pam Robson. *Maps and Mazes: A First Guide to Map Making.* **1993. Brookfield, Conn.: The Millbrook Press. 32p. Grades: 2–5.**

Map-making skills are presented in an easy-to-read format accompanied by opportunities to practice using the skills to make simple maps and mazes. Children enjoy learning about fixing position, scale, and contour as they create two- and three-dimensional maps using the directions in the book. Colorful pictures and easy-to-follow instructions make it easy for children to succeed at making maps and mazes.

Taylor, Barbara. *Be Your Own Map Expert.* Illustrated by Brett Breckon. 1994. New York: Sterling. 46p. Grades: 3–5.

Colorful illustrations, diagrams, and maps accompany the brief text boxes on a variety of different map topics. Activities are included for students to independently explore making maps for a variety of purposes. This hands-on learning assures that students remember the concepts presented, such as bird's-eye view.

Glicksman, Jane. *Cool Geography: Miles of Maps, Wild Adventures, Fun Activities, Facts from Around the World.* Illustrated by Ruta Daugavietis. 1998. New York: Price Stern Sloan. 96p. Grades: 3–6.

Maps, mapmaking, explorers, cultures, and our shifting earth are all components of geography waiting to be explored. Amazing geography activities, far-out factoids, brain busters, and Web sites are all included in this unique geography book. Resources at the end of the book include addresses for locating worldwide pen pals, answers to brain busters, a time line of geography history, a glossary, and an index.

Johnson, Sylvia A. *Mapping the World.* 1999. New York: Atheneum Books for Young Readers. 32p. Grades: 3 and up.

This brief look at the history of mapmaking is filled with interesting facts that make the reader stop and think. Mercator's projection was invented over 400 years ago and is still used today with pictures taken from space. The ability to fly in hot air balloons and airplanes provided mapmakers a new perspective for drawing maps. In the late 1950s, Landsat satellites made possible dramatic changes in mapmaking by recording infrared wavelengths that provided more detailed information about the earth. *Mapping the World* is a 2000 Orbis Pictus Honor Book.

Mapmakers Toolkit. 1999. Mac/Win. Watertown, Mass.: Tom Snyder Productions. Grades: 4 and up.

Using the over 450 maps included in this software students can learn history, science, literature, social studies, and geography. The maps can be studied and printed as they are or students can customize the maps to meet their needs. Included in the collection are maps that display the precipitation, temperature, land use, population density, and vegetation.

National Inspirer. 1997. Mac/Win. Watertown, Mass.: Tom Snyder Productions. Grades: 4 and up.

Students work in cooperative groups as they travel across the United States searching for resources and commodities in order to complete their scavenger hunt. The scavenger hunt requires students to work together to determine which states they will visit and to determine the order of their visits. Once the route is calculated they enter it into the computer to determine their score. Since much of the work does not require the use of the computer, this is a great activity for a one-computer classroom. This software program is part of the Inspirer Geography series.

Steger, Will, and Jon Bowermaster. *Over the Top of the World: Explorer Will Steger's Trek Across the Arctic*. 1997. New York: Scholastic. 63p. Grades: 4 and up.

From Siberia to northern Canada, a team of six adventurers crossed the frozen Arctic Ocean using dog teams, sleds, and canoes. Their daily adventures were chronicled via the Internet to share with schoolchildren the wonders of the Arctic and the impact of pollution on the Arctic. Interspersed with the diary entries are text boxes of information on: life in the Arctic, pollution, clothing, food requirements, native inhabitants of the area, and information about the personalities of the dogs on the sled teams.

Bramwell, Martyn. *Polar Exploration: Journeys to the Arctic and Antarctic*. Illustrated by Marje Crosby-Fairall and Ann Winterbotham. 1998. New York: DK. 48p. Grades: 4 and up.

Bramwell describes the exploration of the Arctic and Antarctic from the first attempts in the 1600s to recent expeditions. Eyewitness accounts and vivid narrative involve the reader in the incredible stories of courageous adventurers. Remarkable photographs, exploded diagrams, and brief text boxes are used to tell these chilling stories. This is one of the DK Discoveries series.

Armstrong, Jennifer. *Shipwreck at the Bottom of the World: The Extraordinary True Story of Shackleton and the Endurance*. 1998. New York: Crown. 134p. Grades: 5 and up.

In the harsh unforgiving world of the Antarctic, Shackleton and his men attempted to become the first explorers to journey from one side of this icy continent to the other. While they did not succeed, their harrowing attempt is compelling reading. With Shackleton's leadership this band of adventurers stayed together and supported one another, which was ultimately credited with the fact that all twenty-eight men survived the ordeal. This book was given the 1999 Orbis Pictus Award for Outstanding Nonfiction for Children. Additional information on Shackleton's journey can be found at www.lpb.org. This book is also available in audiocassette.

EXPLORATIONS

1. After reading *Mapping Penny's World* (Leedy, 2000), call students' attention to the map keys and compass roses on each map.
2. After reading *Mapping Penny's World* (Leedy, 2000), place construction paper, glue, scissors, markers, and clay in a map center for students to create their own three-dimensional maps.

3. While reading *Which Way to the Revolution?: A Book About Maps* (Barner, 1998), point out the different map keys for each map. Then provide the students with a simple map of the school or schoolyard and have them create a map key for the map.

4. After reading *The Whole World in Your Hands* (Berger and Berger, 1993), have students work with an adult in their household to create a floor plan of their house or apartment. Then have them draw a fire escape route on the floor plan.

5. After reading *The Whole World in Your Hands* (Berger and Berger, 1993), peel an orange to show students how the peel comes off and resembles a flattened globe as demonstrated on page 36 in the book.

6. Prior to reading *Sweet Clara and the Freedom Quilt* (Hopkinson, 1993), show the students the quilt on the endpages of the book. Ask them what they see in the quilt squares. After reading the book, have students write out the directions for traveling north based on the quilt squares. Remind them that this is a creative writing activity and to use their imaginations.

7. After reading *Maps and Mazes: A First Guide to Map Making* (Chapman and Robson, 1993), have the students decide on an appropriate scale and create an accurate floor plan of the classroom.

8. *Be Your Own Map Expert* (Taylor, 1994) explains the concept of a bird's-eye view map. Children can use their imagination to create a bird's-eye view map of the schoolyard. Then they can display their maps in the classroom to compare them.

9. After reading *Be Your Own Map Expert* (Taylor, 1994), students can use Mapmakers Toolkit software to create their own maps. These maps can be placed on the bulletin board to share with others in the class.

10. *Cool Geography: Miles of Maps, Wild Adventures, Fun Activities, Facts from Around the World* (Glicksman, 1998) explains the continental drift theory. To help students understand this concept, the author suggests that the students place tracing paper over a world map to trace the landmasses. Then they cut out the landmasses and see if they can fit them together.

11. *Mapping the World* (Johnson, 1999) contains pictures of ancient maps that depict the world very differently than maps today. Using Mapmakers Toolkit software have students print maps from different time periods to see the changes over time. Creating transparencies from the maps enables students to transpose the maps as they examine them for changes.

12. One way for students to practice their map skills is to work in teams using National Inspirer software to travel around the United States searching for resources.

13. Prior to reading *Over the Top of the World: Explorer Will Steger's Trek Across the Arctic* (Steger and Bowermaster, 1997), have students predict what food the explorers packed and what clothing they took with them. While reading the book, have students compare what was actually taken with what they had on their lists.

14. Prior to reading *Polar Exploration: Journeys to the Arctic and Antarctic* (Bramwell, 1998), have students brainstorm reasons why explorers travel to the Arctic and Antarctic. As they read the book have them make note of the reasons for the explorations.

15. Shackleton's leadership is credited with all twenty-eight of his men surviving the ordeal. While reading *Shipwreck at the Bottom of the World: The Extraordinary True Story of Shackleton and the Endurance* (Armstrong, 1998), have students write down notes when they encounter evidence of his leadership. Periodically, have the students share their notes with each other.

GOVERNMENT

America's founding fathers immediately realized the need to establish a government and formulate laws. A written constitution was needed to protect the rights of citizens and to limit the power of the national government. The Constitution spells out the powers of the federal government. In order to keep the federal government from becoming too strong the Constitution provided for the separation of powers by setting up three branches of government. The collection of materials that follows provides fascinating insights into the history of American government.

The study of government encompasses social studies thematic strands two, six, seven, and ten. The second social studies strand includes time, continuity, and change. This includes the study of history to enable students to learn about the past and to understand why and how things change and develop. Strand six focuses on structures of power, authority, and governance as students examine their rights and responsibilities as citizens. Strand seven addresses production, distribution, and consumption and the government's role in economic policymaking. Strand ten deals with civic ideals and practices essential to being productive citizens.

BOOK AND MEDIA CHOICES

Quiri, Patricia Ryon. *The Constitution*. 1998. New York: Children's Press. 48p. Grades: 1–2.

This very simple explanation of the framing of the Constitution of the United States is intended for the very young primary student. It discusses the need for a set of rules to govern the brand new country. The book is illustrated with color paintings and photographs. The book closes with a brief bibliography, a list of organizations, online sites for obtaining additional information, a short glossary, and an index.

Pascoe, Elaine. *The Right to Vote*. 1997. Brookfield, Conn.: The Millbrook Press. 48p. Grades: 2–5.

With freedom comes responsibilities, and this book helps young people understand why it is important to exercise their right to vote. It tells the history of voting in America from the revolution to the voting rights struggles of women and African Americans. The Voting Rights Act of 1965 and the twenty-sixth amendment, which changed the voting age from twenty-one to eighteen years of age, are explained. At the end of the book is a section on understanding the Bill of Rights, a glossary, suggestions of books for further reading, and an index. This is one of the Land of the Free series.

Stein, R. Conrad. *The Powers of Congress.* 1995. New York: Children's Press. 32p. Grades: 3–5.

This book begins with Congress threatening to use its power to impeach Richard Nixon if he does not resign. Throughout the book examples from American history identify Congress's powers and demonstrate that Congress is the voice of the American people. The book explains that the founding fathers argued over how to represent each state in Congress and it was decided to form two houses, the Senate and the House of Representatives, to assure each state would be equally represented. Included in the book are a glossary, a timeline, and an index. This is one of the Cornerstones of Freedom series.

West, Delano C., and Jean M. West. *Uncle Sam and Old Glory: Symbols of America.* Illustrated by Christopher Manson. 2000. New York: Atheneum. Unp. Grades: 4 and up.

Some of the symbols of America discussed in this book include Uncle Sam, Smokey the Bear, the log cabin, and buffalo. One page of the two-page spread is a woodcut of the symbol and the other page contains the text describing the symbol and explaining why it is a symbol of America. Filled with fascinating facts, this is a book students return to again and again.

Feinberg, Barbara Silberdick. *Constitutional Amendments.* 1996. New York: Twenty-First Century Books. 80p. Grades: 5–8.

When the Constitution was first written, most people believed that time would show that there would always be certain things that would not be covered. Most people believed that there should be some sort of provision to make changes or additions to the Constitution. After heated discussions, Article Five was written to allow for amendments to the Constitution. The book discusses the twenty-seven amendments that have been made in the two hundred years since the Constitution was written. It closes with a glossary, sources used, suggestions for further reading, and an index. It is part of the Inside Government series.

Lindop, Edmund. *Political Parties.* 1996. New York: Henry Holt. 64p. Grades: 5–8.

When George Washington became president of the United States, he avidly disapproved of political parties. He feared that they would become so powerful they would negate the vote of the common people. Even before there were political parties, factions, such as the Federalists and the Anti-Federalists, were attempting to control the vote. Included in the appendix of the book is a glossary, sources used, suggestions for further reading, an index, and notes about the author. This book is part of the Inside Government series.

EXPLORATIONS

1. Prior to reading *The Constitution* (Quiri, 1998), have the students talk about rules that govern them when in the classroom. Ask them to describe what would happen in the classroom if they did not have rules.

2. While reading *The Powers of Congress* (Stein, 1995), stop after each example of Congress exercising its power. Discuss the example with students and help them understand the context surrounding the event.

3. After reading *The Right to Vote* (Pascoe, 1997), have one-half of the class work in small groups to write about why they believe it is important to vote. Have the other half of the class work in small groups to write about what they think happens when people do not vote. Then have the groups share their writings with the entire class.

4. *Constitutional Amendments* (Feinberg, 1996) explains the process for making amendments to the constitution. Students can examine the school's student handbook or the classroom rules and discuss what they would need to do to make changes in the rules.

5. Divide the class in half and have each group become a fictitious political party and decide on five tenets their party supports. Then have three or four from each party debate their tenets. Information provided in *Political Parties* (Lindop, 1996) helps students as they design their political parties.

BIOGRAPHY

The subjects of biographies provide positive role models for students. Biographies enable students to explore the lives of real-life people who impacted the world. Reading biographies and viewing biographical videos give students background information about the historical times in which the subjects lived. Students are curious about famous people and people they consider heroes. Heroes are those individuals whose self-sacrifices have benefited others (Sanchez, 1998). Further, Sanchez states that having students read about and study the lives of heroes in the context in which they lived, provides students role models for their own lives. Biographers transfer their fascination with their subjects to books and media, so that others may appreciate the lives and works of famous and interesting people.

As students study about the lives of famous people their study reflects content strands three, four, and five. Strand three deals with students' understanding of the relationships between people and their environments. Strand four addresses how individual development and identity are influenced by culture, groups, and institutional influences. Strand five focuses on the interactions among individuals, groups, and institutions. The people in these biographies made a difference in society through their words and actions.

BOOK AND MEDIA CHOICES

Bedard, Michael. *The Divide*. Illustrated by Emily Arnold McCully. 1997. New York: Doubleday Book for Young Readers. Unp. Grades: K–3.

When Willa Cather was nine years old, her family sold most of their belongings and boarded a train to Nebraska to begin a new life. Willa is determined that this wide prairie will never be home and so she refuses to unpack the few precious mementos of her former life. Gradually, she comes to love the prairie and the other settlers. In later years she would refer to this time as the most important of her life. The book concludes with an afterword on Willa Cather's life and writing.

Livingston, Myra Cohn. *Let Freedom Ring: A Ballad of Martin Luther King, Jr.* Illustrated by Samuel Byrd. 1992. New York: Holiday House. 32p. Grades: 1–3.

This celebration of the life of Martin Luther King, Jr. includes his own words written in bold text drawn from his speeches and sermons. Full-page color illustrations expand on the succinct text. The book ends with captions for the artwork and citations for the direct quotes taken from his speeches and sermons.

Wallner, Alexandra. *Betsy Ross*. 1994. New York: Holiday House. Unp. Grades: 1–4.

Betsy Ross designed the first American flag; however, there is no proof that she sewed the first American flag. This is the story of a hardworking woman who survived three husbands and some of her children. She ran a business and supported her family at a time when few women did.

Breckler, Rosemary. *Sweet Dried Apples: A Vietnamese Wartime Childhood*. Illustrated by Deborah Kogan Ray. 1996. Boston: Houghton Mifflin. Unp. Grades: 1–4.

Jessica Huong Dang fled Vietnam as a young child. This is the story of how war changed her life. When her father went to war, her grandfather, the village herb doctor, came to live with the family. He taught Jessica and her brother to find and dry herbs. The war closed in and her grandfather died, so Jessica, her mother, and brother fled their country in a boat.

Towle, Wendy. *The Real McCoy: The Life of an African-American Inventor*. Illustrated by Wil Clay. 1993. New York: Scholastic. Unp. Grades: 1–6.

Some say the expression "the real McCoy" was used to describe an oil cup invented by Elijah McCoy. The oil cup provided a continuous supply of oil, which meant that the train did not have to periodically stop to be oiled. His oil cup was superior to the ones created by others who copied his invention, so people began asking for "the real McCoy." He was the son of slaves who escaped to Canada on the Underground Railroad. His parents sent him to school in Scotland where he studied engineering. He eventually settled in the United States. As an African American the only work he could find was as a fireman/oilman for the Michigan Central Railroad.

Van Steenwyk, Elizabeth. *When Abraham Talked to the Trees.* **Illustrated by Bill Farnsworth. 2000. Grand Rapids, Mich.: Eerdmans Books for Young Readers. Unp. Grades 1–6.**

This is an anecdotal story of young Abraham Lincoln. His strong desire and his struggle to learn to read, write, and speak are described. His love of words is evident as he memorizes books and sermons to recite again and again to anyone who will listen, even if it is just the trees.

Adler, David A. *A Picture Book of Amelia Earhart.* **Illustrated by Jeff Fisher. 1998. New York: Holiday House. Unp. Grades: 2–4.**

Amelia Earhart was the first woman to fly across the Atlantic Ocean. Her intense passion for flying, her strong will, and her determination enabled her to excel in a male-dominated field. Young readers enjoy learning about this inspiring aviation pioneer. As with other books in the Picture Book Biography series this one provides students with readable text and colorful illustrations that encourage younger students to read and learn about the subjects.

Wallner, Alexandra. *Abigail Adams.* **2001. New York: Holiday House. Unp. Grades: 2–4.**

This prolific letter writer left Americans an intimate look into her own remarkable life, as well as the lives of the second president of the United States, her husband John Adams, and the sixth president, her son John Quincy Adams. While believing that her place in life was to be a wife and mother, she also believed in equality for all Americans and spoke out against slavery and for women's rights. The book provides students with information on daily living in colonial America and in the context of historic events.

The Song of Sacajawea. **1993. Video. Lancaster, Penn: Rabbit Ears Productions/ Microleague Multimedia. 30 min. Grades: 2–4.**

This animated video introduces students to Sacajawea, Lewis and Clark's seventeen-year-old guide as they traveled from the Dakotas to the Pacific Ocean. The video indicates that she lived to one hundred years of age, when in fact she died at a much younger age.

Raphael, Elaine, and Don Bolognese. *Daniel Boone: Frontier Hero.* **1996. New York: Scholastic. Unp. Grades: 2–5.**

This charming book is illustrated with color drawings that depict the life of frontier hero, Daniel Boone. It begins when Daniel was a boy in eastern Pennsylvania and continues with his life as a married man moving his family from North Carolina to Kentucky. The book ends with instructions for drawing the people, a Conestoga wagon, a canoe, and a log cabin using a grid. This book is part of the Drawing America series.

Adler, David A. *Christopher Columbus: Great Explorer*. Illustrated by Lyle Miller. 1991. New York: Holiday House. 48p. Grades: 2–5.

As a youngster, Christopher Columbus read of the travels of Marco Polo and wanted to follow in his footsteps with the hopes of achieving great wealth. In order to achieve his dreams of great wealth he had to find sponsors to support his travels. Queen Isabella financed his journey in search of a shorter route to China. Instead, he landed on an island in South America. The book tells how the landing of these European sailors impacted the lives of the Native Americans by introducing deadly diseases that killed them and by forcing many of them into slavery. Columbus's exploits encouraged other explorers to set sail in search of new lands. The book concludes with an index. This is one of the Picture Book Biography series. This book is also available on cassette from Live Oak Media, Pine Plains, New York.

Turner, Ann. *Abe Lincoln Remembers*. Illustrated by Wendell Minor. 2001. New York: HarperCollins. Unp. Grades 2 and up.

This fictionalized chronicle of one of our most distinguished presidents briefly describes his youth, his march to the presidency, and his life during the turmoil of the Civil War. Not intended to be a biography, this book touches the senses of the reader and provides a somewhat sentimental journey through Lincoln's life. Each student, depending upon the age and developmental level, will get something different from the book.

Stanley, Fay. *The Last Princess: The Story of Princess Ka'iulani of Hawai'i*. Illustrated by Diane Stanley. 2001. New York: HarperCollins. Unp. Grades: 2 and up.

Unlike the other 49 states, Hawaii had a royal family and this is the story of Princess Ka'iulani. She never ruled the islands, but as a teenager she went to Washington to appeal to President Cleveland to not annex her country to the United States and to allow Hawaii to maintain its freedom. Her pleas were futile. Lush paintings capture the beauty of the islands and the racially-mixed inhabitants. This book was named an American Library Association Notable Book and given the Carter G. Woodson Award from the National Council of Social Studies.

Kroll, Steven. *William Penn: Founder of Pennsylvania*. Illustrated by Robert Himler. 2000. New York: Holiday House. Unp. Grades: 3–5.

This book about the founder of Pennsylvania is also a story of the beginnings of the Quaker movement in America. William's Quaker beliefs of equality and conscience shaped his life. At a time when laws prohibiting religious freedom were growing stricter, Penn continued to speak out for his beliefs for which he was frequently imprisoned. The land grant for Pennsylvania was given to William for repayment of debts that King Charles II owed William's father. Pennsylvania provided the Quakers the religious freedom they sought. The book ends with a list of important dates in Penn's life and an author's note.

Lasky, Kathryn. *Vision of Beauty: The Story of Sarah Breedlove Walker*. Illustrated by Nneka Bennett. 2000. Cambridge, Mass.: Candlewick Press. 48p. Grades: 3–6.

Madame C. J. Walker built a cosmetic empire at a time when few women and few African Americans were business owners. She employed other African American women and gave them opportunities to become financially successful. Additionally, she fought for equal rights for African Americans and for women. She serves as a role model for young women.

Giblin, James Cross. *The Amazing Life of Benjamin Franklin*. Illustrated by Michael Dooling. 2000. 48p. New York: Scholastic. Grades: 3–5.

Benjamin Franklin was a noted statesman dedicated to the American cause of freedom. He worked tirelessly both in America and Europe to assure the fledgling nation's success. He is remembered for the hospitals and libraries he established, his Poor Richard's Almanack, his experiments with electricity, and his numerous inventions. The book concludes with a list of the important dates in his life, his inventions, sayings from his Almanack, a list of historic sites associated with him, a bibliography, an artist's note, and an index.

William Penn and Pennsylvania. 1998. Bala Cynwyd, Penn.: Schlessinger Video Productions-Library Video Company. 23min. Grades: 3–7.

The intriguing life of William Penn and his founding of the Quaker colony in Pennsylvania are examined in this video. Re-enactments featuring William Penn are used to facilitate students' understanding of the role of this early settler in establishing a colony for the peaceful, loving Quakers. A teacher's guide is included. This is one of the Colonial Life for Children series videos.

Sullivan, George. *Paul Revere*. 2000. New York: Scholastic. 128p. Grades: 3–7.

Paul Revere's own writing about his famous ride introduces this enjoyable biography. The introduction includes information explaining how primary and secondary sources were used to locate information about this American hero. Unhappy with written accounts of his famous ride, Paul Revere wrote an eight-page letter to the Massachusetts Historical Society describing his ride. Excerpts from this letter are included in the book. The book concludes with a chronology of Paul Revere's life, a bibliography of primary and secondary sources, books for further reading, addresses for obtaining additional information, and an index. This book is one of the In Their Own Words Series.

Maestro, Betsy C. *Struggle for a Continent: The French and Indian War 1689-1763*. Illustrated by Giulio Maestro. 2001. New York: HarperCollins. 48p. Grades: 3–6.

This is an informative examination of 74 years of fighting that helped to determine the destiny of the United States. Pictures, maps, and portraits highlight the people and places described in this book. This is one of the American Story series.

Harness, Cheryl. *Remember the Ladies: 100 Great American Women*. 2001. New York: HarperCollins. 64p. Grades: 3 and up.

The contributions of women throughout American history are briefly described in short biographies of 100 influential women. Writers, architects, nurses, athletes, and politicians are some of the careers chosen by these women. The book includes a pictorial timeline, a glossary, a bibliography, other resources, and a note from the author.

Krull, Kathleen. *Lives of Extraordinary Women: Rulers, Rebels (and What the Neighbors Thought)*. Illustrated by Kathryn Hewitt. 2000. New York: Harcourt Brace. 95p. Grades: 4–6.

This collection of brief biographies introduces readers to 20 remarkable women from history and serves as a starting point for further research. Women in this book include both well-known ones, such as Joan of Arc and Marie Antoinette, and lesser-known ones such as Gertrude Bell and Aung San Suu Kyi. This book is also available in audiocassette and CD versions.

Christian, Mary Blount. *Who'd Believe John Colter?* Illustrated by Laszlo Kubinyi. 1993. New York: Macmillan. 64p. Grades: 4–6.

This biographical fiction tells the story of an actual adventurer and explorer who joined Lewis and Clark on their westward journey. His penchant for telling tall tales meant people rarely believed what he said. He discovered Old Faithful in Yellowstone Park, but no one believed him until many years later. His delightful tales of early America provide an interesting twist to the history of this time.

Jeffrey, Laura S. *Barbara Jordan: Congresswoman, Lawyer, Educator*. 1997. Springfield, N.J.: Enslow Publishers. 112p. Grades: 4–8.

With the support, discipline, and encouragement of her parents, Barbara Jordan worked hard to overcome her impoverished background and succeed. When she reached law school, she realized that the separate but equal education she had as an African American was not the same as her Caucasian classmates. Throughout her careers as congresswoman, lawyer, and educator she worked to assure that African Americans had the same opportunities as Caucasians. The book includes a chronology from her birth in 1936 to her death in 1996.

Whitelaw, Nancy. *Clara Barton: Civil War Nurse*. 1997. Springfield, N. J.: Enslow. 128p. Grades: 4–8.

Clara Barton's father instilled in his daughter the importance of serving her country. Her service to America involved collecting food, medicine, and bandages for wounded soldiers and then delivering the supplies to them on the battlefield. After the Civil War, she established a bureau to identify missing soldiers. Her work also included providing assistance to people suffering from natural disasters. Throughout her life Clara Barton suffered debilitating bouts of depression. This is one of the Historical American Biographies Series. Other books in this series are on the lives of Susan B. Anthony, Stonewall Jackson, John Wesley Powell, Benjamin Franklin, Robert E. Lee, and Paul Revere.

White, Alana J. *Sacagawea: Westward with Lewis and Clark*. 1997. Springfield, N.J.: Enslow. 128p. Grades: 4 and up.

Sacagawea was a vital, courageous member of this team of explorers who journeyed from Saint Louis to the Pacific Northwest. She served as a guide and translator as the explorers encountered different Native American tribes. In Lewis and Clark's journals they acknowledge how invaluable she was to them in their travels. Maps, black-and-white photographs, and black-and-white renditions of paintings accompany the text. This is one of the Native American Biographies series.

Hart, Philip S. *Up in the Air: The Story of Bessie Coleman*. 1996. Minneapolis, Minn.: Carolrhoda Books. 80p. Grades: 4 and up.

Imagine dreaming of being a pilot. However, you are a black woman in a time when there are no black pilots and certainly no black women pilots. Yet, this was the dream of young Bessie Coleman from Waxahachie, Texas. This wonderful book with compelling black-and-white photographs depicts Bessie Coleman's dream. She regarded every obstacle as a challenge and worked at menial jobs to obtain her dream.

Pinkney, Andrea Davis. *Let It Shine: Stories of Black Women Freedom Fighters*. Illustrated by Stephen Alcorn. 2000. San Diego, Calif.: Gulliver Books. 107p. Grades: 4 and up.

From lesser-known Biddy Mason to well-known Sojourner Truth, ten black women freedom fighters are profiled in this hard to put down book. Their courage and perseverance when confronted with overwhelming odds challenges readers to make an effort no matter how small to right the injustices they encounter in their lives. The book includes an introduction and suggestions for further reading.

Lalicki, Tom. *Spellbinder: The Life of Harry Houdini*. 2000. New York: Holiday House. 88p. Grades: 5 and up.

Harry Houdini was born in Budapest, Hungary. He was renowned less for being a magician than for being an escape artist. He found that his audiences were impatient with his magical prowess and clamored for him to perform his marvelous escape routines. While some of his feats have been replicated, most of his escape routines have not. Excellent black-and-white photographs are found throughout the book including pictures of playbills and advertisements of his shows. The book ends with a chronology that links events in Harry's life with momentous events in history. A bibliography and index are also included.

EXPLORATIONS

1. Prior to reading the biographies have students decide on a definition of a hero and list the characteristics of a hero. After reading several biographies ask them to determine which of the people they learned about would be considered a hero based on their definition and the characteristics of a hero. They should be able to support their responses by using examples from the person's biography.

2. After reading several biographies, have students take on the role of one of the people and create diary entries by that person using Diary Maker software. The entries should be based on actual events in the person's life and students need to refer back to the biographies to write the entries.

3. Prior to reading *The Divide* (Bedard, 1997), have students share memories of moves they have made and how they felt when they moved. Willa Cather did not like leaving behind her former life when she moved to Nebraska. Eventually, she came to see the move as a new beginning rather than an ending. Help students draw comparisons between moves they have made and Willa Cather's move. Then help them to see the move as a new beginning and an opportunity for new experiences.

4. After reading *The Divide* (Bedard, 1997), read aloud one of Willa Cather's books to the students.

5. After reading *Let Freedom Ring: A Ballad of Martin Luther King, Jr.* (Livingston, 1992), have the students participate in choral readings of the ballad.

6. As the teacher reads *Betsy Ross* (Wallner, 1994), the students create sketches depicting events in her life. The students can then write brief captions for the drawings that can be displayed on the bulletin board. Younger students may need help writing their captions.

7. Prior to reading *Sweet Dried Apples: A Vietnamese Wartime Childhood* (Breckler, 1996), have students share things they have learned from their grandparents.

8. Reading *Sweet Dried Apples: A Vietnamese Wartime Childhood* (Breckler, 1996) may for some children trigger memories of fleeing war in their homeland. These students need an opportunity to share their experiences in a warm, loving, supporting environment.

9. Prior to reading *A Picture Book of Ameila Earhart* (Adler, 1998), print maps of the United States using Mapmakers Toolkit software or have students use maps in their social studies textbook. As the story is read, have students locate the different places mentioned in the book on their maps.

10. After reading *Sacagawea: Westward with Lewis and Clark* (White, 1997) and viewing *The Song of Sacajawea* (Rabbit Ears Productions, 1993), have students create a compare-and-contrast chart of the data presented in each of them.

11. When students find the grids for drawing pictures at the end of the book *Daniel Boone: Frontier Hero* (Raphael and Bolognese, 1996) they immediately reach for paper and pencil and begin drawing. Provide them with bulletin board space to hang their artwork. Before hanging their artwork have them talk about their pictures.

12. After reading *Christopher Columbus: Great Explorer* (Adler, 1991), have students use Inspiration software to make a concept map showing the challenges he faced, his achievements, and things he accomplished.

13. Prior to reading *The Real McCoy: The Life of an African-American Inventor* (Towle, 1993), ask the students if they have heard of the expression "the real McCoy." After reading the book, have students research the lives of other inventors and then make brief oral presentations to their classmates.

14. After reading *William Penn: Founder of Pennsylvania* (Kroll, 2000), have students create cause-and-effect concept maps of events in his life. They may want to focus on the impact of his religious beliefs on events in his life.

15. Benjamin Franklin led an interesting life. If he were alive today he would be the focus of news reports about the things he did and the things he invented. Students can write news reports about events in his life after reading *The Amazing Life of Benjamin Franklin* (Giblin, 2000).

16. After reading *Paul Revere* (Sullivan, 2000), have students visit www.seacoastnh.com/history/rev/revere.html to learn about Paul Revere's other ride.

17. In the note from the author at the end of *Remember the Ladies: 100 Great American Women* (Harness, 2001), she invites readers to make a list of their own favorite 100 American women. After reading the book, have students make their own list.

18. After reading *Who'd Believe John Colter?* (Christian, 1993), have students retell their favorite part of his life to a partner.

19. After reading *Barbara Jordan: Congresswoman, Lawyer, Educator* (Jeffrey, 1997), students can compare themselves to her by completing these sentences: "I am like Barbara Jordan because . . ." and "I am not like Barbara Jordan because . . ." Students may need guidance as they use higher-order thinking skills to form their comparisons.

20. Biography boxes are one way for students to share with other students information they

learn by reading biographies. After reading a biography, students place objects reflective of the subject's life in a box with the name of the subject on the lid. As they talk to their classmates about the person they ask them why they think the different objects are used to represent the person. For example, for *Clara Barton: Civil War Nurse* (Whitelaw, 1997), bandages and a letter requesting information about a missing relative who fought in the Civl War could be used to represent events in her life.

21. In *Sacagawea: Westward with Lewis and Clark* (White, 1997) students learn how invaluable she was to Lewis and Clark. The contributions of support people are oftentimes not recognized. Students can interview school support personnel and write about their interviews in a class newsletter.

22. After reading *Spellbinder: The Life of Harry Houdini* (Lalicki, 2000), have students brainstorm a list of possible ways he escaped from handcuffs, ropes, straitjackets, and milk cans. Then they can compare their ideas with his actual escape secrets found at www.pbs.org/wgbh/amex/houdini.

23. Prior to reading *Up in the Air: The Story of Bessie Coleman* (Hart, 1996), remind students that it has been said that Bessie Coleman was a woman ahead of her time. As students are reading, have them search for information to explain why she was considered ahead of her time.

24. *Let It Shine: Stories of Black Women Freedom Fighters* (Pinkney, 2000) is a book for reading aloud one story at time. After reading the story, provide students opportunities to discuss the women's lives and the hardships they overcame to make changes in their lives and the lives of many others.

REFERENCE BOOKS

These reference books contain specific details about people, places, and events in American history. They provide multiple sources of information that assures that the material is presented from a variety of perspectives. Students can search these reference books for specific information, by reading only portions of the books.

BOOK AND MEDIA CHOICES

Johnstone, Michael. *Explorers.* 1997. Cambridge, Mass.: Candlewick Press. 32p. Grades: 3–6.

The History News book series consists of newspapers each written on a different theme. This book is filled with fictionalized accounts of explorations many written in the first person. The explorations range from 1500 B.C. to 1960. These accounts are very much like the Sunday magazine sections found in today's newspapers. They are easy-to-read and contain numerous pictures and diagrams. There are other books written in this same style covering topics such as medicine, the Aztecs, and the Romans.

Harness, Cheryl. *Remember the Ladies: 100 American Women.* **2001. New York: HarperCollins. Unp. Grades: 3 and up.**

This ambitious study of American women is made readable by the brief text passages and beautiful, detailed illustrations. Well-known women such as Helen Keller and Margaret Sanger are interspersed with lesser-known, but interesting women such as Annie Smith Peck and Elizabeth Gurley Flynn. The biographical information on these noted women is arranged by time and periods. The book concludes with a timeline, a glossary, a bibliography, a list of recommended readings, historic sites, women's organizations, and a note from the author.

Clinton, Catherine. *Scholastic Encyclopedia of the Civil War.* **1999. New York: Scholastic Reference. 112p. Grades: 4–8.**

Divided into five chapters, before 1861, 1862, 1863, 1864, and 1865 and after, this book provides a comprehensive exploration of the Civil War. The pages are divided into categories such as camp lingo, food and rations, details about individual places and people, eyewitness accounts, and battles-at-a-glance. The book ends with an extensive index.

McCormick, Anita Louise. *Native Americans and the Reservation in American History.* **1996. Springfield, N. J.: Enslow. 128p. Grades: 4–8.**

Native Americans who had lived on this continent for centuries, greeted the first European settlers that arrived in North America. The Native Americans were offered "treaties," as well as warfare in exchange for land that was theirs. The newcomers shoved, bullied, and killed the Native Americans to get their land. The dark legacy surrounding the treatment of the Indians is explored in this well-written text. The book has suggestions for further reading, an index, a timeline, and is part of the In American History series.

Krull, Kathleen. *Lives of the Presidents: Fame, Shame (and What the Neighbors Thought).* **Illustrated by Kathryn Hewitt. 1998. San Diego, Calif.: Harcourt Brace. 96p. Grades: 4–8.**

Many historical books and facts have been written about the presidents of the United States. But not as much has been written about their roles as fathers, husbands, and neighbors. This book examines the presidents in a much more anecdotal manner and looks at them as pet owners, persons with bad habits, ailments, poor attitudes, and odd sleep habits. Forty-two presidents are discussed, some of them with more information than others. Caricatures of each president and some wives are included. The book closes with a selected bibliography. Presidents are listed in chronological order.

Adams, Simon. *Visual Time Line of the 20th Century.* **1996. New York: DK. 48p. Grades: 4 and up.**

The book is divided into the following sections: 1900-1917 – The End of an Era, 1918-1941 – Between the Wars, 1941-1989 – The World Divided, and 1990-2000 – The Final Decade. As evidenced by the entries this has been a century of almost continuous warfare beginning with World War I and ending with the Persian Gulf War. Brief textboxes, color and black-and-white photographs, diagrams, and charts contain a wealth of information about the 20th century.

Rubel, David. *The United States in the 20th Century.* **1995. New York: Scholastic. 232p. Grades: 4 and up.**

The chapters in the book are divided into eras, such as the Progressive Era, the Great Depression, and World War II. Each era include information on politics, life in the twentieth century, arts and entertainment, and science and technology. A timeline extends across the bottom of each two-page spread. Every right-hand page has a features box that spotlights people or events that impacted the era. There is a glossary and an index. This is one of the Scholastic Timelines series that includes *The United States in the 19th Century* (Rubel, 1996).

Rubel, David. *The Scholastic Encyclopedia of the Presidents and Their Times.* **1997. New York: Scholastic. 232p. Grades: 4 and up.**

Information about the presidents is interspersed with information about their personal lives, the political times in which they lived, and the lives of other important figures of the time. Placing the lives of the presidents in the context of important events of their times makes this an excellent resource for studying the presidents and American history. Brief text boxes enhanced with a wide variety of photographs, illustrations, and charts make this a reference source that students return to again and again. At the end of the book is a short, engrossing history of the White House.

Sandler, Martin W. *Presidents.* **1994. New York: HarperCollins. 94p. Grades: 4 and up.**

This anecdotal book of interesting tidbits about our presidents is filled with black-and-white and color photographs. The very human side of the presidents and their families are portrayed, as well as information about their pets. One photograph shows President Lyndon Johnson seated in the Oval Office holding his dog, both of them with their heads thrown back singing a duet.

St. George, Judith. *So You Want to Be President?* **Illustrated by David Small. 2000. New York: Philomel Books. 52p. Grades: 4 and up.**

This delightful Caldecott Medal winner answers questions young readers would not think to ask about the presidents of the United States. Cartoon-like drawings accompany many little-known, interesting facts about the presidents. For example, there is a two-page spread of President Taft being lowered by a crane into a tub specially built to accommodate his large girth. The book ends with thumbnail biographical sketches of the presidents through William J. Clinton.

Mayo, Edith P., editor. *The Smithsonian Book of the First Ladies: Their Lives, Times and Issues.* 1996. New York: Henry Holt. 302p. Grades: 4 and up.

Forty-three remarkable women have served as first ladies and this is the first comprehensive biography written about them for young people. There are eleven highlighted entries about issues important to American women, as well as 127 works of art that make this book especially appealing to young readers. The author of the book is the curator of the First Ladies exhibit at the Smithsonian Institute. The book ends with a bibliography, suggestions for further reading, and a comprehensive index.

Bock, Judy, and Rachel Kranz. *The Scholastic Encyclopedia of the United States.* 1997. New York: Scholastic. 140p. Grades: 4 and up.

Students undertaking a study of the individual states find this book a useful, beginning resource. Each state has its own two-page spread that includes a basic facts column on the left side containing information, such as population, size, flower and motto, and a fascinating facts column on the right side that includes the state's firsts, bests, mosts, and famous people. In between the two columns is information on the history, geography, and industry of the state. At the end of the book is a map of the United States, places to visit in each state, a bibliography, and an index.

Miller, Marilyn. *Words That Built a Nation: A Young Person's Collection of Historic American Documents.* 1999. New York: Scholastic. 172p. Grades: 5 and up.

When studying American history, documents are important artifacts from which to learn about the past. Words have helped to shape America, and the documents collected here provide evidence of the importance of words in America's past. Speeches, book chapters, and declarations had a profound impact on American life. Supporting information and illustrations set the context for the documents. Information is provided about the author or authors of the documents and the public's response to these famous texts. An index is included.

TEACHER RESOURCES

This section contains resources for teaching social studies. These resources include books, contact information for professional organizations, and Internet sites. One of the books listed is a catalog of free social studies resources for teachers. This book is updated yearly and can be found in many school, public, and university libraries.

BOOKS

Cook, Deanna F. *The Kid's Multicultural Cookbook: Food and Fun Around the World.* **1995. Charlotte, Vt.: Williamson. 159p. Grades: P and up.**

This combination of recipes, traditions, and customs from across the globe even includes ideas for theme parties. The recipes include step-by-step instructions and are easy for children to follow.

Zemelman, Steven, Patricia Bearden, Yolanda Simmons, and Pete Leki. *History Comes Home: Family Stories across the Curriculum.* **1999. York, Maine: Stenhouse. 176p. Grades: K–6.**

These projects help students see how history is all around them and helps them connect history to their daily lives.

Pratt, Linda, and Janice J. Beaty. *Transcultural Children's Literature.* **1999. Upper Saddle River, N. J.: Merrill. 403p. Grades: K–8.**

Chapters in this book focus on different geographic regions on the globe. Each chapter is separated into different countries of the region. Books pertaining to that country are summarized and classroom applications for the book are given.

Educator's Guide to FREE Social Studies Materials. **2000-2001. Randolph, Wis.: Educator's Progress Service. 233p. Grades: K and up.**

In this guide, teachers will find free videos, films, filmstrips, lesson plans, print resources, and Web resources. To assist teachers in locating items in the book there are title, subject, source, and what's new indexes. There is also a sample letter to use to request the materials.

Roberts, Patricia L. *Literature Based History Activities for Children, Grades 1–3.* **1998. Boston: Allyn and Bacon. 236p. Grades: 1–3.**

Children's literature and hands-on activities come together to assure students enjoy learning history.

King, David C. *Colonial Days: Discover the Past with Fun Projects, Games, Activities, and Recipes.* **1998. New York: John Wiley and Sons. 118p. Grades: 1–8.**

Interspersed with directions for creating colonial crafts, playing games, and cooking are brief anecdotes about life in colonial times shared by the fictitious Mayhew family. Children enjoy this hands-on approach to learning about life in the 13 original colonies.

Caduto, Michael J. and Joseph Bruchac. *Keepers of the Earth: Native American Stories and Environmental Activities for Children.* **Illustrated by John Kahionhesfadden and Carol Wood. 1997. Golden, Colo.: Fulcrum. 209p. Grades: 4–8.**

Native American tales on various topics are combined with hands-on activities to extend the reading. The tales and activities span the content areas and teach children to value the Earth and all living things.

Roberts, Patricia L. *Literature Based History Activities for Children, Grades 4–8.* **1998. Boston: Allyn and Bacon. 236p. Grades: 4–8.**

Combining ideas, activities, and children's literature to support the history curriculum helps motivate students to learn about history.

Allen, Michael G., and Robert L. Stevens. *Middle Grades Social Studies: Teaching and Learning for Active and Responsible Citizenship.* **1988. Boston: Allyn and Bacon. 180p. Grades: 6–8.**

The social studies curriculum is presented through interdisciplinary instruction with a focus on service learning.

Hess, Fredrick M. *Bringing the Social Sciences Alive: 10 Simulations for History, Economics, Government, and Geography.* **1999. Boston: Allyn and Bacon. 220p. Grades: 7–12.**

The simulations in this book enliven classroom lessons and actively involve students in their learning.

PROFESSIONAL ORGANIZATIONS

The National Association of Economic Educators
Maryland Council on Economic Education
Towson University
8000 York Road
Towson, MD 21252-0001
410-830-3796
http://ecedweb.unomaha.edu/naee.htm

National Council for Geographic Education
16A Leonard Hall
Indiana University of Pennsylvania
Indiana, PA 15705-1087
412-357-6290

National Council for the Social Studies
3501 Newark Street, NW
Washington, DC 20016-3199
202-966-7840
http://ncss.org
Journals: *Social Education, Social Studies and the Young Learner, Middle Level Learning*

INTERNET SITES

American Memory: Historical Collections for the National Digital Library
http://memory.loc.gov/
> The collections of the Library of Congress are only a click away at this site. There are learning pages for students and teachers, lesson plans, and media analysis tools.

Ben's Guide to Government for Kids
http://bensguide.gpo.gov/
> Materials on this site are grouped according to grade levels and include materials for parents and teachers. There is also information on the site's namesake Benjamin Franklin.

EconEdLink
www.ncee.net
> The purpose of this site is to provide materials to assure that students in kindergarten through twelfth grade develop an understanding of economic principles. This site includes lesson plans, information on current events, a catalog of publications, and links to other useful sites.

Lesson Plans and Resources for Social Studies Teachers
www.csun.ed./~hcedu013/index.html
> This site has won numerous awards and features lesson plans and links to other Web sites for enhancing social studies education.

Mr. Dowling's Electronic Passport
www.mrdowling.com
> This award-winning site has an impressive collection of information and links related to social studies and history. A great deal of the information is text-based and written for students in sixth grade and up.

Presidential Exploration
http://library.advanced.org/11492/index2.html
> Students can learn what it takes to become president at this Web site. They can also find information on each president and his presidency.

Xpeditions

www.nationalgeographic.com\xpeditions\home.html

Sponsored by National Geographic, this site has geography resources for teachers, librarians, parents, and students. Included is an interactive atlas, Blue-Ribbon Web sites, Family Xpeditions, standards-based lesson plans, and Xpedition Hall. Xpedition Hall is an interactive virtual world that supports learning the geography standards. Xpeditions is a partner in the educational program, MarcoPolo.

REFERENCES

Athanases, Steven Z. 1998. "Diverse Learners, Diverse Texts: Exploring Identity and Difference through Literary Encounters." *Journal of Literacy Research* 30, no. 2 (June): 273-296.

Beck, Cathy, Shari Nelson-Faulkner, and Kathryn Mitchell Pierce. 2000. "Historical Fiction: Teaching Tool or Literary Experience?" *Language Arts* 77, no. 6 (July): 546-555.

Davis, John C., III, and Jesse Palmer. 1992. "A Strategy for Using Children's Literature to Extend the Social Studies Curriculum." *Social Studies* 83, no. 3 (May-June):125-128.

Diary Maker. 1997. New York: Scholastic.

Dooley, Norah. 1991. *Everybody Cooks Rice*. Minneapolis, Minn.: Carolrhoda Books.

Edgington, William D. 1998. "The Use of Children's Literature in Middle School Social Studies: What Research Does and Does Not Show." *Clearing-House* 72, no. 2 (November-December): 121-125.

Farris, Pamela J., and Carol J. Fuhler. 1994. "Developing Social Studies Concepts through Picture Books." *The Reading Teacher* 47, no. 5 (February): 380-387.

Freeman, Evelyn B., Barbara A. Lehman, and Patricia L. Scharer, eds. 1999. "Inspirations." *The Reading Teacher* 52, no. 6 (March): 622-629.

Goforth, Frances S. 1998. *Literature and the Learner*. Belmont, Calif.: Wadsworth.

Gravelek, James R., and Taffy E. Raphael. 1996. "Changing Talk about Text: New Roles for Teachers and Students." *Language Arts*, 73, no. 3 (March): 182-192.

Inspiration. Version 6. 1999. Portland, Ore.: Inspiration Software.

Kincade, Kay M., and Nancy E. Pruitt. 1996. "Using Multicultural Literature As an Ally to Elementary Social Studies Texts." *Reading Research and Instruction* 36 (Fall): 18-32.

Knight, Margy Burns. 1996. *Talking Walls Continued*. Gardiner, Maine: Tilbury House.

Lee, Lauren. 1996. *Japanese Americans*. Cultures of America. Tarrytown, N. Y.: Benchmark Books, Marshall Cavendish.

Lott, Carolyn, and Stephanie Wasta. 1999. "Adding Voice and Perspective: Children's and Young Adult Literature of the Civil War." *English Journal* 88, no. 6 (July): 56-61.

Mapmakers Toolkit. 1999. Watertown, Mass.: Tom Snyder Productions.

Microsoft PowerPoint. 2000. Redmond, Wash.: Microsoft Corporation.

Microsoft Publisher. 2000. Redmond, Wash.: Microsoft Corporation.

Moss, Marissa. 1999. *Emma's Journal: The Story of a Colonial Girl.* Young American Voices. San Diego, Calif.: Harcourt Brace.

Murray, Yvonne I., and José Velazquez. 1999. "Promoting Reading among Mexican American Children." ERIC Digest, ED 438150.

National Council for Geographic Education. 1994. *Geography for Life: National Geography Standards.* [Online]. Indiana, Pa.: National Council for Geographic Education. Available: www.nationalgeographic.com/resources/ngo/education/standardslist.html [cited 28 November 2000]

National Council for the Social Studies. 1994. *Curriculum Standards for the Social Studies.* [Online]. Washington, D.C.: National Council for the Social Studies. Available: www.ncss.org/standards/2.0.html [cited 28 November 2000]

Nelson, Lynn R., and Trudy A. Nelson. 1999. "Learning History Through Children's Literature." ERIC Digest ERIC Clearinghouse for Social Studies/Social Science Education, Bloomington, Ind. ED 435586.

Phillips, David, and Steven Ferry. 1996. *Greek Americans.* Cultures of America. Tarrytown, N.Y.: Benchmark Books, Marshall Cavendish.

Ranson, Clare. 1996. "Cartography in Children's Literature." Paper Presented at the Annual Conference of the International Association of School Librarianship in Worcester, England, July. ERIC, ED 400859.

Rubel, David. 1996. *The United States in the 19th Century.* Scholastic Timelines. New York: Scholastic.

Sanchez, Tony R. 1998. "Using Stories about Heroes to Teach Values." ERIC Clearinghouse for Social/Studies/Social Sciences Education, Bloomington, Ind. ERIC, ED 424190.

Seda, Milagros M., Olga Z. Liguori, and Carmen M. Seda. 1999. "Bridging Literacy and Social Studies: Engaging Prior Knowledge through Children's Books." *TESOL Journal* 8, no. 3 (Autumn): 34-38.

TimeLiner. Version 4.0. 1999. Watertown, Mass.: Tom Snyder Productions.

Whitehead, Sandra. 1996. *Lebanese Americans.* Cultures of America. Tarrytown, N.Y.: Benchmark Books, Marshall Cavendish.

Yopp, Ruth Helen, and Hallie Kay Yopp. 2001. *Literature-Based Reading Activities. 3d ed.* Boston: Allyn and Bacon.

Chapter 5

Health

Reading books to children about health-related issues provides opportunities for discussions and learning to take place in the classroom and library. Teachers and librarians who read and talk to children about important issues such as these show children that their health is important and establish open lines of communication with children who may not be in healthy environments. Scales (2000) discusses the developmental assets that children need to reach their full potential. Included in these assets are positive peer influence, cultural competence, restraint, self-esteem, achievement motivation, and values. Scales contends that while schools cannot by themselves be responsible for student's developmental assets, they can build on these developmental assets through health education classes. Particularly beneficial are activities that require students to see how their personal health issues relate to social implications such as the right to smoke and the right of others to not be exposed to second-hand smoke.

Sharing books and videos with students about abuse and neglect helps them to understand what they are and to understand that children do not have to be victims. Discussing abuse with children helps to foster a safe, supportive environment for reporting abuse. Creating a safe environment for disclosure of abuse provides children with a chance to escape the abuse (Sechrist, 2000). Further, Sechrist contends that oftentimes siblings and peers are the first ones to know about the abuse and can serve as a liaison between the abused children and responsible adults.

The Joint Committee for National School Health Education Standards developed standards to serve as guidelines for promoting health literacy, which is defined as the ability to understand and use health information to maintain a healthy lifestyle (Summerfield, 1995). The standards require students to demonstrate the ability to obtain valid health information, use the information appropriately, make health-related decisions, and advocate healthy lifestyles. Books and media on proper nutrition, safety, hygiene, and other health-related issues are an excellent way to involve children in learning how to maintain a healthy lifestyle.

This chapter includes a range of health-related topics that have a life-long impact on students. Sections in this chapter include hygiene and safety, nutrition, families, and growth and development. The subsections under families include family constellations, divorce, adoption and foster care, and homelessness. Under the growth and development section are subsections including birth and growth, feelings, friendship, self-esteem, manners, and aging and death.

HYGIENE AND SAFETY

Part of growing up and becoming independent is learning to stay healthy and safe. One of the first things parents teach children is about safety; staying away from hot stoves; not talking to strangers; and tying their shoelaces so as not to trip on them. Other things children learn about are hygiene, exercise, first aid, and safety. The books in this section help students learn to take care of themselves. These are books for sharing with students in the classroom and for sending home to share with their parents.

BOOK AND MEDIA CHOICES

Manning, Mike. *Wash, Scrub, and Brush.* Illustrated by Brita Granstrom. 2001. Morton Grove, Ill.: Albert Whitman. Unp. Grades: P–K.

The text in this book is woven through the large, colorful illustrations. The readers follow several children as they prepare to go to a party. One child has to have head lice removed before attending the party. At the end of the party they all need to be scrubbed again. The book concludes with a glossary.

Carle, Eric. *From Head to Toe.* 1997. New York: HarperCollins. Unp. Grades: P–1.

This book is definitely not just for reading, it is also for participating. The healthy movements included in the book have been carefully selected because they are a fun way for youngsters to exercise. Colorful collage animals demonstrate each movement on the left side of the two-page spread and then challenge children to mimic the movement. The child on the right side of the page mimics the movement and choruses "I can do it!" For example, on one page a cat arches its back and asks the child if she can do it? The child on the next page is depicted arching her back with the cheerful refrain "I can do it!" The repetitious refrain combined with the successful completion of simple movements helps to build children's self-confidence.

Showers, Paul. *Sleep Is for Everyone.* Illustrated by Wendy Watson. 1997. New York: HarperCollins. 32p. Grades: P–1.

The importance of sleep is explained in simple terms and cartoon-like illustrations. The effect of the lack of sleep on the human body is illustrated by a tale of scientists who stayed awake for days. Over time they could not concentrate to read and they made mistakes. Finally, they fell asleep in their chairs. The book ends with a description of what happens during sleep. This book is part of the Let's-Read-and-Find-Out Science series.

Keller, Laurie. *Open Wide: Tooth School Inside.* **2000. New York: Henry Holt. Unp. Grades: P–3.**

Dr. Flossman, a dentist, begins the day by taking roll and making sure that all thirty-two teeth are present. This light-hearted informative look at teeth includes a visit from the tooth fairy. Children relate to the cartoon-like drawing and the antics of the thirty-two teeth.

Asthma, Asthma, You Can't Stop Me. **1998. Video. Chino, Calif.: KidSafety of America. 18 min. Grades: P–4.**

Youngsters who are dealing with asthma relate to Amanda and how she has learned to manage her condition.

McGinty, Alice B. *Staying Healthy: Good Hygiene.* **1998. New York: Franklin Watts. 24p. Grades: K–2.**

Color photographs of children and large text with word pronunciation guides make this a book for young readers to explore on their own. Not only does this book tell children about ways to take care of their body; it also tells them why it is important to take care of themselves. Teachers and librarians help children make connections between the healthy habits of the children in the book and the children in the classroom. This book is one of The Library of Healthy Living series that contains books on dental care, nutrition, exercise, safety, and sleep.

Keeping Clean: Handwashing for Health. **1999. Video. El Dorado, Calif: One Hundred Percent Educational Videos. 15 min. Grades: K–2.**

In this video students learn what germs are and that hands are the primary means of germs entering the body. The importance of proper handwashing in order to remain healthy is explained in this video.

Royston, Angela. *A Healthy Body.* **2000. Des Plaines, Ill.: Heinemann Library. 32p. Grades: K–2.**

For young readers this book provides an introduction to the importance of staying healthy through exercise. The book explains the role of muscles and joints in exercise. Practical tips are included such as the proper procedure for lifting heavy objects and the importance of sleep. The book concludes with a glossary, an index, and a bibliography.

Tooth Wisdom. 1999. Video. El Dorado, Calif: One Hundred Percent Educational Videos. 15 min. Grades: K–2.

Children learn about the functions and importance of teeth in this video. They learn proper techniques for brushing and flossing and why it is important to brush and floss. The roles of dentists and hygienists are explained.

MacGregor, Cynthia. *Ten Steps to Staying Safe*. 1999. New York: The Rosen Publishing Group. 24p. Grades: K–2.

The large, easy-to-read print enables beginning readers to read this book on their own; however, it is one that needs to be discussed with an adult as it is read. The steps presented are common sense, such as walking with a buddy and carrying emergency money for phone calls, but they need to be discussed with children and practiced through role-play. The last step cautions children to remain calm and listen to their instincts. An index concludes the book.

Brown, Laurie Krasny, and Marc Brown. *Dinosaurs Alive and Well: A Guide to Good Health*. 1990. Boston: Little, Brown. 32p. Grades: K–2.

The comic book style of the illustrations appeal to young readers who recognize themselves in the young dinosaurs portrayed in the book. Young readers learn about the importance of taking care of themselves and then through pictures and words learn the basics of taking care of themselves. Topics discussed include bathing, exercising, dealing with feelings, friendship, sneezes, first-aid tips, getting help from grown-ups, and getting enough sleep. This book provides young readers with the knowledge to begin learning how to take care of themselves. This book is one of the Dino Life Guides for Families series.

All about Health and Hygiene. 2001. Video. Bala Cynwyd, Penn.: Schlessinger Video Productions-Library Video Company. 23 min. Grades: K–4.

Students know that being sick is not fun and they are interested in learning how to stay well. This video explains why and how people get sick and includes ideas for staying healthy. The program includes a teacher's guide. This is one of the Human Body for Children series.

Sanders, Pete. *Bullying*. 1996. Brookfield, Conn.: Copper Beech Books. 32p. Grades: K–5.

Color photographs of children role-playing bullying situations and comic strips of bullying demonstrate to children how to deal with bullies. Chapters include information on the definition of bullying, why people bully, standing up to bullies, bullying at school, racist bullying, and ideas about what to do about bullying. Readers are told that the first step in stopping bullying is to talk to someone. The book concludes with a list of organizations to help children who are being bullied and an index. This is one of the What Do You Know About series.

McGruff's Bully Alert. **2001. Video. Chatsworth, Calif.: AIMS Multimedia. 15 min. Grades: K–5.**

McGruff explains to two children what a bully is and ways to deal with bullies such as ignoring them, talking to them, and telling adults about them. This is one of the McGruff series.

Be Cool, Play It Safe!: A Children's Safety Video. **1999. Video. Eugene, Ore.: EMP International. 43 min. Grades: K–5.**

Brief four-minute segments present safety scenarios on topics that include burns, falls, cycling accidents, and drug abuse. A multicultural group of children are seen in the video and women are pictured in nontraditional roles.

McGruff on Self-Protection: Preventing Child Abuse and Neglect. **1993. Video. Chatsworth, Calif.: AIMS Multimedia. 23 min. Grades: K–6.**

Crime Dog McGruff helps children understand child abuse and neglect using dramatizations. He tells children that they have the right to be safe and they need to discuss harmful situations with a trusted adult. This is one of the McGruff series.

McGruff's Self-Care Alert. **1991. Video. Chatsworth, Calif.: AIMS Multimedia. 17 min. Grades: K–6.**

Children who stay at home alone after school relate to the four children in this video who talk about how they take care of themselves when they are home alone. Tips are included for dealing with feelings of loneliness. This is one of the McGruff series.

Gibbons, Gail. ***Emergency.*** **1994. New York: Holiday House. Unp. Grades: 1–3.**

This basic book for youngsters is about different types of transportation for emergency personnel from police cars to helicopters. Under the illustrations of the vehicles are short descriptions of how they are used in emergency situations. A brief look at police vehicles, ambulances, and fire trucks used in the past concludes the book.

Parsons, Alexandra. ***I'm Happy, I'm Healthy.*** **Illustrated by Ann Johns, John Shackell, Paul Banville, and Stuart Harrison. 1996. New York: Franklin Watts. 29p. Grades: 1–3.**

This delightfully illustrated and photographed book is a welcome "first" book on health care for the young child. Subjects covered include fuel for the body, eating and drinking, care of muscles and lungs, cleanliness, being ill, and information about the brain. The book concludes with a glossary, an index, and some useful addresses for health organizations.

Rathmann, Peggy. *Officer Buckle and Gloria*. 1995. New York: G.P. Putnam's Sons. Unp. Grades: 1–6.

Officer Buckle was always thinking up safety tips and he loved to tack them up on his bulletin board. He frequently gave safety lectures at the local elementary school where his tips were ignored until Gloria, a police dog, began accompanying him and demonstrating his safety tips as he read them. Throughout the book and on the endpapers students find a collection of small notes filled with safety tips. This book was awarded the Caldecott Medal.

Boelts, Maribeth, and Darwin Boelts. *Kids to the Rescue!: First Aid Techniques for Kids*. Illustrated by Marina Megale. 1992. Seattle, Wash.: Parenting Press. 71p. Grades: 1–6.

This is a basic first-aid book with illustrations and easy-to-read instructions. Bleeding, broken bones, poisoning, eye injuries, and burns are just a few of the emergencies covered in the book.

Parker, Steve. *Professor Protein's Fitness, Health, Hygiene, and Relaxation Tonic*. Illustrated by Rob Shone. 1996. Brookfield, Conn.: Copper Beech Books. 48p. Grades: 2–5.

Off-beat humor and clever illustrations combine to tell students about exercise, personal hygiene, and diet. Professor Protein combines information about the body with practical, easy-to-understand instructions for taking care of the body. For example, a cross-section drawing of a tooth labels the parts of the tooth and explains why it is important to brush and floss. Then, directions are given for proper brushing and flossing. The book ends with a body chart, a glossary, and an index.

Glibbery, Caroline. *Join the Total Fitness Gang*. 1998. Milwaukee, Wis.: Gareth Stevens. 32p. Grades: 2–6.

Do you know how to deal with a nosebleed? Can you do anything about muscle cramps? What can you do about perspiration odor? These are a few of the many questions that youngsters begin to think about as they are growing up. This book cautions students about drugs, cigarettes, and dieting. The color photographs make each subject discussed very realistic. At the bottom left of each two-page spread is a short question about the topic. The answer is found on the right-hand page. At the end of the book are a glossary, a list of books to read, some videos, Web sites, and an index.

Peacock, Carol Antoinette, Adair Gregory, and Kyle Carney Gregory. *Sugar Was My Best Food: Diabetes and Me.* **Illustrated by Mary Jones. 1998. Morton Grove, Ill.: Albert Whitman. 55p. Grades: 3 and up.**

One summer, Adair Gregory went from being a normal nine-year-old boy to a nine-year-old boy with diabetes. He tells his own story about the ups and downs of altering his lifestyle as he learned to cope with his illness. When he developed diabetes he did not know any other children with the disease and he wrote this book to tell other children with diabetes that they are not alone. Children with the disease and those who want to learn more about the disease find this book easy-to-read and informative.

Reef, Catherine. *Stay Fit: Build a Strong Body.* **1993. New York: Henry Holt. 64p. Grades: 4–8.**

A truly healthy person is one who is physically fit and this book explains the importance of exercise to staying fit. Chapters on stretching and building strength, devising a fitness program, joining a team, safety considerations, and nutrition are included in this book. The author writes for children and does not talk down to them or preach. She provides examples and suggests students give themselves rewards for keeping fit. At the conclusion of the book is a list of books for further reading and an index.

Gold, Susan Dudley. *Arthritis.* **2001. Berkeley Heights, N.J.: Enslow. 48p. Grades: 4 and up.**

Amanda was eleven years old and at summer camp when she became ill. After seeing a number of doctors it was discovered that she had arthritis. Most people think that arthritis is a disease of the elderly. Few people realize that arthritis can be contracted at any age. This book explains all of the components of arthritis including causes, diagnosis, care, and treatment. The final chapter is called Research: Hope for Tomorrow. The book concludes with a list for further reading, addresses for more information, a glossary, and an index. This is part of the Health Watch series. Other books in this series include Alzheimer's disease, asthma, attention deficit disorder, bipolar disorder and depression, cancer, cystic fibrosis, diabetes, epilepsy, heart disease, multiple sclerosis, and muscular dystrophy.

Chaiet, Donna, and Francine Russell. *The Safe Zone: A Kid's Guide to Personal Safety.* **Photographs by Lillian Gee. 1998. New York: Morrow Junior Books. 160p. Grades: 5 and up.**

Self-defense is the topic of this book for young adults. They are cautioned to be aware of their surroundings and to learn to communicate with the person who is threatening their safety. Readers are instructed to think about possible options when confronted by danger and to practice the skills in the book, so that when confronted by danger they will be able to act quickly. Further, they are cautioned about using physical force to defend themselves; however, the book does include information on fighting back. Ideas and strategies for staying safe at home, for staying safe away from home, and dealing with bullies are also included in the book. While younger children will not be able to read the book on their own, librarians and teachers may want to share the ideas presented in the book with them.

Gutman, Bill. *Hazards at Home.* 1996. New York: Twenty-First Century Books. 80p. Grades: 6 and up.

Scenarios of potential home safety hazards provide opportunities for class discussions of appropriate actions to take. This home safety book points out potential dangers in an average home, describes accidents, how to prevent them, and how to treat injuries. The book is written in a simple, explanatory style with colorful photographs and diagrams. It closes with a bibliography, organizations to contact for additional information, and an index. This book is one of the Focus on Safety series of books.

EXPLORATIONS

1. As the teacher reads *From Head to Toe* (Carle, 1997) students enjoy getting out of their seats and mimicking the movements of the animals. Students can be challenged to think of other animal movements to mimic.

2. Before reading *Sleep Is for Everyone* (Showers, 1997), ask students how they behave or feel when they do not get enough sleep at night.

3. Prior to reading *Staying Healthy: Good Hygiene* (McGinty, 1998), create a Hygiene Box filled with items mentioned in the book, such as a washcloth, soap, toothbrush, and a hairbrush. Pull the items from the box and have the children identify the objects and tell how they are used. After reading the story, have the names of the objects in the box printed on index cards and have the students match names to the actual object.

4. *A Healthy Body* (Royston, 2000) explains to children the importance of getting enough sleep. After reading the book, provide the children with a sleep chart to post on their refrigerator. Enlist their parents' help to record how many hours the children sleep each night. At the end of the week have the students return the completed charts to school to determine how many hours of sleep they get each night.

5. After reading each step and its description in *Ten Steps to Staying Safe* (MacGregor, 1999), discuss the steps with the students. Then have them role-play the steps. It may be helpful to explain to them that by role-playing the steps they will be better prepared to act quickly should the need arise.

6. After reading each section of *Dinosaurs Alive and Well: A Guide to Good Health* (Brown and Brown, 1990), have students stand up and pantomime the activities such as bathing, exercising, and sneezing.

7. While reading *Bullying* (Sanders, 1996), call students' attention to the body language of the children in the illustrations. Have them discuss what can be learned about people and their feelings by carefully reading their body language.

8. After reading *Emergency* (Gibbons, 1994), ask children how emergency personnel know when and where to show up. This would be the time to show children on a telephone how to dial 911 and to tell them the importance of staying calm, speaking distinctly, and staying on the phone line. Allow children opportunities to role-play reporting an emergency.

9. In *I'm Happy, I'm Healthy* (Parsons, 1996) foods are given one-star, two-star, and three-star ratings based on their location in the food pyramid. Create a classroom chart to record the food served in the cafeteria at lunch and the ratings of the food. This activity helps children become familiar with the food pyramid and which foods they need to eat each day.

10. The United States Department of Agriculture's (USDA) Web site at www.nal.usda.gov/fnic/Fpyr/pyramid.html has ethnic/cultural food guide pyramids for Native American, Spanish, Asian, and Latin American people. Sharing these pyramids with students from diverse backgrounds helps them to feel a part of the classroom community and gives them an opportunity to talk about foods from their countries. Students can create a unique class food pyramid including foods from the different cultures represented in the classroom.

11. Prior to reading *Officer Buckle and Gloria* (Rathmann, 1995), tape small safety tips around the classroom or library for students to discover.

12. After reading *Officer Buckle and Gloria* (Rathmann, 1995), share with students that the idea for the book came from a creative writing class assignment that required Rathmann to find a piece of paper lying on the floor and start a story from the information on the paper (Peck and Hendershot, 1997). Have the students look at school and at home for abandoned grocery lists, notes, or "things to do" lists. Then have them write stories based on the papers they found.

13. Prior to reading each section of *Kids to the Rescue!: First Aid Techniques for Kids* (Boelts and Boelts, 1992), ask children if they have ever faced a similar first-aid situation and how they responded. Share the text with the students and have them pantomime the correct response.

14. Have students work in pairs to select one section of information in *Professor Protein's Fitness, Health, Hygiene, and Relaxation Tonic* (Parker, 1996) to present to their classmates. Students should bring in appropriate props and encourage their classmates to participate in the presentation. For example, when presenting the section on exercise warm-up routines they could have their classmates do the warm-up routines with the presenters.

15. *Join the Total Fitness Gang* (Glibbery, 1998) has two-page spreads on important health topics for students. Before reading each section, tell the students the topic and ask them to share what they know about the topic. After reading the section have the students write down the key ideas they learned in the section. Have them discuss the ideas they wrote down. For example, one section deals with drugs and has photographs of children who briefly tell their stories about drugs and alcohol. Allow children opportunities to talk about their encounters with drugs and alcohol.

16. Prior to reading *Sugar Was My Best Food: Diabetes and Me* (Peacock, Gregory, and Gregory, 1998) have students tell what they know about diabetes and record their responses in an Inspiration software concept map. While reading, have them record additional information they learn in the concept map. After reading the book, have the students generate questions about diabetes that they can research and add to the concept map.

17. After reading *Stay Fit: Build a Strong Body* (Reef, 1993), help students devise a fitness program and set goals for themselves. Classmates with similar goals can form a support group to help each other achieve their goals. The group may want to devise a chart to record their progress and plan rewards for themselves when they meet their goals as suggested in the book.

18. Before reading *Hazards at Home* (Gutman, 1996), have students brainstorm a list of possible hazards found in homes. Divide the class into six groups, one for each chapter. Each group is to skim through their chapter and create a checklist of possible home hazards. Each group's checklist can be duplicated for all of the students, who take the list home and assess the hazards in their house. They can discuss the assessment with their parents and decide what needs to be changed.

NUTRITION

Eating the right foods is one component of staying healthy, as food is fuel for the body and gives it the energy to move and grow. The food pyramid is a graphic representation of the foods the body needs and the number of portions needed of each food. Maintaining good nutrition while they are growing impacts students' health for the rest of their lives. Knowing what foods they need to eat helps students make wise choices at mealtime and snacktime. Since adults are the ones making food purchases in the home, it is important to share nutrition information with them. This can be done by sending the books home with students and by including the adults in activities related to proper nutrition.

The delights and pleasures of food are extolled in verses by a variety of noted poets in *Food Fight* (Rosen, 1996). Children enjoy looking through the book to discover if their favorite foods are included. Sharing the poems with children is one way to introduce a unit on nutrition.

Rosen, Michael, editor. *Food Fight*. 1996. San Diego, Calif.: Harcourt Brace. 46p. Grades: 2–5.

Short poems, long poems, funny poems, and thought-provoking poems all sing the praises of the poets' favorite foods. Thirty-three children's poets have written poems in celebration of food to benefit Share Our Strength's mission to eliminate hunger and support its causes. Lively watercolor illustrations surround the verses.

BOOK AND MEDIA CHOICES

Tofts, Hannah. *I Eat Vegetables*. Photographed by Rupert Horrox. 1998. New York: Zero to Ten. Unp. Grades: P–1.

Colorful, fresh vegetables photographed on vibrant painted backgrounds with foldout pages entice children to read the book and perhaps even convince them to taste some of the vegetables. For example, below the word "tomato" in the top left corner of a two-page spread, tomatoes roll across the page. Lifting the flap on the right-hand side displays cut tomatoes with these words: leaves, seeds, half, and slices. Each vegetable is depicted in a similar manner and students can learn the names of the vegetables and a variety of other vocabulary words.

ized *Picture of Health/Magic in the Kitchen*. 1998. Video. New York: Columbia TriStar – Sony Pictures Entertainment. 50 min. Grades: P–1.

Youngsters join Jim Henson's bear as he starts his morning with a woodland workout and then serves his friends breakfast. The importance of exercise and nutrition are demonstrated in this musical adventure. This is part of the Bear in the Big Blue House series.

De Bourgoing, Pascale, and Gallimard Jeunesse. *Vegetables in the Garden*. Illustrated by Gilbert Houbre. 1994. New York: Scholastic. Unp. Grades: P–2.

This beautifully photographed book contains transparent pages and slick pages showing a number of different kinds of vegetables. It explains how they grow and whether we eat the underground part or the aboveground part. The book encourages readers to plant their own garden and to enjoy the crops they grow. This is one of the First Discovery series.

Gibbons, Gail. *Apples*. 2000. New York: Holiday House. Unp. Grades: K–3.

Here is information about the fruit tree grown in more parts of the world than any other fruit. Information about how they grow, their various parts, and tidbits from pollination to pickling are included. There are also instructions on planting and caring for apple trees. In Gibbons's own inimitable style, the text and bright, colorful pictures appeal to the young child. At the end of the book is Gibbons's trademark series of little-known, illustrated facts.

Kalbacken, Joan. *The Food Pyramid*. 1998. New York: Children's Press. 48p. Grades: 1–3.

This colorfully photographed book introduces the food pyramid to young children. The pyramid levels are described and examples are provided of the foods in each level. Young readers learn why it is important to eat a variety of foods and what the different foods do for the body. A bibliography, a list of Web sites, a short glossary, and an index are included. This book is one of the True Book series.

Kalbacken, Joan. *Vitamins and Minerals*. 1998. New York: Children's Press. 48p. Grades: 1–3.

Large, easy-to-read print introduces children to the importance of vitamins and minerals to maintain strong, healthy bodies. Young readers learn what foods contain which vitamins and minerals and what each of the vitamins and minerals do for the body. A bibliography, a list of Web sites, a short glossary, and index are included. This book is one of the True Book series.

***Doug's Chubby Buddy*. 2000. Video. Burbank, Calif.: Disney Educational Productions. 25 min. Grades: 1–8.**

The issue of eating disorders is explored in this video, as Patti Mayonnaise is getting ready to participate in track. Patti's excessive dieting and exercising is dangerous and this video forms the basis for classroom discussions of the hazards of eating disorders.

Patent, Dorothy Hinshaw. *Where Food Comes From*. Photographs by William Muñoz. 1991. New York: Holiday House. 40p. Grades: 2–4.

Readers may be surprised to learn that their food starts with the sun. From green plants to grains, to meat to dairy products, readers are introduced to where foods come from. The last chapter explains how foods are put together for meals using familiar favorite children's food such as pizza and tacos. Muñoz's rich, colorful, close-up photographs of food in the garden, pasture, barn, and grocery store cause the reader to pause and linger.

Patent, Dorothy Hinshaw. *Nutrition: What's in the Food We Eat?* Photographs by William Muñoz. 1992. New York: Holiday House. 40p. Grades: 2–4.

Appetizing, colorful photographs of nutritious foods cause the reader's mouth to water while perusing this book. Basic information on the right foods to eat and why they are important to good health is the focus of the book. Aimed at young readers, this book explains proper nutrition and why it is so important. A recipe for soft pretzels, the Food Guide Pyramid, a glossary, and an index conclude the book.

***Mysteries of the Food Pyramid*. 2000. Video. Kansas City, Mo. MarshMedia. 15 min. Grades: 4–6.**

Viewers join two students as they discover the mysteries of the food pyramid and learn about good nutrition. This video comes with a teacher's guide and is closed-captioned.

Chandler, Gary, and Kevin Graham. *Natural Foods and Products*. 1996. New York: Henry Holt. 63p. Grades: 4–6.

Success stories of entrepreneurs, who grow and create natural foods and products that are environmentally safe, are the subject of this book. One of the success stories is about growing organic grapes. Another one tells about how growing colored cotton eliminates the need for costly and environmentally unfriendly dyeing of the cotton fiber. At the end of each story is an address for additional information on the food or product. This is one of the Making a Better World series.

***Protein: How Cows and Carrots Become People*. 2000. Video. Lake Zurich, Ill.: Learning Seed. 18 min. Grades: 4–8.**

This video shows children the importance of adequate protein in the diet. It includes protein for both traditional and vegetarian diets.

***Nutrition and Diet*. 1994. Video. Bala Cynwyd, Penn.: Schlessinger Video Productions-Library Video Company. 30 min. Grades: 5–8.**

Students learn that proper nutrition is a cornerstone of good health throughout their lives. The food pyramid is explained and the importance of proper exercise is discussed. Students learn about developing healthy eating habits.

EXPLORATIONS

1. Have students bring in a variety of raw vegetables to categorize and taste. Before reading *I Eat Vegetables* (Tofts, 1998) or *Vegetables in the Garden* (De Bourgoing and Jeunesse 1994), have children decide on different ways to categorize the vegetables, such as by color, shape, or taste. While reading the book, have the children taste or smell each vegetable as it is introduced.
2. After reading *Apples* (Gibbons, 2000), provide students a variety of different apples to taste. Have them determine if the different varieties have different tastes and have them try to describe the tastes. Record and graph the class favorites.
3. Gail Gibbons has written and illustrated numerous nonfiction books for children that can be placed on a table in the classroom or library for an author/illustrator study. An author/illustrator study expands students' opportunities to respond aesthetically to books as they explore the connections between the text and the illustrations as Madura (1995) discovered with her primary-age students.
4. After reading *The Food Pyramid* (Kalbacken, 1998), have students maintain a food diary for two or three days. Then have them examine their food diaries to determine what changes they should make in their diets. Students can be encouraged to share their findings with their parents.
5. To help students apply what they have learned from *Vitamins and Minerals* (Kalbacken,

1998) conduct a class survey to record what they ate for breakfast, lunch, or dinner. Using the information in the book help students determine what vitamins and minerals were in the foods they ate. Help them determine which vitamins or minerals were not in their foods.

6. As *Where Food Comes From* (Patent, 1991) is read aloud, have students draw a diagram of the food chain. Then have them write down the steps in the process.

7. Prior to reading *Nutrition: What's in the Food We Eat?* (Patent, 1992), have students make a list of their favorite foods. After reading, have them decide whether or not their favorite foods are nutritious.

8. *Natural Foods and Products* (Chandler and Graham, 1996) has information on starting an indoor garden. Students can plant a garden and grow vegetables in the classroom.

9. At the end of each section in *Natural Foods and Products* (Chandler and Graham, 1996) is an address for obtaining additional information on the topic. Have students select one of the organizations to write to for information. When the information arrives, they can present what they learned to their classmates by creating HyperStudio stacks on the computer.

FAMILIES

This portion of the chapter includes sections on family constellations, divorce, adoption and foster care, and homelessness. Exploring single-parent families, divorced families, adoptive families, families with aging grandparents, and homeless families in books provides opportunities for children to explore and discuss these issues from different points of view. By evaluating the characters' actions they gain insight into their own actions when faced with similar situations. After reading these books students need opportunities to relate the books to their own lives. Engaging in discussions after reading the books provides them a chance to clarify their understanding, verify what they have read, and reflect on the information they have learned (Goforth, 1998).

FAMILY CONSTELLATIONS

Reading books about different family constellations assures that children find families similar to their own between the pages of a book, which enables them to find personal meanings in the text. The books in this section reflect a variety of family constellations and *Families* (Morris, 2000) introduces this topic with colorful photographs and easy-to-read text.

Morris, Ann. *Families*. 2000. New York: HarperCollins. 32p. Grades: P–4.

Eye-catching color photographs from around the world celebrate all kinds of families. Large-print text under the photographs tells how families work together, play together, and help one another. Families composed of aunts, uncles, and cousins, as well as families composed of grandparents and foster parents are shown enjoying each other's company. The index has a thumbnail of the photograph and identifies the country where the photograph was taken. On the last page of the book is a line drawing of the world so students can locate the countries represented in the book.

BOOK AND MEDIA CHOICES

Luthardt, Kevin. *Mine!* 2001. New York: Atheneum Books for Young Readers. Unp. Grades: P–1.

Sharing is a difficult lesson for young children to learn, but an essential lesson for getting along in the world. When a stuffed dinosaur arrives in the mail, two brothers in unison think "Mine!" The ensuing battle leaves the dinosaur torn with stuffing spilling out. Mom mends the dinosaur and the boys realize that sharing the dinosaur is better than having no dinosaur at all.

Ballard, Robin. *My Day, Your Day.* 2001. New York: Greenwillow. Unp. Grades: P–1.

When children are dropped off at day care and their parents go to work, they may each seem to be going in very different directions; however, the author of this book shows how similar their daily actions really are. For example, one small girl is building with blocks on the left side of the two-page spread, while on the right side is a brief statement about building with blocks and three scenes of the girl's father on his construction job.

Spinelli, Eileen. *When Mama Comes Home Tonight.* Illustrated by Jane Dyer. 1998. New York: Scholastic. Unp. Grades: P–2.

Lyrical verse and pastel pictures tell the tale of a working mother's evening at home with her child. Motherly chores and childcare take up her evening that ends with a lullaby and tucking a sleepy child into bed. Working mothers and their children find themselves portrayed in the pages of this book.

Wood, Douglas. *What Dads Can't Do.* Illustrated by Doug Cushman. 2000. New York: Simon and Schuster Books for Young Readers. Unp. Grades: P–2.

All the wonderful things that dads do for their children are seen through the eyes of a young child, who is convinced that there are lots of things dads cannot do. For example, since dads need extra practice putting worms on a fishing hook, the child lets dad bait his hook. An adorable dinosaur son and his dad bring smiles to readers' faces as they share memorable moments together. This is a book for young and old readers as both recognize themselves in the pictures. A mom does not appear in this book and children who live with their fathers want to see families like theirs.

Wood, Douglas. *What Moms Can't Do*. Illustrated by Doug Cushman. 2000. New York: Simon and Schuster Books for Young Readers. Unp. Grades: P–2.

This companion book to *What Dads Can't Do* (Wood, 2000) looks at mothers through the eyes of a young child, who discovers that moms are inept at things, such as keeping salamanders in their shirts or keeping toads in their pockets. Moms even need help reading books to children. Once again readers young and old will see themselves in the story and make connections between their lives and the lives of the characters. A father does not appear in this book.

Benjamin, Amanda. *Two's Company*. 1995. New York: Penguin Books. Unp. Grades: P–3.

Maddy and her mother have a special relationship, just the two of them. Then one day Simon enters their lives and suddenly Maddy's mother begins spending more and more time with him. When the subject of marriage comes up, Maddy is opposed to the idea. Her mother's reassurances and kind, thoughtful actions help Maddy accept and welcome Simon into the family. This book shows children that becoming a blended family can be a wonderful experience and it also provides parents with ideas for helping children accept the changes in their lives.

Viorst, Judith. *Super-Completely and Totally the Messiest*. Illustrated by Robin Preiss Glasser. 2001. New York: Atheneum Books for Young Readers. Unp. Grades: K–2.

This is the story of two very different siblings, one very neat and one very messy. In spite of her best attempts the messy one will never be neat and her older sister comes to realize that and to appreciate her sister just the way she is. Children recognize themselves and their siblings in this story of two loving sisters, who happen to be very different.

Galindo, Mary Sue. *Icy Watermelon*. Illustrations by Pauline Rodriguez Howard. 2001. Houston, Tex.: Pinata Books. Unp. Grades: K–2.

On a warm summer afternoon mother brings out icy cold watermelon for the children to share with their grandparents as they spend the waning moments of the day seated on the front porch. The watermelon reminds the grandparents of when they met and they share the story with their grandchildren. This story evokes fond remembrances of family gatherings and the stories that are shared with family members. The text of the book is written in both Spanish and English.

Pfister, Marcus. *The Happy Hedgehog*. Translated by J. Alison James. 2000. New York: North-South Books. Unp. Grades: K–3.

Mikko enjoyed spending time in his garden learning the names of the plants and their healing powers. His grandfather thought Mikko was wasting his time in his garden and told him to go out and accomplish something useful. Mikko visited with other animals in the forest all trying to be the biggest, the strongest, or the smartest, but none of them seemed happy. He returned to his garden where he was happy just the way he was.

Smothers, Ethel Footman. *Auntee Edna.* **Illustrated by Wil Clay. 2001. Grand Rapids, Mich.: Eerdmans Books for Young Readers. Unp. Grades: K–6.**

Spending the night with old-fashioned Auntee Edna is the last thing Tokee wants to do, but her mother insists. Auntee Edna does not even have a television. In this heartwarming story, Tokee discovers her family heritage and learns to value her aunt's knowledge and ways. The book ends with a recipe for Auntee Edna's homemade tea cakes.

Nolen, Jerdine. *In My Momma's Kitchen.* **Illustrated by Colin Bootman. 1999. New York: Harper Trophy. Unp. Grades: K and up.**

The kitchen is the heart of this African American family and a young child describes all the wonderful family gatherings that occur in this warm, loving atmosphere. Readers of all ages and cultures relate to the family gatherings.

Bercaw, Edna Coe. *Halmoni's Day.* **Illustrated by Robert Hunt. 2000. New York: Dial Books for Young Readers. Unp. Grades: 1–4.**

When her grandmother, Halmoni, arrives from Korea, Jennifer is concerned about what her classmates will think of her grandmother who dresses differently from the other grandmothers and does not speak English. On Grandparent's Day, Jennifer's mother interprets as Halmoni shares a story about her father and tells Jennifer and her classmates how proud she is of her granddaughter who reminds her of her own father. When Halmoni's father returned from the Korean War, he lost his voice. Halmoni and her father learned to communicate with one another through simple gestures much the same way that Halmoni and Jennifer communicate since they do not speak one another's language.

That's a Family. **2000. Video. San Francisco, Calif.: Women's Educational Media. 35 min. Grades: 1–6.**

This video features children talking about their nontraditional families that include ethnically mixed, lesbian mothers, divorced, and single-parent households. Throughout the video the families are seen doing everyday family activities and it is evident that what makes a family is the love and care the family members have for one another.

Fraustino, Lisa Rowe. *The Hickory Chair*. Illustrated by Benny Andrews. 2001. New York: Scholastic. Unp. Grades: 2–4.

Louis is a special child with a special grandmother. They are especially close and Louis feels he can actually "see" her even though he was born blind. When Gran dies while Louis is still young, she reveals in her will that she has hidden notes around her house telling each family member what she has left them. Louis is certain she has left him the rocker they sat in together, day after day. But he does not find his note until he is a grown man.

Bowen, Keith, with Dan Gutman. *Katy's Gift*. 1998. Philadelphia, Penn.: Courage Books. Unp. Grades: 2–4.

The culture of the Amish people is introduced in this heart-warming book of a brother and sister who put their own wishes aside to provide for their sibling. Important values are imparted as the siblings learn that money must be earned and just because they want something does not mean it can be theirs. The technology-free life of the Amish is introduced in this book.

Zucker, David. *Uncle Carmello*. Illustrated by Lyle Miller. 1993. New York: Macmillan. Unp. Grades: 2–4.

Sometimes children who speak only English have relatives who speak little or no English. Not only do they have difficulty communicating with them, they also have difficulty relating to the relatives' customs and life styles. This heartwarming story tells of a boy's visit to his dreaded Italian uncle and the boy's discovery that his uncle is respected and beloved by many and most importantly, in his own way, he cares deeply for the boy.

Jenness, Aylette. *Families: A Celebration of Diversity, Commitment, and Love*. 1990. Boston: Houghton Mifflin. 47p. Grades: 2–6.

Family diversity is explored through 17 children and their families in what was first a photographic exhibition at the Children's Museum in Boston. Now through text and photographs the shapes and sizes of families are examined. The book begins with children's written comments about what makes a family and what families do. Children's reactions to the photographic exhibit of these blended families, single-parent families, gay and lesbian families, and families formed through adoption and foster care indicate that young readers want to read about families like their own, which may not be the two-parent family. Throughout the book readers are shown that love is what really makes a family.

EXPLORATIONS

1. Prior to beginning a study of families, have the children draw a picture of their family and share the pictures with their classmates.
2. Prior to reading *Mine!* (Luthardt, 2001), have students talk about times they have had

to share with others and discuss their feelings about sharing. Assure students that it is okay not to want to share everything they have with siblings, friends, or classmates. This may lead to a discussion of things they do not want to share.

3. Prior to reading *When Mama Comes Home Tonight* (Spinelli, 1998), share the pictures with the students and have them predict what will happen in the story.

4. Before reading *What Dads Can't Do* (Wood, 2000), have students brainstorm a list of things their dads can and cannot do, or for younger students, have them draw pictures. Compare their lists with the things presented in the book.

5. After reading *What Moms Can't Do* (Wood, 2000), have older students discuss the humor in the book. Then have them discuss the things their moms can and cannot do.

6. After reading *Two's Company* (Benjamin, 1995), provide students an opportunity to discuss the book and share similar experiences.

7. After reading *Super-Completely and Totally the Messiest* (Viorst, 2001), place the book in the reading center for students to revisit and examine the detailed drawings depicting the zany antics of the messy younger sister.

8. *Icy Watermelon* (Galindo, 2001) is a book for reading aloud on a warm sunny day. After a page is read in English, it can be read in Spanish, if possible. Then at the end of the story, the students can share icy watermelon slices and share memories of their grandparents.

9. After reading *The Happy Hedgehog* (Pfister, 2000), help children retell the story by creating a story map of the animals and what they were each doing in the story in order to be happy.

10. After reading *Auntee Edna* (Smothers, 2001), have students create their own zoo-zoo with a button and some string. As they work have them share stories about visits with their relatives.

11. Prior to reading *In My Momma's Kitchen* (Nolen, 1999), have children make a list of all the things that happen in their kitchens.

12. Prior to reading *Halmoni's Day* (Bercaw, 2000), have students share ways that they communicate without words.

13. Prior to reading *Halmoni's Day* (Bercaw, 2000), have students draw pictures of their grandparents or bring in photographs of their grandparents.

14. After reading *Katy's Gift* (Bowen, 1998), students can write their own story about a sibling or friend using Imagination Express, Destination: Neighborhood. This software enables students to add animation and sounds to their stories. These electronic stories can be shared with their classmates.

15. Prior to reading *Uncle Carmello* (Zucker, 1993), place the students in small groups to share their stories about making visits to relatives. Then ask the children to tell about one of their favorite relatives. Read the book to the students and then discuss why the boy's feelings about his uncle changed.

16. Prior to reading the book *Families: A Celebration of Diversity, Commitment, and Love* (Jenness, 1990), have students write down what makes a family and what families do.

After reading the book, have students add to their lists about what makes a family and what families do.

DIVORCE

Books in this section include both fiction and nonfiction selections dealing with the feelings and emotions children experience when their parents divorce. Some of these books provide students with practical suggestions for coping with divorce and the inherent changes in their lives. These books also provide teachers, librarians, and parents with insight into divorce from children's perspectives.

BOOK AND MEDIA CHOICES

Bernhard, Durga. *To and Fro, Back and Slow*. 2001. New York: Walker. Unp. Grades: P–2.

This book of opposites is a very powerful book about a child who moves back and forth between her parents' houses. The illustrations aptly portray the contrast between the child's two houses and help to assure children in similar situations that they are not the only ones living in two different homes.

Powell, Jillian. *Talking about Family Breakup*. 1999. Austin, Tex.: Raintree Steck-Vaughn. 32p. Grades: K–4.

The emotional and practical problems that children experience when families break up are explored in this book. Color photographs of different families accompany the large print. The book is broken into chapters covering topics such as why families break up, what happens when families break up, what children can do, and how things will change, and what life will be like in the future. The books ends with a glossary, books to read, and an index.

Santuco, Barbara. *Loon Summer*. Illustrated by Andrea Shine. 2001. Grand Rapids, Mich.: Eerdmans Books for Young Readers. Unp. Grades: K and up.

This is the story of a young girl and her father who spend their first summer after the divorce at their house on a lake. The discovery of a family of loons reminds the girl of when her parents were married and they came to the house as a family. At the end of the story she comes to accept the fact that from now on her mother will not be at the lake house and that like the loons, she will return again next year with her father.

Vigna, Judith. *I Live With Daddy*. 1997. Morton Grove, Ill.: Albert Whitman. Unp. Grades: 1–4.

This is the story of Olivia, a child of divorced parents, who lives with her father. Her mother is a career television reporter who travels a great deal. The daughter is assured by her father that the divorce had nothing to do with her and that both her parents love and care for her. For

Writer's Day she decides to write a book about her mother who is supposed to come for the program. Her mother does not arrive, so she regrets having written a book about her mother and dedicates the book to her father. Her mother arrives after the program long enough to tell her she loves her and that she has to go back to work. Olivia shows her father the book dedicated to the best dad ever.

Best, Cari. *Taxi! Taxi!* **Illustrated by Dale Gottlieb. 1994. Boston: Little, Brown. Unp. Grades: 2–4.**

Scheduled Sunday afternoon visits are surprise-filled excursions in Papi's taxi that create happy memories for Tina and her father. Sometimes Papi does not come and Mama tells Tina that he is busy driving people around the city. This realistic portrayal of scheduled visits with a noncustodial parent assures children of divorce that they are not alone and that other children share their experiences and feelings.

When Your Mom and Dad Get Divorced. **1991. Video. Pleasantville, N.Y.: Sunburst Communications. 20 min. Grades: 2–4.**

Students learn in this video that divorce is never their fault. Real-life scenarios are used to portray different ways for children to cope with the upheavals in their lives. A teacher's guide is included.

Field, Mary B. *My Life Turned Upside Down, But I Turned It Rightside Up: A Self-Esteem Book about Dealing with Shared Custody.* **Illustrated by Bruce Van Patter. 1994. Secaucus, N. J.: Childswork/Childsplay. 70p. Grades: 2–6.**

A young girl tells her story about living with divorced parents. Many youngsters relate to how she has to learn to deal with forgetting things at one parent's house and remembering the different rules at each house. As each problem is encountered, the reader turns the book upside down to read about how the young girl solved her problem. This book is filled with practical advice for youngsters and basically reminds them that they must take responsibility for themselves.

Bode, Janet, and Stan Mack. *For Better, For Worse: A Guide to Surviving Divorce for Preteens and Their Families.* **2001. New York: Simon and Schuster Books for Young Readers. 162p. Grades: 3–6.**

Through interviews and surveys the authors gathered stories from preteen children and their families about the impact of divorce on their lives. The children's words tell of the pain and anguish they have experienced because of the divorce, but they also tell of their hope for the future. Part one of the book is written for the children of divorce and part two of the book is written for their parents. This very readable book fulfills the request of one child of divorce who asked that the authors write a book that when you finished reading it you would feel better.

EXPLORATIONS

1. Rather than reading *Talking about Family Breakup* (Powell, 1999) to the entire class, this may be a book the teacher or librarian shares individually with students.
2. After reading *Loon Summer* (Santuco, 2001), invite students to talk about changes in their lives over which they have no control. Provide them an opportunity to discuss how they have adjusted to the changes.
3. Some students in the class may see their own mother or father reflected in the parents in *I Live with Daddy* (Vigna, 1997). Even intact families may have one parent similar to the mother in this book. Allow students who want to discuss their parents the opportunity to do so, while allowing children who do not wish to participate in the discussion to sit silent.
4. Many children have had experiences similar to those of Tina in *Taxi! Taxi!* (Best, 1994). After reading this book the teacher may simply ask for students' thoughts about the book. This may be a time when the teacher remains silent and listens to the students to see where the discussion takes them.
5. *For Better, For Worse: A Guide to Surviving Divorce for Preteens and Their Families* (Bode and Mack, 2001) is in part based on children's journals. In the book children commented on how writing and talking about their problems made them feel better. Children of divorce and children from intact families wrote about the problems in their lives. Students in the classroom can write in their journals about the problems in their lives and be given an opportunity to talk about their problems.

ADOPTION AND FOSTER CARE

Adoption and foster care are not as secretive and mysterious as they once were. These books help students understand that their feelings and questions about adoption and foster care are normal. They find answers to their questions in these books that include both fiction and nonfiction titles.

BOOK AND MEDIA CHOICES

Say, Allen. *Allison*. 1997. Boston: Houghton Mifflin. Unp. Grades: P–3.

When Asian American Allison puts on a kimono she realizes that she looks more like her doll Mei Mei than she does her American parents. Allison's parents explain how they adopted her from another country. The sober watercolor illustrations beautifully portray Allison's emotions as she grapples with learning about her adoption.

Weitzman, Elizabeth. *Let's Talk about Foster Homes*. Illustrated by Seth Dinnerman. 1996. New York: The Rosen Publishing Group. 24p. Grades: K–2.

Children will find practical factual advice in this book, such as in a foster home they can expect different rules to apply than they would have had in their own homes. Foster children are encouraged to talk about their feelings of anger and sadness, and they are reminded that these feelings are normal. The large text encourages young readers to return to the book again and again to read it on their own. The book includes a short glossary and an index. This is one of The Let's Talk Library series.

Little, Jean. *Emma's Yucky Brother*. Illustrated by Jennifer Plecas. 2001. New York: HarperCollins. 64p. Grades: K–3.

When Emma's family adopts four-year-old Max, Emma discovers that brothers can be pests; however, Emma also learns that Max needs a sister to love and care for him. This book presents a realistic look at the adoption process and the adjustment required when an adopted child becomes a member of the family. This is an I Can Read book.

Lewis, Rose A. *I Love You Like Crazy Cakes*. Illustrated by Jane Dyer. 2000. Boston: Little, Brown. Unp. Grades: K–3.

The author, a single parent, shares her personal experiences of adopting a daughter from China. The joy and happiness she feels as she cares for her new daughter shine through in this marvelous story. The watercolor illustrations capture the happiness and wonder that flows through the story.

Peacock, Carol Antoinette. *Mommy Far, Mommy Near: An Adoption Story*. Illustrated by Shawn Costello Brownell. 2000. Morton Grove, Ill.: Albert Whitman. Unp. Grades: 1–5.

In this touching story, a young girl shares her feelings about having a Chinese birthmother, and an American mother who adopted her. The child struggles to understand why she has two mothers. After seeing a Chinese mother and daughter at the playground, she realizes that her Chinese mother would look like the Chinese mother on the playground. Her adopted mother assures her that her Chinese mother loved her and that she is surrounded by a family who loves her. Having adopted two daughters from China the author writes from her personal experiences.

Giannetti, Charlene C. *Who Am I?* Illustrated by Larry Ross. 1999. New York: Price Stern Sloan. 95p. Grades: 4–6.

Written in a question-and-answer format, this book provides children with answers to tough questions they have about adoption as they reach their preteen years. The book ends with information about athletes, entertainers, journalists, business people, and writers who were adopted. This is one of the Plugged In series.

EXPLORATIONS

1. After reading *Mommy Far, Mommy Near: An Adoption Story* (Peacock, 2000), *I Love You Like Crazy Cakes* (Lewis, 2000), and *Allison* (Say, 1997), provide students opportunities to ask questions about adopting children from other countries. Help the students to see that family members do not have to all look alike and come from the same countries.

2. *Let's Talk about Foster Homes* (Weitzman, 1996) is a book to share one-on-one with a student in a foster home. Oftentimes, children feel comfortable sharing their feelings about their home situation with a teacher or librarian. This book is an excellent starting place for discussing students' concerns about foster care.

3. Prior to reading *Emma's Yucky Brother* (Little, 2001), ask students what they know about adoption.

4. After reading *Emma's Yucky Brother* (Little, 2001), encourage students to discuss the story from each character's point of view.

HOMELESSNESS

Homeless people are seen on the side of the road, living under overpasses, and camping out on city sidewalks. Many children and entire families are now included in the number of homeless people in America. The books in this section deal with this important topic by enabling students to view homelessness from the perspective of the homeless. The last book in this section tells the stories of real homeless children in their own words.

BOOK AND MEDIA CHOICES

McGovern, Ann. *The Lady in the Box*. Illustrated by Marni Backer. 1997. New York: Turtle. Unp. Grades: 1 and up.

Based on the author's personal observations, this story tells about a sister and brother, who help a homeless lady sleeping on the sidewalk in their neighborhood. By making contact with the woman they begin to learn about the plight of the homeless and take steps to help the woman and other homeless citizens in their neighborhood. Rich, dark illustrations fill the pages of the book. A note from the author about volunteering at centers for the homeless concludes the book.

Bunting, Eve. *December*. Illustrated by David Diaz. 1997. San Diego, Calif.: Harcourt Brace. Unp. Grades: 2–4.

On Christmas Eve a homeless mother and her son lay in their cardboard home trying to stay warm when a Christmas angel appears at their door in the form of a homeless old woman. They invite her in to share their warmth and the young boy hesitantly shares his Christmas cookies.

After the visit from the angel their lives change. The next Christmas finds the boy and his mother in their own apartment. Caldecott award-winning artist David Diaz painted the rich, dark illustrations that accompany the text.

Hubbard, Jim. *Lives Turned Upside Down: Homeless Children in Their Own Words and Photographs.* 1996. New York: Simon & Schuster Books for Young Readers. 40p. Grades: 3–7.

Told through the words and photographs of five children, four of whom are homeless and one of whom has a home with no electricity, this book describes the lives of homeless families who have been in touch with various shelters. The stories tell of the determination and perseverance of these young people who strive to better themselves and their families. The author is the founder of a program called Shooting Back that attempts to empower at-risk youth by giving them the tools needed for creative expression such as cameras. The books ends with contact information for agencies that aid homeless people and for Shooting Back.

EXPLORATIONS

1. After reading *The Lady in the Box* (McGovern, 1997), ask students what they think they can do to help the homeless in their town. This discussion might encourage students to pursue an authentic learning activity involving social action to assist homeless children (Fitzgibbons and Tilley, 1999). Students could collect books for a homeless shelter or conduct a food drive for the local food bank.
2. *December* (Bunting, 1997) and *Lives Turned Upside Down: Homeless Children in Their Own Words and Photographs* (Hubbard, 1996) both deal with homelessness as seen through the eyes of homeless children. Whereas *December* is realistic fiction and has a happy ending, *Lives Turned Upside Down* is about real children who hope for a better life. Help students to discern the differences in the way the material in these two books is presented.

GROWTH AND DEVELOPMENT

This section includes books on growing up and growing older—from dealing with a new sibling, to discovering body parts, and understanding aging. Throughout life, events occur that surprise and delight, such as a new baby and discovering bodily changes; however, sometimes children's initial reactions to the changes are fear and frustration. These books help children see that their reactions to these things are a normal part of growing up. Graves shares his remembrances of growing up through a collection of poems to read aloud and discuss with children. These poems introduce many of the topics covered in this chapter.

Graves, Donald. *Baseball, Snakes, and Summer Squash: Poems About Growing Up.* **1996. Honesdale, Pa.: Wordsong/Boyds Mills Press. 80p. Grades: 4–8.**

Through an unsentimental look at his own childhood, Graves affords readers intimate glimpses into childhood. The poems encompass familiar topics such as his first baseball glove, making pies with his grandfather, losing himself in a book, being sent to his room, his special dog, and fishing for eels. The poems are written in free verse and illustrated with black-and-white drawings. Although the main character is a boy, the sentiments and experiences revealed in these poems also appeal to girls.

BIRTH AND GROWTH

Being born and growing up are the most personal topics that children hear and read about. During all the stages of life, it is important to be aware of the changes taking place and to appreciate all that life has to offer. Through poetry Arnold Adoff causes readers to stop, notice, and take delight in their lives and the multitude of experiences that surround them.

Adoff, Arnold. *Touch the Poem.* **Illustrated by Lisa Desimini. 2000. New York: Blue Sky Press. Unp. Grades: K–3.**

This joyous and spirited collection of poems entices children to think of the many things they touch each day of their lives. The poems cause children to stop and reflect on small delights, such as peaches, ice cream cones, bubble baths, and cold windowpanes. The colorful photographs are a feast for the eyes.

There are books in this section on a range of topics including sex education, new siblings, deafness, stuttering, and growing up.

Book and Media Choices

Leonard, Marcia. *Babies Help Out.* **Photographs by Dorothy Handelman. 2001. New York: HarperCollins. Unp. Grades: P.**

Adorable photographs of babies helping out as only babies can, entertain young readers and the adults in their lives. For example, straightening shelves actually involves pushing everything off of the shelves and fixing breakfast requires that it be spread all over the table top. This book is part of the Hanna Books series.

Wong, Janet S. *Grump.* **Illustrated by John Wallace. 2001. New York: Margaret K. McElderberry Books. Unp. Grades: P–K.**

A very tired mother becomes a very grumpy mother when her baby refuses to take a nap. Mothers and children will recognize themselves in this familiar tale of a mother who falls asleep before the baby.

Royston, Angela. *Where Do Babies Come From?* **1996. New York: DK. 37p. Grades: P–1.**

When a child first begins to ask where babies come from, this is a book to share with the child. Beginning with where plants come from, to where animals come from, to where human beings come from, this book uses large-print text and brightly colored photographs to answer these questions. It also shows that babies grow into children who grow into adults who may be mothers and fathers. An introductory note to parents provides advice about sharing this book with young children.

Intrater, Roberta Grobel. *Two Eyes, a Nose, and a Mouth.* **1995. New York: Scholastic. Unp. Grades: P–1.**

Close-up photographs of the faces of Americans of all ages and nationalities introduce very young readers to the variety of features on people's faces. The book helps readers to see the variety, but more importantly reminds them that if everyone looked alike the world would be a dull place. This is demonstrated by a two-page spread of thumbnail shots of the face of one child and another two-page spread of shots of people of different ages and ethnic backgrounds.

Paul, Ann Whitford. *Hello Toes! Hello Feet!* **Illustrated by Nadine Bernard Westcott. 1998. New York: DK INK. Unp. Grades: P–2.**

This delightful poem of a little girl's adventures throughout the day is accompanied by bright cartoon-like illustrations. The little girl begins her day by greeting her toes and feet. She takes the reader along with her as she tries on different kinds of shoes, runs, jumps, and shuffles through the day. Young readers identify with her antics and want to try them too.

Talking Hands. **2000. Video. Alpharetta, Ga.: Small Fry Productions. 30 min. Grades: P–2.**

This simple introduction to American Sign Language encourages young viewers to participate and learn the language while they watch.

Lachtman, Ofelia Dumas. *Pepita Takes Time.* **Illustrated by Alex Pardo DeLange. 2000. Houston, Tex.: Pinata Books. Unp. Grades: K–2.**

Pepita becomes involved in watching things around her, such as a spider spinning a web and ladies making tortillas, and is always late. One day she misses the bus taking her classmates to the zoo and spends the morning on a bench in the school office and the afternoon in the school library. She realizes that always being late impacts her family and friends, as well as hurting herself. She resolves to be more thoughtful of others by being on time. This book is written in both English and Spanish. The English text is on the top half of the page and the Spanish text is on the bottom half of the page.

Millman, Isaac. *Moses Goes to School*. 2000. New York: Farrar Straus Giroux. Unp. Grades: K–3.

This is the story of Moses, a hearing-impaired child, and his first day at a school for the deaf. Parts of the text are translated into American Sign Language using small diagrams at the bottom of some of the pages. Hearing-impaired students and those who are not enjoy this engaging story.

Arnold, Tedd. *Parts*. 1997. New York: Scholastic. Unp. Grades: K–3.

Told in poetry form, this delightful tale of a young boy describes his reactions when he thinks he is falling apart. He finds hair in his comb, lint in his navel, and he loses a tooth. He is convinced his brains are coming out of his nose and his skin is shriveling up at the beach. He yells at his parents for not telling him all of this is "natural." All children have different responses to "new" things happening to them and delight in this youngster's responses. Arnold's artwork is cartoonish enough to show this example of hyperbole.

Henkes, Kevin. *Julius the Baby of the World*. 1990. New York: Greenwillow Books. Unp. Grades: K–3.

Anyone who has ever suddenly been presented with a baby brother or sister relates to Lilly's feelings toward her new baby brother, Julius. She goes from loving the idea of having a baby brother to finding the reality of having a baby brother really disgusting. Lilly enchants readers with her various ways of communicating her intense dislike of the new sibling. Not until her cousin expresses disdain for her brother, does Lilly begin to appreciate him.

Scheidl, Gerda Marie. *Tommy's New Sister*. Illustrated by Christa Unzner. 1999. New York: North-South Books. Unp. Grades: K-3.

Tommy likes his family just the way it is—a mom, a dad, a dog, and himself. Then his mom goes to the hospital and comes home with a baby sister who cries and cries. He tries different ways to get rid of her including trying to pack her in a box and mail her to grandma. Eventually, he comes to realize that his sister needs him and his parents appreciate his taking care of her.

***Nine Month Miracle*. 1995. Mac/Win. Atlanta, Ga.: A.D.A.M. Software. Grades: K and up.**

Human reproduction and birth are explored in this multimedia CD. For young students there is a story about reproduction and interactive games. For older students there is more in-depth information about the miracle of life. In-body photography, animations, sounds, video, and a dictionary provide multimedia support for learning about this fascinating topic.

Lears, Laurie. *Ben Has Something to Say: A Story about Stuttering*. Illustrated by Karen Ritz. 2000. New York: HarperCollins. Unp. Grades: K–4.

Ben does not talk much because he does not want to be teased about his stuttering. After school on Fridays he goes to a junkyard with his dad, an auto mechanic, to look for parts. When the new junkyard guard dog, Spike, fails to bark during a robbery the owner contemplates sending the dog to the pound. In order to save the dog, Ben, who has never spoken in front of the junkyard owner, decides to speak up for Spike.

Cole, Babette. *Mommy Laid an Egg! or Where Do Babies Come From?* 1993. San Francisco, Calif.: Chronicle Books. Unp. Grades: 2–4.

A difficult topic for discussion for most adults is handled in a truly hilarious manner that should take the embarrassment away. The parents decide to share the facts of life with their son and daughter. They explain that dinosaurs deliver babies, that babies are found under stones or grown in clay pots from seeds. The children decide to explain the facts of life to their parents using child-drawn posters and simple language.

What Kids Want to Know about Sex and Growing Up. 1992. Video. Beverly Hills, Calif.: Pacific Arts Video. 60 min. Grades: 3 and up.

This Children's Television Workshop video provides students with an open, honest discussion of sex. Two teenagers are the hosts of the program and two adult counselors join them. The counselors talk with groups of children and with individual children in a straightforward manner.

Just Around the Corner for Boys. 2000. Video. Kansas City, Mo.: MarshMedia. 15 min. Grades: 4–7.

Using an easygoing presentation style, an older male teenager explains puberty to younger boys. The use of a teenage host makes this a unique video on this sensitive topic. The companion video is *Just Around the Corner for Girls*.

EXPLORATIONS

1. *Where Do Babies Come From?* (Royston, 1996) answers children's questions about where babies come from and *Julius the Baby of the World* (Henkes, 1990) answers children's questions about how their lives will change once a new baby arrives. Sharing these books with children encourages them to ask questions about this life-changing event. Students are eager to share their stories of life with a new sibling and need opportunities to talk about their feelings.
2. After reading *Two Eyes, a Nose, and a Mouth* (Intrater, 1995), take digital photographs of the eyes, noses, and mouths of the students to include in a HyperStudio stack. As

the stack is projected, the students can guess whose facial features are being displayed. This activity helps develop students' powers of observation.

3. *Hello Toes! Hello Feet!* (Paul, 1998) is just the book for sharing outdoors on a warm spring day. Students enjoy imitating the characters' walking, jumping, sliding, crunching, and toe wiggling. Children identify with the characters and enjoy imitating their actions (Kane, 1994).

4. After reading *Pepita Takes Time* (Lachtman, 2000), have students share what happened to them when they were late for an event. Then have the students brainstorm a list of things to do to help them arrive on time.

5. Prior to reading *Moses Goes to School* (Millman, 2000), ask children what they know about deafness and American Sign Language. After reading the book, allow them to practice the sign language in the book.

6. While reading *Parts* (Arnold, 1997), stop after each of the boy's discoveries and ask the students what they think is happening to the boy. Then read what he thinks is happening. For example, after the boy finds the hair in his comb, stop reading and ask the students why they think there was hair in his comb. Listen to their responses and then read about how the boy thinks he is going bald. Continue reading the book in this manner.

7. After reading *Tommy's New Sister* (Scheidl, 1999), invite the students to talk about what it was like in their house when a new baby arrived.

8. After reading *Ben Has Something to Say: A Story about Stuttering* (Lears, 2000), discuss with students how to listen and respond to people who stutter.

FEELINGS

Everyone has feelings and children need to know that feelings are normal. They may need help understanding their feelings and learning to deal with them appropriately. In the pages of these books students find children with feelings similar to ones they have experienced and they learn how these children deal with their feelings. Students may benefit from being able to role-play dealing with different feelings.

BOOK AND MEDIA CHOICES

Curtis, Jamie Lee. *Today I Feel Silly & Other Moods that Make My Day.* Illustrated by Laura Cornell. 1998. New York: Joanna Cotler Books. Unp. Grades: P–2.

Moods are bewildering to young children. They do not always understand why they feel the way they do. This book explores different moods from a child's perspective and reassures the readers that changing moods are a normal part of life. This humorous book encourages readers to laugh at and accept their moods.

Evans, Lezlie. *Sometimes I Feel Like a Storm Cloud.* **Illustrated by Marsha Gray Carrington. 1999. Greenvale, N.Y.: Mondo Publishing. Unp. Grades: P–2.**

Simile is used to describe typical childhood emotions and feeling by comparing them to things familiar to children. For example, a child tells about feeling like a flattened balloon when she's lost her air and feeling sad. Vibrant drawings fill the pages as the child experiences different feelings throughout the day.

Bang, Molly. *When Sophie Gets Angry – Really, Really Angry . . .* **1999. New York: Scholastic. Unp. Grades: P–1.**

When Sophie gets angry enough to erupt, she runs and runs, she cries, and then she climbs her favorite tree and drinks in nature all around her. When she has calmed down she returns to her loving family and life resumes. This book was named a Caldecott Honor book and given the Charlotte Zolotow Award.

When Sophie Gets Angry – Really, Really Angry . . . **2000. Video. New Rochelle, N.Y.: Spoken Arts. 7 min. Grades: P–1.**

Once familiar with this story students are eager to watch the short video or listen to the cassette recording. The book is read by Carrie Fisher. A discussion guide is included with the video.

Yolen, Jane. *How Do Dinosaurs Say Good Night?* **Illustrated by Mark Teague. 2000. New York: Scholastic. Unp. Grades: P-2.**

Young children's feelings of anger and fear of turning out the light and going to sleep are playfully described as speculation rises about how young dinosaurs react to being told to turn out the lights and go to sleep. Different dinosaurs are depicted on each page as possible scenarios are acted out. The names of the dinosaurs are posted somewhere in the bedroom. The surprise ending will make this a favorite with young and old readers.

Spelman, Cornelia Maude. *When I Feel Angry.* **Illustrated by Nancy Cote. 2000. Morton Grove, Ill.: Albert Whitman. Unp. Grades: P–3.**

A lovable bunny shows readers a variety of options for managing anger and ways to prevent anger in this picture book. Children easily relate to the situations faced by the bunny. A note from the author tells adults of the importance of helping children understand that anger is a normal emotion and that there are acceptable ways of dealing with anger.

Modesitt, Jeanne. *Sometimes I Feel Like a Mouse: A Book About Feelings*. Illustrated by Robin Spowart. 1992. New York: Scholastic. Unp. Grades: K–2.

Written for the very young child, this book is a first step towards acknowledging and understanding feelings. Feelings are compared to animals; for example a scurrying squirrel is used to show how excitement feels. Sharing the book with a significant adult in their lives helps children understand that everyone has a variety of feelings. The large, simple text with pastel drawings assures that beginning readers are able to read the text on their own.

Henkes, Kevin. *Wemberly Worried*. 2000. New York: Greenwillow Books. Unp. Grades: K–2.

Anyone who has ever worried relates to Wemberly, who worries about everything even though her parents and grandmother assure her there is no reason to worry. All the childhood worries about starting school, such as finding the bathroom and having a mean teacher, overwhelm Wemberly. This is a book for sharing with students prior to school or during those sometimes traumatic first days of school. It is one that is returned to throughout the school year. This book is also available on cassette from Live Oak Media, Pine Plains, New York.

***When You're Mad, Mad, Mad!: Dealing with Anger*. 1993. Video. Pleasantville, N.Y.: Sunburst Communications. 27 min. Grades: 5 and up.**

Students are assured that angry feelings are normal, but anger does not have to lead to angry behavior. Techniques are demonstrated for dealing with anger in constructive ways.

EXPLORATIONS

1. Before reading *Today I Feel Silly & Other Moods that Make My Day* (Curtis, 1998), ask students to talk about when they are happy and when they are sad. Also, have them share what they do when they are feeling happy or sad.
2. *Sometimes I Feel Like a Storm Cloud* (Evans, 1999) and *Sometimes I Feel Like a Mouse: A Book About Feelings* (Modesitt, 1992) show children that feelings are a normal part of life. Both of these books use objects or animals to represent feelings. Students can create their own personal feelings book using objects or animals that depict their different moods.
3. Prior to reading *When Sophie Gets Angry – Really, Really Angry . . .* (Bang, 1999), compile a list on the blackboard of how children react when they are angry. After reading the book, compare Sophie's ways of dealing with anger with the ones on the list. Guide students as they each create their own list of acceptable ways to deal with anger.
4. Prior to reading *Wemberly Worried* (Henkes, 2000), have the children share what worries them.

FRIENDSHIP

One of the first experiences children have outside of the family is making friends. The many facets of friendship are examined in these books. How to make friends, what it means to be a friend, and the value of friends are topics explored in these books.

BOOK AND MEDIA CHOICES

Tafuri, Nancy. *Will You Be My Friend?* 2000. New York: Scholastic. Unp. Grades: P–2.

Young readers enjoy this delightful tale of a shy bird befriended by a small brown rabbit. Learning to be a friend sometimes means overcoming shyness and young children can relate to the feelings of the animals in this story. The large easy-to-read text encourages emergent readers to read this book on their own. The large, simple illustrations appeal to young readers.

Wells, Rosemary. *Timothy Goes to School.* 2000. New York: Viking. Unp. Grades: P–2.

Timothy no sooner starts kindergarten than he is ready to quit. He cannot compete with Claude who wears all the right clothes and never makes mistakes. Then he meets Violet and discovers that friendship and shared laughter are better than being perfect.

Larson, Kirby. *The Magic Kerchief.* Illustrated by Rosanne Litzinger. 2000. New York: Holiday House. Unp. Grades: P–3.

A sharp-tongued old lady, Griselda, gives shelter one night to a poor old woman. In return the woman gives Griselda a magic kerchief and assures her that with it she will receive great riches. Griselda does not believe the old woman, but puts the kerchief on anyway as she leaves for town. To her amazement every time she opens her mouth to scold or complain, only compliments come forth. In the end Griselda learns that riches come in many shapes and sizes.

Leedy, Loreen. *How Humans Make Friends.* 1996. New York: Holiday House. Unp. Grades: K–2.

An alien from another planet returns home after an expedition to observe earthlings and presents a slideshow to his fellow aliens explaining how humans meet and greet friends, including things they do, how they get along, how they solve conflicts, and how they say good-bye. The aliens have amusing side conversations during the presentation. Young readers learn about how to be a friend as they turn the pages of the book and explore the imaginative slides. The cartoon-like illustrations are perfect for the text and appeal to most young readers.

DiTerlizzi, Tony. *Ted*. 2001. New York: Simon and Schuster Books for Young Readers. Unp. Grades: K–2.

A young boy meets a large, pink creature with a button in his belly that immediately suggests activities that get the boy in trouble with his father. The father insists that Ted is an imaginary friend and that the boy creates all of the havoc himself. When the boy is forbidden to associate with Ted, Ted runs away. The boy leaves a note for his father and sets out to find Ted. The twist at the end of the book leaves all readers satisfied.

Vainio, Pirkko. *The Best of Friends*. Translated by J. Alison James. 2000. New York: North-South Books. Unp. Grades: K–3.

This loving story of two unlikely friends, a bear and a hare, helps children understand the importance of friendship and accepting each other in spite of differences in size and shape.

Judd, Naomi. *Love Can Build a Bridge*. Illustrated by Suzanne Duranceau. 1999. New York: HarperCollins Children's Books. Unp. Grades: K–3.

This song for world peace with accompanying realistic illustrations of small children caring for each other reminds young readers that their daily actions and caring ways spread the message of peace and harmony. A tape of the song performed by the Judds accompanies the book and the lyrics for the song are on the last page of the book.

Halperin, Wendy Anderson. *Love Is . . .* 2001. New York: Simon and Schuster Books for Young Readers. Unp. Grades: 1–3.

Saint Paul's timeless words defining love have been adapted in this finely detailed picture book. By carefully examining the contrasting illustrations across the two-page spreads, readers begin to realize that they make choices in how they respond to everyday situations. These choices impact their lives and the lives of those around them. Responding to situations with love rather than anger, envy, or selfishness positively impacts lives.

***Friendship: The Good Times . . . The Bad Times*. 1990. Video. Pleasantville, N.Y.: Sunburst Communications. 24 min. Grades: 6–8.**

This video shows students the importance of friendship in their lives and how to be a good friend. A teacher's guide is included.

EXPLORATIONS

1. After reading *Will You Be My Friend?* (Tafuri, 2000), provide students opportunities to retell the story using a flannel board or with bird and bunny puppets.
2. After reading *The Magic Kerchief* (Larson, 2000), show students the magic kerchief that they are going to get to take turns wearing during the day. Remind them that when they are wearing the kerchief they must be sure to speak only kind words and to display kind actions.

3. After reading *How Humans Make Friends* (Leedy, 1996), students want to create their own slide show. Using HyperStudio they can create presentations to share with their classmates. Ideas presented in the book can be expanded, such as the dwelling places, the learning building, the play zone, and special lessons.

4. Prior to reading *The Best of Friends* (Vainio, 2000), have students share their ideas about friendship. Have them write down or draw pictures of things that friends do when they are together. After reading the book, have them compare what they wrote down to the events in the story.

5. After reading *Love Can Build a Bridge* (Judd, 1999), share with students times the teacher or librarian has witnessed them helping one another. For example, when one student spills a box of crayons on the floor, others may have stopped to help pick up the crayons.

6. After reading *Love Can Build a Bridge* (Judd, 1999), play the tape for students to sing along.

7. After reading *Love Is . . .* (Halperin, 2001), have students first discuss and then illustrate incidents in their lives and different ways of responding. For example, how would they respond to being shoved while in line waiting for the bus.

SELF-ESTEEM

Sharing books that contain positive gender role models and are quality literature can help build positive self-esteem in children. When selecting books Heine et al. (1999) suggest that the characters be examined using these guidelines: character's personal traits, issues the character encounters, how the character solves problems, character's relationships, how the character does not fit traditional stereotypes, and does the character represent people not usually found in children's literature. The authors caution that not every book will meet all of the guidelines. When students are allowed to ask questions and suggest topics for discussion they become more engaged in the dialogue (Almasi and McKeown, 1996). Siemens (1994) found that by making time to let thoughts wander and providing a safe environment for questioning and responding to stories, her second graders pondered deep questions important to themselves. Students' engagement and personal responses to books are important if they are to benefit from the books.

BOOK AND MEDIA CHOICES

Moss, Thylias. *I Want to Be Me*. Illustrated by Jerry Pinkney. 1993. New York: Dial Books for Young Readers. Unp. Grades: P–2.

Prize-winning poet, Thylias Moss, takes readers on a journey of discovery through the eyes of a young girl deciding what she wants to be. The girl realizes that she wants to be all that she can be in order to experience life to the fullest. The warm, inviting illustrations of Jerry Pinkney help readers imagine all the possibilities that exist in the universe.

What's Respect? **1995. Video. Pleasantville, N.Y.: Sunburst Communications. 13 min. Grades: P–2.**

This music video features a young boy who learns about respect. Some of the topics covered are the importance of respect for property, rules, and the environment.

Garland, Michael. *Icarus Swinebuckle.* **2000. Morton Grove, Ill.: Albert Whitman. Unp. Grades: P–3.**

Glorious life-like illustrations set in eighteenth-century London accompany this retelling of the Greek myth of Icarus. However, in this version Icarus is a pig that neglects his work to concentrate on building wings to fly. He soars into the clouds and then plummets into the river. The crowd that gathered to watch him applaud his efforts and he sets his sights even higher. This captivating tale shows children the importance of believing in themselves and their dreams.

Barnwell, Ysaye M. *No Mirrors in My Nana's House.* **Paintings by Synthia Saint James. 1998. San Diego, Calif.: Harcourt Brace. Unp. Grades: K–2.**

A young child discovers that looking deeply into her Nana's eyes reveals the beauty of the world around her. Had there been a mirror in the house it would have reflected the poverty that surrounded her; instead she saw only the love in her Nana's eyes. Included with the book is an audio CD of the song sung a capella by Sweet Honey in The Rock and a recording of the text. This book won a National Parenting Publications Award and a Parent's Guide Children's Media Award.

Pinkney, Sandra L. *Shades of Black: A Celebration of Our Children.* **Photographs by Myles C. Pinkney. 2000. New York: Scholastic. Unp. Grades: K–2.**

The diversity in the appearance of African American children is highlighted through crisp, colorful photographs and poetic language. As they struggle with their personal identity this book helps them to appreciate and accept their unique appearances. The expressive faces of the children as they compare their skin, hair, and eyes to familiar objects light up the pages of this book to be shared with children of all races.

Sanders, Eve. *What's Your Name? From Ariel to Zoe.* **Photographs by Marilyn Sanders. 1995. New York: Holiday House. Unp. Grades: K–3.**

Nothing is quite as personal and special as a name. Large color photographs of children are accompanied by short descriptions of the meaning of the child's first name or where the name came from and personal statements about the children featured in the photographs. Names from A to Z are included in the book and a pronunciation guide for the names can be found at the end of the book.

Lucado, Max. *You Are Special.* Illustrated by Sergio Martinez. 1997. Wheaton, Ill.: Crossway Books. 31p. Grades: 1 and up.

This allegory describes a country of small wooden creatures called Wemmicks and their creator, a woodworker named Eli. The Wemmicks award stickers to one another based on their perceived behavior—stars for good things and dots for not-so-good things. Punchinello seems to only attract dots and is miserable. When he meets a stickerless Wemmick he wants to know why she does not have any stickers. She suggests he go see Eli and learn what the stickers mean. Children who have difficulty building self-esteem profit from the message in this book.

Young, Ed. *Voices of the Heart.* 1997. New York: Scholastic. Unp. Grades: 3 and up.

Through 26 Chinese characters combined with the character for the heart, Ed Young explores feelings and emotions all coming from the heart. For example, "joy" reflects a happy heart. By combining the characters for an older person and the heart, he explains that insightful words from an elder assure good luck and bring joy to the heart. Each character is represented in a seemingly three-dimensional collage that gives the feeling of texture.

Pinkney, Andrea Davis. *Let It Shine: Stories of Black Women Freedom Fighters.* Illustrated by Stephen Alcorn. 2000. San Diego, Calif.: Harcourt Brace. 107p. Grades: 4 and up.

Pinkney has selected ten women from Sojourner Truth to Shirley Chisholm whom she calls freedom fighters. From 1797 to the present, she tells the stories of these courageous women who fought for their beliefs. Each of these women had special unique characteristics as a child and as they grew, their determination to right civil injustices grew as well. These leaders in the civil rights struggle modeled for others how to work to overcome injustice, to believe in oneself, and to persist against all odds. These inspiring stories offer hope to all who struggle against injustice.

Hansen, Joyce. *Women of Hope: African Americans Who Made a Difference.* 1998. New York: Scholastic. 32p. Grades: 5 and up.

The women featured in this book, such as Maya Angelou, provide inspirational role models for young people. These are women who believed in their ability to make their world a better place and by their words and actions they made their world a better place. They have made a difference while engaged in a variety of careers including poet, educator, lawyer, doctor, and astronaut. The left side of each two-page spread features a large photograph of the women and the right side contains information about their lives and triumphs. Above each photograph is a thought-provoking quote by each woman and below the photograph their place of birth, birth date, and for some, the date of their death. Twelve women are featured in this book and a list of additional inspirational women, as well as an annotated bibliography, are included at the end of the book.

Birdseye, Debbie Holsclaw, and Tom Birdseye. *Under Our Skin: Kids Talk about Race.* **Photographs by Robert Crum. 1997. New York: Holiday House. 32p. Grades: 5–8.**

In a world filled with prejudice, hate crimes, and riots, the problems surrounding racial diversity become more and more important. The authors wondered if preteens would talk about their experiences with racism. They found that the students wanted to share their feelings and their thoughts. Six young people from six different races share their lives with readers.

Peer Pressure. **1994. Video. Bala Cynwyd, Penn.: Schlessinger Video Productions-Library Video Company. 30 min. Grades: 5 and up.**

Youngsters discuss problems they have encountered when giving into peer pressure. Peer educators provide students with ways to overcome peer pressure. A teacher's guide is included and this video is closed-captioned. This is one of the Schlessinger Teen Health Video Series.

Self-Esteem. **1994. Video. Bala Cynwyd, Penn.: Schlessinger Video Productions-Library Video Company. 30 min. Grades: 6 and up.**

Teens talk about their thoughts on their own self-image and an adult self-esteem expert leads discussions on self-esteem. The importance of developing a healthy self-esteem is the message in this video. A teacher's guide is included and this video is closed-captioned. This is one of the Schlessinger Teen Health Video Series.

EXPLORATIONS

1. In *I Want to Be Me* (Moss, 1993) the young girl searches for what she wants to be and discovers her own unique talents that make her who she is and make her special. Students can write down in their journals what makes them special.
2. After reading *Icarus Swinebuckle* (Garland, 2000), have students share their dreams and ideas for the future.
3. Prior to reading *No Mirrors in My Nana's House* (Barnwell, 1998), ask students what adults in the students' lives do to make them feel special.
4. *No Mirrors in My Nana's House* (Barnwell, 1998) comes with a CD of the book and the song. Children enjoy singing the song and quickly learn the words. Singing the song helps them remember the words as they read the book.
5. After reading *What's Your Name? From Ariel to Zoe* (Sanders, 1995), have the students ask their parents about the origins of their names. Then take the students' pictures with a digital camera, insert their pictures into Microsoft Publisher, and type in the information they gathered about their names. Older students are able to complete this activity on their own, but younger students will need assistance. Print out the pages to form a class book of the students.
6. Prior to reading *You Are Special* (Lucado, 1997), have children discuss why they are special. The teacher or librarian can begin the discussion by talking about special char-

acteristics of the children in the group and encouraging the students to talk about why their classmates are special.

7. After sharing *Voices of the Heart* (Young, 1997) with students have them pick a feeling or emotion to create their own symbol to represent. Provide the students with wallpaper samples to create collages of their symbol; encourage them to include a heart in their collage. Students can also write an explanation for elements in their collage.

8. After reading *Let It Shine: Stories of Black Women Freedom Fighters* (Pinkney, 2000), have students think about an important, special woman in their lives. The students then write about what makes the woman important and special to them.

9. Each of the women profiled in *Women of Hope: African Americans Who Made a Difference* (Hansen, 1998) have moving words and powerful thoughts to share with readers. These stories can be rewritten into scripts for Readers Theatre. While Readers Theatre is usually reserved for fiction, Young and Vardell (1993) advocate its use with nonfiction and provide a variety of examples for using it across the curriculum. Students can select one of the women from the book, prepare a script, practice the script, and present it to their classmates.

10. Sharing the stories of the students in *Under Our Skin: Kids Talk about Race* (Birdseye and Birdseye, 1997) provides an opportunity for students to discuss racial issues in the classroom. By learning more about the diverse cultures represented in the classroom students develop empathy and understanding for each other.

MANNERS

Good manners require showing others common courtesies, in other words treating them respectfully. There are those who believe that the knowledge of how to behave is essential to success in life. Sharing books about manners and offering students opportunities to practice good manners facilitates the creation of a classroom environment conducive to learning. Humor, common sense, and a Hasidic legend are found in the books in this section, and they all provide examples of appropriate manners to use in a variety of social situations.

BOOK AND MEDIA CHOICES

Riehecky, Janet. *"Excuse Me."* Illustrated by Gwen Connelly. 1992. Chanhassen, Minn.: The Child's World. 32p. Grades: P–1.

This short, simple book shows young readers when to say, "Excuse me." Everyday situations are portrayed in the pictures, such as when you reach in front of someone or want to get the teacher's attention. This is a book to be shared with young readers who are soon able to read it on their own due to the simple text and the illustrations that illustrate exactly what the text says.

Tryon, Leslie. *Patsy Says.* 2001. New York: Atheneum Books for Young Readers. Unp. Grades: P–2.

Patsy tries her best to teach an unruly batch of first graders manners before their parents arrive at the end of the week for Open House. It seems as though the students will never learn, but on the big day they surprise Patsy, their teacher, and the principal with their impeccable manners. The delightfully, clever illustrations have readers young and old giggling at the antics of the first graders.

Naylor, Phyllis Reynolds. *"I Can't Take You Anywhere!"* Illustrated by Jef Kaminsky. 1997. New York: Aladdin Paperbacks. Unp. Grades: P–2.

Oftentimes even when they try to behave, accidents just seem to happen to growing children. They can relate to Amy Audrey Perkins, who gets left behind rather than taken out in public. She convinces her parents to take her to Aunt Linda's wedding where she behaves perfectly. The relatives are so surprised that they become klutzes and make all sorts of silly messes.

Cole, Babette. *The Bad Good Manners Book.* 1995. New York: Alfred A. Knopf. Unp. Grades: P–2.

Learning good manners can be fraught with hazards as demonstrated in this wonderful book. The trials and tribulations encountered while attempting to behave correctly have readers young and old chuckling as they read. The funny, detailed drawings have readers returning to the book again and again to carefully examine the catastrophes on each page.

Williams, Suzanne. *My Dog Never Says Please.* Illustrated by Tedd Arnold. 1997. New York: Dial Books for Young Readers. Unp. Grades: P–2.

Disgusted with her parents' constant reminders about her manners and her younger brother's halo, Ginny Mae dreams of becoming a dog. Dogs never say please, they lick their plates, and they go outside barefooted. With her parents' blessing, she moves outside to take up life with her dog. Children relate to Ginny Mae's feeling and thoroughly enjoy Tedd Arnold's hilarious drawings.

Buehner, Caralyn. *It's a Spoon, Not a Shovel.* Illustrated by Mark Buehner. 1995. New York: Dial Books for Young Readers. Unp. Grades: K–2.

Learning manners is fun with a silly collection of animals portrayed in somewhat ordinary daily situations in not-so-ordinary locations. For example, a pair of pythons is enjoying tea curled up, over and around living room chairs in the middle of the jungle. Manners are taught through a series of multiple-choice questions with each answer designated by a letter. The letters that correspond to the correct answers are hidden in the accompanying illustrations. Also, the locations of correct answers in each picture are printed upside down on the last page of the book.

Lauber, Patricia. *What You Never Knew About Fingers, Forks, and Chopsticks.* **Illustrated by John Manders. 1999. New York: Simon and Schuster. Unp. Grades: 1–3.**

Learning that most of the people in the world eat with fingers or chopsticks, rather than knives, forks, and spoons surprises young readers. This investigation of the origin and use of eating utensils shows the one common denominator of people all over the world, the use of fingers when eating. Delightful illustrations accompany the text that begins with the Stone Age, through ancient civilizations, the Middle Ages, and on to the eighteenth through twenty-first centuries. The book includes a bibliography.

Kimmel, Eric A. *Gershon's Monster: A Story for the Jewish New Year.* **Illustrated by Jon J. Muth. 2000. New York: Scholastic. Unp. Grades: 1–4.**

Rather than change his behavior, Gershon sweeps his misdeeds into the cellar every Friday. Once a year he stuffs them into a large bag and throws them into the sea. The reckless lifestyle and sinful nature of this selfish man threatens the lives of his son and daughter. When faced with the prospect of losing them, he offers his life in their place and they are all spared. This retelling of a Hasidic legend concludes with instructions on how to make amends for one's misdeeds.

Table Manners for Kids. **1993. Video. Chicago: Public Media Video. 34 min. Grades: 1–6.**

Throughout a six-course meal children learn about table etiquette including an introduction to different silverware, which forks to use when, and where to place the napkin when they leave the table.

James, Elizabeth, and Carol Barkin. *Social Smarts: Manners for Today's Kids.* **Illustrated by Martha Weston. 1996. New York: Clarion Books. 104p. Grades: 4 and up.**

Manners in every culture focus on treating individuals with respect and consideration. It stresses the importance of good manners as a way to assure that appropriate social skills are used. Each chapter focuses on appropriate manners for different social situations: when meeting people, at school, at the table, at social affairs, during difficult times, on the phone, in public, and on vacation. A mythical advice columnist offers advice to students about manners. This format opens the way for discussions about the correct manners in a wide variety of situations.

EXPLORATIONS

1. To encourage students to reflect on manners, use a large sheet of white paper as a tablecloth on a low table. Stand a selection of books on manners on the table for students to read during the day. After they read the book, ask them to write about what they learned on the tablecloth. At the end of the week share their reflections with the entire class.
2. After reading *"Excuse Me"* (Riehecky 1992), have students role-play the situations in

the pictures. Have them freeze in action to discuss the situation and the appropriate responses to what has happened.

3. After reading *Patsy Says* (Tyron, 2001), have the students role-play the situations in the story as they practice their manners.

4. After reading *"I Can't Take You Anywhere!"* (Naylor, 1997), have students talk about times when they made messes in public. Then help them to discover ways not to make messes, for example, by not touching things they have been told not to touch.

5. *The Bad Good Manners Book* (Cole, 1995) is a book that lends itself to expressive reading. After the teacher models reading the book with expression, students can be encouraged to practice reading the book with expression and then read it aloud to their classmates.

6. After reading *The Bad Good Manners Book* (Cole, 1995), have children observe the manners of other students on the bus, in the hallways, on the playground, and in the cafeteria. Then give them an opportunity to share their observations.

7. In *My Dog Never Says Please* (Williams, 1997) the plot conflict is character against self. Have the students determine what the problem is, who owns the problem, and what is causing the problem. Then have them talk about other conflicts that arise between parents and children.

8. After reading *My Dog Never Says Please* (Williams, 1997), have the students brainstorm other advantages to being a pet rather than a child. Use their ideas to create a classroom story about a child who becomes a pet or have them write their own stories. They may want to refer back to the book in order to model their writing after the author's style.

9. After reading *It's a Spoon, Not a Shovel* (Buehner, 1995), have students talk about appropriate table manners and how to set a table. Encourage them to observe the table manners in the cafeteria. On a designated day prior to lunch, have the students set their classroom desks with napkins, plastic forks, spoons, and knives, as well as a cup for their milk. After the students pick up their meals in the cafeteria bring them back to the classroom to eat at their desks and practice good table manners.

10. In *What You Never Knew About Fingers, Forks, and Chopsticks* (Lauber, 1999) students discover cultural differences in manners and that manners change over time. Ask students to share cultural differences in manners that they have encountered. "Manners" from *A Suitcase of Seaweed and Other Poems* (Wong, 1996) tells of her dilemma about the proper way to eat with chopsticks, as what is considered proper by her Korean relatives is different from what is considered proper by her Chinese relatives.

11. *Gershon's Monster: A Story for the Jewish New Year* (Kimmel, 2000) is about not dealing with mistakes. Admitting mistakes and taking actions to correct them is often not easy. Students benefit from discussing and role-playing how to do this.

12. In *Social Smarts: Manners for Today's Kids* (James and Barkin, 1996) there are letters to a mythical advice columnist. Read the letters to the students and have them discuss how they would handle the situation. Then read the advice of the columnist.

AGING AND DEATH

Books with older characters often have stereotypical views of them. Additionally, our society is age-segregated; however, sharing books about older people helps students examine the concept of growing old and the role of the elderly. Reading books with older characters helps students develop a more balanced perspective on aging and helps them relate to older people (Crawford, 1996; Laney, et al., 1997).

Books about death help children to understand the grieving process, and by coming to terms with death, students can experience the affirmation of life and hope (Bargiel, et al., 1997). Conflicting emotions exhibited by characters in realistic fiction books dealing with death add depth and dimension to the characters that enable students to identify with them. Sharing books on death with children leads to discussions of this difficult topic that most would prefer to avoid. Teachers and librarians may feel unprepared to discuss death with children and may need assistance from school district support personnel. When teachers and librarians share their personal experiences with death, students feel more comfortable sharing their experiences. Rudman (1995) offers these guidelines: before the age of five children do not understand that death is permanent, between the ages of five and eight they think they have control over death, and not until they are nine are able to understand that death is permanent.

Students who have recently experienced the death of a loved one should be given the choice about whether or not they are ready to listen and respond to books on death. A teacher suggested that a university student read books about death to her second grade reading partner, whose grandmother had recently died. The student expressed concern about reading the books to the child, concerned that the child may not be ready to discuss the death of her grandmother. She decided to bring in a variety of books, including two on the death of a loved one, and let the child decide which ones they would read. The child did not select either of the books about death. Another consideration when selecting books about death to read in the classroom is the age and developmental stage of the children. Some of the books in this section portray aging and growing old in a very realistic and very humorous manner. Children are sure to discover their grandparents and older relatives in the pages of these books.

BOOK AND MEDIA CHOICES

Winch, John. *Keeping Up with Grandma*. 2000. New York: Holiday House. Unp. Grades: P–3.

When Grandma sets out to explore the great outdoors, Grandpa reluctantly goes along; however, he has trouble keeping up with Grandma. Charming illustrations depict the problems Grandpa encounters as he accompanies Grandma while she canoes, horseback rides, dances, and even sails. At the suggestion of their grandchild they go back home and resume their lives.

Schick, Eleanor. *Mama*. 2000. Tarrytown, NY: Marshall Cavendish. Unp. Grades: K–3.

In this poignant story a young girl remembers her last days with her dying mother, tells of her father's withdrawal, and shares the love and support she receives from her caregiver. In the end the child's life goes on and she realizes that her mother will always be with her in her heart when she sings, when she sees the moon, and when she is sad. Muted watercolor paintings portray the sadness of the child as she copes with the loss of her mother and the accompanying changes in her life.

Barron, T. A. *Where Is Grandpa?* Illustrated by Chris K. Soentpiet. 2000. New York: Philomel Books. Unp. Grades: K–3.

Fond, loving remembrances of a deceased grandpa are shared on the front porch steps by a grieving family in this heartwarming story. When his grandson asks where is heaven, the boy's mother responds that heaven is any place where loved ones have shared time. Suddenly, the boy realizes that his grandpa is still with him.

Shriver, Maria. *What's Heaven?* Illustrated by Sandra Speidel. 1999. New York: St. Martin's Press. Unp. Grades: K–4.

When Rose Fitzgerald Kennedy died her great-grandchildren began asking questions about death. The thought-provoking questions and the difficult answers to the questions fill this book. The narrative format helps children see that all families struggle for answers when a loved one dies. The pastel illustrations set the tone for this somber book that in the end reminds children that those they love live on within them in their memories.

Wild, Margaret. *Old Pig.* Illustrated by Ron Brooks. 1998. New York: Penguin Putnam. Unp. Grades: K–4.

This is a beautiful story about a grandmother and her granddaughter who live together and share all the responsibilities and joys of life. As Old Pig realizes her life is nearing its end, she settles all of her business accounts and takes her granddaughter on a walk around the neighborhood to feast on the delights she finds. This healthy interpretation of the end of life is sure to help students when faced with the death of a loved one.

Bahr, Mary. *If Nathan Were Here.* Illustrated by Karen A. Jerome. 2000. Grand Rapids, Mich.: Eerdmans Books for Young Readers. Unp. Grades: 1–3.

The adults around him including a sympathetic teacher, Miss Brickley, accept a young boy's grief over the death of his best friend, Nathan. To help the students in her class come to terms with their classmate's death; she has them fill a memory box of items that remind them of Nathan. Nathan's best friend has a difficult time deciding what to include. He sorts through his memories and finally makes his decision.

Johnson, Angela. *When I Am Old with You*. Illustrated by David Soman. 1990. New York: Orchard Books. Unp. Grades: 1–3.

This is a heartwarming tale of a young child fantasizing about being old one day with his grandaddy. Together they will ride the tractor, walk on the beach, and sit on the porch and rock. The timeless, boundless bond between grandchildren and grandparents is celebrated in this book. Readers recognize themselves in the book and think fondly of their own special relationships with their grandparents. This is a Corretta Scott King Honor Book.

Brown, Laurie Krasny, and Marc Brown. *When Dinosaurs Die: A Guide to Understanding Death*. 1996. Boston: Little, Brown. 32p. Grades: 1–4.

The cartoon dinosaurs and comic book layout assure that this book appeals to children. Children's concerns and questions about death are explained in everyday situations that children can understand. Why people die, feelings about death, religious customs associated with death, and ways to remember someone are some of the topics covered. A glossary of unfamiliar terms is included at the end of the book. This book is one of the Dino Life Guides for Families series.

Cole, Babette. *Drop Dead*. 1997. New York: Dial Books for Young Readers. Unp. Grades: 2–4.

Growing old is part of the cycle of life and two curious grandchildren quiz their grandparents about being "bald old wrinklies." The grandparents describe the fun they had throughout their lives and speculate on what will happen to them when they drop dead. This light-hearted look at aging is sure to generate questions from curious children as they grapple with trying to understand growing old and dying.

Coville, Bruce. *My Grandfather's House*. Illustrated by Henri Sorensen. 1996. Mahwah, N. J.: Bridgewater Books. Unp. Grades: 2–4.

Based on his own personal experience, Bruce Coville tells the story of his grandfather's death and burial. Soft, muted illustrations convey the sadness and uncertainty surrounding the death of a loved one. The visit to the funeral home includes an illustration of grandfather in his coffin where the realization of death takes hold as the child feels the cool, smooth skin of his grandfather's hand. Children's questions and concerns about death are addressed in the warm, loving atmosphere of a family setting.

Spelman, Cornelia. *After Charlotte's Mom Died*. Illustrated by Judith Friedman. 1996. Morton Grove, Ill.: Albert Whitman. Unp. Grades: 3–6.

Sharing this book is one way to encourage children to talk about their unspoken feelings and fears about the death of a parent. The single parent in this book is struggling with his own grief and does not at first recognize the child's grief. An observant teacher or librarian may be the one cognizant of a child's needs following the death of a parent and this book is but one option for providing support.

EXPLORATIONS

1. Prior to reading *Mama* (Schick, 2000), provide children who wish to share their experiences with the death of a family member an opportunity to do so. After reading the book help children to see that through memories loved ones live on in their hearts.

2. Prior to reading *Mama* (Schick, 2000), have students share their experiences with death. For some students their only experiences with death may be the death of a pet. Encourage the students to share their experiences if they feel comfortable doing so.

3. After reading *What's Heaven?* (Shriver, 1999), provide students opportunities to share their memories of loved ones.

4. Prior to reading books about older people have the students draw pictures of how they think they will look when they are old. Ask them questions about the pictures such as "Why did you include glasses in your picture?"

5. *Old Pig* (Wild, 1998) is not just a book about death. It is also about taking the time to enjoy the beauty and wonder of nature. Students can explore the school playground to discover the beauty and wonder of nature. Then they can share their discoveries with their classmates.

6. Before reading *When I Am Old with You* (Johnson, 1990), ask students what they like to do with their grandparents.

7. *When I Am Old with You* (Johnson, 1990) and *Drop Dead* (Cole, 1997) present two very different perspectives about growing old. Have students compare the grandparents in the books and then ask them what they think they will be like when they are old.

8. *Drop Dead* (Cole, 1997) can be used to engage students in a discussion of stereotypes of older people, since these grandparents look old, but do not act old.

9. *When Dinosaurs Die: A Guide to Understanding Death* (Brown and Brown, 1996) is divided into short chapters. Reading one or two chapters at a time and discussing them with children affords them an opportunity to learn about death. This is a book to share throughout the year and not just after a death.

10. *My Grandfather's House* (Coville, 1996) offers a realistic portrayal of the death of a grandparent and could be used to prepare a child for the impending death of a sick grandparent.

11. *After Charlotte's Mom Died* (Spelman, 1996) is a book not just for students, but also for teachers and librarians who may be at a loss for what to do for a child faced with the death of a parent. Privately sharing this book with the child is one way for a teacher to let the child know that support is available and that the child is not alone.

TEACHER RESOURCES

This section includes books, professional organizations, and Internet sites for teachers and librarians to locate resources to use as they teach these very important and very personal topics.

BOOKS

Educator's Guide to FREE Health, Physical Education & Recreation Materials. 2000-2001. Randolph, Wis.: Educator's Progress Service. 233p.

In this guide, teachers will find free videos, films, filmstrips, lesson plans, print resources, and Web resources. To assist teachers in locating items in the book there are title, subject, source, and what's new indexes. There is also a sample letter to use to request the materials.

Herod, Leslie. *Discovering Me: A Guide to Teaching Health and Building Adolescents' Self-Esteem.* 1999. Boston: Allyn and Bacon. 265p. Grades: 6 and up.

Helping teenagers develop positive self-esteem through problem-solving activities provides them with practice in essential life skills. This book offers activities to involve students in learning ways to increase their self-esteem.

PROFESSIONAL ORGANIZATIONS

American Dietetic Association
216 W. Jackson Blvd., Ste. 800
Chicago, IL 60606-6995
312-899-0040

American Heart Association National Center
7272 Greenville Avenue
Dallas, TX 75231
800-AHA-USA1
www.americanheart.org

American Red Cross National Headquarters
431 18th Street, NW
Washington, DC 20006
800-797-8022
www.redcross.org

American School Food Service Association
700 South Washington Street, Suite 300
Alexandria, VA 22314
703-739-3900

American School Health Association

P.O. Box 708

Kent, OH 44240

330-678-1601

www.ashaweb.org/

National Aging Information Center

330 Independence Avenue, SW – Room 4656

Washington, DC 20201

202-619-7501

www.nih.gov/nia

INTERNET SITES

Food and Drug Administration (FDA)

www.fda.gov/

This site includes links to FDA news, product approvals, and safety alerts. For children there are links to information on food safety, vaccines, tobacco, and other topics of interest to children. Also available from the children's Web page is a link to a Web site for parents.

KidsHealth

www.kidshealth.org/

Created by medical experts, this site provides excellent information about children's health with links for parents, children, and teens. Much of the site is text-based and children may not be able to read and understand it on their own. This extensive site has a search engine.

United States Department of Agriculture (USDA)

www.nal.usda.gov/fnic/Fpyr/pyramid.html

Included here is a guide for using the food pyramid and black line masters for printing copies of the pyramid. Ethnic/cultural food guide pyramids are also available.

REFERENCES

Almasi, Janice F., and Margaret G. McKeown. 1996. "The Nature of Engaged Reading in Classroom Discussions of Literature." *Journal of Literacy Research* 28, no. 1 (March): 107-146.

Bargiel, Susie, Cathy Beck, Dick Koblitz, Anne O'Connor, Kathryn Mitchell Pierce, and Susan Wolf. 1997. "Bringing Life's Issues into the Classrooms." *Language Arts* 74, no. 6 (October): 482-490.

Crawford, Patricia A. 1996. "Exploring Books that Connect the Generations." *Language Arts* 73, no. 5 (September): 352-358.

Fitzgibbons, Shirley A., and Carol L. Tilley. 1999. "Images of Poverty in Contemporary Realistic Fiction for Youth." Paper presented at the Third International Forum on Research in School Librarianship, Annual Conference of the International Association of School Librarianship in Birmingham, Ala., November. ERIC, ED 437060.

Goforth, Frances S. 1998. *Literature and the Learner.* Belmont, Calif.: Wadsworth.

Heine, Pat, Christine Inkster, Frank Kazemek, Sandra Williams, Sylvia Rachke, and Della Stevens. 1999. "Strong Female Characters in Recent Children's Literature." *Language Arts* 76, no. 5 (May): 427-434.

HyperStudio. Version 4. 2000. Torrance, Calif.: Knowledge Adventure.

Imagination Express, Destination: Neighborhood. 1995. Redmond, Wash.: Edmark.

Inspiration. Version 6. 1999. Portland, Ore.: Inspiration Software.

Kane, Karen. 1994. "Stories Help Students Understand Movement." *Strategies* 7, No. 7 (May): 13–17.

Laney, James D., Jo Lynn Laney, T. Joy Wimsatt, and Patricia A. Moseley. 1997. "Children's Ideas about Aging Before and After an Integrated Unit of Instruction." Paper presented at the annual meeting of the American Educational Research Association Conference in Chicago, Ill., March. ERIC, ED 408109.

Madura, Sandra. 1995. "The Line and Texture of Aesthetic Response: Primary Children Study Authors and Illustrators." *The Reading Teacher* 49 no. 2, (October): 110-118.

Peck, Jackie, and Judith Hendershot. 1997. "Meet Officer Buckle and Gloria through Their Creator's Own Story." *The Reading Teacher* 50 no. 5, (October): 404-408.

Rudman, Masha Kabakow. 1995. *Children's Literature: An Issues Approach.* 3rd ed. White Plains, N. Y.: Longman.

Scales, Peter C. 2000. "Building Students' Developmental Assets to Promote Health and School Success." *The Clearing House* 74, no. 2 (Nov./Dec.): 84-88.

Sechrist, William. 2000. "Why Teach Children about Child Abuse and Neglect?" *The Education Digest* 66, no. 2 (October): 45-49.

Siemens, Lisa. 1994. "'Does Jesus Have Aunties?' and 'Who Planned it All?': Learning to Listen for 'Big' Questions." *Language Arts* 71, no. 5 (September): 358-361.

Summerfield, Liane M. 1995. National Standards for School Health Education. ERIC Digest. ED387483.

Young, Terrell A., and Sylvia Vardell. 1993. "Weaving Readers Theatre and Nonfiction into the Curriculum." *The Reading Teacher* 46, no. 5 (February): 396-406.

Chapter 6

Sports, Recreation, and Dance

Physical education, dance, sports, and games all have unique vocabularies for students to learn in order to understand and fully participate in the activities. One way to help students learn the necessary vocabulary words is by reading aloud to them books on these topics. Reading books to the students and making them available in a reading corner encourages students to read the books on their own. Trade books can introduce topics, facilitate independent explorations, and suggest extension activities (Farris and Fuhler, 1994). One way to extend what children have learned from books is to have them write about what they learned. Duthie's (1994) students learned to write nonfiction by studying the writing styles of nonfiction books and working through the writing process. Students who are interested in a sport or game can write about why the activity interests them. Their interest is often such that they work at the sport rather than play. The following video introduces the origins of several popular sports and games.

Sports and Games: Vol. 16. 1990. Video. Ann Arbor, Mich.: Schoolmasters Video. 30 min. Grades: 3–6.

The origins of a variety of sports and games are explored in this video. Some of the sports and games included are tennis, basketball, soccer, checkers, and hide-and-seek. This is one of the Tell Me Why Video Encyclopedia Series.

The National Association for Sport and Physical Education (NASPE, 1992) developed Content Standards for Physical Education classes to clarify what physically educated students should know and be able to demonstrate. These standards include benchmarks to assess students' competency in movement forms, ability to maintain a physically active lifestyle, and understanding of the importance of physical activity. These standards state that a physically educated student:

1. Demonstrates competency in many movement forms and proficiency in a few movement forms.
2. Applies movement concepts and principles to the learning and development of motor skills.

3. Exhibits a physically active lifestyle.
4. Achieves and maintains a health-enhancing level of physical fitness.
5. Demonstrates responsible personal and social behavior in physical activity settings.
6. Demonstrates understanding and respect for differences among people in physical activity settings.
7. Understands that physical activity provides opportunities for enjoyment, challenge, self-expression, and social interaction.

Dance allows students to express themselves through movement. One way for students to respond to literature is through creative movement (Schoon, 1997-1998). Imitating the movement of characters in books enables children to practice motor skills. Movement involves the whole child and they respond with enthusiasm and excitement (Kane, 1994). The *National Standards for Arts Education* (ArtsEdge, 1992) established guidelines for what young people should be able to know and do in the arts. The following content standards are for dance.

1. Identifying and demonstrating movement elements and skills in performing dance.
2. Understanding choreographic principles, processes, and structures.
3. Understanding dance as a way to create and communicate meaning.
4. Applying and demonstrating critical and creative-thinking skills in dance.
5. Demonstrating and understanding dance in various cultures and historical periods.
6. Making connections between dance and healthful living.
7. Making connections between dance and other disciplines.

The content standards for physical education and dance serve as guidelines for teachers as they develop their classroom curriculum. The sections in this chapter include sports, athletes, recreation, dance, dancers, and teacher resources.

SPORTS

The books in this section encompass a variety of sports and help to address the physical education content standards. By participating in sports children learn sportsmanship and the importance of teamwork. All of these activities require physical activity, which is essential to lifelong health and well-being. Learning to play different sports and games provides students with ways to spend their leisure time throughout their lives. Children who are not interested in reading other books may be interested in reading these books to learn about sports and games they want to learn to play. The excitement and passion of sports attract players of all ages. *Hoops* (Burleigh, 1997) speaks to basketball players.

Burleigh, Robert. *Hoops.* **Illustrated by Stephen T. Johnson. 1997. Unp. Grades: 3–8.**

The graceful, intense passion of basketball is captured in this poem, while the energized, dynamic nature of the sport is captured in the illustrations. While the ball sails through the air, the players' bodies are frozen in motion. Basketball enthusiasts and poetry lovers both enjoy this book, which is to be savored and appreciated again and again.

BOOK AND MEDIA CHOICES

Morris, Ann. *Teamwork.* **1999. New York: William Morrow. 32p. Grades: K–2.**

The importance of teamwork is shown in a multicultural collection of photographs of people working in teams around the world. The importance of teamwork and the benefits of working together are explained. Sparse text in large print makes this a book young readers can read on their own. The book ends with an index of the photographs in the book and tells where each was taken. The last page of the book is a world map with the question "Where in the world were these photographs taken?"

Knotts, Bob. *Track and Field.* **2000. New York: Children's Press. 48p. Grades: K–3.**

Large, easy-to-read text and color photographs attract young readers to this book. Track-and-field events are described including sprints, marathons, high jumps, and field events. One chapter describes noted track-and-field athletes. The book also includes a list of books and resources for further research, a glossary, and an index. This book is part of A True Book series.

Shannon, David. *How Georgie Radbourn Saved Baseball.* **1994. New York: Blue Sky Press. Unp. Grades: 2–4.**

In America in the future, there are no longer four seasons during the year, only winter. This story tells of the humiliation of a ballplayer named Boss Swaggert, who constantly struck out when he played baseball. When he became rich and powerful, he banned anything dealing with baseball. With baseball banned spring, summer, and fall no longer came. Then Georgie was born and he only spoke in baseball lingo. Eventually, Georgie brought baseball back and with baseball the seasons returned. Both baseball fans and those who are not fans enjoy this book.

Young, Robert. *Game Day: Behind the Scenes at a Ballpark.* **Photographs by Jerry Wachter. 1998. Minneapolis, Minn.: Carolrhoda Books. 48p. Grades: 2–5.**

What strikes the reader about this book is that not only is it the story of the activities that take place before a game, it is also testimony to the many people that work behind the scenes on game day to assure that all runs smoothly. Color photographs give young sports fans glimpses into behind-the-scenes activities and excitement. Included is a text box about the special mud used to rub on baseballs to remove the shine so that they can be seen more easily. The mud comes from a secret spot in the Delaware River.

Brown, Fern G. _Special Olympics._ 1992. New York: Franklin Watts. 64p. Grades: 3–5.

The Special Olympics provides opportunities for individuals with mental retardation to participate in organized athletic events. Information is given on the history of Special Olympics and the rules for competition. The importance of volunteers to the success of Special Olympics is stressed. Included in the book is a section on what schools can do. The book ends with a glossary and an index.

Jackson, Collin. _The Young Track and Field Athlete._ 1996. New York: DK. 32p. Grades: 3–6.

This typical DK volume is filled with color photographs and brief text dealing with track-and-field events, such as the long jump, high jump, discus throwing, and hurdles. Warm-up exercises for young athletes are described and shown in photographs. Starting positions and moves for each event are depicted.

Hoyt-Goldsmith, Diane. _Lacrosse: The National Game of the Iroquois._ Photographs by Lawrence Migdale. 1998. New York: Holiday House. 32p. Grades: 3–7.

Lacrosse is more than a sport to the Iroquois Indians, it is part of their heritage. This book is a photo essay that tells the history of the sport, information about this fast-paced sport, and the importance of the sport to the Iroquois. It follows the lives of a three-generation family with drawings, paintings, and photographs. There is a glossary and an index.

Buckley, James Jr. _America's Greatest Game: The Real Story of Football and the National Football League._ 1998. New York: Hyperion Books for Children. 64p. Grades: 3 and up.

Color photographs of NFL players and coaches fill the pages of this book. From the early years of football starting in 1876 to the present, this book contains fascinating information and absorbing football facts. For example, football was originally a running game and it was not until 1906 that it was legal to pass the football. Throughout the book are textboxes of interesting information, such as the one showing how helmets changed over the years.

Lineker, Gary. _Soccer._ 2000. New York: DK. 45p. Grades: 4–6.

Young soccer players enjoy this easy-to-read book with color photographs and step-by-step directions explaining soccer skills. The book begins with a brief history of the game, the needed equipment and clothing, diagrams of the field, and diagrams of the officials' signals. The book concludes with a glossary, an index, and addresses for obtaining additional information about the game.

Vicario, Arantxa Sanchez. *The Young Tennis Player*. 1996. New York: DK. 45p. Grades: 4–8.

A professional tennis player wrote this book. She shares her enthusiasm for the game by giving young tennis players the information they need to get started playing. Diagrams for correct foot positions and diagrams of ball trajectories aid readers as they attempt the different movements shown in the pictures. The color photographs of children demonstrating correct positions and swings enhance this book's appeal for students. At the end of the book is a glossary, tennis rules, an index, and useful addresses for obtaining additional information.

Mullin, Chris, and Brian Coleman. *The Young Basketball Player*. 1995. New York: DK. 45p. Grades: 4–8.

This book begins with a brief history of basketball and a diagram of the court with the players and officials noted. Different skills needed to play the game are described in text and photographs. There are brief descriptions of the basketball leagues, a glossary, rules, an index, and useful addresses at the end of the book.

Anderson, Dave. *The Story of the Olympics*. 1996. New York: William Morrow. 160p. Grades: 4 and up.

This fascinating history of the Olympics provides detailed information about some of the famous athletes who have competed in the games. The distinct, individual personalities of the athletes and their intense training routines are examined and provide interesting, personal glimpses into their lives. The history of the games is framed in the politics of the times and includes incidents such as Hitler's snub of Jesse Owens.

Layden, Joseph, and James Preller. *NBA Game Day*. 1997. New York: Scholastic. 64p. Grades: 4 and up.

The authors asked 26 sport photographers to provide them with photographs showing what it is like to play in the NBA. This book is a behind-the-scenes look at game day in the NBA. Students recognize the famous players and may be surprised to see them with joints wrapped in ice bags and soaking in whirlpools. Amazing photographs, such as Dennis Rodman seemingly floating horizontally above the floor as he flies to catch a ball, fill the book.

Stewart, Mark. *Basketball: A History of Hoops*. 1998. New York: Franklin Watts. 160p. Grades: 4 and up.

A picture of James Naismith holding a basketball and a peach basket begins this history of basketball. Also included is a picture of the gym where basketball was born in 1891. The book includes information on the history of both college and professional basketball. A basketball timeline is included, as are numerous appendices of basketball facts and figures. An index concludes the book.

Jackman, Joan. *The Young Gymnast.* 1995. New York: DK. 45p. Grades: 5–8.

Audiences marvel at the feats of gymnasts as they twist, turn, leap, and roll. Photographs of young gymnasts demonstrating a variety of moves and step-by-step instructions for completing complex maneuvers spill across the pages of this book. Also included are photographs of the apparatuses used and the competition arena. The book ends with a glossary, an index, and a list of useful addresses.

***Nitty Gritty Basketball: Fundamentals.* 1999. Video. Philadelphia, Penn.: Golden Aura Publishing. 48 min. Grades: 5 and up.**

Students demonstrate fundamental basketball skills and drills, including ball handling, dribbling, shooting, and rebounding. Live action clips of students practicing basketball techniques assure that viewers are encouraged to try the techniques.

Silverstein, Alvin, Virginia Silverstein, and Robert Silverstein. *Steroids: Big Muscles, Big Problems.* 1992. Hillside, N.J.: Enslow Publishers. 112p. Grades: 5 and up.

This no-nonsense look at the dangers of steroids describes steroids and why people use them. Some athletes feel that if they do not use them they cannot succeed since other athletes in their sport are using them. Young people use them to enhance their appearance and to build up their body for competitions. Some young people continue to use steroids even though they know that they can be addictive and that they may lead to dangerous, aggressive behavior. This is part of the Issues in Focus series.

Jacobs, Jeff. *Hockey Legends.* 1995. New York: Friedman/Fairfax. 120p. Grades: 7 and up.

Most of the book is dedicated to great hockey players, but it also includes information on the greatest moments in the game, the dynasties, a chronology, hall of fame, all-time records, club addresses, and an index. Large color photographs capture the excitement of the game and the exuberance of the players.

EXPLORATIONS

1. After reading *Teamwork* (Morris, 1999), divide the students into three member teams. Then have them work together to create the letters of the alphabet with their bodies.
2. Many children enjoy participating in the events they read about in *Track and Field* (Knotts, 2000) and *The Young Track and Field Athlete* (Jackson, 1996). Help them organize some of the running and jumping events described in the book during recess.

3. After reading *How Georgie Radbourn Saved Baseball* (Shannon, 1994), the students can create a sequence map of the main events in the story. Younger students may need assistance deciding which events to include in the map.

4. Place *Game Day: Behind the Scenes at a Ballpark* (Young, 1998), *America's Greatest Game: The Real Story of Football and the National Football League* (Buckley, 1998), *NBA Game Day* (Layden and Preller, 1997), and *Basketball: A History of Hoops* (Stewart, 1998) on a table for students to leisurely read. Provide them with pencils and sticky notes to record comments about the books or to highlight their favorite parts of the books. They then place the sticky notes in the book.

5. Students learn by reading *Special Olympics* (Brown, 1992) that the games depend on volunteers. Children can be encouraged to find out about how they can volunteer to help at a Special Olympics event in their neighborhood.

6. To introduce children to the skills, vocabulary, and equipment of different sports played in physical education class, books on the sport can be shared with them and placed in the classroom for them to read on their own.

7. After reading *The Story of the Olympics* (Anderson, 1996), students can obtain additional information from the International Olympic Committee Web site at www.olympic.org and from the United States Olympic Committee at www.usoc.org.

ATHLETES

Children look up to athletes and want to emulate them. The athletes in these books are role models for children. While reading about the lives of the athletes, children discover the perseverance and hard work required for success. Books in this section address content standards six and seven. While reading books about athletes, students come to appreciate and to respect differences among people, which are addressed in content standard six. Also, students learn that participation in sports involves challenge, self-expression, and social interaction, which are addressed in content standard seven.

Some of the books on athletes contain information on several different athletes in the same book. These are examples of nonfiction books that do not have to be read from beginning to end. This distinction from fiction books that are usually read from beginning to end should be pointed out to the students. Some students are overwhelmed by the prospect of reading an entire book. These students welcome being able to read only the portions of the book that are of interest.

BOOK AND MEDIA CHOICES

***The Magic School Bus Plays Ball.* 1996. Video. New York: Scholastic. 30 min. Grades: 1–4.**

This animated video has the Friz and her students learning physics as they play "frictionless baseball." The video features the voice of Lily Tomlin.

***Michael Jordan's Playground.* 1991. Video/DVD. New York: Fox Broadcasting. 40 min. Grades: 1 and up.**

Students are introduced to Michael Jordan as he offers encouragement to a high school basketball player who was cut from his school team. Michael shares his personal experiences and the dedication and hard work it took to become a basketball star.

Gutelle, Andrew. *Baseball's Best: Five True Stories.* Illustrated by Cliff Spohn. 1990. New York: Random House. 48p. Grades: 2–4.

Young readers enjoy reading this book about five baseball greats because they can read it on their own. These brief introductions to the careers of Babe Ruth, Joe DiMaggio, Jackie Robinson, Roberto Clemente, and Hank Aaron capture the imagination of young baseball players. Both photographs and illustrations accompany the stories.

Krull, Kathleen. *Wilma Unlimited: How Wilma Rudolph Became the World's Fastest Woman.* Illustrated by David Diaz. 1996. San Diego, Calif.: Harcourt Brace. Unp. Grades: 2–4.

This is the inspiring story of a young African American child whose leg was crippled by polio. She overcame the disability through grueling hours of physical therapy and practice. She won a scholarship to Tennessee State University making her the first member of her large family to ever attend college. In 1960, she represented America at the Olympic games in Rome. With a twisted ankle she won the 100-meter dash, the 200-meter dash, and the 400-meter dash making her the fastest woman in the world. This is an example of a picture book that portrays a strong, positive, contemporary female character, who serves as a role model for females (Heine et al., 1999.)

***Awesome Athletes.* 1995. Win. Portland, Ore.: Creative Multimedia. Grades: 2–8.**

This multimedia presentation includes video clips of athletes and online links to additional resources. Children learn about the history of sports, rules, and sports heroes. The CD includes games that enhance reading, spelling, and memory skills. This may be just the program for reluctant readers who are interested in sports figures. This software program was produced in cooperation with *Sports Illustrated.*

Jordan, Roslyn M., and Deloris Jordan. *Salt in His Shoes.* Illustrated by Kadir Nelson. 2000. New York: Simon and Schuster Books for Young Readers. Unp. Grades: 2 and up.

Michael Jordan's mother and sister wrote a loving tribute to this great basketball player. His determination, hard work, and belief in his abilities enabled him to excel. The expressive faces of the characters and the attention to detail in the illustrations make this a picture book to linger over and read again.

Sullivan, George. *Glovemen: Twenty-Seven of Baseball's Greatest.* **1996. New York: Atheneum Books for Young Readers. 72p. Grades: 4 and up.**

This well-illustrated volume contains professional and personal data about famous baseball fielders. Sullivan considers fielders to be the under-sung heroes of baseball and wrote this book as a salute to them and their special abilities. The introduction to the book explains how vitally important fielders are to the game of baseball and chronicles the development of the baseball glove. The book ends with a listing of fielding averages and Gold Glove Awards.

Myers, Walter Dean. *The Greatest: Muhammad Ali.* **2001. New York: Scholastic. 172p. Grades: 4 and up.**

Few students today know that Muhammad Ali was once Cassius Clay. This intriguing biography reveals his complex nature and enables readers to fully appreciate this great athlete who continues to persevere as he copes with Parkinson's disease.

Sullivan, George. *Quarterbacks!: Eighteen of Football's Greatest.* **1998. New York: Atheneum Books for Young Readers. 60p. Grades: 4 and up.**

Following an introduction to the role of the quarterback, this book profiles famous quarterbacks. Each profile begins with biographical facts, as well as team information. The profiles focus on the quarterbacks' career highlights. While the level of the reading material may be challenging to some students, the subject matter motivates them to read the book. Interspersed throughout the text are photographs of the players achieving their career highlights. The placement of the photographs breaks up the long strings of text so as not to overwhelm the reader. At the end of the book young football fans are delighted to discover the listings of All-Time Records.

Osborn, Kevin. *Scholastic Encyclopedia of Sports in the United States.* **1997. New York: Scholastic. 220p. Grades: 4 and up.**

Beginning with the 1770s through the 1990s brief biographical information and pictures are shown of famous athletes throughout American history. The athletes are grouped by time periods and within each time period they are arranged alphabetically. Each athlete has a career capsule, as well as data about their personal and professional lives. The book concludes with an index.

Long, Barbara. *Jim Thorpe: Legendary Athlete.* **1997. Springfield, N. J.: Enslow. 128p. Grades: 4 and up.**

Illustrated with black-and-white photographs, this well-researched biography deals with the life of famous Native American athlete, Jim Thorpe. Born into the Sac and Fox tribe in Oklahoma,

Thorpe was known for his amazing athletic skill. He did not like school and repeatedly ran away. One day his father took him back to school in their horse-drawn wagon traveling 23 miles. Taking several short cuts Thorpe ran home and arrived before his father. Thorpe competed in the 1912 Olympic games, but he was not well known to Olympic fans. This is one of the Native American Biographies series.

America's Greatest Olympians. 1996. Video/DVD. Atlanta, Ga.: Turner Entertainment. Grades: 4 and up.

This is a collection of clips and stories featuring American athletes as they competed in the Olympics. Greg Louganis and Mary Lou Retton are just two of the amazing athletes showcased on this video.

Green, Carl R. Jackie Joyner-Kersee. 1994. New York: Crestwood House, McMillan. 48p. Grades: 5 and up.

Little did a skinny young African American girl born in east St. Louis, Illinois, in the sixties know that she would one day be acclaimed as the premier athlete in the world. Wanting a better life for their children, the Joyners worked hard to achieve their goal. Jackie achieved recognition in both academics and athletics. As she grew, she demanded more and more of herself until she began breaking records, one by one. Jackie won medals in the 1984, the 1988, and the 1992 Olympics. This book concludes with a glossary and an index.

Jim Ryun, America's Great Miler. 1998. Video. New York: Blake & Associates. 58 min. Grades: 6 and up.

While still in high school, Jim Ryun broke the four-minute mile. This video features highlights of his career and interviews with former coaches, competitors, and family members.

Lindop, Laurie. Athletes. 1996. New York: Twenty-First Century Books. 128p. Grades: 6 and up.

There is no question that the ten women covered in this book are outstanding contemporary athletes; but more than that, they are outstanding role models for girls today. There are some sports that were closed to females at one time, such as marathon swimming, horse racing, as well as basketball and some areas of track competition. Several of the athletes described in this book excelled in all of these sports. Their stories tell of sacrifice, self-discipline, and determination to achieve excellence in their respective fields. There are source notes, a list of books for further reading, and an index. This book is part of the Dynamic Modern Women series that includes books about Political Leaders, Scientists and Doctors, and Champions of Equality.

Wilma Rudolph. **1995. Video. Bala Cynwyd, Penn.: Schlessinger Video Productions-Library Video Company. 30 min. Grades: 7 and up.**

As a child Wilma Rudolph was partially paralyzed by polio. Through determination and hard work she overcame her paralysis and earned three Olympic gold medals in track and field. This is part of the American Women of Achievement Video Collection. Other titles in this award-winning series include Abigail Addams, Jane Addams, Marian Anderson, Susan B. Anthony, Clara Barton, Emily Dickinson, Amelia Earhart, Helen Keller, and Sandra Day O'Connor.

EXPLORATIONS

1. Students can make their own baseball cards based on the information in *Baseball's Best: Five True Stories* (Gutelle, 1990) and *Glovemen: Twenty-Seven of Baseball's Greatest* (Sullivan, 1996).

2. After reading the book *Wilma Unlimited: How Wilma Rudolph Became the World's Fastest Woman* (Krull, 1996) or viewing *Wilma Rudolph* (Bala Cynwyd, Penn.: Schlessinger Video Productions-Library Video Company, 1995), provide students the opportunity to discuss what they can learn from her life. When the teacher is removed from actively participating in the discussion, students tend to speak to one another and become more engaged in the discussion.

3. In *Salt in His Shoes* (Jordan and Jordan, 2000) Michael Jordan's mother puts salt in his shoes to make him grow. Students can ask their parents and relatives about other superstitions. Then the class can discuss the different superstitions and hypothesize as to how they came about.

4. Have students look through books on athletes such as *Athletes* (Lindop, 1996), *Glovemen: Twenty-Seven of Baseball's Greatest* (Sullivan, 1996), *Scholastic Encyclopedia of Sports in the United States* (Osborn, 1997), and *Quarterbacks!: Eighteen of Football's Greatest* (Sullivan, 1998) and select their favorite athlete. Then compile a class list of favorite athletes and the sports they played. Students can create a short oral presentation about why the athletes they selected are their favorite.

5. Some students relate to *Jim Thorpe: Legendary Athlete* (Long, 1997) because he did not like school. Have students look through the book to determine reasons why he did not like school. Then have students share their thoughts on school.

6. One of the striking things about *Jackie Joyner-Kersee* (Green, 1994) is the strong support system she had throughout her life. She had family, friends, and coaches who helped her accomplish her goals. Have students think about and discuss who provides them with support in their lives.

RECREATION

This section of the chapter includes books and media on recreational activities for children including games and some sports. Participation in recreational sports and games provides opportunities for students to meet the physical education content standards. Materials on physical activities in this section include swimming, music and movement, hopscotch, jacks, cycling, snowboarding, skateboarding, sidewalk games, karate, ice-skating, volleyball, and mountain climbing.

BOOK AND MEDIA CHOICES

Schuurmans, Hilde. *Sidney Won't Swim.* **2001. Watertown, Mass.: Charlesbridge. Unp. Grades: P–2.**

Sidney is faced with taking swimming lessons with his classmates at the local pool. He dreams up all sorts of reasons why he cannot get into the water including the fact that if he gets wet he turns into a monster. His friends push him into the pool chanting for him to turn into a monster. Once they realize the near disastrous consequences of their actions they work together to get Sidney safely into the water.

Palmer, Hap. *Can Cockatoos Count by Twos? Songs for Learning through Music and Movement.* **1996. CD. Topanga, Calif.: Hap-Pal Music. Grades: K–3.**

Combining music and movement actively involves students as they learn and practice math and language skills such as addition, subtraction, telling time, and rhyming. Singing along and moving as they learn aids student retention of the concepts. A teaching guide with suggested activities and extensions comes with this CD.

Lankford, Mary D. *Hopscotch Around the World: Nineteen Ways to Play the Game.* **1992. New York: A Beech Tree Paperback Book. 48p. Grades: 1–3.**

Hopscotch is played around the world and has been traced to Roman soldiers who some think brought the game to England. Each two-page spread tells the name of the game in that country, an introduction to how the game is played in that country, a diagram of the playing field, and step-by-step instructions for the variation of the game. The book concludes with a bibliography and index.

Erlbach, Arlene. *Sidewalk Games Around the World.* **Illustrated by Sharon Lane Holm. 1997. Brookfield, Conn.: The Millbrook Press. 64p. Grades: 1–5.**

Some of the sidewalk games in the book resemble those played in the United States and others are ones that American children find new and different. A brief introduction is given about the country in which the game is played, followed by the rules for playing the game. In some instances instructions are given for creating the equipment needed to play the game.

Lankford, Mary D. *Jacks around the World.* **Illustrated by Karen Dugan. 1996. New York: Morrow Books. 40p. Grades: 2–5.**

This companion book to *Hopscotch Around the World* (Lankford, 1992) provides a multicultural look at the popular children's game of jacks. Around the world the rules are basically the same.

Brief information is given about the country where the game is played, the name of the game, and a pastel illustration of children playing the game. Instructions are given for playing the game as it is played in each country. In some countries the knucklebones of sheep are used for playing jacks and directions for making knucklebones from flour, water, salt, and glycerin are included. The book concludes with a bibliography and an index.

Shoemaker, Joel. 1995. *Skateboarding Streetstyle*. Minneapolis, Minn.: Capstone Press. 48p. Grades: 2–6.

Youngsters interested in learning about or reading about skateboarding enjoy this introduction to this fast paced sport. Information on purchasing a skateboard and the needed equipment, as well as tricks for completing various moves and safety measures, are included in this slim volume. At the end of the book is a glossary, a brief bibliography, and an index. This is one of the Action Sports series.

Sullivan, George. *Snowboarding: A Complete Guide for Beginners*. 1997. New York: Cobblehill. 48p. Grades: 3–6.

Have you ever thought of whooshing down a mountainside on a snowboard? This book offers information to get you started in this fast growing sport. There is information on the equipment used, basic skills to master, advanced techniques, and safety tips. A young snowboarder demonstrates the skills needed to sail through the air on a fiberglass board. The book concludes with a glossary and resources that provide additional information on skateboarding.

Iguchi, Bryan. *The Young Snowboarder*. 1997. New York: DK. 37p. Grades: 3–8.

Information about the development of snowboarding and equipment needed are combined with step-by-step instructions for the beginner. Photographs showing the individual actions required to complete the moves accompany the instructions. At the end of the book are a glossary, an index, and useful addresses for obtaining additional information.

***Karate for Kids: Intermediate Instruction and Exercise*. 1994. Video. West Long Beach, N.J.: Kultur Video. 35 min. Grades: 3 and up.**

This three-volume set begins with stretches and basic techniques and progresses to advanced moves. While learning how to defend themselves with karate, students also develop positive self-esteem and become physically fit.

Mitchell, David. *The Young Martial Arts Enthusiast.* 1997. New York: DK. 65p. Grades: 3 and up.

There are 15 popular martial arts noted in this book with the focus on judo, karate, kung fu, and tae kwon do. The book advises readers that most martial arts techniques cannot be self-taught. The photographs in this work carefully demonstrate correct posture and stance, but proper training by a qualified instructor is essential. The martial arts require strict self-discipline. The book concludes with useful addresses, magazines, training schools, a glossary, and an index.

Morrissey, Peter. *The Young Ice Skater.* 1998. New York: DK. 37p. Grades: 3–8.

Do you know what a snowplow is? Do you understand tango on ice? The answers to these questions and more are found in this book about ice-skating. This book traces ice-skating back to its roots as transportation in the tenth century. Photographs illustrate the most basic steps, as well as edges, turns, spins, and ice dancing. The book includes a glossary, useful addresses for additional information, and an index.

Foeste, Aaron. *Ice Skating Basics.* Photographed by Bruce Curtis. 1998. New York: Sterling. 96p. Grades: 4–8.

For readers interested in learning to ice-skate, this book is the place to begin. Included are chapters on purchasing the proper equipment, skating basics, instructions for adult beginners, instructions for parents who want to teach their children to skate, and advanced skating maneuvers. Color photographs accompany the step-by-step instructions. An index is included.

Edwards, Chris. *The Inline Skater.* 1996. New York: DK. 37p. Grades: 4–8.

Inline skating started in the 1700s in Belgium. This book begins with a history of the sport and discusses necessary gear, the importance of warming up, and various movements used in the sport. Photographs of five young inline skaters accompany the text and demonstrate the moves used in this fast-paced sport. At the end of the book are a glossary, an index, and a list of useful addresses.

Gutman, Bill. *Volleyball: Start Right and Play Well.* Illustrated by Ben Brown. 1990. Freeport, N.Y.: Marshall Cavendish. 64p. Grades: 4 and up.

A brief history of volleyball sets the stage for learning to play the game. The first section of the book contains information about the game and the equipment used to play the game. The second section of the book gives directions for the skills and maneuvers used in playing the game. Illustrations accompany the directions. The book ends with a glossary of terms.

Rouse, Jeff. *The Young Swimmer.* **1997. New York: DK. 37p. Grades: 5–8.**

This book introduces swimming through short text blurbs and color photographs. It begins with a history of the sport and the basic skills needed to begin swimming. Detailed step-by-step instructions and accompanying photographs explain the sequence of moves involved in different swimming strokes. Information on synchronized swimming and competitions is also included. The book concludes with a glossary, an index, and addresses for obtaining additional information.

Parks, Deborah. *Climb Away!: A Mountaineer's Dream.* **1996. Parsippany, N.J.: Silver Burdett Press. 142p. Grades: 5 and up.**

This personal account of her mountain-climbing hobby describes Parks's adventures from her first "real mountain" to her more recent climbing experiences. As much as she loves the mountains she climbs, Deborah Parks seems to love the people she meets on her trips as much. As a child she was often warned by family and friends that she was going to get hurt, get in trouble, come to a bad end, to which she always replied "Who says?" While she does include much about the technical aspects of her climbs, she has written an "easy-to-read" book that readers find hard to put down.

Jenkins, George H. *Cycling.* **1994. Vero Beach, Fla.: Rourke Corporation. 48p. Grades: 5 and up.**

Cycling is not only a sport; it is a common form of transportation. Included in the book are chapters on cycling competitions, road racing, and track racing. Color photographs furnish close-up views of the cyclists in action. Safety cautions are given for riders and information on protective clothing. The book concludes with a glossary, sources of additional information, and an index. This is one of the Pro-Am Sports series.

EXPLORATIONS

1. Prior to reading *Sidney Won't Swim* (Schuurmans, 2001), ask students to share their experiences about learning to swim.
2. While listening to *Can Cockatoos Count by Twos? Songs for Learning through Music and Movement* (Palmer, 1996), have students participate in the movements described in the teacher's guide.
3. Using Mapmakers Toolkit software the students create a map of the world and select a stamp to represent hopscotch and another stamp to represent jacks. As they play the different versions of hopscotch (Lankford, 1992) and jacks (Lankford, 1996) have them place the appropriate stamp on the country where the version of the game is played.
4. In *Jacks Around the World* (Lankford, 1992) students learn that knucklebones are used to play jacks. The book has a simple recipe for making knucklebones that requires no baking. Children enjoy making knucklebones and playing jacks with them.

5. Using *Sidewalk Games Around the World* (Erlbach, 1997) have the students work in groups to learn one of the games in the book. Then provide them time to teach the game to the other students in the class.

6. After reading *Skateboarding Streetstyle* (Shoemaker, 1995), have children discuss all the safety equipment used in skateboarding and why it is important to use the equipment.

7. After reading *Snowboarding: A Complete Guide for Beginners* (Sullivan, 1997) or *Ice Skating Basics* (Foeste, 1998), ask students to write a brief safety manual for beginners.

8. After reading *Volleyball: Start Right and Play Well* (Gutman, 1990), have students make connects between the vocabulary used in volleyball and the vocabulary used in other sports. For example, players serve the ball in both tennis and volleyball.

9. In *Climb Away!: A Mountaineer's Dream* (Parks, 1996) the author writes of her passion for mountain climbing and how she set goals for herself to attain. Encourage students to look in the book to find out what she had to do to attain her goals. Help them relate the author's goal setting to their own lives.

10. After reading *Climb Away!: A Mountaineer's Dream* (Parks, 1996), have students write about their favorite form of recreation.

DANCE

Books in this section help students become aware of the movement that is inherent in the act of dancing, whether they are dancing a Native American dance, a ballet, or simply moving and swaying to music. Students learn that some dances have specific steps and movements, but that they can also create their own dance steps and movements by simply responding to music they hear on a recording or the music they hear in nature. Materials in this section help assure that students meet dance content standards one through five as they learn about dance and practice dance steps.

BOOK AND MEDIA CHOICES

Walton, Rick. *How Can You Dance?* Illustrated by Ana Lopez-Escriva. 2001. New York: G. P. Putnam's Sons. Unp. Grades: P–1.

Lively, bouncy youngsters are delighted to have an opportunity to move and dance. This book shows them how to use their boundless energy to dance at every opportunity, when they are mad, or fearful, or on the beach, or lying on the floor. Simple directions are given for dances for every occasion.

Ancona, George. *Let's Dance.* 1998. New York: Morrow Junior Books. Unp. Grades: P–2.

Stunning color photographs and simple text encourage children to examine the pictures and read the text to learn about dancing around the world. Small text boxes tucked into the corners of the pictures provide additional information about the country and the dance depicted. Students learn that dances are used to celebrate and to tell stories.

How to Be a Ballerina. 1997. Video/DVD. New York: Sony Wonder. 40 min. Grades: K–3.

This video is of the children's class at the Royal Academy of Dance. Viewers follow along as the students warm up, rehearse, and perform scenes from Sleeping Beauty.

Backstage at the Ballet. 1992. Video. Chandler, Ariz.: Bridgestone Multimedia Group. 25 min. Grades: K–5.

This behind-the-scenes tour of a production of *The Nutcracker* introduces students to the performers and stagehands. Students are able to see the backstage preparations for a performance. This is one of the Field Trip Video Series.

Time to Dance. 2000. Video. Wynnewood, Penn.: Library Video. 28 min. Grades: 1–6.

Allison Crosby, a professional dance instructor, teaches a group of young girls a variety of dance steps in a series of dance lessons. This video introduces youngsters to the joy of dancing. A Spanish version of this video is available.

George Balanchine's The Nutcracker. 1997. DVD. Burbank, Calif.: Warner Home Video. 92 min. Grades: 1 and up.

Tchaikovsky's *The Nutcracker* is a favorite Christmas tradition. This video is Peter Martins's adaptation of George Balanchine's version of this famous ballet featuring the New York City Ballet. Kevin Kline narrates the video.

Smith, Cynthia Leitich. *Jingle Dancer*. Illustrated by Corneilius Van Wright and Ying-Hwa Hu. 2000. New York: Morrow Junior Books. Unp. Grades: 2–4.

A young Native American girl, Jenna, practices jingle dancing by imitating her grandmother's steps on the videotape playing on the television. Jenna wants to be able to jingle dance at the next powwow. In order for her dress to sing, she needs four rows of jingles. Since there is not enough time to mail order the tins for creating jingles she sets off to borrow them from other dancers in her family and community. This heartwarming story provides students a glimpse into the rich culture and community of Native Americans.

Esbensen, Barbara Juster. *Dance with Me.* **Illustrated by Megan Lloyd. 1995. New York: HarperCollins. 32p. Grades: 2–4.**

The movement of dance is found all around us in the wind, in a garden, in the dust, in the tide, and in a basketball game. These poems awaken in the reader a sense of how the daily rhythms of life form their own unique dances. The poems challenge readers to appreciate and discover dance movements all around them. The National Council of Teachers of English gave this book their 1994 Excellence in Poetry Award.

Bussell, Darcey, and Patricia Linton. *The Young Dancer.* **1994. New York: Dorling Kindersley. 65p. Grades: 3–8.**

The importance of learning basic steps and movements is essential to develop the leg strength needed for ballet. The basic steps and movements are depicted in photographs of young male and female dancers. There is a short section on mime and make-up. The book also includes a short description of a selection of ballets. A listing of useful addresses, a glossary, and an index are included.

Swan Lake. **1997. DVD. Santa Monica, Calif.: PolyGram Filmed Entertainment: MGM. 106 min. Grades: 3 and up.**

This beautiful, classic ballet by Tchaikovsky is based on an old folktale. This is a romantic tale of princesses who were changed into swans and rescued by a prince.

Castle, Kate. *My Ballet Book.* **1998. New York: DK. 61p. Grades: 4 and up.**

This beautifully photographed book explains the life of a ballerina from dress, to practice, to performing, to backstage events, to make-up, to the world of ballet. Young ballerinas enjoy looking at the photographs and reading the brief text entries that describe life as a ballerina. The book concludes with a glossary, an index, and useful addresses.

EXPLORATIONS

1. After reading *Let's Dance* (Ancona, 1998), play a musical selection and let the children spontaneously create their own dances of celebration.
2. The poems in *Dance with Me* (Esbensen, 1995) lend themselves to interpretation through movement. For example, while the teacher reads "Invitation to the Wind" have the students imagine themselves as the wind. Then have students stand and gently sway moving their arms and gradually slowly twirling and spinning. Movement allows students to creatively express their reactions to words (Schoon, 1997-1998).
3. Prior to reading *Jingle Dancer* (Smith, 2000), ask students to share their knowledge of ethnic dances. Students from other countries may be familiar with dances that are native to their heritage.

4. Prior to reading *My Ballet Book* (Castle, 1998), have students relate their experiences with ballet lessons.

5. After reading *My Ballet Book* (Castle, 1998), have students make comparisons between the life of a ballet dancer and the life of a pro-football or basketball player.

DANCERS

Students may not be aware of the hard work and dedication necessary for dancers to succeed in their profession. In these books students learn of the long hours and years of practice that dancing requires. One of the books recounts the trials and tribulations of a teenage boy from Russia who came to America to dance. Books in this section address content standard three as students discover that dance is a way to create and communicate meaning. Also, content standard five is addressed as students recognize the place of dance in different cultures.

BOOK AND MEDIA CHOICES

Gregory, Cynthia. *Cynthia Gregory Dances Swan Lake*. Photographs by Martha Swope. 1990. New York: Simon and Schuster Books for Young Readers. Unp. Grades: 4–6.

Ballerina Cynthia Gregory takes readers along as she goes about her routine on the day of a performance. Young ballerinas enjoy this behind-the-scenes look at the life of a ballerina. This is one of the Time of My Life Book series.

Lang, Paul. *Maria Tallchief: Native American Ballerina*. 1997. Springfield, N. J.: Enslow. 128p. Grades: 4 and up.

This well-researched biography of the first Native American prima ballerina in this country, Maria Tallchief, is unusual in several ways. First, there is historical representation of the Osage Indian tribe into which she was born. Also, there is a biographical section on George Balanchine. Both of these sections relate to the subject of the book, but it is unusual to find them in the detail presented in this book. These sections furnish a context for understanding her life. She studied dance and music from the time she was three and her most significant performance was Balanchine's Firebird. This is one of the Native American Biographies series.

Morris, Ann. *Dancing to America*. Photographs by Paul Kolnik. 1994. New York: Dutton Children's Books. 40p. Grades: 5 and up.

This is the story of Anton, a teenage Russian ballet dancer, who immigrated to the United States with his parents to pursue his dreams of becoming a famous ballet dancer. Beautiful color photographs and engaging text draw the reader into this moving story of a boy and his family in search of the freedom and opportunity not available in their native country. The challenges of learning a new language, new customs, and a new style of ballet are overcome as Anton works to reach his goal.

EXPLORATIONS

1. As students read *Maria Tallchief: Native American Ballerina* (Lang, 1997) have them write down obstacles in her life and how she overcame them.
2. Reading *Cynthia Gregory Dances Swan Lake* (Gregory, 1990) and *My Ballet Book* (Castle, 1998) provides students with a more in-depth look at ballet. Reading two books on the same topic furnishes students a more balanced view. Students can be encouraged to make comparisons between the books.
3. Prior to reading *Cynthia Gregory Dances Swan Lake* (Gregory, 1990), have students listen to Swan Lake playing softly in the background as they complete assignments in the class.
4. In *Dancing to America* (Morris, 1994) students learn how Anton came to America to dance. Have students from other countries share with their classmates why they came to America.

TEACHER RESOURCES

This section includes professional books, professional organizations, and Internet sites to support teachers and librarians as they work to assure that students develop the skills necessary to participate in sports and recreational activities throughout their lives. Many resources available to teachers and librarians are free for the asking.

BOOKS

Gallas, Karen. *The Languages of Learning: How Children Talk, Write, Dance, Draw, and Sing Their Understanding of the World.* 1995. New York: Teachers College Press. 169p. Grades: K–4.

This teacher/researcher draws upon her own classroom experiences as she describes how children learn including her English-as-a-Second Language students. Her rich descriptions and examples provide readers a glimpse into her classroom. The book includes a bibliography and an index.

Grant, Janet Miller. *Shake, Rattle, and Learn: Classroom Tested Ideas that Use Movement for Active Learning.* 1995. York, Maine: Stenhouse. 112p. Grades: K–6.

This book explores the relationship between movement and learning and provides teachers ideas for incorporating movement into their classrooms.

Zakkai, Jennifer Donohue. *Dance as a Way of Knowing.* **1997. York, Maine: Stenhouse. 152p. Grades: K–6.**

Children's natural inclination to move is used to help them develop creativity and to learn. The author addresses teaching students to become responsible movers in the classroom. Students are encouraged to use creative problem solving and learn through discovery as they move.

Chepko, Steveda F., and Ree K. Arnold. *Guidelines for Physical Education Programs: Standards, Objectives, and Assessments for Grades: K–12.* **2000. Boston, Mass.: Allyn and Bacon. 287p. Grades: K–12.**

Whether developing curriculum or looking for innovative ways to assess students' learning this book is a useful resource.

Harris, Jane A., Anne M. Pittman, Marlys S. Waller, and Cathy L. Dark. *Dance a While: Handbook for Folk, Square, Contra, and Social Dance.* **2000. Boston, Mass.: Allyn and Bacon. 538p. Grades: K and up.**

Combined in this book is information on dance instruction, descriptions of major forms of dance, and directions for dances. This is a wonderful reference source for dance teachers.

Educator's Guide to FREE Health, Physical Education & Recreation Materials. **2000-2001. Randolph, Wis.: Educator's Progress Service. 233p. Grades: K and up.**

In this guide teachers will find free videos, films, filmstrips, lesson plans, print resources, and Web resources. To assist teachers in locating items in the book there are title, subject, source, and what's new indexes. There is also a sample letter to use to request the materials.

Fronske, Hilda. *Teaching Cues for Sport Skills.* **2001. Boston, Mass.: Allyn and Bacon. 318p. Grades: 1 and up.**

This is a resource book for physical education teachers and coaches who are looking for visual and verbal cues to use when teaching sports.

Jeziorski, Ronald M. *The Importance of School Sports in American Education and Socialization.* **1994. Portola Valley, Calif.: Warde Publishers. 128p.**

This book is an excellent source of information on all the reasons why school sports programs need to be fully funded.

Silby, Caroline, and Shelley Smith. *Games Girls Play: Understanding and Guiding Young Female Athletes.* **2000. New York: St. Martin's. 304p.**

Written from personal experiences and examples taken from case studies this book contains handy checklists, strategies, and ideas for parents and coaches as they work with female athletes.

Thompson, Jim. *Positive Coaching: Building Character and Self-Esteem through Sports.* **1995. Portola Valley, Calif.: Warde Publishers. 400p.**

The benefits of providing positive support and encouragement to young athletes is the focus of this book.

Wilson, Susan M. *Sports Her Way: Motivating Girls to Start and Stay with Sports.* **2000. New York: Simon & Schuster. 224p.**

This useful guide contains suggestions for encouraging girls to become involved in sports by focusing on the positive impact of sports on girls' lives. Involvement in sports helps to build positive self-esteem and provides girls with skills to maintain healthy lifestyles.

PROFESSIONAL ORGANIZATIONS

American Alliance for Health, Physical Education, Recreation, and Dance
1900 Association Drive
Reston, VA 20191
703-476-8316
www.aahperd.org/

National Association for Sport and Physical Education
1900 Association Drive
Reston, VA 20191
703-476-3410
www.aahperd.org/naspe/naspe-main.html
Journals: *Strategies, Journal for Physical Education, Recreation and Dance, Research Quarterly for Exercise and Sport, Journal for Health Education*

INTERNET SITES

PE Central
www.pecentral.org
Designed for health and physical education teachers, parents, and students, this site includes links to a wide variety of resources. One link is to top physical education Web sites.

SIRC

www.SPORTQuest.com/

This site is a collection of searchable bibliographic databases on sports, fitness, and sports medicine.

Sports Illustrated for Kids

www.sikids.com/

This Web site designed for upper elementary and middle school students includes news clips, games, comics, and puzzles.

REFERENCES

ArtsEdge. 1992. *National Standards for Arts Education*. [Online]. Available: http://artsedge.kennedy-center.org/professional_resources/standards/natstandards/standards_k4.html [cited 14 October 2000]

Duthie, Christine. 1994. "Nonfiction: A Genre Study for the Primary Classroom." *Language Arts* 71, no. 8 (December): 588-595.

Farris, Pamela J., and Carol J. Fuhler. 1994. "Developing Social Studies Concepts through Picture Books." *The Reading Teacher* 47, no. 5 (February): 380-387.

Heine, Pat, Christine Inkster, Frank Kazemek, Sandra Williams, Sylvia Rachke, and Della Stevens. 1999. "Strong Female Characters in Recent Children's Literature." *Language Arts* 76, no. 5 (May): 427-434.

Kane, Karen. 1994. "Stories Help Students Understand Movement." *Strategies* 7, no. 7 (May): 13-17.

Mapmakers Toolkit. 1999. Watertown, Mass.: Tom Snyder Productions.

National Association for Sport and Physical Education. 1992. *The Content Standards in Physical Education*. [Online] Available: www.aahperd.org/naspe/naspe-main.html [2000, November 30]

Schoon, Susan. 1997-1998. "Using Dance Experience and Drama in the Classroom." *Childhood Education* 74, no. 2 (Winter): 78-82.

Chapter 7

Art

Through the visual arts children can develop alternative ways of seeing their world. These visualizations help feed their imaginations with the necessary resources to become productive citizens in the future (Marantz, 1992). The *National Standards for Arts Education* (ArtsEdge, 1992) establishes a framework for assuring that students understand and appreciate the visual arts. Incorporating the visual arts into the classroom optimizes student learning and achievement because these arts provide a common basis of understanding for diverse learners (Stephen, 1996). Images span cultures and create common understandings between cultures in ways that words cannot. Students from different countries speaking different languages can learn and communicate through images. Additionally, the visual arts enable librarians and teachers to provide instruction in a variety of modalities to assure that each student has the opportunity to learn in their preferred learning style. Using different modalities to present instruction reinforces the content and helps assure retention of the material. Art, as well as creative dramatics, provides venues for children to explore, reflect, organize, and respond to their learning.

The *National Standards for Arts Education* (NSAE) *Visual Arts Standards* (ArtsEdge, 1992) establish a framework for assuring that students understand and appreciate the visual arts. The *Visual Arts Standards* are

1. Understanding and applying media, techniques, and processes.
2. Using knowledge of structures and functions.
3. Choosing and evaluating a range of subject matter, symbols, and ideas.
4. Understanding the visual arts in relation to history and cultures.
5. Reflecting upon and assessing the characteristics and merits of their work and the work of others.
6. Making connections between visual arts and other disciplines.

Examining images and reacting to the images should involve higher-order thinking skills and creativity (Stephen, 1996). Through the visual arts students can learn that there are many interpretations and no one correct answer. Children need guidance as they learn to describe what they see. They need a supportive, comfortable atmosphere as they take risks to interpret works of art. As they learn to respond to art, they develop a deeper understanding of themselves and their environment (Weigmann, 1992). Through art and literature children learn about themselves, their environment, and their relationship to their environment. By providing children with a variety of books, writing materials, and art materials, parents, teachers, and librarians encourage the development of children's cognition and literacy (Hale, 1996).

Art and children's literature help students establish connections between content areas (Flood, Hamm, Herrington, and Turk, 1993). Visual arts standard six focuses on students being aware of the connections between the visual arts and their content area curriculums. These connections or links enable children to use their prior knowledge as a basis for new learning. Helping students to make these connections assures that they have a full, rich understanding of the material they are learning. Drawing from several disciplines to facilitate understanding, to discover new solutions to old problems, and to communicate with others through images requires holistic literacy (Weigmann, 1992). Weigmann describes holistic literacy as the ability to simultaneously use skills from different disciplines to facilitate comprehension, devise new solutions, and create visuals to communicate with others. Combining art, children's literature, and content area material fosters holistic literacy, supports critical thinking, and encourages creativity. Sections in this chapter include artists, art appreciation, art in children's literature, creating art, and teacher resources.

ARTISTS

Learning about the lives of artists enables children to better appreciate and understand the artists' works. Many artists depict important people and events in their lives through their work. Carefully looking at artists' works can provide interesting insight into their lives and the historical times in which they lived. Visual arts standard four relates to students understanding how history and culture impact artists' works. By studying about artists and their work, students can learn to make connections between the work and the artists. Making these connections requires higher-order thinking skills and demonstrates to children that there is no one right conclusion. They can compare their conclusions to those of their classmates and learn to justify their answers. Studying a body of work by a particular artist enables students to see the changes in the artist's style of work over the years. They can possibly relate these changes in style to changes in the artist's life.

BOOK AND MEDIA CHOICES

Mayhew, James. *Katie and the Sunflowers*. 2001. New York: Orchard Books. Unp. Grades: P–2.

When the rain prevents Katie and her grandmother from working in the garden, they decide to go to the museum. While Grandma rests on a bench in the museum, Katie embarks on a lively romp through the postimpressionists' paintings hanging on the walls. As she explores the paintings she introduces young readers to the works of Vincent van Gogh, Paul Gauguin, and Paul Cézanne. At the end of the book readers find information about the postimpressionist style of painting and brief introductions to the three artists whose works are included in the book.

Venezia, Mike. *Pierre Auguste Renoir*. 1996. Chicago: Children's Press. 32p. Grades: 1–3.

Young children learn about Renoir's impressionist paintings through this book. Impressionists painted outdoors, used bright colors and light, quick brush strokes to create naturalistic, alive paintings that were at first not accepted by art patrons. He painted portraits and large outdoor scenes of people enjoying themselves. Cartoons in the book catch children's attention, and the teacher can then lead them to more closely explore the reproductions found in the book. These carefully chosen reproductions appeal to children. This book is one of the Getting to Know the World's Greatest Artists series.

Anholt, Laurence. *Camille and the Sunflowers*. 1994. Hauppauge, New York: Barron's Educational Series. Unp. Grades: 1–4.

A story about Vincent van Gogh's "The Sunflowers" is recounted in this tale of a young boy and his family who befriend van Gogh when he moves to their town. The real people depicted in some of van Gogh's paintings are interwoven in this tale. Among the author's watercolor illustrations are actual reproductions of some of van Gogh's most famous paintings including "The Sunflowers." This book introduces a fascinating artist to young children. It is a delightful representation of van Gogh's life in a small village where he painted his surroundings and the people of the village.

Littlesugar, Amy. *Marie in Fourth Position*. Illustrated by Ian Schoenherr. 1996. New York: Philomel Books. Unp. Grades: 1–4.

Marie van Goethem was the model for Edgar Degas' sculpture "La Petite Danseuse." Unusual for its time, this almost life-size sculpture was made of wax on a wire base and was dressed in a real tutu, with ballet slippers, and human hair. Most sculptures created during this time were made of marble. This is a fictional representation of a real event in which an ordinary child, not a real beauty was used as a model. She considered herself a ballet "rat." Degas, however, saw her as a butterfly and convinced her that indeed she was a butterfly.

***Degas and the Dancer*. 1999. Video. Toronto, Ontario: Devine Entertainment. 56 min. Grades: 2 and up.**

Forced to paint ballerinas in order to pay his bills, Degas meets a floundering young ballerina, Marie van Goethem. This temperamental pair forges a common bond and each provides something the other needs. Based on a true story, this account is fictionalized.

LeTord, Bijou. *A Bird or Two: A Story about Henry Matisse*. 1999. Grand Rapids, Mich.: Eerdmans Publishing. Unp. Grades: 2–4.

As a child, the author's first "picture books," were her father's books of Matisse's paintings. His trademark bright, joyful colors and his style are captured in the book's illustrations. Through lyrical, poetic text the author's enthusiasm for her subject is shared with young readers.

Stanley, Diane. *Leonardo da Vinci*. 1996. New York: HarperCollins. Unp. Grades: 2 and up.

The genius and passion of Leonardo is evidenced by his many inventions, his work as a painter and sculptor, as well as his work as a scientist. The text is enhanced by drawings from Leonardo's notebooks and Stanley's beautiful illustrations. The book includes a pronunciation guide, a bibliography, and a list of books for further reading. This book was awarded the 1997 Orbis Pictus Award and was named an American Library Association Notable Book.

Mason, Anthony. *Famous Artists: Picasso*. 1994. Hauppauge, N.Y.: Barron's. 32p. Grades: 3–6.

Short blocks of text are interspersed with colorful graphics that enhance comprehension of the text. Reproductions of the artist's works and illustrations capture the readers' attention and encourage them to read the text to learn more about the artist's life and work. Each two-page spread has a section depicting a technique the artist used. Readers are encouraged to try the technique on their own. Through this book students can see how Picasso's work changed from classical realism to abstract surrealism. At the end of the book is a timeline of the artist's life, a brief history of art, a list of museums and galleries owning Picasso's work, a short glossary, and an index. Students enjoy reading the stories behind Picasso's most famous paintings. This book is one of the series, An Introduction to the Artist's Life and Work.

Turner, Robin Montana. *Georgia O'Keeffe*. 1991. Boston: Little, Brown. 32p. Grades: 3–6.

Georgia O'Keeffe decided to become an artist at a time when women were not expected to be artists, nor were they given opportunities to become artists. In spite of this Georgia became an artist. She struggled to be taken seriously as an artist and to develop and paint in her own style. Male artists criticized her vibrant use of color. She painted larger-than-life flowers to make people notice the beauty she found in them. The details of her life help the reader to appreciate her art. This is one of a series of books Portraits of Women Artists for Children.

Turner, Robin Montana. *Mary Cassatt.* 1992. Boston: Little, Brown. 32p. Grades: 3–6.

Mary Cassatt became a painter at a time when it was not considered a proper ambition for a woman. She was a friend of Edgar Degas. Cassatt is noted for her loving portraits of mothers and children. Her work captures this special bond and allows the observer to focus on this close loving relationship featuring caring, tender, adoring mothers who acknowledge how special their children are. Her family trait of stubbornness led to her becoming a member of an independent group of impressionists. Her bright colors and loose brush strokes were reasons given for her work not being accepted in salons and galleries. Later in life she tightened her brush strokes and softened the colors she used in her paintings. This is one of a series of books Portraits of Women Artists for Children.

Visconti, Guido. *The Genius of Leonardo.* Illustrated by Bimba Landmann. 2000. New York: Barefoot Books. Unp. Grades: 3–6.

With quotations taken from the notebooks of Leonardo DaVinci, Visconti has written a story told by one of Leonardo's apprentices. Everyone said Leonardo was a genius and the apprentice did not understand the meaning of the word genius, but knew there was almost nothing that Leonardo could not do or did not want to know about. When war came to Italy, Leonardo stopped painting, stopped going to the market, stopped working on his designs for a flying machine, and only designed weapons and machinery of war. Following this period the king of France invited Leonardo to visit his country. Leonardo went, and took the painting of the Mona Lisa with him.

Monet: *Shadow and Light.* 2001. DVD. Toronto, Ontario: Devine Entertainment. Grades: 3–8.

Students learn to appreciate the work of this great artist as they watch this moving story unfold. This DVD has a variety of menu options that provide behind-the-scenes information and versions in different languages. As with other films in this series, the artists interact with youngsters and this assures that students relate to the artists and their lives. This title is also available on videocassette and is part of The Artists' Specials series. Other artists profiled in this award-winning series include Goya, Rembrandt, Winslow Homer, Mary Cassatt, and Degas.

Sills, Leslie. *Inspirations: Stories about Women Artists.* 1989. Niles, Ill.: Albert Whitman. 56p. Grades: 4–6.

Georgia O'Keeffe, Frida Kahlo, Alice Need, and Faith Ringgold are the artists portrayed in this book. Their inspiring life stories, their struggles, and their triumphs are interspersed with personal photographs and reprints of their works. The illustrations and the text are beautifully interwoven to provide poignant glimpses into the lives of these famous women artists. Through the text, the works depicted in the book become more meaningful and cause readers to stop and reflect on what is shown in the art. Art reproductions in color and black-and-white of various art forms created by these artists are included. The stories of the artists' early days are of special interest to children.

Gherman, Beverly. *Norman Rockwell: Storyteller with a Brush*. Illustrated by Norman Rockwell. 2000. New York: Atheneum. 59p. Grades: 4–6.

In the pages of this book readers learn how Rockwell drew upon his life experiences as he painted. This very readable biography includes several reproductions of Rockwell's illustrations that show readers how his life experiences became subjects for his paintings. The book includes credits for the illustrations and an index.

Krull, Kathleen. *Lives of the Artists: Masterpieces Messes (and What the Neighbors Thought)*. Illustrated by Kathryn Hewitt. 1995. San Diego, Calif.: Harcourt Brace. 96p. Grades: 4–6.

The short, chatty, brief biographies of the artists appeal to children. Each artist is represented by an attractive caricature. One slightly disappointing factor is the absence of true reproductions of the artists' works. Each selection is followed by interesting open-ended questions about selected works of the artists; however, the questions deal with art that is not depicted in the book. Internet searches of museum collections, as well as other art books could be used to locate these works.

Greenberg, Jan, and Sandra Jordan. *Chuck Close, Up Close*. 1998. New York: DK. 48p. Grades: 4–6.

Learning disabilities made school an unpleasant place for Chuck Close. His learning disabilities made him different, and he learned to compensate for them. Throughout trying times in his life, art provided him solace. He could not play games as well as other children, so instead he entertained them with puppet shows using puppets he created. His parents supported his artistic endeavors. He tells how his learning disabilities impacted his art by causing him to focus intently on small portions of his work at one time. Working from photographs, he creates grids to make larger-than-life portraits of his friends. The same photograph is often used to create a variety of portraits using different techniques and materials.

Welton, Jude. *Monet*. 1992. London: Dorling Kindersley. 64p. Grades: 4–6.

Photographs, illustrations, and reproductions graphically depict the life of this artist. Captions and brief blocks of text provide fascinating information on Monet's life and work. Photographs of various objects of interest to Monet add a sense of reality to the story of his life and his work. For example, the caption under a photograph of a replica of fabric used in one of his paintings describes how the fabric impacted the color and style of the painting. The book ends with a timeline of his life, a glossary, a map of galleries and museums that house his works, and an index.

Stanley, Diane. *Michelangelo*. 2000. New York: HarperCollins Children's Books. 48p. Grades: 4–7.

The lively narrative is lavishly illustrated, which makes this a very readable book. To facilitate his understanding of human anatomy he dissected corpses that enabled him to paint and sculpt the human form in exquisite detail. Students enjoy reading about his life and learning the stories behind his most famous works.

Rohmer, Harriet, editor. *Just Like Me: Stories and Self-Portraits by Fourteen Artists*. 1997. San Francisco, Calif.: Children's Book Press. 32p. Grades: 4–8.

In the pages of this book students see artists from ethnically diverse backgrounds who share their art and their backgrounds with children. Stories of the artists' lives written by the artists are accompanied by photographs of them as youngsters and as they look today. Their self-portraits are found on the page opposite the narrative. A thumbnail sketch of the artist's life is found at the bottom of each narrative.

Love of Art. 1998. Mac/Win. Burbank, Calif.: Topics Entertainment. Grades: 4 and up.

Five CD-ROMs are included in this collection encompassing several great artists. The CDs include: 1) *Starry Night*, an examination of van Gogh's work; 2) *Scrutiny in the Round*, a combination of art, poetry, music, and video; 3) *Painter's Painting*, artists from post-war New York, 4) *Art and Music: The Twentieth Century*, which examines art and music at the beginning of the twentieth century; and 5) *The Claude Monet Collection*, a screen saver of Monet's works.

Kostenevich, Albert, and Lory Frankel. *Henri Matisse*. 1997. New York: Harry N. Abrams. 92p. Grades: 5 and up.

Intended for the enjoyment of readers of all ages, this biography of the twentieth-century artist, Henri Matisse, describes a remarkable life. This French painter has been described as looking more German than French and as seeming robust rather than ascetic. More than 60 reproductions are included and are listed at the back of the book along with an index. This book is one of the First Impressions Introduction to Art series.

EXPLORATIONS

1. Prior to reading *Katie and the Sunflowers* (Mayhew, 2001), show the students the pictures in the book and have them make predictions about what is happening in the book.

2. After reading *Katie and the Sunflowers* (Mayhew, 2001), discuss with the students how the author made up stories about the people in the paintings. Share art reproductions with the students and have them work with a partner to tell a story about what is happening in the painting. Younger children can work with the teacher to create a class story about a painting.

3. After reading about the lives of several different artists, students can create a class timeline depicting noted events in each artist's life. Then students can add important world events to the timeline to place the artist's life in a historical perspective.

4. Have students bring in a photograph of themselves or a member of their family. Students recreate the photograph several times using different materials each time, such as charcoal, pastels, watercolors, and tempera paints.

5. To help students understand how Chuck Close works, create grids on transparencies. Have students place the transparencies over a school picture of themselves. On manila drawing paper have them pencil in a larger grid to use to enlarge the photograph.

6. On a large world map on the classroom wall students can place the name of an artist in the country of their birth. They could then research to find out about life in that country during the artist's lifetime.

7. The biographies of the artists include information on important times in their lives. Students can create pictures depicting important times in their lives.

8. While reading to students about an artist's life, they can draw sketches to help them remember important events. These sketches can then be shared in small groups as the students recall what they heard about the artist's life.

9. After reading about impressionists, students can be given an opportunity to create their own impressionist paintings. Remind them that they will need to use short brush strokes of different colors to give an impression of how the object looks in nature.

10. The artists' lives are often filled with challenges and disappointments, yet they continue to believe in themselves and overcome challenges in order to pursue their art. As students discuss artists' lives share with them the importance of believing in themselves and their abilities.

11. Often the biographies of artists do not tell all of the details of their lives. Have students select an artist and independently research to discover more about the artist. Once the research is complete, they can become their artists and have their classmates interview them to learn more about the artists' lives. The students could be asked to identify sources of inspiration, such as places, people, or events in the artists' lives that appear in their art.

12. Students can also be encouraged to use their research to create their own biography of an artist's life.

13. Famous artists come from a variety of ethnic backgrounds. Have students examine the reproductions of their artwork to determine the influence of their backgrounds on their art.

14. Students can compare the lives of two or more of the artists using a large compare-and-contrast chart.

ART APPRECIATION

Children need to be surrounded by examples of art to learn to make decisions about what they like and what interests them. They only learn to appreciate that with which they are familiar. Children need to know that their tastes will change as they mature and what they like as children may or may not appeal to them when they become adults. A wide variety of art in the classroom provides students with exposure to different artists. Reproductions can be found in calendars and magazines—additionally, some libraries have reproductions that can be checked out and many museums have reproductions for sale. Having a variety of artwork to examine helps students learn to understand how the visual arts reflect history and culture, which relates to visual arts standard four.

Teachers and librarians can model the visual literacy vocabulary students will need to discuss their reflections on the reproductions. By using visual literacy terminology children develop a deeper understanding of the terms and are able to use the terms in all content areas (Weigmann, 1992). By using the terms to express their perceptions and interpretations of reproductions, children deepen their understanding of the words. Being able to think visually and express themselves visually enhances their critical-thinking ability. As children learn to describe what they see using terms such as line, color, shape, direction, texture, and scale, they develop a deeper understanding of themselves (Weigmann, 1992). Visual arts standard five requires students to describe, analyze, and compare their artwork and the artwork of others.

Stephens and Hermus (1999) developed art clue cards to help students develop their skills of observation and interpretation as they critically examined art reproductions. Students were first introduced to the artist and the reproduction. Then working in small groups they used the art clue cards to guide their careful examination of the reproduction. Visual literacy elements pertinent to the reproductions were briefly explained on the cards. Students might be asked to examine the artist's use of color, balance, shapes, people, media, mood, or the center of focus. As students are examining color, they might be encouraged to determine how the colors in the painting make them feel. For example, when examining a cubist painting, they might be asked to determine the different shapes used in the painting.

BOOK AND MEDIA CHOICES

Micklethwait, Lucy. *Spot a Cat*. 1995. New York: Dorling Kindersley. Unp. Grades: P–2.

More than 12 famous paintings are reproduced in this very basic book for young children challenging them to locate the cats in each reproduction. Most of the pages have very large words in sentences made up of five or six words. There is a picture list at the end of the book that credits each painting in the book and tells its location either in a museum or a private collection. Students who enjoy this book also enjoy *Spot a Dog* (Micklethwait, 1995). This book is part of A Child's Book of Art series.

Delafosse, Claude, and Gallimard Jeunesse. *Animals.* **Illustrated by Tony Ross. 1993. New York: Scholastic. Unp. Grades: K–2.**

Animals are found in primitive cave paintings, Escher's lithographs, Calder's mobiles, and Matisse's collages. Realistic to abstract works in a variety of media show the pervasiveness of animals in the art world. The transparencies and cut-out pages can be flipped to provide different perspectives on the works depicted in the book. This book is one in a series titled A First Discovery Art Book. Teachers report that students return again and again to books in this series and that the pages withstand repeated readings.

Delafosse, Claude, and Gallimard Jeunesse. *Portraits.* **Illustrated by Tony Ross. 1993. New York: Scholastic. Unp. Grades: K–2.**

Realistic, fanciful, and abstract portraits are explored in this book for young readers. Portraits are created in stained glass, on old brooms, in stone and clay, and in oil. Famous portraits such as the *Mona Lisa* and *American Gothic* are reproduced. This book is one in a series titled A First Discovery Art Book.

Baumbusch, Brigitte. *Animals Observed.* **1999. New York: Stewart, Tabori, and Chang. 29p. Grades: K–3.**

Both the text and the artwork in this book lend themselves to class discussions. The artwork includes colorful paintings, prints, sculptures, drawings, carvings, and mosaics that appeal to young children. This book combines attractive pictures with brief descriptions. Animals fascinate children and readers enjoy discovering in these works of art familiar animals seen from a variety of perspectives. In addition, imaginative, mythical creatures are introduced. The book concludes with a picture list naming the artwork and where it is located. This book is one of the Art for Children series the purpose of which is to expose children to a wide variety of art from around the world and throughout time.

Baumbusch, Brigitte. *Looking at Nature.* **1999. New York: Stewart, Tabori, and Chang. 29p. Grades: K–3.**

Realistic to abstract to fanciful recreations of nature delight young children as they are introduced to a wide variety of art forms. For younger students, the large print can be read aloud and the pictures shared with them. Older students want to read the smaller text that describes the images depicted. This book is one of the Art for Children series.

Blizzard, Gladys S. *Come Look with Me: Enjoying Art with Children.* **1990. Charlottesville, Va.: Thomasson-Grant. 32p. Grades: K–5.**

A grandmother's desire to share works of art with her grandchildren led to the publication of this book. As she traveled, she mailed her grandchildren postcards of museum works depicting children. On the back of each postcard were questions to make her grandchildren carefully observe and think about the reproductions. These postcard reproductions were turned into a book. The left side of the two-page spread is a full-page reproduction of a work of art. On the right side of the spread are open-ended questions accompanied by information about the artist and the painting. This is one of the Come Look with Me book series.

The Louvre: Museums of the World for Kids. **1995. Mac/Win. New York: Voyager CD-ROMs. Grades: K and up.**

Included on this CD is a stunning collection of masterpieces by known and unknown artists from around the world all found in the Louvre Museum. Full-screen images, maps, timelines, descriptions of paintings, games, and audio narration help students learn to examine and appreciate the artwork. This is one of the Museums of the World for Kids series.

With Open Eyes. **1995. Mac/Win. New York: Voyager CD-ROMs. Grades: K and up.**

Two hundred works of art from the Art Institute of Chicago are on this CD. The works are from artists from around the world, from 3000 B.C. to the present, and represent a wide variety of art styles. Full-screen images, maps, timelines, descriptions of paintings, games, and audio narration help students learn to examine and appreciate the artwork. Students can also create a scrapbook of their favorite pieces.

Collins, Pat Lowery. *I Am an Artist.* **Illustrated by Robin Brickman. 1992. Brookfield, Conn.: The Millbrook Press. Unp. Grades: 1–4.**

Looking at the world of nature with an artist's eye enables the reader to see the multitude of colors in a seashell, the lines in a leaf, and to feel feathery when watching a bird. Simple poetic words and colorful, simple illustrations celebrate the beauty of nature and the creativity of the artist. The illustrations begin with black-and-white sketches flowing into full-color illustrations.

Micklethwait, Lucy. *A Child's Book of Art.* **1993. New York: DK. 64p. Grades: 1–4.**

This book introduces art to children by using well-known works of art to illustrate and give greater meaning to familiar words. It is divided by categories rather than time periods and deals with animals, colors, shapes, traveling, and activities. The artworks chosen are colorful and varied. Children can become familiar with great artworks by connecting them to words they know, but may not yet fully understand. These intriguing reproductions will be returned to again and again as there is much to see in each illustration. With this book children can begin to develop a lasting appreciation for art, as well as words. Parents, teachers, and children enjoy perusing these pictures together.

Micklethwait, Lucy. *A Child's Book of Play in Art.* 1996. New York: DK. 45p. Grades: 2–6.

This collection of reproductions is for parents, teachers, and librarians to share with children. This book provides children opportunities to explore similarities and differences in paintings. These explorations of varieties of paintings help children develop their own appreciation for art.

Jeunesse, Gallimard. *Paint and Painting.* 1993. New York: Scholastic. 48p. Grades: 3–5.

Like other books in this series, glossy, colorful pages can be manipulated to reveal basic information about paints and painting. This book begins with cave painting and ends with the paintings' restoration. The book ends with a bibliography, people and words to know, an index, and a timeline. This is one of the Scholastic Voyages of Discovery series.

Who Is the Artist? Degas, Renoir, Cassatt? 2001. Video. Glenview, Ill.: Crystal Productions. 20 min. Grades: 3 and up.

This video teaches students to recognize the paintings of Degas, Renoir, and Cassatt. Students learn to compare the artists by examining their styles of painting and the subjects of their paintings. This is one of the Who Is the Artist? series.

Van der Meer, Ron, and Frank Whitford. *The Kids' Art Pack.* 1997. London: Dorling Kindersley. Unp. Grades: 3 and up.

To truly appreciate art it helps to understand how art is created and the problems that artists are attempting to solve. Sections in the book include: How Art Is Made, Picturing Reality, Light and Color, Movement, Pattern and Composition, Stories and Puzzles, and Style and Subject. Art reproductions, mobiles, pop-up activities, and pockets with removable objects teach complex art ideas such as depth perception and optical illusion. The art reproductions are on flaps that can be lifted to reveal information about the art and the artist. Tucked into a pocket at the end is an activity book of ideas for students to use to explore a variety of techniques while creating their own original artwork. This would make an excellent gift for a young artist.

Thomson, Peggy, and Barbara Moore. *The Nine-Ton Cat: Behind the Scenes at an Art Museum.* 1997. Boston, Mass.: Houghton Mifflin. 96p. Grades: 4 and up.

A day in the National Gallery of Art in Washington, D.C. is described from dawn until dusk. While some 77 color illustrations and 39 black-and-white illustrations are shown, the book describes some of the things that happen to the holdings rather than just showing them. This book also explains why 800 keys are needed by the museum, how art treasures are tracked down, how a 500-year-old picture can have its color restored, and how a nine-ton cat can be hoisted.

Salomon, Stephanie. *Come Look with Me: Exploring Native American Art with Children.* 1997. New York: Lickle Publishing. 32p. Grades: 4 and up.

Color images of artwork from 12 different tribes are explored in this book. Underneath each image is a description of the artwork including the materials from which it was constructed. A number of questions designed for children age five through ten, but provocative enough to intrigue adults, accompany each image. Information is provided about the tribe and the importance of the artwork to the tribe. Each piece of art is unique and sure to pique the curiosity of children. The purpose of this series, Come Look with Me, is to encourage children to experience art with enjoyment.

Richmond, Robin. *Children in Art.* 1992. Nashville, Tenn.: Ideals Children's Books. 48p. Grades: 4 and up.

The artist describes this book as a trip to a museum where paintings are arranged topically rather than by period. This collection of children in art is arranged according to what the children are doing, such as play, music and dance, families, outings, and appearances. Reproductions by a variety of artists from Matisse to Rockwell are included. The stories behind the paintings, their meanings, and interpretations make interesting reading. At the end of the book the current locations of the paintings are given. Some of the children are posed in silks and finery and many are unposed enjoying themselves. The author explains that many paintings appear to be strange because the artists compose with their feelings rather than just painting what they observe.

Panzer, Nora. *Celebrate America in Poetry and Art.* 1994. New York: Hyperion Paperbacks for Children. 96p. Grades: 4 and up.

Poetry that celebrates 200 years of American history is illustrated by works of art from the National Museum of American Art, Smithsonian Institution. The illustrations include paintings, sculptures, drawings, and photographs that visually depict events in American history, American life, and American landscapes. The powerful combination of art and poetry captures the essence of America and makes the book a delight for both the eyes and the ears. Brief biographical notes are included about the artists and the poets.

Masterworks from the Collection: The Metropolitan Museum of Art. 1998. Mac/Win. New York: Macromedia. Grades: 4 and up.

While viewing the artwork, students can create their own portfolio of favorites by saving them in the Notebook provided in the software. Additional information on the artwork, such as short essays, is provided on the CD that enables students to learn more about the piece.

Friedman, Nancy. *California: The Spirit of America*. 1998. New York: Harry N. Abrams. 120p. Grades: 6 and up.

This eclectic book of art and art forms describes the state of California from early days to the present. All art is celebrated from dance to films to graphic arts to sculpture to paintings. Commerce and culture are included, as well as politics and literary arts. The book concludes with a selective listing of great people and places, a perennial calendar of events and festivals, a listing of places to go, and a list of credits. The books in this series, Art of the State, examine individual states from a unique perspective and provide information about the states through art.

EXPLORATIONS

1. After reading *Animals Observed* (Baumbusch, 1999), provide the students with small sheets of colored tissue paper to create a collage of their family pet or another animal.
2. Some paintings in these books appear more than once. Have students locate them and hypothesize as to why they appear in several of the books.
3. In *A Child's Book of Play in Art* (Micklethwait, 1996) on pages 38 and 39 are reproductions of van Gogh's bedroom in Arles, one painted by van Gogh and one painted by Lichtenstein. Students familiar with *Camille and the Sunflowers* (Anholt, 1994) recognize that the bedroom is the same one illustrated in that book. Have students compare and contrast the three paintings.
4. Share an illustration with the students and have them describe what they see in the illustration. Clarify for the students that they are to state only what they see in the picture, not to infer what is happening in the picture. Then allow them to share their inferences.
5. At the end of *A Child's Book of Play in Art* (Micklethwait, 1996) the story behind the reproduction, "Captain Thomas Lee," on page 37 is explained. This painting was sent to Queen Elizabeth I to request money, land, and power for Captain Lee's faithful service. Ask students to paint a picture to relay a message using art instead of words.
6. Prior to sharing *The Kids' Art Pack* (Van der Meer and Whitford, 1997) ask students to tell about their visits to art museums.
7. While students are reading *The Kids' Art Pack* (Van der Meer and Whitford. 1997), have them create illustrations to try out the different techniques such as depth perception or optical illusion.
8. Provide each student with a sheet of black construction paper and pastels to create a self-portrait using Picasso's style. Be sure to have mirrors available for them. Have them

begin with an oval that they divide in half. On the left half of the oval create a profile (this half will be looking sideways) and on the right half of the oval draw half of a self-portrait (this half will be looking straight ahead).

9. Have students visit the Louvre Web Museum at http://sunsite.unc.edu/louvre/ to select a painting or sculpture they would like to have hanging in their bedroom. Then have them write a paragraph telling why they selected that particular piece.

ART IN CHILDREN'S LITERATURE

A large part of the appeal of children's literature is the colorful illustrations that enhance and explain the text or tell the entire story as in wordless picture books. These illustrations express the visual meanings just as words express verbal meanings (Kiefer, 1991). The Caldecott Medal honors outstanding illustrations in children's literature and these books are an excellent starting point for examining different art styles. One indication of the value and importance of the artwork found in children's literature is the fact that museums showcase the artwork in displays. In children's literature the entire book is seen as a work of art, rather than just one illustration from the book. Examining the art in children's literature enables students to make connections between the visual arts and literature, which addresses visual arts standard six.

Using four different illustrated versions of the story of *Noah's Ark*, Stewig (1994) had students examine and reflect on the illustrations after the books were read aloud. Students were provided guidance in discussing visual elements, such as color, shape, dimension, and texture. Asking students to compare and contrast the visual elements in the books elicited the most detailed comments. After reading and discussing the illustrations in the four books students selected their favorite version and wrote about why it was their favorite version. The ideas in their essays were less fully developed than the thoughts expressed in the discussions and were not reflective of the rich, detailed observations made during the discussions.

One version of *Noah's Ark* (Stewig, 1994) had a nude picture of Adam and Eve. Upon first viewing the illustration some students snickered or smiled. When given the opportunity to select illustrations to discuss, the students did not select that illustration. Some books about artists and their work contain nude reproductions and teachers have to decide how they will handle the works in their classes.

An undergraduate university student enrolled in a children's literature class was dismayed to have her third grade partner discover a nude reproduction in a corner of a pop-up scene in the book they were reading. Prior to bringing the book into the class the university student had screened the detailed art book for nudes. The student made a brief comment about the work and then moved on to another page in the book.

Examining several books by a favorite children's illustrator can be an excellent introduction to visual elements such as line, shape, color, texture, and space. Hodges (1999) had students examine Eric Carle's books to introduce them to elements of line, shape, color, texture, and space. From Carle's work students moved to studying the collages created by Matisse when he was no longer able to paint. Studying the familiar work of Eric Carle provided them with the background to understand and appreciate Matisse's work.

Wells (1999) uses picture books in her art classes to activate students' prior knowledge and provide a common ground for art lessons. She reads the book aloud to the students, and then uses the book's illustrations to present an art concept prior to the students' independent explorations of the art concept. For example, when presenting the concept of depth, students examined the pictures in the book to determine how the artist created the illusion of depth on a flat surface. Over the course of several classes students first painted the background, then the middle ground, and finally the foreground of their pictures to achieve the illusion of depth in their illustrations.

BOOK AND MEDIA CHOICES

dePaola, Tomie. *The Art Lesson*. 1989. New York: Putnam and Grosset. Unp. Grades: K–3.

This is an autobiographical picture book from a children's book illustrator who knew as a very young child that he wanted to be an artist. Faced with teachers who expected him to copy their artwork, he was devastated because he knew that true artists never copy. He and his art teacher reached a compromise that satisfied them both. Tomie de Paola's bright simple artwork has great appeal to children. After hearing the story read aloud, beginning readers want to read it on their own. An audiocassette version of the book with a teacher's guide is available.

Lionni, Leo. *Matthew's Dream*. 1991. New York: Alfred Knopf. Unp. Grades: K–3.

After a trip to a museum and a late night dream filled with colors and shapes, Matthew begins to look at things from a different perspective. The pile of junk in his attic habitat becomes shapes and colors that he translates onto large canvases depicting the joy and happiness in his life.

Weitzman, Jacqueline Preiss, and Robin Preiss Glasser. *You Can't Take a Balloon into the Metropolitan Museum*. 1998. New York: Dial. 37p. Grades: 1–3.

As a truly unique introduction to art, this book will find a place in many collections. An errant balloon floats through New York City pursued by a faithful museum guard, while the owner, a little girl, and her grandmother tour the famed Metropolitan Museum of Art. There is a connection between the travels of the balloon and the artwork being viewed on the museum tour. These parallel travels depict the relationship between life and art. This beautifully illustrated book combines cartoon quality drawings with photographic reproductions of paintings, architecture, sculptures, and urns. The judicious use of color draws the eye of the viewer to particular parts of the finely, detailed black-and-white illustrations. The provenance of each artwork is explained at the end of the book.

Bedard, Michael. *The Clay Ladies.* **Illustrated by Les Tait. 1999. New York: Tundra Books of Northern New York. Unp. Grades: 2–4.**

Grandparents share important stories or life lessons with their grandchildren. This grandmother tells her grandson about the clay ladies on her shelf. The clay busts are of two sculptors who taught the grandmother to sculpt. More than that they taught her to observe and to really see things, to live in harmony with nature, and to feel the life in the clay. Readers of all ages relate to the life lessons shared in this story. A delightful story so realistically told that it is difficult to believe it is fiction; it is the story of two eccentric artists told through the eyes of a neighborhood child.

Reeves, Howard W., editor. *Wings of an Artist: Children's Book Illustrators Talk about Their Art.* **1999. New York: Harry N. Abrams. 36p. Grades: 2–5.**

An eclectic collection of illustrators shares the importance of art in their lives through text and illustrations. The striking thing about this book is the wide variety of media and styles used by the illustrators. These fanciful, sensuous, realistic, dreamy, and intriguing illustrations appeal to a wide audience of children. Children see that there is a place for different kinds of illustrations. All forms of expression are welcomed and appreciated. Children appreciate the brevity of the text and the large colorful illustrations.

Wiesner, David. *Sector 7.* **1999. New York: Clarion Books. Unp. Grades: 2–6.**

A routine trip to the Empire State Building becomes anything but routine when a mischievous cloud whisks a boy away to Sector 7. Once there the boy designs a collection of sea creature clouds. The grownups at Sector 7 want only standard cloud formations, but these extraordinary, imaginative clouds have other ideas. Look up on any cloudy day to see if the clouds have once again fashioned themselves into sea creatures. This book was named a Notable Children's Book in the Language Arts.

Marcus, Leonard S. *A Caldecott Celebration: Six Artists and Their Paths to the Caldecott Medal.* **1998. New York: Walker. 49p. Grades: 3–6.**

Marcus presents an intimate look at the work involved in creating illustrations that have captured the Caldecott medal. Robert McCloskey, Marcia Brown, Maurice Sendak, William Stieg, Chris Van Allsburg, and David Wiesner are the illustrators profiled in this book. The creative processes the artists used as they created their award-winning illustrations are described. A glossary of terms helps readers comprehend the text.

Lawrence, Jacob. *The Great Migration*. 1993. New York: HarperCollins Children's Books. Unp. Grades: 3 and up.

A series of 60 original paintings were reunited to tell the story of the northward movement of African Americans during the early twentieth century. They left the South in search of a better life for their families. These paintings portray the hardships, conflicts, and rejection they encountered. From their struggles comes a power, triumph, and beauty that is portrayed in these paintings and the sparse, poignant text that accompanies them. The book concludes with the poem "Migration" by Walter Dean Myers.

***Words with Wings: A Treasury of African-American Poetry and Art*. Selected by Belinda Rochelle. 2001. New York: HarperCollins. Unp. Grades: 4 and up.**

The 20 pieces of art in this book are accompanied by poems of 13 poets. The artwork is strong and vivid and admirably matches the poetry. The African American artists and writers selected here are superb examples of excellence in their fields. The book lists the poems, the poets, the artists, and their artworks in the table of contents and concludes with notes about the poets and artists.

EXPLORATIONS

1. Prior to reading *The Clay Ladies* (Bedard, 1999), show the students the illustrations. Have them predict what they think is happening in the story. Write their predictions on chart paper. After reading the story, review the predictions and compare them to what actually happened in the story.

2. Before reading *The Clay Ladies* (Bedard, 1999), have students share their experiences when visiting their grandparents or older relatives. Ask them to tell about lessons they have learned from their grandparents or older relatives.

3. After reading *The Clay Ladies* (Bedard, 1999), provide each child with a ball of clay. Ask them to feel the life in the clay and tell what they feel in the clay. Then have them create what they feel.

4. Before reading *Wings of an Artist: Children's Book Illustrators Talk about Their Art* (Reeves, 1999), have students share their personal experiences with art and its impact on their lives.

5. The authors in *Wings of an Artist: Children's Book Illustrators Talk about Their Art* (Reeves, 1999) provide a brief description of what is depicted in their illustration. Have students select one page of a picture book that appeals to them. Pretend that they are the illustrator of that page, relate the picture to their own lives, and write about what it means to them.

6. Using one of the illustrations from *Sector 7* (Wiesner, 1999), have students write a detailed description of what they see in the illustration, as well as describe what they think is happening in the picture.

7. Have students close their eyes and listen as the teacher reads one of the selections from

A Caldecott Celebration: Six Artists and Their Paths to the Caldecott Medal (Marcus, 1998). During the reading the students are to visualize what is happening. Once the selection is read they are to draw a picture depicting what the illustrator did to help create the award-winning illustrations.

8. After reading *The Great Migration* (Lawrence, 1993), have students draw a series of paintings to tell of their lives or a class experience.

9. After reading *The Great Migration* (Lawrence, 1993), have students carefully examine the illustrations to determine what techniques were used to depict the strong emotions expressed. Have them create a series of pictures depicting a move they made. Discuss techniques to use to assure that the pictures portray their feelings about moving.

10. Once students have been introduced to *A Caldecott Celebration: Six Artists and Their Paths to the Caldecott Medal* (Marcus, 1998) and *Wings of an Artist: Children's Book Illustrators Talk about Their Art* (Reeves, 1999) they want to independently explore the artists' books. A collection of these books in the classroom library assures that students make connections between the artists' books and their personal stories.

11. After reading *Words with Wings: A Treasury of African-American Poetry and Art* (Rochelle, 2001), have older students examine several anthologies of poetry and books of art and attempt to "match up" poems with art selections. Then the students can scan them into a computer and make their own classroom book. Remind the students to list the sources for their artwork and poems.

12. Ask students to interview an older relative or neighbor to learn about people in their lives that taught them important lessons.

13. Once students have studied several illustrators, they can be encouraged to select their favorite and then create their own book using one of that illustrator's techniques.

CREATING ART

Giving children opportunities to create art helps them to understand the time and effort involved in the creative process. Art should be integrated into other academic subjects rather than taught as a detached stand-alone course (Stephen, 1996). Infusing art into the curriculum assures that learning occurs in a rich, integrated manner as the learner draws on prior knowledge from a variety of disciplines to create new knowledge and understanding (Stephen, 1996). As students create their own artwork, they learn about media, techniques, processes, and the structures and functions of art, which addresses visual arts standards one and two.

Slemmers's (1999) students examined two of Monet's paintings of autumn leaves before creating their own Impressionist paintings. Students discovered how the time of day, seasons, and weather conditions affect how things look. They also learned that artists frequently paint the same objects over and over. Students understanding of impressionism was evidenced by their concern that their paintings looked as well when viewed up close as when seen from a distance. As students learn how to use the techniques of artists, they are incorporating visual arts standard three.

BOOK AND MEDIA CHOICES

Gibbons, Gail. *The Art Box*. 1998. New York: Holiday House. Unp. Grades: P–2.

Simple drawings with bright colors and large print make this a wonderful introduction to art for the very young reader. Artists' tools and materials are introduced in colorful illustrations with large print. Out of the art box comes a collection of tools and materials used to create art that springs from the artist's imagination. The primary colors and their combinations are illustrated.

George, Lindsay Barrett. *My Bunny and Me*. 2001. New York: Greenwillow Books. Unp. Grades: P–2.

A young boy draws a rabbit and then imagines all the wonderful things he and the rabbit would do if it were alive. Then in the end he realizes that if the rabbit were real he would turn it loose and let it roam free.

Edwards, Pamela Duncan. *Warthogs Paint: A Messy Color Book*. Illustrated by Henry Cole. 2001. New York: Hyperion. Unp. Grades: P–2.

On a dreary rainy day the warthogs decided to add some color to their world by painting. As they paint, the colors run together and form new colors. Students enjoy exploring what happens when colors are mixed just as the warthogs do.

McPhail, David. *Drawing Lessons from a Bear*. 2000. Boston: Little, Brown. Unp. Grades: P–2.

In this charming story a young bear follows his passion for drawing and grows up to become an artist. Readers are told that they too can be artists if that is what they choose to do. The end pages of the book contain brief drawing lessons for young artists.

Greenfield, Eloise. *I Can Draw a Weeposaur and Other Dinosaurs*. Illustrated by Jan Spivey Gilchrist. 2001. New York: Greenwillow Books. 32p. Grades: K–2.

A young girl's imagination unleashes a variety of one-of-a-kind dinosaurs including a Speedasaurus and a Florasaurus. In her poems and paintings the dinosaurs come to life spilling from the drawing paper to fill her bedroom. The adorable child in the illustrations and her clever, friendly dinosaur creations appeal to young readers who themselves are eager to take the time to dream and paint.

Emberley, Ed. *Picture Pie 2: A Drawing Book and Stencil.* **1996. Boston: Little, Brown. Unp. Grades: K–4.**

This book is just one book in an extensive collection of drawing books written by Caldecott Medal winner Ed Emberley. Using a stencil of simple shapes, the book shows step-by-step instructions on how everything from elephants, to dogs, to trains can be drawn. The back of the book contains a section for inquiring minds and explains other methods and time-saving activities that can be utilized. Using fractions, shapes, and proportion, students can create variations of the objects drawn in the book.

HyperStudio. Version 4. **2000. Mac/Win. Torrance, Calif.: Knowledge Adventure. Grades: K–8.**

This presentation software includes a variety of drawing tools for students to use to create their own works of art. Students enjoy creating interactive multimedia presentations to share what they have learned. Graphics, sounds, and movies are easily incorporated into student presentations.

Kid Pix Studio. **1994. Mac/Win. Duncan, S.C.: The Learning Company. Grades: K–8.**

This software program allows young artists to express themselves by using the computer to paint, draw, and edit photographs. Children can create slide shows and digital picture books using a variety of multimedia tools. This is an easy-to-use software program that children enjoy exploring and using in a wide variety of ways.

Corbett, Grahame. *You Can Draw Fantastic Animals.* **1997. London: Dorling Kindersley. 21p. Grades: 1–6.**

Drawing animals requires studying the animal's proportions, drawing basic outline shapes, and then sketching in the animal's features. Instructions and diagrams are provided for drawing dogs, cats, birds, horses, sea animals, and wild animals. Tips and techniques are included for adding detail touches to the drawings. Also included are photographs and drawings to help young artists create realistic representations of animals.

Gamble, Kim. *You Can Draw Amazing Faces.* **1997. London: Dorling Kindersley. 21p. Grades: 1–6.**

Drawing an egg shape and adding circles and curves for the eyes, ears, nose, and mouth enables students to draw a face. Directions are provided for adding hair, glasses, character, and expressions. Instructions are given for drawing with a variety of materials, and techniques specific to each material are included. Gamble uses simplistic designs to illustrate proper size and proportion in faces emphasizing the difference in pencil and brush strokes to achieve a realistic result. She also includes instructions for caricatures and how they are used. Both photographs and drawings are used to make her points.

Baxter, Leon. *The Drawing Book*. 1990. Nashville, Tenn.: Ideals Publishing Company. 62p. Grades: 1–6.

The simplicity in art is emphasized in this book through a variety of drawing activities for young artists. They are encouraged to create without fear. The crayon pictures appeal to students. Drawing with grids is explored, as are artistic principles of line, composition, perspective, shape, and color. These principles are presented with step-by-step instructions and detailed descriptions. For example, vanishing points are explained in text and illustrations, and then students are encouraged to explore them on their own.

Sirett, Dawn. *My First Paint Book*. 1994. London: Dorling Kindersley. 48p. Grades: 2–6.

This book is a basic how-to book for beginning artists. A variety of painting techniques is introduced for children to try out with their own creations. Instructions are given for making kites, friezes, t-shirt designs, pins, and frames.

Jeunesse, Gallimard. *The History of Printmaking*. 1995. New York: Scholastic. 50p. Grades: 3–6.

Printmaking dates back to prehistoric times when cave dwellers dipped their hands in red clay and left their handprints on the walls of caves. This book includes information on engraving, lithography, collage, silk screening, comic strips, and computer graphics. Readers enjoy the interactive nature of this book that includes stickers, transparent pages, a wheel to turn, and flaps to lift. The book ends with a bibliography, addresses for art museums, people to know, words to know, alphabets, and an index. This is one of the Scholastic Voyages of Discovery series.

Welton, Jude. *Drawing: A Young Artist's Guide*. 1994. London: Dorling Kindersley. 45p. Grades: 3 and up.

This introduction to drawing helps students examine artists' techniques and learn to use them to create their own unique drawings. Reproductions by various artists are used throughout to demonstrate the techniques. Then young artists are encouraged to try the techniques in their own drawings. Shading, use of color, outline, shape, texture, patterns, composition, perspective, and the use of imagination are topics included in this book. The works come from the Tate Gallery in London.

Goodman, Marilyn J. S., and Natalie K. Lieberman. *Learning through Art: The Guggenheim Museum Collection.* **1999. New York: Guggenheim Museum Publications. 63p. Grades: 3 and up.**

Individual works from the Guggenheim Museum in New York are featured in this book. Each reproduction is accompanied by activities that enable children to explore school subjects through the art. Some activities encourage students to carefully look at the work and ask questions. Many of the activities enable students to explore different artistic techniques. The pages are coated so that students can write and draw on the pages with a washable marker, wipe off the pages, and complete the activity again.

Art Smart: Basic Drawing for Beginners. **2000. Video. Slidell, La.: Video Specialties. 60 min. Grades 5 and up.**

Students are introduced to elemental art terms and techniques. Close-ups of the artist's sketchpad enable students to see exactly what is being drawn.

EXPLORATIONS

1. Have students create their own masterpieces throughout the year to display on the classroom walls. At the end of the year have each student select one or two of their best pieces to hang in the classroom gallery. Invite parents to the gallery opening. Classical music playing in the background and refreshments set the right tone for the event.

2. After reading *My Bunny and Me* (George, 2001), have students draw a picture of a favorite animal and tell a story about what they would do with the animal if it were alive.

3. Share books by Leo Lionni and explore the different materials he uses to create collages. Teachers can collect wallpaper sample books and fabric remnants on sale to create a collection of materials for making collages.

4. After sharing the above books with students have them work with a partner to create their own pop-up, fold-out, cut-out or shape book to depict the different art techniques that they have learned.

5. Provide students with an art center in the classroom with a variety of materials and drawing books. Encourage them to draw pictures using the techniques described in the books. Use their works to decorate the art center. An art center in a crowded classroom may just consist of small boxes of drawing materials that students take to their desks to use.

6. Calder's mobiles require delicate balancing if they are to move freely and easily. Have students create mobiles depicting a subject they are studying in class. They can work together to get the mobiles to balance.

7. The shapes from the stencils in Ed Emberley's *Picture Pie 2: A Drawing Book and Stencil* (1996) can be cut out of felt and applied to a flannel board to demonstrate how the shapes can be used to create a variety of pictures.

8. Using the caricature techniques in *You Can Draw Amazing Faces* (Gamble, 1997), stu-

dents can create caricatures of themselves. These can be hung in the front of the room for open house to see if parents can figure out which one is their child.

9. Students of all ages enjoy mixing the primary colors to make new colors. Small vials of water tinted with food coloring can be used for this purpose. Be sure to have paper towels on hand to mop up spills.

10. A variety of different colored transparencies can be displayed on the overhead projector and overlapped to show children what happens when colors are combined.

11. Drawing with colored pencils provides students opportunities to create different textures by applying the color heavily, and then by scratching with a sharp object they can create designs.

12. Drawing with pastels or colored chalk on black and then white construction paper enables students to explore how colors interact.

TEACHER RESOURCES

The books and Internet sites in this section contain useful resources for teachers as they work to integrate art into their content area teaching. The National Art Education Association also provides resources for teachers.

BOOKS

Kohl, MaryAnn F. *Scribble Art: Independent Creative Art Experiences for Children*. Illustrated by Judy McCoy. 1994. Bellingham, Wash.: Bright Ring. 158p. Grades: K–5.

These activities are great for placing in an art center for children to explore art on their own. Children enjoy having the freedom to create their own artwork and do not hesitate to let their imaginations roam as they work with a variety of art materials.

Moline, Steve. *I See What You Mean: Children at Work with Visual Information*. 1992. York, Maine: Stenhouse. 148p. Grades: K–6.

Visual literacy requires students to interpret pictures, symbols, and words. This book provides information on teaching visual literacy to students by having them create their own visuals based on their learning. Examples of children's work are interspersed throughout this useful resource for classroom teachers.

Cornett, Claudia E. *The Arts as Meaning Makers: Integrating Literature and the Arts Throughout the Curriculum*. 1999. Upper Saddle River, N. J.: Merrill. 456p. Grades: K–12.

Chapters are included for integrating literature, visual arts, art, drama, dance and movement, and music throughout the curriculum. Separate chapters for each of the arts include seed strategies, ideas for extending learning through the arts.

Brookes, Mona. *Drawing with Children: A Creative Method for Adult Beginners, Too.* **1996. New York: Putnam. 272p. Grades: K and up.**

This book provides teachers and librarians a way to integrate art into the content area curriculum using the Monart Drawing Method. Teachers and librarians do not need to have art training to use this method to teach students how to draw to express themselves.

Kohl, MaryAnn F., and Kim Solga. *Discovering Great Artists: Hands-On Art for Children in the Styles of the Great Masters.* **Illustrated by Rebecca VanSlyke. 1997. Bellingham, Wash.: Bright Ring. 141p. Grades: 6 and up.**

The activities in this book enable students to experiment with the styles and techniques of the great masters. Students become involved in painting, drawing, sculpting, photographing, and other techniques as they create their own masterpieces. The book includes a resource section and an index.

PROFESSIONAL ORGANIZATION

National Art Education Association
1916 Association Drive
Reston, VA 20191-1590
703-860-8000
www.naea-reston.org/
Journal: *Journal of Art Education*

INTERNET SITES

ArtsEdge
http://artsedge.kennedy-center.org/
> This site is supported by the Kennedy Center for the Performing Arts, the National Endowment for the Arts, and the U. S. Department of Education. Materials and resources on this site assist teachers as they use technology to place art at the center of the classroom curriculum. ArtsEdge is a partner in the educational program, MarcoPolo.

ArtsEdNet
www.artsednet.getty.edu/
> This is the Getty Museum's art education Web site. This site contains lesson plans, links to galleries and exhibitions, other resources for teachers, and a search engine.

Art Teacher on the Net
www.artmuseums.com/
> There are art projects on this site for every area of the curriculum and across grade levels. There is a teacher forum and a link for parents.

Global Children's Art Gallery

www.naturalchild.com\gallery

Children under the age of 12 can have their artwork displayed at this site. Children's artwork from all over the world is displayed here.

WebMuseum, Paris

www.ibiblio.org/wm/

If you are looking for a large collection of artwork try the Famous Paintings section of this site.

REFERENCES

ArtsEdge. 1992. *National Standards for Arts Education*. [Online]. Available: http://artsedge.kennedy-center.org/professional_resources/standards/natstandards/standards_k4.html [cited 14 October 2000]

Flood, Nicole, Brenda Hamm, Tina Herrington, and Christine Turk. 1993. "Teaching the Whole Enchilada: Through Children's Literature in the Content Areas." *Reading Horizons*, 33, no. 4 (December): 359-365.

Hale, Judy A. 1996. "Determining Relationships between Young Children's Cognitive Stage of Development and Art Stage of Development as They Relate to Literacy." Paper presented at the Southern Early Childhood Association Conference in Little Rock, Ark., March. ERIC, ED 394938.

Hodges, Peter T. 1999. "Books Arts Aesthetics: Eric Carle and Henri Matisse." *Arts and Activities* 126, no. 1 (September): 52–53.

Kiefer, Barbara. 1991. "Accent on Art." *The Reading Teacher* 44, no. 6 (February): 406-414.

Marantz, S. S. 1992. *Picture Books for Looking and Learning: Awakening Visual Perceptions Through the Art of Children's Books*. Phoenix, Ariz.: The Oryx Press.

Slemmers, Paula M. 1999. "Repetition Makes an Impression." *Arts and Activities* 126, no. 1 (September): 26-27.

Stephen, Veronica P. 1996. "The Visual Arts and Qualitative Research: Diverse and Emerging Voices." Paper presented at the Annual Meeting of the Association of Teacher Educators. St. Louis, Mo., February. ERIC, ED 394 980.

Stephens, Pamela Geiger, and Cynthia Rhule Hermus. 1999. "Clueing into Art Observation and Interpretation." *Arts and Activities* 126, no. 1 (September): 50-51.

Stewig, John Warren. 1994. "Children's Observations about the Art in Picture Books." Imagery and Visual Literacy: Selected Readings from the Annual Conference of the International Visual Literacy Association, Tempe, Ariz. October. ERIC, ED 380069.

Weigmann, Beth A. 1992. "Visual Literacy, Science Process Skills, and Children's Books." Paper presented at the Annual Conference of the International Visual Literacy Association Pittsburgh, Penn. September/October. ERIC, ED 363328.

Wells, Judy. 1999. "Cultivate a Love for Reading and Art." *Arts and Activities* 126, no. 2 (October): 34-35.

Chapter 8

Music

Integrating music into the curriculum furnishes students a way to learn and to articulate what they have learned (Gilles, Andre, Dye, and Pfannenstiel, 1998). One way to do this is through shared singing which provides students opportunities for singing along while reading the words to a song (Smith, 2000). This activity reinforces reading skills for emerging readers. The integration of music and reading mutually reinforces the content of both subjects. Singing and accompanying hand movements actively involve children in their learning, which fosters retention of the material.

The *National Standards for Arts Education* (ArtsEdge, 1992) seeks to ensure the quality and accountability of arts education for all students. Included in these standards are content standards for music education, which follow.

1. Singing, alone and with others, a varied repertoire of music.
2. Performing on instruments, alone and with others, a varied repertoire of music.
3. Improvising melodies, variations, and accompaniments.
4. Composing and arranging music within specified guidelines.
5. Reading and notating music.
6. Listening to, analyzing, and describing music.
7. Evaluating music and music performances.
8. Understanding relationships between music, the other arts, and disciplines outside the arts.
9. Understanding music in relation to history and culture.

These standards establish competencies that ensure students have the skills and knowledge to use music as a form of communication and a mode of thought and action (NSAE, 1992). Students' successful attainment of these competencies is vital to their development. Music is all around them and is an integral part of their ability to understand and positively communicate their feelings. The poems in *Song and Dance* (Hopkins, 1997) assure that readers hear the music that surrounds them every day.

Hopkins, Lee Bennett, compiler. *Song and Dance*. Illustrated by Cheryl Munro Taylor. 1997. New York: Simon and Schuster. 32p. Grades: 2–4.

Lee Bennett Hopkins carefully selected 16 poems from poets as diverse as Carl Sandburg and Langston Hughes and as modern as Charlotte Zolotow and Ashley Bryan to show readers that song and dance is everywhere. The brief poems are all accompanied by bright, active, colorful illustrations. The poems speak to the music of the soul and to the rhythms inside everyone. They express the songs that live within each of us, as well as the joy of the movements of dance. This book, as with others in this chapter, enables students to explore the connections between their lives and music.

This chapter contains sections on instruments, musicians and composers, types of music, songs, reference materials, and teacher resources. The section on instruments offers a variety of books that introduce young readers to the instruments of the orchestra and to instruments from around the world. The lives of classical and contemporary musicians and composers are presented in traditional biographies and fictionalized accounts that provide a unique perspective on their lives. Readers are exposed to different types of music that reflect a variety of cultures. Books with collections of songs and individual songs encourage students to read along as they sing the words to familiar songs. The music reference books contain useful resources for teachers, librarians, and students. Teacher resources conclude the chapter.

INSTRUMENTS

These books and media in this section provide an introduction to musical instruments. Music education standards addressed in this section are: standard two, which involves performing on instruments, standard six, which requires students to listen and analyze music, and standard seven, which has students evaluating music and musical performances. Readers find themselves in the photographs of students with their musical instruments and relate to them. Some of the books in this section such as *The Young Person's Guide to the Orchestra* (Ganeri, 1996) include a CD that enables students to hear the musical instruments as they read about them. The last book in this section presents the hard work and meticulous detail that goes into making an instrument.

BOOK AND MEDIA CHOICES

***Sesame Street: Let's Make Music*. 2000. Video. New York: Sony Music Entertainment. 40 min. Grades: P–K.**

When Telly Monster loses his tuba his friends decide to introduce him to other instruments for making music. Students learn along with Telly that pots, pans, spoons, and bottles can all be used to make music. This is one of the My Sesame Street series.

Moss, Lloyd. *Our Marching Band.* **Illustrated by Diana Cain Bluethenthal. 2001. New York: G. P. Putnam's Sons. Unp. Grades: P–2.**

The children in the neighborhood begin to play musical instruments and decide to practice every day. The horrendous noise they make causes all the grown-ups to complain. However, with practice they improve and the mayor declares that they shall be the band for the Fourth of July parade. The rhyming lyrical text makes this a fun book to read aloud.

Lithgow, John. *The Remarkable Farkle McBride.* **Illustrated by C. F. Payne. 2000. New York: Simon and Schuster. Unp. Grades: K–3.**

Child prodigy, Farkle McBride, introduces children to the instruments of the orchestra as he learns to play each one. Young readers delight at the onomatopoeia and repetition found in the lyrical text and are eager to participate in reading this book. Imaginative, playful illustrations accompany the text.

Austin, Patricia. *The Cat Who Loved Mozart.* **Illustrated by Henri Sorenson. 2001. New York: Holiday House. Unp. Grades: K–3.**

Music communicates emotions and feelings and forges bonds. In this heartwarming story, the music of Mozart bonds a young musician and a stray cat she has taken into her life. Her attempts to bond with the cat failed, until one day the cat jumped on the piano bench to join her as she practiced a Mozart sonata for a piano recital. Each day as she practiced, the cat returned and they formed a special bond.

Pillar, Marjorie. *Join the Band!* **1992. New York: HarperCollins. Unp. Grades: 1–3.**

This book of color photographs begins with students arriving at school with their instruments. The students are amazed that their teacher knows how to play all the different instruments. The photographs show students putting their instruments together, cleaning them, and practicing. After approximately 100 hours of practice the concert begins. The students are amazed at how good they sound together and each thinks that being in the band is the best part of school.

Rubin, Mark. *The Orchestra.* **Illustrated by Alan Daniel. 1992. N.Y.: Firefly Books. Unp. Grades: 1–4.**

Come along as two children discover that music is all around us. The author defines musical terms such as tempo, harmony, and melody in easy-to-understand language and through an illustration of lines woven over several pages. The members of the orchestra introduce the children to the instrument families and explain how the instruments in each family are related. This easy-to-read, understandable text provides a wonderful introduction to music and the orchestra.

Levine, Robert. *The Story of the Orchestra*. Illustrated by Meredith Hamilton. 2001. New York: Black Dog and Leventhal. 96p. Grades: 1–5.

This book is comprised of two sections; one on classical composers and one on the instruments of the orchestra. Included with the book is a CD of 41 selections by noted composers. What make this book and CD combination unique is that throughout the book are notes indicating a track on the CD that corresponds to the information presented in the book. The title and composer of the selection are given and readers are told what to listen for in the recording.

Hausherr, Rosemarie. *What Instrument Is This?* 1992. New York: Scholastic. 38p. Grades: 2–4.

Students become involved in this book as they guess the names of eighteen instruments. On the right-hand page is a color picture of a child playing an instrument with a question below. Turning the page reveals the answer to the question. The top half of the page contains a black-and-white photograph of a child playing the instrument with a brief description of how the instrument is played. The book ends with a glossary and ideas for parents to help them provide support for their children as they learn to play musical instruments.

Moss, Lloyd. *Zin! Zin! Zin! a Violin*. Illustrated by Marjorie Priceman. 1995. New York: Simon and Schuster Books for Young Readers. Unp. Grades: K–4.

Rhyming text and flowing artwork sweep the reader along as some of the instruments of the orchestra are introduced in this unique counting book. As the number of instruments on stage increase by one number, terms such as solo, duo, trio, and quartet are introduced. This is a fun book to read and a fun book to listen to again and again. Students do not realize all they are learning as they explore this book. This is a Caldecott Honor Book.

***Zin! Zin! Zin! a Violin*. 1999. Video. Westport, Conn.: Weston Woods Studios. 10 min. Grades: K–4.**

Once children have listened to this book read aloud, or have read it themselves, they are thrilled to watch this short video. This recording was selected as a Notable Children's Video.

Hayes, Ann. *Meet the Orchestra*. Illustrated by Karmen Thompson. 1991. San Diego, Calif.: Harcourt Brace. Unp. Grades: 2–6.

An intriguing collection of wild animals in formal attire introduces the instruments of the orchestra. These appealing animals and the clever, informative text make learning about the instruments fun. Using colors, sounds, and metaphors the author describes the sounds of the instruments. These unique descriptions of the sounds coupled with the animal musicians appeal to young and old.

Ganeri, Anita. *The Young Person's Guide to the Orchestra*. 1996. San Diego, Calif.: Harcourt Brace. 56p. Grades: 3–6.

This masterful introduction to the orchestra is accompanied by a CD narrated by Ben Kingsley, who gives a guided tour of the instruments. As each instrument is introduced, listeners can hear it played. At the end of the CD the entire orchestra plays. Each section of the orchestra is explained. Chapters include information on the instruments in different sections of the orchestra, famous composers, orchestras of the world, instruments of the world, playing in an orchestra, and running an orchestra. A glossary follows the index.

Doney, Meryl. *Musical Instruments*. 1995. Danbury, Conn.: Franklin Watts. 32p. Grades: 3–6.

This brief book provides information about musical instruments from around the world, from Australia to Zimbabwe, from Bolivia to Mozambique. Students enjoy learning about the origins of the instruments and delight in creating their own instruments using the simplified instructions the author provides. There is a section of useful information, hints on making music, a glossary, and an index. This book is one of the World Crafts series.

Parker, Josephine. *Music from Strings*. 1992. Brookfield, Conn.: The Millbrook Press. 48p. Grades: 3–6.

From simple one-stringed instruments to multi-stringed harps and pianos, the string family members are explored. A history of the stringed instrument, a description of how it is played, and information about a famous musician noted for playing the instrument provide fascinating information about the different stringed instruments. Color photographs, illustrations, and paintings accompany the brief text. A glossary and index are included.

***Musical Instruments*. 1993. New York: Scholastic. 46p. Grades: 3–6.**

This book describes how blowing, rubbing, plucking, and scraping instruments makes music. The description of how instruments are made is accompanied by dazzling graphics. Color paintings and photography enhance the brief text. The book ends with listings of musical resources, brief composer biographies, a timeline, and an index. This is one of the Scholastic Voyages of Discovery series

***Microsoft Musical Instruments: Exploring the Amazing World of Music*. 1994. Win. Redmond, Wash.: Microsoft Corporation. Grades: 3–8.**

As students click on the instruments, buttons, and icons on this computer CD, the sounds of the musical instruments fills the air. Unless the entire class is involved in using the CD a set of headphones will be needed for the computer. Learning about instruments and their families by clicking on the computer screen gives students control of their learning and helps assure they retain what they learn.

Cornelissen, Cornelia. *Music in the Wood*. Photographed by John MacLachlan. 1995. New York: Delacorte Press. 48p. Grades: 3 and up.

Enhanced by black-and-white photographs this book follows a luthier, Marten Cornelissen, as he creates a baroque cello. It begins as he selects just the right pieces of wood and finishes as he presents the instrument to cellist Roel Dieltiens. The luthier's wife, whose pride in her husband's meticulous work is evident, wrote this narrative. Their faithful companion, an English springer spaniel named Willie, is shown as he waits patiently for Marten to finish his work oblivious to the wood shavings piling up on him. Included is a CD recording of Roel Dieltiens playing his new cello.

EXPLORATIONS

1. Prior to introducing these books to the students, have them share their knowledge of musical instruments by completing a prediction chart of the instrument families. Students can place pictures or drawings of the instruments on the chart in what they think are the correct families. Once they have read *The Young Person's Guide to the Orchestra* (Ganeri, 1996) or *The Orchestra* (Rubin, 1992) students can reexamine the chart to check their predictions.

2. While reading *What Instrument Is This?* (Hausherr, 1992), pause to allow students an opportunity to guess the name of the instrument.

3. Students need to be able to see real musical instruments and to hear them played as they learn about them. One way to provide students this opportunity is to have students in the class who play musical instruments bring them into the class for their classmates to examine and to hear. A school band director might be asked to come to the class with a few instruments for the students to see and hear.

4. As the students read *Zin! Zin! Zin! a Violin* (Moss, 1995) have them write down the adjectives used to describe each instrument, such as the trombone's "mournful moan" and "silken tone." While listening to the different instruments encourage students to work with a partner to add their own descriptive adjectives to the list. This builds descriptive vocabulary, as well as information about making music.

5. After reading *Meet the Orchestra* (Hayes, 1991), students can research the names of the animals in the book and then discuss why they think the illustrator matched a particular animal to an instrument.

6. While listening to the CD from *Music in the Wood* (Cornelissen, 1995) students can paint a picture of what they hear.

MUSICIANS AND COMPOSERS

The books in this section include traditional biographies and fictionalized accounts of the musicians' and composers' lives. The fictionalized accounts contain factual biographical information, but provide the authors opportunities to tell about their subject from a unique perspective (Ketner, 1999). The biographies enable readers to learn about talented musicians and composers, as well as about the times in which they lived. Media in this section support standard nine, which involves an understanding of how history and culture impacts musicians and composers.

BOOK AND MEDIA CHOICES

Schroeder, Allan. *Satchmo's Blues.* **Illustrated by Floyd Cooper. 1996. New York: Bantam Doubleday Dell Books for Young Readers. Unp. Grades: K–3.**

A youngster named Louis Armstrong spent many hot summer nights in New Orleans peeking under the swinging doors of Economy Hall listening to jazz. He especially enjoyed the cornet player and longed to emulate him. After seeing a cornet in a pawnshop window for five dollars Louis did odd jobs to earn the money to buy it and after months of hard work, the horn was his.

Raschka, Chris. *Charlie Parker Played Be Bop.* **1992. New York: Orchard Books. Unp. Grades: K–3.**

Sparse, rhythmic text inspired by one of Parker's songs gives students a feel for the sound of jazz without hearing a note. His illustrations reflect the sway and movement of jazz. Students enjoy repeating the phrases and nonsense refrains.

Charlie Parker Played Be Bop. **2000. Audiocassette. Pine Plains, N.Y.: Live Oak Media. Grades: K–3.**

The book is read twice on the audiocassette. It is read slowly the first time to assure that all the words are heard. The second time it is read to the beat of the music playing in the background.

Battle-Lavert, Gwendolyn. *The Music in Derrick's Heart.* **Illustrated by Colin Bootman. 2000. New York: Holiday House. Unp. Grades: K–4.**

This delightful story of an uncle teaching a young boy how to play the harmonica is accompanied by beautiful, soft-color illustrations. The boy is told that he must play from the heart and feel the music. He practices all summer long. At the end of the summer the uncle's arthritis is so pronounced he is unable to play anymore, but the boy now plays from the heart.

Mathis, Sharon Bell. *Ray Charles*. Illustrated by George Ford. 2001. New York: Lee and Low Books. Unp. Grades: K–4.

The music of Ray Charles is recognized around the world. In this biography, young readers learn about his childhood when he lost his sight and how he eventually became a famous jazz and blues musician. The book includes an introduction and an afterword to update this new addition of the book. This book won a Corretta Scott King Award.

The *Very Best of Ray Charles*. 2000. CD. Rhino Records, Los Angeles, Calif. Grades: K and up.

The 16 tracks on this CD offer a broad range of Ray Charles's hit songs and make a great introduction to his music for listeners of all ages. One track features a duet with Willie Nelson.

Children's *Classics*. 1998. CD. New York: Sony Music Entertainment. Grades: K and up.

Leonard Bernstein and the New York Philharmonic Orchestra perform *Peter and the Wolf*, *Carnival of the Animals*, and *Young Person's Guide to the Orchestra*. Young musicians join the Philharmonic to perform *Carnival of the Animals*.

Mozart's *Magic Fantasy: A Journey through the Magic Flute*. 1995. CD. Pickering, Ontario: Children's Group. Grades: K and up.

This delightful children's story is one to listen to again and again as students discover the magic of Mozart. This is one of the Classical Kids series.

Rachlin, Ann. *Chopin*. Illustrated by Susan Hellard. 1993. Hauppauge, N.Y.: Barron's Educational Books. Unp. Grades: 1–3.

Filled with fascinating facts about Chopin, this look at his childhood engages the interest of young readers in his life. He began composing at age seven and played in public at eight. Fascinating facts about his music and his life keep readers interested in learning about this famous composer. For example, his Minute Waltz was his description of a dog chasing its tail. This book is one of the Famous Children series, which includes books on Bach, Brahms, Handel, Haydn, Mozart, and Schumann.

Rachlin, Ann. *Tchaikovsky*. Illustrated by Susan Hellard. 1993. Hauppauge, N.Y.: Barron's Educational Books. Unp. Grades: 1–3.

Peter Tchaikovsky's early years are described in this short biography. His world of governesses and boarding schools will be unfamiliar to many young readers. However, hearing about a youngster near their own age appeals to young children, who naturally draw comparisons between their lives and his. This book is one of the Famous Children series that tell of the early years of famous composers.

Venezia, Mike. *Wolfgang Amadeus Mozart*. 1995. Chicago: Children's Press. 32p. Grades: 1–4.

Mozart's musical career from three years of age to his death at thirty-five years is briefly explored in this biography. His father and older sister were both accomplished musicians. From an early age he was surrounded by music and encouraged to play for audiences. The large easy-to-read text in this book makes it accessible to young readers who want to read on their own. This book is one of the Getting to Know the World's Greatest Composers series.

Livingston, Myra Cohn. *Keep on Singing: A Ballad of Marian Anderson*. Illustrated by Samuel Byrd. 1994. New York: Holiday House. Unp. Grades: 1–4.

This moving ballad tells of the racial discrimination faced by Marian Anderson, the first black woman singer invited to sing at the Metropolitan Opera. Some of the lines of the ballad are Anderson's own words taken from her autobiography. Author notes at the end of the book explain terms such as "Jim Crow" and amplify other information such as the name of the teacher who was moved to tears upon hearing Anderson sing.

Venezia, Mike. *Aaron Copland*. 1995. Chicago: Children's Press. 32p. Grades: 1–4.

The author combines photographs, paintings, and cartoons to elicit the attention of children as they learn about this famous composer and conductor. As a child, Aaron Copland pestered his sister to teach him to play the piano and began composing music. The world was changing rapidly as he grew and jazz was coming into existence. He added bits of jazz to his classical compositions to enlarge his audience.

Tchaikovsky Discovers America. 1993. CD. Pickering, Ontario: Children's Group. Grades: 1 and up.

Storytelling and classical music combine to introduce young listeners to the world of classical music. Selections from Tchaikovsky's work serve as a backdrop for his adventures in America with a group of young friends. This is one of the Classical Kids series.

Pinkney, Andrea Davis. *Duke Ellington: The Piano Prince and His Orchestra*. Illustrated by Brian Pinkney. 1998. New York: Hyperion Books for Children. Unp. Grades: 2–5.

Dark, swirling, colorful paintings engulf the bouncy, lively text as the story of Duke Ellington's magical music unfolds. The images and text convey the feelings evoked by the music of Duke Ellington. The author's and illustrator's passion for their subject shines through in this award-winning book. Students will be interested to know that Duke Ellington rebelled against staid piano lessons as a child. Later, when he heard ragtime music he realized the piano did not have to be constrained, and he taught himself to play. The book ends with an extended list of sources for further reading. This book won the Coretta Scott King award, is a Caldecott Honor Book, and was named an Outstanding Nonfiction book by the 1999 Orbis Pictus Award Committee.

Duke Ellington: The Piano Prince and His Orchestra. 2000. Video. Westport, Conn.: Weston Woods Studio. 15 min. Grades: 2–5.

This iconographic video based on the book includes a soundtrack with some of Duke Ellington's original music. This book is also available in audiocassette.

Krementz, Jill. A Very Young Musician. 1991. New York: Simon and Schuster Books for Young Readers. Unp. Grades: 2–5.

This is a photo essay of a young trumpet player, Josh Broder. It describes his life in the fifth grade, his private music lessons, his music camp, and his practice sessions. One section of the book is devoted to a discussion of the instruments in the orchestra. On his eleventh birthday, his parents took him to a Wynton Marsalis concert on Long Island. Prior to the concert, he had an opportunity to meet Wynton and play the trumpet for him.

Nichol, Barbara. Beethoven Lives Upstairs. Illustrated by Scott Cameron. 1993. New York: Orchard Books. Unp. Grades: 3–5.

A series of letters between Christoph and his uncle tell the fictionalized story of Beethoven at a time when he lived in Vienna as a boarder in Christoph's and his mother's home. This account of Beethoven's life introduces him to young readers through the eyes of another child. This unique perspective appeals to young readers and encourages them to find out more about this musician's life. Beautiful illustrations evoke the emotions the young boy feels as he learns to appreciate the eccentric boarder. This book is also available on audiocassette.

Vernon, Roland. Introducing Gershwin. 1990. Parsippany, N.J.: Silver Burdett. 32p. Grades: 3–6.

Photographs, illustrations, and posters are used throughout the book to explain George Gershwin's rise in the music world. He had limited education and never learned theory or had formal musical training. His talent was instinctive and natural. He sought music teachers to provide him the formal training he thought he needed; however, the teachers were afraid they would destroy his natural ability. When he was only twenty, he was hired to compose the entire score of a musical comedy that was an instant success. The book also includes a timeline of his life, a glossary, and an index.

Ellis, Veronica Freeman. *Wynton Marsalis.* **1997. Austin, Tex.: Raintree Steck-Vaughn. 48p. Grades: 3–6.**

This famous trumpeter was given his first trumpet at age six by trumpeter, Al Hirt. While best known for his work with jazz, he has won Grammy awards for both jazz and classical recordings. As a composer his foremost interest is to use music to teach people mutual respect. This is one of the Contemporary African American Series.

***Making Music.* 1995. Mac/Win. New York: Voyager CD-ROMs. Grades: 3 and up.**

Students enjoy using this interactive CD to compose and perform musical compositions. The easy-to-use interface enables students to draw notes on the screen and play them back using different instruments. While they compose music, students also learn about musical notation, rhythm, and musical variation. A composition book is provided for them to store their work. The success of this CD led to the creation of *Making More Music*.

Clay, Julie. *The Stars that Shine.* **Illustrated by Dan Andreasen. 2000. New York: Simon and Schuster. 101p. Grades: 4–6.**

This unusual collection of childhood memories and dreams were gathered from country music stars. The stories are a blend of biography and fiction. Each story is followed by biographical information on the star and background material on the story.

Lester, Julius. *The Blues Singers: 10 Who Rocked the World.* **Illustrated by Lisa Cohen. 2001. New York: Hyperion Books for Children. 47p. Grades: 4–6.**

This collection of short biographies is a grandfather's remembrances he is sharing with his granddaughter. Singers in the book include among others Bessie Smith, Ray Charles, Mahalia Jackson, Muddy Waters, and Little Richard. One memorable thing about some of the stories is that the singers express regret about not learning to read and write or not finishing high school and college. The book concludes with a bibliography and a list of recommended listening recordings.

Devine, Daniel, and Richard Mozer. *Handel's Last Chance.* **2000. Video. Music by Georg Frideric Handel. Toronto, Ontario: Devine Entertainment. 51 min. Grades: 4–8.**

Handel faces ruin if his newest composition is not well received by audiences. Church choirs who sing off key and a washerwoman who wants him to rescue her young son, Jamie, from jail, confront him. Handel rescues the youngster from jail and in turn the youngster saves the production with his beautiful singing voice. Students enjoy the period costumes, the men in wigs, and the bully who gets his due as they listen to Handel's moving musical works. This is one of the Great Composers series of videos.

Orgill, Roxane. *Shout, Sister Shout! Ten Girl Singers Who Shaped a Century*. 2001. New York: Margaret K. McElderry Books. 148p. Grades: 6 and up.

Readers learn about the lives and music of ten, twentieth-century female singers who shaped popular music in this readable collection of biographies. The singers include: Sophie Tucker, Ma Rainey, Ethel Merman, Judy Garland, Anita O'Day, Joan Baez, Bette Midler, Madonna, and Lucinda Williams. These women provide strong role models for young girls and perhaps it would be better not to refer to the singers as "girls." The book ends with a list of compact discs containing recordings by the singers, a bibliography, and an index.

EXPLORATIONS

1. Prior to reading *Satchmo's Blues* (Schroeder, 1996), discuss with students strategies they use to obtain things they really want. After reading the book, compare their strategies with those of Louis Armstrong's hard work and perseverance in order to purchase his cornet.

2. In *Beethoven Lives Upstairs* (Nichol, 1993) students discovered a great deal of personal information about Beethoven through the letters exchanged between a boy and his uncle. After reading about another composer, students can write letters to a fictitious aunt or uncle telling about that composer.

3. Create a graph of two-inch squares with enough boxes for the names of key people in a composer's life across the top and down the sides. List the people's names across the top and down the left side. In the box where the people intersect, write down how they related or interacted with one another.

4. After reading about several musicians and composers, have students create a timeline depicting their births and important events in their lives to determine if they lived during the same time periods. To place their lives in a historical perspective students can find world events that occurred during the musicians' or composers' lifetimes and add them to the timeline.

5. Students can draw stair steps and record one important event in the composer's life on each step.

6. After reading about two or more of the musicians, have students complete an inventory of each of the composers' likes and dislikes, favorite foods, and characteristics. Then have them look for comparisons among the composers.

7. After reading about a musician, allow students opportunities to listen to the musician's music while they draw pictures representative of the music.

8. After reading *The Stars that Shine* (Clay, 2000), have students share their own memories of the past and dreams for the future. Older students can type their stories and create their own book of memories.

9. *The Blues Singers: 10 Who Rocked the World* (Lester, 2001) is for reading aloud and discussing with the class. Older students enjoy being read aloud to and these short biographies can be read at the beginning of a class period to help focus and relax the students to prepare them for learning.

10. After viewing the video, *Handel's Last Chance*, have students discuss the tactics the young bully uses throughout the video to make Jamie's life miserable. Then ask students to brainstorm ideas for dealing with bullies.

11. After viewing *Handel's Last Chance*, have students discuss whether or not they liked the music they heard. Then have them try to determine why they liked or did not like the music.

12. After reading about the singers in *Shout, Sister Shout!* (Orgill, 2001) encourage students to create a short presentation on one of the singers and to bring in samples of their music to share with their classmates.

TYPES OF MUSIC

The books and media in this section provide information on different genres and styles of music including jazz, blues, classical, opera, and African American. As students develop an understanding and appreciation of different styles of music they are meeting the goals of music standard six, which addresses the ability to describe music. Additionally, they learn the place of music in history and culture, which addresses standard nine.

BOOK AND MEDIA CHOICES

Velasquez, Eric. *Grandma's Records*. 2001. New York: Walker. Unp. Grades: K–3.

During the summer while his parents work, Eric stays with his grandmother in El Barrio, Spanish Harlem. Together they listen and dance to her scratchy, old records of Puerto Rican music. Then one night they have an opportunity to attend a live concert. The book ends with information about three Puerto Rican musicians mentioned in the story.

Myers, Walter Dean. *The Blues of Flats Brown*. Illustrated by Nina Laden. 2000. New York: Holiday House. Unp. Grades: 1–3.

The meanest man in Mound Bayou, Mississippi, severely abuses his junkyard dogs, Flats and Caleb. They run away and survive by singing and playing the blues always one step ahead of their master. One night their master hears Flats singing a song about him and his hard heart melts. Flats and Caleb live out their lives playing and singing the blues on the waterfront in Savannah, Georgia.

Schroeder, Alan. *Carolina Shout!* Illustrated by Bernie Fuchs. 1995. New York: Dial Books for Young Readers. Unp. Grades: 1–3.

Prior to World War II, street vendors relied upon short, informal songs called "Shouts" to advertise their wares. Each shout reflected the personality of the vendor. This book celebrates and records this historical musical art form that has ceased to exist. George and Ira Gershwin used three shouts in their opera *Porgy and Bess*.

Vagin, Vladimir. *Peter and the Wolf*. 2000. New York: Scholastic. Unp. Grades: 1–4.

This retelling of Sergei Prokofiev's timeless classic is accompanied by bright, colorful illustrations. Knowing the story behind the music makes the music more meaningful and enjoyable to children. Even without the music this tale makes exciting reading. The book includes a listing of the characters, their musical themes, and brief musical measures. At the end of the book is a very brief biography of the composer.

***Prokofiev: Peter and the Wolf*. CD. New York: ELEKTRA/ASYLUM. Grades: 1–4.**

This Sergei Prokofiev classic is narrated by Patrick Stewart. This rendition is a delight to hear and introduces students to a beloved classic.

Bryan, Ashley. *All Night, All Day: A Child's First Book of African-American Spirituals*. 1991. New York: Atheneum. 48p. Grades: 1 and up.

America's most unique contribution to song literature is African American spirituals, 20 of which are included in this collection. People all over America sing these songs; however, few are aware of the songs' origins. Slaves first sang these songs and their creation ended with slavery. Each song has a piano accompaniment created by David Manning Thomas and guitar chords are noted. The essence of the songs is captured in brightly-colored primitive art illustrations that enhance the spirituals.

Price, Leontyne. *Aida*. Illustrated by Leo and Diane Dillon. 1990. San Diego Calif.: Gulliver Books. Unp. Grades: 3–6.

Giuseppe Verdi's opera tells the story of an Ethiopian Royal Princess, Aida, and is considered one of the greatest love stories of all time. Opera diva, Leontyne Price, tells the story from Aida's point of view. The rich, dark illustrations and the powerful story capture children's imaginations and introduce them to this popular opera.

Weatherford, Carole Boston. *The Sound That Jazz Makes*. Illustrated by Eric Velasquez. 2000. New York: Walker. Unp. Grades: 3–6.

The history of jazz is recounted in rhyming stanzas that young readers enjoy listening to and reading on their own. The musical text and the rich oil paintings create a symphony for the senses that shows readers the power of jazz to portray human suffering and jubilation. Jazz's history is traced from its African origins on drums carved from trees to its influence on today's rappers with their electric boom boxes. The introduction of famous jazz musicians and the rich vocabulary used throughout the book all provide students with ideas for further exploration.

Igus, Toyomi. *i see the rhythm.* **Paintings by Michele Wood. 1998. San Francisco: Children's Book Press. 32p. Grades: 3–7.**

Five hundred years of African American music is celebrated in this lively, colorful book. From slave songs, to swing, to rock 'n roll, to hip-hop, the contributions of African Americans to music are chronicled. While looking at the paintings and listening to the music, the narrator wrote poems about the musical scenes. Each type of music is depicted in a two-page spread that includes a full-page color painting, a poem, a timeline, and a brief paragraph about the music. The timeline includes both historical and musical events. This book won the Coretta Scott King Illustrator Award.

Medearis, Angela Shelf, and Michael R. Medearis. *African-American Arts: Music.* **1997. New York: Twenty-First Century Books. 80p. Grades: 4–8.**

This detailed account of the history of African-American music includes: blues, ragtime, jazz, gospel, rhythm and blues, soul, rock and roll, and rap. The development of each style is chronicled, a description of the music is given, and famous musicians associated with each style are noted. Books for further reading and an index conclude the book. This book is one of the African-American Arts series that celebrates African Americans' contributions to the arts.

Husain, Shahrukh. *The Barefoot Book of Stories from the Opera.* **Illustrated by James Mayhew. 1999. New York: Barefoot Books. 80p. Grades: 4 and up.**

Opera is a form of music to which most children are not exposed, but there are many operas that have great attraction to children. This book describes the stories of seven operas written and composed by masters such as Mozart, Rimsky-Korsakov, and Wagner. Each story begins with an introduction that sets the stage for the opera and provides a brief amount of information about the composer. Knowing the stories makes the reader eager to see and hear the opera, especially if it is performed in English; however, even if performed in another language, knowing the story makes it more enjoyable.

Switzer, Ellen. *The Magic of Mozart: The Magic Flute, and the Salzburg Marionettes.* **Photographs by Costas. 1995. New York: Atheneum Books for Young Children. 90p. Grades: 4 and up.**

A biography of Mozart begins the book and sets the stage for the story of *The Magic Flute*. The second portion of the book retells the story of *The Magic Flute* accompanied by color photographs of the Salzburg marionettes as they perform the opera. The last section of the book provides a brief, fascinating history of the Salzburg marionettes, and a behind-the-scenes look at how they magically come to life in the hands of experienced puppeteers.

EXPLORATIONS

1. Prior to reading *Carolina Shout!* (Schroeder, 1995), have students sing jingles to their favorite commercials. After reading the book, help students make comparisons or connections between the "shouts" and present-day jingles.

2. After reading *Peter and the Wolf* (Vagin, 2000), provide students an opportunity to listen to the symphony. After listening to the symphony, have the students reenact the story while the symphony plays.

3. Provide students with background information on the origins of the songs in *All Night, All Day: A Child's First Book of African-American Spirituals* (Bryan, 1991). Using a document camera or overhead transparencies project the words of the song for the entire class to see, have students carefully examine the words of the song, and discuss the song's meaning.

4. Some of the vocabulary in *The Sound That Jazz Makes* (Weatherford, 2000) may hinder students from fully comprehending the text. After reading the book have students create a list of the unfamiliar words or familiar words that are used in an unfamiliar context. Have students work in small groups with each group researching definitions for the words. One group can be responsible for typing the words and their definitions into the computer. This glossary of terms can then be attached to the end of the book.

5. *The Sound That Jazz Makes* (Weatherford, 2000) briefly introduces a variety of famous jazz musicians. Working in groups the students can use *African-American Arts: Music* (Medearis and Medearis, 1997) to find out more about the musicians and present their information to their classmates.

6. While reading *i see the rhythm* (Igus, 1998), have students take brief notes to describe the different kinds of African American rhythmic music. Students can then be divided into groups to conduct further research on various types of music and to find recordings of the music to share with their classmates.

7. After reading *The Magic of Mozart: The Magic Flute, and the Salzburg Marionettes* (Switzer, 1995) or *Aida* (Price, 1990), have students create puppets to use to retell the story.

8. After reading the stories in *The Barefoot Book of Stories from the Opera* (Husain, 1999), have students consult with a library media specialist about obtaining recordings of the opera for the class to hear.

SONGS

This section has books and media with a wide range of familiar songs including a Native American lullaby, familiar folk songs, and popular children's songs. The lyrics to many of the songs are included to enable students to read the words as they sing along. As students read the books in this section and listen to and sing the songs, they are meeting music content standard one that focuses on singing a variety of music. As they learn to read music in order to sing the songs, they are addressing content standard five. Content standard nine is acknowledged when students discover how music chronicles events in American history. For example, the Star Spangled Banner, which recounts the Battle of Baltimore during the War of 1812.

BOOK AND MEDIA CHOICES

Zelinsky, Paul O. *The Wheels on the Bus*. 10th Anniversary Special Edition. 2000. New York: Dutton's Children's Books. Unp. Grades: P–1.

Not only do children get to read the words to the song over and over again in this book, they can also move parts of the book over and over again. For example, the windshield wipers on the bus move back and forth across the front of the bus. The luscious illustrations on the cover of the book and in the book shimmer with foil. Children enjoy imitating all the sounds heard on the bus as it travels through the town.

Holt, Lenny. *The Seals on the Bus*. Illustrated by G. Brian Karas. 2000. New York: Henry Holt. Unp. Grades: P–1.

This variation on a favorite song has children singing and reading along as they imitate the sounds of a bus full of animals. They can hiss with the snakes, errp with the seals, and holler for help with the people on the bus as they travel through town. Children delight in the reactions of the people on the bus to their beastly fellow passengers. These reactions are vividly portrayed in the faces of the bus riders.

Sing It! Say It! Stamp It! Sway It! Volume 1. 1997. Audiocassette/CD. Worcester, Mass.: 80-Z Music. Grades: P–1.

Twenty-seven short, early childhood songs and chants youngsters enjoy singing and moving to are on this recording by Peter and Ellen Allard. Lyrics, motions, and classroom activities are included.

Kellogg, Steven. *A-Hunting We Will Go!* 1998. New York: HarperCollins. Unp. Grades: P–1.

An author's note at the end of the book explains that this folk song dating from the 1600s has an accompanying game and that traditionally participants have been encouraged to create their own verses. The author has created his own delightful verses with a merry band of animals accompanying two children as they make their way to bed. This whimsical, rollicking tale and the fanciful illustrations make this a favorite story for reading aloud whether headed to bed or not.

***Smithsonian Folkways Children's Music.* 1998. Audiocassette. Washington, D.C.: Smithsonian Institute. Grades: P–1.**

Childhood favorites such as "Twinkle, Twinkle Little Star" are included on this recording. Also included are the musical arrangements and the text of the songs. Various artists perform these songs.

Miller, J. Phillip, and Sheppard M. Greene. *We All Sing with the Same Voice.* Illustrated by Paul Meisel. 2001. New York: HarperCollins. Unp. Grades: P–2.

Young fans of *Sesame Street* will recognize this song that embraces the sameness of children all over the world. The colorful, lively illustrations depict children from different nations singing, dancing, and playing. This book includes a music CD for singing along with the song.

***We Three Kings.* Illustrated by Olga Zharakova. 1993. New York: Scholastic. Unp. Grades: P–2.**

Vibrant, colorful torn and cut paper shapes have been used to create collages to illustrate this carol. Gold paint and pencil were used to provide features for the people and animals formed from the paper. Four to five lines of the song are found on each page amidst the colorful collages. The end pages contain the song and musical score.

Weiss, George David, and Bob Thiele. *What a Wonderful World.* Illustrated by Ashley Bryan. 1995. New York: Atheneum Books for Young Readers. Unp. Grades: P–3.

The lyrics of this song speak of the wonders and promise of the universe. Lively, vibrant artwork depicts the harmony of people of different backgrounds. A puppet show portrays the words of the song Louis Armstrong made famous. He appears in person at the puppet show and as one of the puppets.

Raffi. *Raffi: Children's Favorites.* 1993. New York: Omnibus Press. 172p. Grades: P–3.

Fifty-one familiar children's songs with lyrics and guitar chords are included in this book. Favorites such as, *Goodnight Irene* and *Wheels on the Bus* are included. These songs lend themselves to both classroom and campfire sing-alongs.

***Singable Songs for the Very Young.* 1996. CD. Cambridge, Mass.: Rounder Records. Grades: P–3.**

Young children enjoy singing along with Raffi to favorite songs like *Baa Baa Black Sheep* and the *More We Get Together.* In *Brush Your Teeth,* he gently reminds them of the importance of brushing their teeth and in *Eating to Grow,* he informs the children how important eating is to growth even though they cannot see the growth.

Baby Beluga. **1996. CD. Cambridge, Mass.: Rounder Records. Grades: P–3.**

This is one of Raffi's most beloved recordings. Students embrace Baby Beluga in this simple salute to the whale and his environment. *This Old Man* and *Kumbaya* are other favorite tunes included on this CD.

Farjeon, Eleanor. ***Morning Has Broken.*** **Illustrated by Tim Ladwig. 2001. Grand Rapids, Mich.: Eerdmans Books for Young Readers. Unp. Grades: P–4.**

This inspirational song has made its way to the pages of a picture storybook with beautiful watercolors. The wonder of nature and the greatness of the universe are explored in words and pictures. Young readers familiar with the song sing along as the text is read.

The Farmer in the Dell. **Illustrated by John O'Brien. 2000. Honesdale, Penn.: Boyds Mills. Unp. Grades: K–2.**

When the farmer falls in the dell, it takes a concerted effort to pull him out. Children enjoy the repetition and predictable sequence of this nursery rhyme and sing along as the pages of the book are turned. The whimsical illustrations delight young and old. This book is a class favorite to read again and again.

Yankee Doodle. **Illustrated by Stephen Kellogg. 1996. New York: Simon and Schuster Books for Young Readers. Unp. Grades: K–2.**

This spirited, rousing song is cleverly illustrated by Stephen Kellogg, who has given young Yankee Doodle a canine friend. Children delight in closely examining the detailed pictures as they learn about America during Revolutionary War days. A note at the end of the book tells of the mystery surrounding the true author of the song. Tucked in the border around the note are definitions of unfamiliar terms or familiar terms with alternate definitions.

Wood, Douglas. ***Northwoods Cradle Song.*** **Illustrated by Lisa Desimini. 1996. New York: Simon and Schuster Books for Young Readers. Unp. Grades: K–2.**

This Menominee lullaby describes the woodlands at night as a mother sings to her sleepy baby. The dark, restful illustrations and the calm, soothing words relax readers and listeners as they share this book. This bedtime story book can also be used in a classroom just before naptime.

Children's Songbook. **1997. Mac/Win. New York: Voyager CD-ROMs. Grades: K–3.**

Included on this CD are 15 traditional songs from around the world. The songs are accompanied by a film, lyrics, games, and information on the song's origin. This CD won the 1997 Best Overall Title for Kids Mac Home Journal's Home Choice Award and the Newsweek Parent's Guide to Children's Software 1997 Editor's Choice Award.

Trapani, Iza. *How Much Is That Doggie in the Window?* 1997. Boston: Whispering Coyote. Unp. Grades: K–3.

The song *How Much Is That Doggie in the Window?* has been cleverly adapted into a heartwarming tale of a young boy who is rewarded for taking care of his family members. While trying to save money to buy the dog, he spends money on his family. He buys his sister frozen yogurt after she falls, his mother chocolate after a bee sting, and his father a box of tissues for his sneezes. The verses and musical score can be found at the end of the book. The author has done similar adaptations of other familiar songs including: *The Itsy Bitsy Spider; Twinkle, Twinkle, Little Star;* and *Oh Where, Oh Where Has My Little Dog Gone?*

Guthrie, Woody. *This Land Is Your Land.* 1998. Paintings by Kathy Jakobsen. Boston: Little, Brown. Unp. Grades: K–3.

This inspiring American folk song was written as Woody Guthrie hitchhiked across America from Los Angeles to New York City. The book is illustrated with folk art paintings that show Americans' diverse heritages. At the end of the song is a three-page spread of the United States and her people. The book ends with a tribute to Woody Guthrie written by Pete Seeger and a biographical scrapbook of Woody.

ature *This Land Is Your Land.* 1997. CD. Cambridge, Mass.: Rounder Records. Grades: K and up.

This father-and-son performance by Woody and Arlo Guthrie has everyone singing along and swaying to the music and is a great accompaniment to the book by the same title.

This Land Is Your Land. 2000. Video. Norwalk, Conn.: Weston Woods Studios. 12 min. Grades: 2 and up.

Family photos and Woody's original sketches add to the enjoyment of this short video.

Wheeler, Jody. *The First Noel.* 1992. Nashville, Tenn.: Ideals Children's Books. Unp. Grades: K–3.

Warm, pastel watercolors illustrate this rendition of a classic Christmas carol. Pastel blue frames surround the watercolor illustrations. Seven verses of the song and the musical accompaniment are included, as well as a brief history of the carol.

Gershwin, George, DuBose Heyward, Dorothy Heyward, and Ira Gershwin. *Summertime: From Porgy and Bess.* **Paintings by Mike Wimmer. 1999. New York: Simon and Schuster Children's Books. Unp. Grades: K–3.**

The graceful, haunting words of George Gershwin are illustrated with lush oil paintings of a family's summer day portraying the day-to-day life of a rural African American family. This classic American song is one children want to hear again and again. The comfort and joy of having an extended family to love and to cherish is evident in these paintings.

Gill, Madelaine. *Praise for the Singing Children: Songs for Children.* **Arrangements by Greg Pliska. 1993. Boston: Little, Brown. 64p. Grades: K–4.**

A variety of cultures and traditions are represented in this collection of hymns. They are categorized by themes: Joy and Celebration, Peace and Freedom, Hope and Faith, and Love and Thanksgiving. The songs suggest a variety of ways for singers to participate including rounds, call-and-response, parts, clapping, and dance.

Ella Jenkins Live at the Smithsonian. **1993. Video/DVD. Washington, D.C.: Smithsonian/ Folkways. 28 min. Grades: K–4.**

Students sing, clap, and move as they watch and listen to this lively video.

Pete Seeger's Family Concert. **1992. CD. New York: Sony Wonder. 40 min. Grades: K–4.**

This favorite folk singer leads students on a rollicking rousing sing-along. Included on this recording are *Skip to My Lou*, *Coming Round the Mountain*, and *Guantanamera*.

Peter, Paul, and Mommy, Too. **1993. Video/DVD. Warner. 90 min. Grades: K–4.**

Students enjoy singing along to songs in this recording such as *Puff (The Magic Dragon)*, *Day Is Done*, *It's Raining*, and *Boa Constrictor*. This recording is also available in audiocassette.

Weeks, Sarah. *Crocodile Smile: Ten Songs of the Earth as the Animals See It.* **Illustrated by Lois Ehlert. 1994. New York: HarperCollins. Unp. Grades: K–4.**

Looking at the earth as animals see it reminds humans that their actions impact the animals' existence. From chopping down trees to making hats of feathers, humans use and abuse animals and their habitats. The lyrics of these ten songs are told from Mother Nature's viewpoint through various animals of the jungle. The brightly-colored collage adds to the mood of the book that is accompanied by an audiocassette. This book is a Caldecott Award Honor Book.

Seeger, Pete. *For Kids and Just Plain Folks.* 1997. Audiocassette. New York: Sony Music Entertainment. Grades: K and up.

This is a great collection to sing along with. Students are familiar with many of the songs on the cassette that includes *If I Had a Hammer, Michael Row the Boat Ashore, This Land Is Your Land,* and *Be Kind to Your Parents.*

Lithgow, John. *Singing in the Bathtub.* 1999. Audiocassette. New York: Sony Music Entertainment. Grades: 1–4.

This multitalented entertainer delights children with his renditions of favorite songs, such as *Swinging on a Star.*

Connelly, Bernardine. *Follow the Drinking Gourd: A Story of the Underground Railroad.* Illustrated by Yvonne Buchanan. 1997. New York: Simon and Schuster. Unp. Grades: 1–4.

Follow the Drinking Gourd is a traditional American folk song used by slaves to communicate the way north to freedom. In this book a young girl, her brother, and her mother set out on the Underground Railroad to find freedom. Dark watercolor illustrations depict the family's journey north. Tucked in the back of the book is a compact disc containing Morgan Freeman's narration of the story with musical accompaniment by Taj Mahal.

Birdseye, Tom, and Debbie Holsclaw Birdseye. *She'll Be Comin' Round the Mountain.* Illustrated by Andrew Glass. 1994. New York: Holiday House. Unp. Grades: 1–4.

Rather than just charming illustrations to accompany the words of the song, this wonderful, creative book has the song embedded in a narrative. The family friend Tootie, whom they have not seen in several years, is coming to visit. In response to questions from young Petunia and Delbert about the impending visitor, the clan responds with the verses to the song. Youngsters listening to the story are sure to sing along. The surprise ending is a delight.

Geis, Jacqueline. *Where the Buffalo Roam.* 1992. Nashville, Tenn.: Ideals Children's Books. Unp. Grades: 1–4.

In 1933, *Home on the Range* was the most popular song in America. The author has adapted and expanded the original song to include additional information about the Southwest. Watercolor illustrations depict the animals and plants mentioned in the verses. When encountering unfamiliar words, such as javelina and cottonwood, readers can refer to the illustrations and the glossary at the end of the book for understanding. The book includes an author's note and a map of the American Southwest.

Child, Lydia Maria. *Over the River and Through the Woods.* **Illustrated by Christopher Manson. 1993. New York: North-South Books. Unp. Grades: 1–4.**

Most who know this traditional holiday song probably do not know it was adapted from a poem. With only two to three lines per page, there is plenty of room for the realistic woodcuts that fill the pages of this engaging book. The trip to the grandparent's house set in the nineteenth century traverses a winter wonderland past children ice fishing, sledding, and playing ice hockey. The last page of the book has the musical accompaniment and six verses of the poem.

Hammerstein, Oscar. *The Surrey with the Fringe on Top.* **Illustrated by James Warhola. 1993. New York: Simon and Schuster Children's Books. Unp. Grades: 1–4.**

A wild romp through the countryside past a rollicking cast of characters combined with rhyming lyrics makes this book fun to read and to sing. A father, his children, and the family pets spend a delightful afternoon together in their magnificent surrey. The musical score can be found on the end pages. This is a wonderful way to introduce students to the musical *Oklahoma.*

Kroll, Steven. *The Story of the Star-Spangled Banner: By the Dawn's Early Light.* **Illustrated by Dan Andreasen. 1994. New York: Scholastic. 40p. Grades: 2–5.**

This book is a narrative account of the events leading up to the battle of Baltimore where a young lawyer witnessed the battle from the deck of a ship anchored in the harbor. A large American flag was raised at Fort McHenry. The heavy shelling and rocketing went on for hours and at one point a comrade asked Frances Scott Key if he could see if the flag was still waving. It was, and Key began to record his thoughts on the back of an envelope as the battle was drawing to a close. These words later became the "Star-Spangled Banner." This book was named A Notable Children's Trade Book in the Field of Social Studies and an American Bookseller Pick of the Lists.

Hodges, Margaret. *Silent Night: The Song and Its Story.* **Illustrated by Tim Ladwig. 1997. Grand Rapids, Mich.: Eerdmans Books for Young Readers. Unp. Grades: 2 and up.**

"Silent Night" was written in Austria by a priest, Joseph Mohr, and the church organist, Franz Gruber, one Christmas Eve when the church organ was broken. Since they could not imagine a Christmas Eve service without music, they composed a simple song for Father Mohr's guitar. The story of how this simple song traveled across the world is chronicled in the book. Brief stories tell how in times of war enemies have laid down their weapons and joined together to sing this carol. The song and musical score are found at the end of the book.

Krull, Kathleen. *Gonna Sing My Head Off! American Folk Songs for Children.* Illustrated by Allen Garns. 1992. New York: Alfred A. Knopf. 147p. Grades: 2 and up.

This collection of favorite songs was compiled for children ages seven and up. The arrangements are written for guitar or piano accompaniment. A short paragraph at the beginning of each song tells something of its place in American history. An introductory note by Arlo Guthrie reminds the readers of happy times associated with singing these familiar tunes and encourages readers to make happy memories as they sing. The colorful illustrations accompanying the songs make this a book to read, as well as to sing. The songs are indexed by first lines and by 23 types of songs, such as animal songs, train songs, and dance songs. This book was named An American Library Association Notable Book.

St. Pierre, Stephanie. *Our National Anthem.* 1992. Brookfield, Conn.: The Millbrook Press. 48p. Grades: 3–5.

Not only does this book describe how "The Star-Spangled Banner" came to be written, it also provides information on how it came to be our national anthem. The patriotism and heroism expressed in all four verses is explained. The book concludes with a chronology, books for further reading, and an index. This book is one of the I Know America series that provides detailed information about distinctly American things.

Kidd, Ronald. *On Top of Old Smoky: A Collection of Songs and Stories from Appalachia.* Illustrated by Linda Anderson. 1992. Nashville, Tenn.: Ideals Children's Books. Unp. Grades: 3–6.

The traditional songs and folk tales compiled for this book are familiar to many readers. The collection includes favorites such as *Jack and the Bean Tree*, *The Frog He Went A-Courting*, and *Billy Boy*. The introduction to the book tells a little about the origins of the people of Appalachia and their songs and tales. The text is accompanied by paintings of Appalachia.

Siegen-Smith, Nikki. *Songs for Survival: Songs and Chants from Tribal Peoples Around the World.* Illustrated by Bernard Lodge. 1996. New York: Dutton Children's Books. 80p. Grades: 4–6.

Songs are an integral part of the lives of tribal people around the world. Revealed in these songs and chants are tribal peoples' reverence for nature and their belief in the importance of living in harmony. Brief paragraphs are included that explain some of the songs and chants. Colorful, primitive drawings illustrate the book. The origin of each song or chant is noted just under the title of the song. Survival International, a group that believes the lives and lands of tribal peoples should be respected, produced the book.

EXPLORATIONS

1. After reading and singing *The Wheels on the Bus* (Zelinsky, 2000) and *The Seals on the Bus* (Holt, 2000), have students make up their own version of the song. Write their version down on chart paper to point to the words as the students read and sing along.

2. *We Three Kings* (*We Three Kings*, 1993), *Silent Night: The Song and Its Story* (Hodges, 1997), and *The First Noel* (Wheeler, 1992) are all familiar Christmas carols. While listening to recordings of the songs, students can draw pictures that come to mind. Then their pictures can be compared with the books' illustrations.

3. After reading *What a Wonderful World* (Weiss and Thiele, 1995) to the students, they can create their own puppets and work in small groups to re-enact the song as the teacher narrates.

4. While the teacher reads *The Farmer in the Dell* (2000), students can complete a flowchart of the actions.

5. *Northwoods Cradle Song* (Wood, 1996) is an excellent choice for reading to young students at naptime. Older students can examine the lyrics to pick out the words that connote sleep.

6. After reading *Northwoods Cradle Song* (Wood, 1996), have students share lullabies they remember from when they were young.

7. Prior to reading *How Much Is That Doggie in the Window?* (Trapani, 1997) to older students, discuss cause and effect with them. After reading, create a class cause-and-effect chart to depict what happens in the story.

8. Prior to reading *Summertime: From Porgy and Bess* (Gershwin, et al. 1999), have students share their favorite summer activities. Write their favorite activities on the board for them to compare their activities with the ones of the child in the story as it is being read aloud. After discussing the book, have students paint pictures of how they spend their time in the summer.

9. *Praise for the Singing Children: Songs for Children* (Gill, 1993) is a book full of songs to sing aloud. Students enjoy clapping and dancing as the songs are sung. Many of these songs can be sung as rounds or by call-and-response.

10. While listening to the tape that accompanies *Crocodile Smile: Ten Songs of the Earth as the Animals See It* (Weeks, 1994), children can create paper collages depicting the importance of taking care of animals and their habitats. Underneath the collages have students post a short description of the message of their collage.

11. Prior to reading *She'll Be Comin' Round the Mountain* (Birdseye and Birdseye, 1994), explain the format of the book to the students. Then as the teacher or librarian reads the narrative, one half of the students sing the first part of the refrain and the other half of the students sing the second part of the refrain, which is in parentheses.

12. Prior to reading *Over the River and Through the Woods* (Child, 1993), encourage students to share their memories of traveling to relatives' houses for Thanksgiving dinner.

13. After reading two versions of the origin of our national anthem, such as *Our National Anthem* (St. Pierre, 1992) and *The Story of the Star-Spangled Banner: By the Dawn's Early Light* (Kroll, 1994), have students compare and contrast the two books.

14. *Gonna Sing My Head Off! American Folk Songs for Children.* (Krull, 1992) and *On Top of Old Smoky: A Collection of Songs and Stories from Appalachia* (Kidd, 1992) are collections of favorite American folks songs for singing aloud. Students enjoy clapping and moving as they sing the songs in these collections. Many of these songs can also be adapted for choral reading.

REFERENCE BOOKS

The music reference books included in this section contain additional information to answer students' questions about the material presented in other books in this chapter. These books serve as resources for teachers and librarians as they seek ways to use music to extend books and enhance students' understanding of the content. These books are also resources for students as they seek greater understanding of the importance of music in their lives.

BOOK AND MEDIA CHOICES

Hart, Avery, and Paul Mantell. *Kids Make Music!: Clapping and Tapping from Bach to Rock.* Illustrated by Loretta Trezzo Braren. 1993. Charlotte, Vt.: Williamson. 60p. Grades: P–4.

Involving children in dance, music, singing, and drama provides a multisensory approach to learning. This collection of music-making activities also includes background information on different kinds of music and dance and instructions for creating simple instruments and activities for students to express themselves through music. There are even instructions for creating minimal-noise backseat musical instruments for long car trips. An index is included.

Lewis, Richard. *All of You Was Singing.* Illustrated by Ed Young. 1994. New York: Aladdin Books. Unp. Grades: 2–5

How music came to earth is explained in this Aztec myth. To the author the myth symbolizes the importance of music to the well-being of life. The collective "you" in the title refers to all of the earth, including the wind, the sky, the sun, the flowers, and the birds. The unity of man, earth, and music resounds throughout this ancient myth. Ed Young's illustrations envelop the entire two-page spread and portray in colors and designs the harmony expressed in the myth.

Barber, Nicola, and Mary Mure. *The World of Music.* 1996. Parsippany, N.J.: Silver Burdett Press. 94p. Grades: 4–8.

Musical instruments from around the world and across time are explored through text, art reproductions, photographs, diagrams, and illustrations. Listen Out For text boxes suggest works of music to listen to for select instruments. The description of the instrument includes a tone range shown on a keyboard. Orchestra diagrams show where the instruments are located during a concert. Interesting musical tidbits appear throughout the chapters. There are chapters on different styles of music including: electronic, medieval, renaissance, baroque, classical, romantic, modern, and folk. Pulse, rhythm, pitch, and melody are also discussed. The book includes a glossary of musical terms, a glossary of composers, and an index.

Wilson, Clive, editor. *The Kingfisher Young People's Book of Music.* 1996. New York: Kingfisher. 128p. Grades: 4 and up.

This book provides information on music from around the world and throughout time. Instruments, great composers, types of music, and the place of music in our lives are all explored. Colorful photographs and illustrations are interspersed with short text boxes and timelines of important events. The layout of the book not only makes it easy to find information, it entices the reader to continue to read and discover more fascinating facts about music. Also included are a glossary and an index.

TEACHER RESOURCES

Books, professional organizations, and Internet sites that provide resources for teachers are included in this section. The professional organizations offer teachers valuable resources as they work to integrate music into their classroom curriculum.

BOOKS

Laughlin, Mildred Knight, and Terri Parker Street. *Literature-Based Art and Music: Children's Books and Activities to Enrich the K-5 Curriculum.* 1992. Phoenix, Ariz.: Oryx Press. 156p. Grades: K–5.

This book has information on children's books to use in art and music classes. Activities are provided for introducing the book, activities for teachers and students, and activities for individual students.

Kline, Tod F. *Classic Tunes & Tales: Ready-to-Use Music Listening Lessons & Activities for Grades K–8.* 1999. Englewood Cliffs, N.J.: Prentice-Hall. 368p. Grades: K–8.

Students develop an appreciation for classical music as they participate in the hands-on activities in this book. The book is spiral bound for ease of copying.

Mitchell, Loretta. *The Music Teacher's Almanac: Ready-to-Use Music Activities for Every Month of the Year.* 1992. Englewood Cliffs, N.J.: Prentice-Hall. 256p. Grades: K–8.

Teachers and librarians find a wealth of activities in this book to help them incorporate music into their lessons. Children enjoy celebrating and this book has music activities to celebrate special days throughout the year.

Campbell, Don G. *The Mozart Effect for Children*. 2000. New York: William Morrow. 272p. Grades: P and up.

This book explains the effect of Mozart and music on children's creativity and intelligence. Included in this book are music and movement exercises to stimulate young minds. The chapters end with a Mozart Musical Menu of suggested compositions for different age groups.

PROFESSIONAL ORGANIZATIONS

American Music Conference
5790 Armada Drive
Carlsbad, CA 92008
800-767-6266
www.amc-music.com/

National Association for Music Education (MENC)
1806 Robert Fulton Drive
Reston, VA 20191
800-336-3768
www.menc.org/
Journals: *Music Educators Journal, Teaching Music, Journal of Research in Music Education, General Music Today*

INTERNET SITES

The Children's Group, Inc.
www.childrensgroup.com/
   This site has a collection of educational resources including music CDs and videos.

Hap-Pal Music, Inc.
www.happalmer.com/
   Hap Palmer's Web site includes annotations and reviews of his songs and videos. One part of the site contains the words and music to his songs, as well as activities for extending the songs to enhance student learning.

Peter and Ellen Allard's Recordings and Songbooks.
http://peterandellen.com
   Teachers of very young students will find recordings of wonderful songs for singing and movement to use in their classrooms.

REFERENCES

ArtsEdge. 1992. *National Standards for Arts Education*. [Online]. Available: http://artsedge.kennedy-center.org/professional_resources/standards/natstandards/standards_k4.html [cited 14 October 2000]

Gilles, Carol, Marilyn Andre, Carolyn Dye, and Virginia Pfannenstiel. 1998. "Talking about Books: Constant Connections through Literature—Using Art, Music, and Drama." *Language Arts* 76, no. 1 (September): 67-75.

Ketner, Carla. 1999. "Bringing Them to Life: Artists, Musicians, and Authors." *Book Links* 8, no. 5 (May): 12-17.

Smith, John A. 2000. "Singing and Songwriting Support Early Literacy Instruction." *The Reading Teacher* 53, no. 8 (May): 646-649.

Appendix

TEACHER RESOURCES

This section contains general teacher resources that are not specific to one subject area. Included in these resources are journals, professional organizations, Internet sites, and media sources such as videos, DVDs, audiocassettes, CDs, and software.

JOURNALS

Listed below are several journals that are excellent sources of information on current children's books. Mailing addresses and Web sites for the journals are provided.

Bookbird: A Journal of International Children's Literature
English Department, 202-E Holmes Hall
Morgan State University
1700 E. Cold Spring Road
Baltimore, MD 21251
410-319-3958
www.ibby.org/Seiten/04_bookb.htm

The Five Owls
2004 Sheridan Avenue South
Minneapolis, MN 55405
612-377-2004
www.fiveowls.com/

The Horn Book Magazine
14 Beacon Street
Boston, MA 02108-9765
617-227-1555
800-325-1170
www.hbook.com/mag.shtml

Multicultural Review
Greenwood Publishing Group
88 Post Road West, Box 5007
Westport, CT 06881-50007
203-226-3571
www.mcreview.com

The New Advocate
Department of Language, Reading and Culture
512 College of Education
P.O. Box 210069
University of Arizona
Tucson, AZ 85721-0069
520-621-1311
www.ed.arizona.edu/departs/lrc/advoc.htm

School Library Journal
P.O. Box 1978
Marion, OH 43306-2078
800-842-1669
www.schoollibraryjournal.com

Voice of Youth Advocates - VOYA
Scarecrow Press
Dept. VOYA
52 Liberty Street
P.O. 4167
Metuchen, NJ 08840
800-537-7107
www.voya.com/

PROFESSIONAL ORGANIZATIONS

The subject areas represented in the book all have their own professional organizations that support the work of teachers and librarians. Information on these subject specific organizations is located at the end of each chapter. The professional organizations listed in this *Introduction* are ones focusing on other areas of interest to teachers. Information about the organizations and the resources they provide can be obtained by contacting the organizations using the addresses, phone numbers, or Web sites listed. The organizations have national, regional, state, and local conferences for teachers and librarians. Conferences are an excellent way for teachers to share ideas with other teachers and to learn new things to enhance their teaching. Additionally, many of the organizations publish journals of interest to elementary and middle schoolteachers. The names of these journals are included in the contact information.

American Library Association
50 East Huron
Chicago, IL 60611
800-545-2433
www.ala.org
Journals: *Booklist, Book Links, Journal of Youth Services, American Libraries*

Association for Childhood Education International
11501 Georgia Avenue, Suite 315
Wheaton, MD 20902
800-423-3563
www.acei.org
Journals: *Childhood Education, Journal of Research in Childhood Education*

The Center for Children's Books
54 East Gregory Drive
Champaign, IL 61820
217-333-8935
www.lis.uiuc.edu/puboff/bccb/index.html
Journal: *The Bulletin of the Center for Children's Books*

Children's Book Council
12 W. 37th Street, 2nd floor
New York, NY 10018-7480
212-966-1990
www.cbcbooks.org/

Council for Exceptional Children
1920 Association Drive
Reston, VA 20191-1589
1-888-CEC-SPED
www.cec.sped.org/
Journals: *Teaching Exceptional Children, Exceptional Children*

International Federation of Library Associations and Institutions
P.O. Box 95312
2509 CH The Hague
Netherlands
www.ifla.org
Journal: *IFLA Journal*

International Society for Technology in Education

480 Charnelton Street
Eugene, OR 97401-2626
800-336-5191
www.iste.org
Journals: *Learning and Leading with Technology, Journal of Research on Computing in Education*

National Association for the Education of Young Children

1509 Sixteenth Street, NW
Washington, DC 20036-1426
800-424-2460
www.naeyc.org
Journal: *Young Children, Early Childhood Research Quarterly*

National Association for Gifted Children

1707 L Street, NW, Suite 550
Washington, DC 20036
202-785-4268
www.nagc.org/
Journals: *Gifted Child Quarterly*

National Middle School Association

4151 Executive Parkway, Suite 300
Westerville, OH 43081
800-528-NMSA (6672)
www.nmsa.org/
Journals: *Middle School Journal, Research in Middle Level Education, Middle Ground*

INTERNET SITES

Annenberg/CPB

www.learner.org

> Annenberg/CPB is a partnership between the Annenberg Foundation and the Corporation for Public Broadcasting (CPB). This partnership produces educational video programs with Web-based and print materials for K-12 teachers and students. This site has a search engine.

AskEric

www.askeric.org

> Lesson plans, a database of professional articles, and a place to ask education-related questions make this a wonderful resource for teachers.

Ask Jeeves for Kids

www.ajkids.com

> This search engine was developed specifically for children to help them find Web-based resources.

DestinationImagiNation

www.dini.org

> DestinationImagiNation is an international nonprofit corporation focusing on developing the creative problem-solving skills of teams of students from around the world. Kindergarten through college students are eligible to enter the tournaments.

Global Schoolhouse

www.gsn.org/

> Lightspan.com and Global Schoolhouse have combined to provide a variety of online learning opportunities. There are links for online collaborative projects, communication tools, and technology professional development.

Highlights' TeacherNet

www.teachernet.com/html/

> This site has an extensive collection of links for teachers, librarians, parents, and children. The sites are grouped by categories: What's New, Lounge, Classroom, Publishers, Features, and Products.

libraryvideo.com

www.libraryvideo.com

> An extensive collection of videos are available on this site. The entries include detailed annotations and suggested grade levels. Some videos have teacher's guides that can be downloaded from the site. The best feature of the site is the ability to download and preview short video clips prior to purchasing.

MarcoPolo

marcopolo.worldcom.com/

> The MarcoPolo program provides no-cost, standards-based Internet content for the K-12 teacher and classroom, developed by the nation's content experts. Online resources include panel-reviewed links to top sites in many disciplines, professionally developed lesson plans, classroom activities, materials to help with daily classroom planning, and powerful search engines. MarcoPolo includes links to six content specific Web sites: 1) EconEdLink (economics), 2) Xpeditions (geography), 3) Edsitement (humanities), 4) Illuminations (mathematics), 5) Science NetLinks, and 6) ArtsEdge.

Pitsco's Ask an Expert

www.askanexpert.com

Real-world experts are available online to answer students' questions. The available experts have links to their Web sites with answers to frequently asked questions (FAQs). If the answers are not found on the Web site, students can e-mail their questions to the expert.

Public Broadcasting System (PBS)

www.pbs.org/

There is a wealth of material on this site with links for children and teachers. The resources are for life-long learners of all ages with a wide variety of interests. The materials available are related to programs presented on PBS.

Scholastic, Inc.

http://scholastic.com

Scholastic Books hosts this Web site with resources for teachers and students. The site also contains interactive games for students.

Smithsonian Institution

www.si.edu/

The Smithsonian Web site contains resources related to arts, sciences, and history. Online collections, lesson plans, publications, and recordings are a few of the resources on this site.

Yahooligans

www.yahooligans.com/

School-related sites and a recreational site for children are found on this Web page. The site also includes links for parents and teachers. The site includes a search engine.

MEDIA SOURCES

Videos, DVDs, audiocassettes, CDs, and software on a wide array of topics are available to enhance student learning. Listed below are companies that provide these resources for teachers and librarians.

VIDEO TAPES

Annenberg/CPB Videos
901 E Street, NW
Washington, DC 20004
800-LEARNER
www.learner.org

Backyard Enterprises, Inc. (early childhood)
8489 W. Third Street
Los Angeles, CA 90048
323-653-4431
www.netwood.net

Midwest Tapes
P.O. Box 820
Holland, OH 43528
800-875-2785
www.midwesttapes.com

Rolland Collection (art)
22-D Hollywood Avenue
Ho-Ho-Kus, NJ 07423
800-597-6526
www.roland-collection.com

***Spencer's Complete Guide to Special Interest Videos*. 4th edition.**
James-Robert Publishing
15838 N. 62nd Street, Suite 103
Scottsdale, AZ 85254
602-483-7007

AUDIO BOOKS

Audio Editions, Books on Cassette and CD
P.O. Box 6930
Auburn, CA 95604
800-231-4261.
www.audioeditions.com

Books on Tape, Inc.
P.O. Box 7900
Newport Beach, CA 92658
800-541-5525
www.booksontape.com

Landmark Audiobooks, Inc.
4865 Sterling Drive
Boulder, CO 80301
800-580-2989
www.landmarkaudio.com

Listening Library
One Park Avenue
Old Greenwich, CT 06870-1727
800-733-3000
www.listeninglib.com

Recorded Books, LLC
270 Skipjack Road
Prince Frederick, MD 20678
800-638-1304
www.recordedbooks.com

SOFTWARE

Educational Resources
1550 Executive Drive
Elgin, IL 60123
800-860-7004
www.edresources.com/

Inspiration Software, Inc.
7412 SW Beaverton Hillsdale Hwy, Suite 102
Portland, OR 97225-2167
800-877-4292
www.inspiration.com

Learning Services
P.O. Box 10636
Eugene, OR 97440
800-877-9378
www.learnserv.com/

Software Express, Inc.
4128-A South Boulevard
Charlotte, NC 28209
800-527-7638
http://swexpress.com

Sunburst
101 Castleton Street
P.O. Box 100
Pleasantville, NY 10570
www.sunburst.com

Tom Snyder Productions
80 Coolidge Hill Road
Watertown, MA 02472
800-342-0236

Subject Index

Author-Illustrator-Title Index

About the Authors

KATHRYN I. MATTHEW was born in Oakland, California. She has lived in Louisiana, Texas, North Carolina, Georgia, Iowa, West Virginia, and Hawaii. She received an Ed.D. in Curriculum and Instruction with an emphasis on technology and reading from the University of Houston. She has worked in elementary schools in Texas and Louisiana as a classroom teacher, English-as-a-Second-Language Specialist, and Technology Specialist. At the university level she has taught children's literature, reading, language arts, technology, and research classes. She and her husband, Chip, divide their time between homes in Ruston, Louisiana, and Sugar Land, Texas.

JOY L. LOWE was born in Minden, Louisiana. She received graduate and undergraduate degrees from Centenary College of Louisiana, Louisiana Tech University, and Louisiana State University. She received a Ph.D. in Library and Information Science from the University of North Texas. A former school and public librarian, she has taught library science at Louisiana Tech University for twenty-five years. She currently lives in Ruston, Louisiana, with her husband, Perry.